Myths  Pre-Columbian America

Donald A. Mackenzie

DOVER PUBLICATIONS, INC.
Mineola, New York

Published in Canada by General Publishing Company, Ltd.,
30 Lesmill Road, Don Mills, Toronto, Ontario.
Published in the United Kingdom by Constable and Company,
Ltd., 3 The Lanchesters, 162–164 Fulham Palace Road, London
W6 9ER.

Bibliographical Note

This Dover edition, first published in 1996, is a republication
of the work originally published by The Gresham Publishing
Company, Ltd., London, n.d. Several of the plates have been
repositioned, and the original color frontispiece depicting Tlaloc,
the rain god, from *Codex Vaticanus A* has been moved to the front
cover in the present edition.

Library of Congress Cataloging-in-Publication Data

Mackenzie, Donald Alexander, 1873–1936.
    Myths of pre-Columbian America / Donald A. Mackenzie.
       p.   cm.
    Originally published: London : Gresham Pub. Co., 1923, in
series: Myth and legend in literature and art.
    Includes bibliographical references and index.
    ISBN 0-486-29379-3 (pbk.)
    1. Indian mythology. 2. Aztec mythology. 3. Maya
mythology. I. Title.
E59.R38M2 1996
299′.72—dc20   96-32395
                                        CIP

Manufactured in the United States of America
Dover Publications, Inc., 31 East 2nd Street, Mineola, N.Y. 11501

PREFACE

In this volume, which deals with the myths and religious practices of pre-Columbian America in their relation to habits of life and the growth of civilization, the question is frankly faced whether these manifestations of ancient culture were of independent origin or had been imported from the Old World. The view has been favoured by some writers that America remained isolated from the rest of the world from early Pleistocene times until it was discovered by Columbus and conquered by the Spaniards, and that we should account for the existence there of habits of life, habits of thought, myths, folk-tales, &c., similar to those found in Asia and elsewhere, by accepting them as proofs of the "psychic unity" of mankind. Even the most highly complex beliefs, myths, and deities should, according to this theory, be regarded as natural products of the human mind. "Similar needs", we are informed, "produce similar results." It was not, however, until comparatively late in the history of man that signs of progress were revealed in the New World. There is nothing of importance older in America, as the Americanists inform us, than 200 B.C., the date usually applied nowadays to the beginning of what is called the "Archaic period". All the great pre-Columbian civilizations, the Maya of Central America, the Peruvian of South America, and the Aztec of Mexico, fall within the Christian era. Indeed, the Aztec

was mediæval and its beginnings are obscure, for it seems
to have been superimposed on an earlier civilization which
may have been as old as the Maya. Thus we find that in
America the early growth and the early fusions of culture
took place after China had been welded into an empire
under the Han dynasties, and after the mixed communities
of China and those of Cambodia and Indonesia had become
seafarers on the Pacific. Much has been made of the
fact that even Mexican civilization was still in, or had
scarcely emerged from, the so-called Age or Stage of Stone
when the Spanish conquests took place, metals having been
used chiefly for ornamental or religious purposes. The
Su-shen, a people of north-eastern Siberia, who have been
called "the Vikings of the East", were, however, as is
shown in this volume, likewise a "Stone Age" people,
although they were known for many centuries to the
Chinese as seafarers and traders. The Indonesians, another
people who used implements and weapons of stone, penetrated the North Pacific and effected settlements in Japan
early in the Christian era, and also discovered and colonized
the islands of Polynesia. In connection with the latter
"drift", the late Mr. Percy Smith refers in his *Hawaiki*
to evidence which tends to show that the earliest Polynesian wanderers left India, an ancient homeland, as far
back as the fourth century B.C. They were not only
daring but expert mariners, and even after settling on the
coral islands of Oceania continued to set out on long and
adventurous voyages of exploration. Smith has, in this
connection, recorded the native story of the experiences of
a great Polynesian seafarer who reached the Antarctic.
"The frozen ocean", referred to in the traditional account
of the voyage, "is", says Smith, "expressed by the term
Te tai-uka-a-pia, in which *tai* is the sea, *uka* (Maori) is ice,
a-pia means—*a*, 'as', 'like', 'after the manner of'; *pia*,

the arrow-root, which, when scraped, is exactly like snow." Another indication of the distances traversed by the ancient Polynesian mariners is obtained by means of the *maraki-hau*, the half human, half monster of ancient Maori carvings, which has two long tusks protruding from its mouth. Smith has identified this "wonder beast" or, as the Hindus would have called it, this *makara*, with the walrus or sea-elephant, which is seen only in high latitudes. Tongan traditions refer to voyages of 2400 and even of 4200 miles. "More often than not", wrote Mr. Percy Smith, "they (the Polynesians) made these adventurous voyages with the definite object of establishing new colonies in which to settle." Their canoes were not exactly similar to those now in use. "Much larger and better sea-going vessels were formerly employed", we are reminded. Ellis, the missionary, writing a century ago, remarked on the resemblance between the larger Polynesian vessels and those used by the ancient Greeks and the heroes of Homer.

The distances between the various small islands of Oceania, which were visited and colonized by the Polynesian wanderers, were greater than is the distance between America and Oceania. A people who reached Easter Island could, it is held, have hardly missed a great continent. That America was reached is possible. The coco-nut palm grew there in ancient times, and it was introduced into the islands of Oceania by the Polynesians. According to the traditions of the Marquesan Islanders, they procured their first coco-nut from the north-east, the direction in which America lies. The coco-nut was anciently grown in Indonesia and in India. Whether it is native to Indonesia or America is, as yet, uncertain. The important point is that the coco-nut was carried across the Pacific by ancient mariners.

But the Polynesians were not, as has been indicated,

the only explorers of the Pacific Ocean. Great and wide-spread movements of eastern seafaring peoples were in progress some centuries before and after the birth of Christ. The Polynesian migrations were connected with these movements, which emanated chiefly from Cambodia, where a complex civilization was in existence as far back as the eighth century B.C.

It is not rash to assume that there was a psychological motive for these ancient race movements. Large numbers of peoples were not likely to have been stirred to face the perils of uncharted seas merely for love of adventure and a desire for change. It is more likely that the daring mariners were searching not merely for " fresh woods and pastures new ", for lonely uninhabited coasts and alluring and peaceful islands, but for something they required, something which they wished to obtain no matter at what cost of labour and endurance. In other words, they were evidently prospecting for precious metals, precious stones, pearls, &c., for which a great demand had grown up in centres of ancient civilization. This view explains why the movements of these ancient drifts followed, as Mr. W. J. Perry was the first to point out, the distribution of the pearling beds of the world, and why, wherever pearls are found, we find also similar complex religious myths, beliefs, and practices. Gold, silver, precious stones, jade and jadeite, obsidian, curative herbs (and those supposed to be curative and life-pro-longing) were similarly searched for and found. In this connection it is of special interest and importance to find that the pre-Columbian civilization of America was deeply impregnated with the religious beliefs and practices and habits of life that obtained among the treasure-seekers of the Old World. The Maya people settled in the most unhealthy parts of Central America, and it is surely not merely a coincidence that it is in these districts precious metals were and are still found. If the chief attraction had not been gold, would not the early colonists have searched for and settled in a country which demanded a smaller toll on human life? As is shown in Chapter I, gold was regarded by the pre-Columbian Americans not only as a precious but as a sacred substance. It was, as the Aztecs called it, "an emanation" or "excretion of the gods", and it was used in the New World in the same manner and for the same purposes as it was used in the Old World. That is a very remarkable fact to which full recognition and consideration must be given. It cannot be explained away by the theory of "psychic unity".

In India gold was, as ancient texts state clearly, "a form of the gods". We are, in these texts, informed explicitly that "gold is immortal life; . . . gold, indeed, is fire, light, and immortality". The ancient Egyptians regarded gold as "the flesh of the gods", and in the Empire period inscriptions of the temple of Wady Abbad, which refer to gold as such, the goddess Isis is made to say to the Pharaoh, Seti I: "I have given thee the gold countries, . . . fine gold, lapis-lazuli, and turquoise." This goddess was also connected with and the giver of the *Artemesia* herb which effected cures, as was believed, being impregnated with her "life substance" like the red jasper called "Blood of Isis". The sun god Ra was believed to have bones of silver, flesh of gold, and hair of lapis-lazuli, and in Asia lapis-lazuli was supposed to be "the essence of gold".

Like the Buddhists of India, China, and Japan, and like the ancient Gauls, the Aztecs of Mexico accumulated precious metals and precious stones and ornaments made of these in symbolic shapes, to increase their store of religious influence or "merit". There is, in short, not a vestige of originality in the Mexican symbolism of gold, silver, and precious stones. The case for "independent origin" is therefore greatly weakened by such a test.

It is, however, when we come to deal with milk-symbolism that the theory of "psychic unity" is subjected to a particularly heavy strain. In Chapter XI, which deals with the milk goddess, and with the complex ideas connected with the agave plant which are fundamental in Mexican religion, it is shown that these ideas and the associated practices are similar to the ideas connected with various milk-yielding plants in India and Europe, and that we must go to Ancient Egypt to trace the history of such arbitrary connections as those of milk-yielding domesticated animals with certain milk-yielding plants, of sea-shells with milk, and of a milk-providing mother goddess with fish. The Mexican goddess, Mayauel, who suckles a fish, and is a personification of the plant which yields a milky juice that ferments and intoxicates, had a long history which dates back far beyond the beginning of civilization in America, and reaches far across the world to the cradle of ancient civilization in the Nile valley.

Throughout this volume many links are traced between the Old and New Worlds, but none is more remarkable than that afforded by the American story of Yappan (Chapter XIII) which so closely resembles, in all its essential features, a characteristic Hindu myth found in the *Mahá-bhárata*. With that piece of evidence alone, a good circumstantial case is made out for the transference to pre-Columbian America of Hindu modes of thought, Hindu myths and deities, and Hindu religious practices, coloured somewhat by influences to which they had been subjected on the way between India and America and after being localized in the New World. It prepares us, too, for the finding of snake-worshipping peoples in the New World, and, likewise, for finding, as we do find, ascetics who engaged in penitential exercises and begged for food as alms, with bowls in their hands, like the Brahmanic and Buddhist religious mendicants. It further prepares us for identifying the elephant-like figures on Maya sculptured stones, declared by some to be badly-drawn birds (see plate at page 32), and also to find that these elephants are represented with conventional ornamentation of symbolic character identical with the ornamentation of the elephant figures on Cambodian sacred stones. That Buddhist influence reached America is clearly indicated by the Quetzalcoatl figures reproduced on plate at page 256. As is well known, the Buddhists blended with their complex faith the myths and religious practices of the various peoples among whom they settled.

Throughout this volume it is shown that there are ample data which point to fusions of myths and beliefs in America, similar to Old World fusions. The American Tlaloc-lore links with the Dragon-lore of China and Japan and with the Nāga-lore of India. When we come to deal with the goddesses, and especially with the goddess of jade or jadeite, water, and herbs—her herb is that of Isis—we again meet with complexes that have no history in the New World, but are similar to those whose history can be traced in the Old World (Chapters VII and XII).

Anthropologists who favour the view that pre-Columbian American religion and civilization were of independent origin have, of necessity, to explain why the myths and practices of the New World assumed at the very beginning those complex features which, in the Old World, resulted from the fusions and movements of many peoples of different racial types, after a lapse of time much greater than that covered by New World civilization from start to finish. Several Americanists have insisted on the homogeneity of the New World peoples and on their isolation from a remote period—some insist on isolation dating as far back as the Ice Ages. They have failed, however, to explain why the American races should have been the last to emerge from a state of savagery, and why, once they emerged, their progress should have been so phenomenally rapid.

Is it possible, granted that America received its population early in Pleistocene times—a contention yet to be proved—that a people who had so long remained in a state of stagnation, should have, once the seeds of civilization were sown, surpassed even the ancient Egyptian and Mesopotamian peoples in the rapidity of their progress? Could they have achieved in a few generations what the earliest civilized peoples in the world achieved only after the lapse of a good many centuries? When questions like these are asked, it becomes difficult to reject the view that the sudden growth of civilization in America resulted from the intrusions of minorities from centres of Old World culture. When, further, it is found that so many myths, deities, beliefs, &c., common to the Old World are found in the New, the contention seems sound that the onus of proof for their faith must be laid on those who favour the theory of independent origin.

DONALD A. MACKENZIE.

CONTENTS

LIST OF PLATES

MAP

The plates at pages 16, 33, 48 (lower illustration), 84, and 153 are reproduced, by kind permission, from *A Glimpse at Guatemala*, by A. P. and A. C. Maudslay.

MYTHS OF
PRE-COLUMBIAN AMERICA

CHAPTER I

The Glamour of Gold

An Ancient Quest—American Superstitions connected with Gold—
Parallel Customs and Beliefs in America, Asia, and Europe—Mexican Gold
a "Divine Emanation"—Jewels laid at Temple Foundations—Mexican Cult
of Gold-workers—The God of Gold—Human Sacrifices—The "Fighting
Chance" Combat—Gold as an Elixir—Jewels offered to Deities in Asia and
America—Religious "Merit" in Wealth—The Mexican Royal Treasure—
Jewels buried with the Dead—Why Warriors wore Jewels—Jewels and Idols
—Culture Links between the Old and New World.

THE famous "footprints" of Buddha, which may
be seen impressed on hard rock in eastern lands, are
essentially relics of early Buddhist missionary enterprise,
while the complex and borrowed symbols that adorn
them remind us of the debt owed by Buddhism to earlier
faiths. There are similarly to be found on the heights
and hollows of pre-Columbian American mythologies,
associated with groups of familiar imported symbols,
undeniable traces, comparable to Buddha's footprints, of
the activities and influence of those early missionary-
prospectors who wandered far and wide in quest of gold
and gems and curative herbs. That ancient quest, like

1

the Arthurian quest of the Holy Grail, had originally
a religious significance. Precious metals and stones and
precious herbs were supposed to be impregnated with
divine influence and consequently to possess life-giving
and life-prolonging properties, and they were greatly
valued by those ancient peoples whose religious ideas
were rooted in the fear of death, of pain, and the frailties
of old age. The search for them was consequently
hallowed by the performances of religious rites. When
Columbus, in 1502, reached Costa Rica (the " Rich
Coast ") and the region since called Veragua, he found
that the natives, who were descendants of settlers from
Maya and other culture centres, practised rigorous fasting
and continence when they went in quest of gold. " A
superstitious notion with respect to gold ", comments
Washington Irving,[1] " appears to have been very prevalent among the natives. The Indians of Hispaniola
observed the same privations when they sought for it,
abstaining from food and from sexual intercourse.
Columbus, who seemed to look upon gold as one of
the sacred and mystic treasures of the earth, wished to
encourage similar observances among the Spaniards, exhorting them to purify themselves for the research of
the mines by fasting, prayer, and chastity."

A similiar spirit of religious fervour originally
attended the search for ginseng (mandrake) in Korea.
This plant—which, as Dr. Rendel Harris shows,[2] was
anciently connected with the goddess Aphrodite and other
goddesses of similar type—is found chiefly by the Koreans
in their Kang-ge Mountains.[3] "It is rare ", Mrs. Bishop
informs us, " and the search so often ends in failure, that

[1] *The Life and Voyages of Christopher Columbus*, Book XV, Chapter VI.
[2] *The Ascent of Olympus.*
[3] Wild ginseng is more valuable than the cultivated variety.

the common people credit it with magical properties and believe that only men of pure lives can find it."[1] The quest of ginseng dates back till early times in the Far East. Like gold dust, ground jade, &c., it was supposed to contain life-renewing and life-prolonging qualities, and it is still in demand among Chinamen sufficiently wealthy to be able to purchase it.[2]

The earliest searchers for precious metals, and other precious or sacred substances, who settled in Spain before the introduction of bronze working in Western Europe, were an intensely religious people from the east, who, as their relics show, adored the mother goddess of the Palm-tree cult. They have been credited by Siret[3] with having introduced those religious ideas and ceremonies that gave origin to Druidism, a feature of which was the Gaulish custom of depositing large quantities of gold and silver in sacred lakes and in sacred groves.

The Aztecs of Mexico venerated precious metals, precious stones, pearls, and herbs, and attached to them a religious value. Their native name for gold was *teocuitlalt*, a word formed from *teotl* ("god") and *cuitlatl* ("an emanation")[4] and signifying "divine emanation".

Gold, silver, pearls, precious stones, &c., were offered with seeds and the blood of human beings to the Mexican gods. These precious or sacred things were not only deposited in temples but laid beneath their foundations. Bernal Diaz, who accompanied Cortez, the conqueror of Mexico, informs us that when the temple of Tenochtitlan (city of Mexico) was being constructed the natives deposited at its foundations offerings of gold,

[1] *Korea and Her Neighbours*, Vol. II, 96 (London, 1898).
[2] A single root of wild ginseng may cost £40.
[3] *L'Anthropologie*, Tome XXX, 1920, pp. 235 *et seq.* (article "La Dame de l'Érable").　　[4] The word is used in a gross sense.

silver, pearls, and precious stones, and "bathed them with the blood of many Indian prisoners of war who were sacrificed ". With the precious metals and gems they "placed there every sort and kind of seed that the land produces, so that their idols should give them victories and riches and large crops ".

Bernal Diaz proceeds to tell how discovery was made by the Spaniards that this practice was formerly prevalent in the conquered state. The Christian Church "to our patron and guide, Señor Santiago " was, he tells, erected on the site of the demolished Aztec temple. When the workmen opened part of the ancient foundations in order to strengthen them, "they found much gold and silver and *chalchihuites* (sacred stones, including jadeite), and pearls and seed pearls and other stones ". A similar discovery was made by a Spanish settler at another part of the temple area.

On being questioned by the Spaniards regarding this custom, the Mexicans said it was true that the natives had formerly deposited precious metals and jewels at the temple foundations, "and that so it was noted in their books and pictures of ancient things ".[1]

There was anciently a Mexican cult and caste of gold-seekers and gold-workers. Their chief centre was at Atzcapotzalco, about three miles to the north-west of Tenochtitlan (city of Mexico). This town was the capital of the Tepaneco people before the Aztecs invaded that region. Their special cult god was Xipe Totec [2] whose name signifies "god of the flaying " or "our lord the flayed ". He was worshipped generally throughout Mexico and very specially honoured at an annual festival.

---

[1] Bernal Diaz, *The True History of the Conquest of New Spain* (English translation ; Hakluyt Society publication ; Book II, Chapter XCII).

[2] Pronounced *She'pe tot'ek.*

Those who neglected homage to him were supposed to suffer punishment by becoming victims of skin diseases, smallpox, and head and eye pains. As Xipe was the source of these afflictions, he was the only deity who could remove them. In this respect he resembled the Anatolian mouse and sun god Smintheus Apollo, who in the *Iliad* shoots arrows of disease from his silver bow, and thus sends "a sore plague" so that the folk begin to perish. The plague rages until the offended god is propitiated with sacrifices, prayers, and songs:

"So all day long worshipped they the god with music, singing the beautiful pæan, the sons of the Achaians making music to the far-darter; and his heart was glad to hear ".[1]

Xipe had animal and human forms. Like the Chinese god of the west, he was a tiger;[2] he was likewise the red spoonbill and the azure cotinga. In human shape he was invariably coloured yellow and tawny, wearing a tasselled cap, a human skin which surrounded the upper part of his body, and a green kilt; he carried a red-rimmed yellow shield and a spear or sceptre.

The rites observed in connection with Xipe's festival were of a particularly savage character. Criminals and prisoners were sacrificed and flayed. Those found guilty of the crime of stealing gold were supposed to have wronged and insulted the god, and they were kept as prisoners until the festival, when they were flayed alive; their hearts were afterwards torn out and their bodies cut up and eaten with ceremony. Youthful warriors meanwhile clad themselves in the skins of victims, and fought a sham battle, taking prisoners who had subsequently to be ransomed. A captive or criminal sacrificed to Xipe

[1] *Iliad*, Book I (Lang, Leaf, and Myers translation, London, 1914 edition).
[2] The Chinese tiger god of the west was connected with metal, as well as with autumn, wind, and the planet Venus.

was supposed to bring luck to his owner—that is, to the warrior who had taken him in battle, or the individual who had been robbed of gold. The owner gave the skin to men who went about begging alms and brought what they received to him. At the end of twenty days after the festival all the human skins, then smelling horribly, were deposited in a cave. Those who had worn them purified themselves by washing, a ceremony which was the occasion of great rejoicings. Victims of those diseases which were supposed to be caused by Xipe assisted in disposing of the human skins. It was believed that by touching the skins they invoked Xipe to cure them.

As the victim, who was doomed to be sacrificed to Xipe, was, during the period preceding the festival, regarded as the adopted son of his owner, it may be that criminals and prisoners were substitutes for sons and that originally parents sacrificed their own children, as did the Irish worshippers of the golden god Crom Cruach. This " king idol of Erin " was, according to one reference, surrounded by " twelve idols made of stones, but he was of gold. . . . To him they used to offer the firstlings of every issue and the chief scions of every clan." Another version tells that Crom Cruach was " adorned with gold and silver, and surrounded by twelve other statues with bronze ornaments ".[1] It is specifically stated in a Gaelic poem :

> To him without glory
> They would kill their piteous, wretched offspring,
> With much wailing and peril,
> To pour their blood around Crom Cruach.

In Gaelic literature there is evidence that criminals and prisoners were given " a fighting chance ". If they could

[1] *Revue Celtique*, Vol. XVI. De Jubainville, *Le Cycle Mythologique Irlandais et la Mythologie Celtique*, Chapter V, section 7.

overcome those selected to guard them and then out-distance them in a race, they were allowed to regain their freedom. A custom of like character obtained in ancient Mexico in connection with the Xipe festival which was consecrated also to the terrible war god Huitzilopochtli, who, like Xipe, had solar attributes. The Mexican's prisoner was painted white and had his hair decorated with tufts of cotton. He was then placed on a great stone shaped like a millstone and attached to it by a rope, which was long enough to allow him freedom of move-ment when engaging in combat. The weapon placed in the hands of the prisoner was a wooden club in the head of which, however, feathers instead of flints were stuck. Against him went in succession strong, young warriors, wearing the skins of Xipe's victims, and armed with swords and shields. In some cases the prisoner was set free if he overcame in single combat five warriors; in others he was attacked by warrior after warrior until he was himself struck down. The story is told of a fierce gladiatorial conflict of this character in which the hero was a general of the Tlascala people, who had assisted Cortez against their hereditary enemies the Aztecs. He had been taken prisoner almost by accident, but refused the offers of Montezuma, the Aztec king, to return home or to accept a high position in his service. He preferred to fight his hated enemies to the death. Accordingly he was tied to the stone, and before he fell he slew eight and badly injured twenty of the Aztec champions.[1]

The belief that Xipe, the cult god of gold-workers, cured diseases of the skin and eyes is of special interest, as gold was not only connected with the sun, "the eye" of heaven, but was of itself, as has been indicated, an

---

[1] Abbé Clavigero, *Storia Antica del Messico*, tom 1, pp. 281-2 (English translation, London, 1787).

elixir.   Being impregnated with divine influence or "life substance" from the divine source of life, it could renew youth and prolong existence in this world and in the next. That is the reason why gold-dust is regarded as an important ingredient in the native medicines of India and China.   "He who swallows gold", says a Chinese text, "will exist as gold; he who swallows jade will exist as long as jade."   Both gold and jade were "the essence of the dark sphere" (heaven)[1].

In India, as far back as Vedic times, gold "that", one text says, "men of old with their progeny sought," was given a religious value.   "Of long life becomes he that wears it," is a highly significant statement.   "Gold, doubtless," runs another passage, "is a form of the gods . . . gold is immortal life . . . gold, indeed, is fire, light, and immortality."[2]

Precious metals and gems radiated divine influence, and the custom was widespread in ancient times of accumulating them in temples and palaces, as well as of wearing them for protection and good luck.   In Lucian's *De Dea Syria* (Chapter XXXII) a description is given of the statue of Hera:

"Without she is gilt with gold, and gems of great price adorn her, some white, some sea-green, others wine-dark, others flashing like fire.   Besides these there are many onyxes from Sardinia and the jacinth and emeralds, the offerings of the Egyptians and of the Indians, Ethiopians, Medes, Armenians, and Babylonians."[3]

The temple is compared to "the rising sun".

"The foundation rises from the earth to the space of two fathoms, and on this rests the temple.   The ascent to the temple

[1] De Groot, *The Religious System of China*, Book I, Vol. I, pp. 272-3.

[2] Whitney, *Atharva Veda Samhita*, XIX, 26, p. 937 (Harvard Oriental Series, Vols. VII, VIII, Cambridge, Mass., 1908), and Eggeling, *Satapatha-Brahmana*, Part V of *Sacred Books of the East*, XLIV, 1900, pp. 187, 203, 236, 239, 348-50.

[3] Professor H. A. Strong's translation, London, 1913.

RUINS OF THE PALACE OF MITLA, MEXICO

The upper view shows the Terrace, and the lower a detail of the sculptured stone-work.

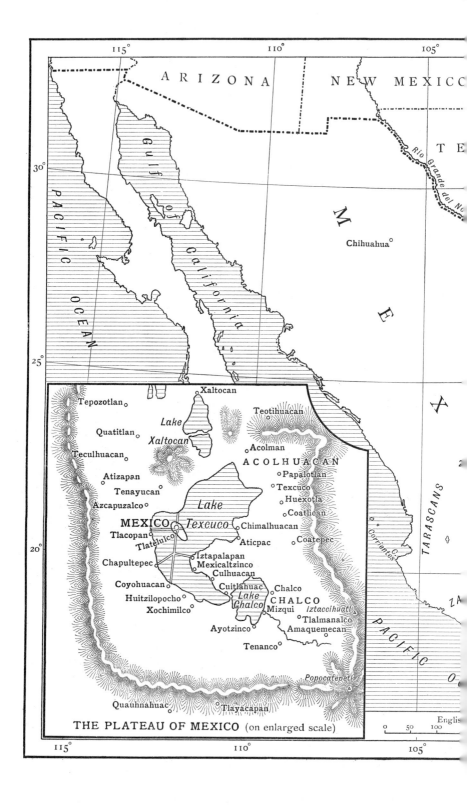

THE PLATEAU OF MEXICO (on enlarged scale)

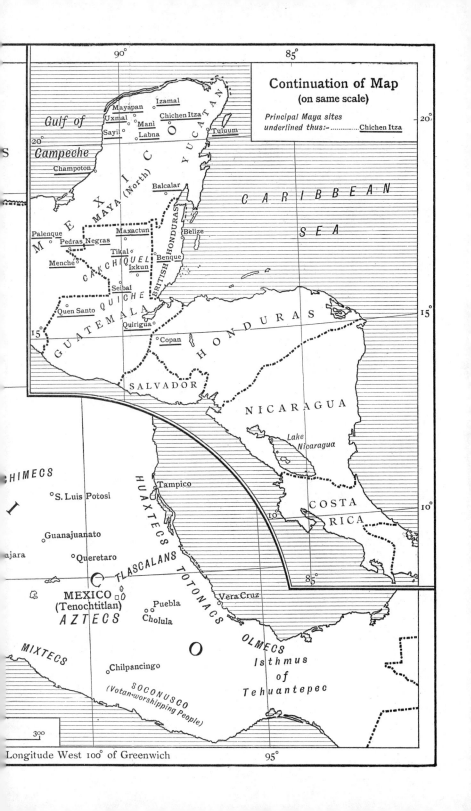

Continuation of Map
(on same scale)

Principal Maya sites
underlined thus:- ....Chichen Itza

90°   85°   20°

Gulf of   Mayapan   Izamal
Campeche   Uxmal Mani Chichen Itza
            Sayil Labna
20°
  Champoton   Tuluum

M E X I C O

                    Balcalar
MAYA (North)
                         C A R I B B E A N
Palenque   Maxactun
Pedras Negras   Belize   S E A
              Tikal
Menche   Benque
CAKCHIQUEL   Ikxun
BRITISH HONDURAS
        Seibal
QUICHE
Quen Santo
            Quirigua   H O N D U R A S   15°
15°
              Copan

GUATEMALA

        SALVADOR

                    N I C A R A G U A

                         Lake
                       Nicaragua

HIMECS
      S. Luis Potosi   C O S T A   10°
I   10°   R I C A
    Guanajuanato
ajara   Queretaro
        TLASCALANS
      C   Vera Cruz
        MEXICO   TOTONACS
      (Tenochtitlan)   Puebla   85°
      A Z T E C S   Cholula
                                   OLMECS
MIXTECS   O   Isthmus
        Chilpancingo   of
              SOCONUSCO   Tehuantepec
          (Votan-worshipping People)

300

Longitude West 100° of Greenwich   95°

is built of wood and not particularly wide: as you mount even the great hall exhibits a wonderful spectacle, and it is ornamented with golden doors. The temple within is ablaze with gold, and the ceiling in its entirety is golden." [1]

Precious metals were not used for decorative purposes alone. At a spring festival they were sacrificed with animals.

"They cut down tall trees and set them up in the court; then they bring goats and sheep and cattle and hang them living to the trees; they add to these birds and garments and gold and silver work. After all is finished, they carry the gods around the trees and set fire under; in a moment all is a blaze." [2]

Reference has been made to the Gaulish custom of depositing gold and silver in sacred groves and lakes. None dared to touch these "gifts of numerous donors". The Romans plundered the sacred treasure of the Celts as the Spaniards did the sacred treasure of the Mexicans.[3]

In the Buddhist Paradise the "stock of merit"—that is, religious merit—was supposed to "grow in the following shapes, viz. either in gold, in silver, in jewels, in beryls, in shells, in stones, in corals, in amber, in red pearls, in diamonds, &c., or in any one of the other jewels,[4] or in all kinds of perfumes, in flowers, in garlands, in ointment, in incense-powder, in cloaks, in umbrellas, in flags,

---

[1] Professor H. A. Strong's translation, London, 1913, Chapters XXIX–XXX.

[2] *Ibid.*, Chapter XLIX.

[3] *Diodorus Siculus*, V, 27; *Strabo*, IV, c. 1, § 13.

[4] In China, gold, jade, pearls, silver, &c., were placed in the mouth of the dead so as to preserve the body from decay and prolong life in the next world. "The same reasons why gold and jade were used for stuffing the mouth of the dead hold good for the use of pearls in this connection" (De Groot, *The Religious System of China*, Book I, Vol. I, pp. 274 *et seq.*). For evidence that in Vedic times in India the pearl was supposed to have life-giving qualities, see H. Bloomfield, *Hymns of the Atharva Veda* in *Sacred Books of the East*, XLII, 1897, IV, 20.

in banners, or in lamps, or in all kinds of dancing, singing, and music ".[1] Sacred objects of merit-increasing gold in the "Land of Bliss" included "nets of gold adorned with emblems of the dolphin, the svastika (swashtika), the nandyavarta, and the moon ".[2]

When Cortez, the famous Spanish plunderer, reached the city of Mexico he came to hear of a great hoard of gold and jewels, which successive Aztec kings had accumulated and increased. Father Diego Duran, a sixteenth century writer, who procured his information from men that had taken part in the Spanish conquest, tells that the treasure was kept in a secret chamber, the small, low door of which had been covered with plaster shortly before the arrival of the Spaniards. The plaster was removed.

"Entering by that narrow and low door, they found a large and spacious room, in the middle of which was a heap of gold, jewels, and precious stones, as high as a man; so high was it, that one was not seen on the other side. . . . At the same time there was in this room a great quantity of piles of very rich cotton cloths and women's finery; there were hanging on the walls a great number of shields and arms, and devices of rich workmanship and colours; there were many piles of vessels of gold, dishes and porringers made according to their style, from which the kings ate, especially four large dishes made like platters, all of gold, very elaborately worked, as big as a large shield, and they were so filled with dust that one understood that many days had passed in which they had not been in service. There were many gold chocolate cups, made and decorated in the same manner of those of the gourds, used for drinking cacao, some with feet and others without; there were in the corners of the room many stones for working all manner of precious stones; in fine, there was in this room the greatest riches ever seen so that the Spaniards were surprised and marvelled."

---

[1] Description of Suktavati, the Land of Bliss, in *Buddhist Mahâyâna Texts* (*Sacred Books of the East*, Vol. XLIX, pp. 16–7).   [2] *Ibid.*, p. 50.

No individual king was allowed to profit by this accumulated treasure. Father Duran says in this connection :

"On the death of the King, the same day that he died, all the treasure that he left of gold, stone, feathers, and arms, and finally all his wardrobe, was put in that room, with much care, as a sacred thing and of the gods".

Bernal Diaz gives fewer details about the secret chamber and its contents. He says that when Cortez and some of his captains entered it—

"they saw such a number of jewels and slabs and plates of gold and chalchihuites (sacred stones) and other great riches, that they were quite carried away and did not know what to say about such wealth".

Andrés de Tápia, one of Cortez's captains, tells that after entering through the door they found—

"a great number of chambers, and in some of them considerable quantity of gold in jewels and idols and many feathers".[1]

Estimates of the value of the treasure vary from £700,000 to a million and a half pounds sterling.

Gold, jewels, and other precious articles were buried with the Mexican dead and especially with the bodies of monarchs, priests, and great warriors. In the narrative of "the Anonymous Conqueror", a companion of Cortez,[2] a description is given of a burial custom :

"They made a pit in the earth with walls of rough stone and mortar, in which they placed the dead seated in a chair. At his

---

[1] Father Diego Duran, *Historia de las Indias de Nueva España y Islas de Tierra Firme*; Bernal Diaz, *The True History of the Conquest of New Spain*, translation by A. P. Maudslay (Hakluyt Society publication); *The Goldsmith's Art in Ancient Mexico* (Marshall H. Saville, New York, 1920).

[2] *Narrative of some Things of New Spain and of the Great City of Temestitan, Mexico,* Cortez Society, Vol. I, p. 49 (New York, 1917).

side they placed his sword and shield, burying also certain jewels of gold. I helped to take from a sepulchre jewels worth three thousand castellanos."

The dead were in need of protection, for the road leading to the Otherworld was beset with many perils. Their sacred jewel-charms were believed to protect souls and withal to stimulate them with their life-conferring qualities as they had protected and stimulated them during the earthly state of existence. The gods themselves were similarly charmed and protected. "Put on thy disguising, the golden garment; clothe thyself with it", a poet sang to the god Xipe Totec.[1]

Tacitus tells us that the Æstyans, who searched for and traded in amber, a life-giving substance, worshipped the mother goddess, regarded the boar as her symbol, and believed that "he who has that emblem about him, thinks himself secure even in the thickest ranks of the enemy, without any need of arms, or any other mode of defence".[2] In like manner Aztec warriors were protected in battle by having their armour and weapons adorned with gold, jewels, and symbols, and by wearing talismans as ornaments. Shields of pure gold were used as votive offerings, but shields richly adorned with life-protecting and stimulating gold, pearls, jadeite, &c., were carried into battle. Lip and nose ornaments, which had a religious significance, were worn by the living and placed in graves with the dead. Idols were as richly decorated with precious or sacred metals and jewels and symbols in the New as in the Old World. Captain Andrés de Tápia, who accompanied Cortez, has described

[1] Seler, *Ancient Mexican Religious Poetry* (*Proceedings of the International Congress of Americanists*, 13th Session, New York), pp. 171–4.

[2] *Manners of the Germans*, Chapter XLV.

two stone idols about three yards high, which he saw in Mexico.

" The stone ", he writes, " was covered over with mother-of-pearl, and over this, fastened with bitumen, like a paste, were (set in) many jewels of gold, and men, snakes, birds, and histories (hieroglyphs) made of small and large turquoises, of emeralds and amethysts, so that all the mother-of-pearl was covered, except in some places where they left it (uncovered) so as to make work with the stones. These idols had some plump snakes of gold (as) girdles, and for collars each (one had) ten or twelve hearts made of gold, and for the face a mask of gold, and eyes of mirror (obsidian or iron pyrites)."[1]

Mexican temples were lavishly decorated with gold and precious stones and other precious or sacred things, including richly coloured feathers. Subject towns and states paid tribute in gold and jewels. The precious metal might be given in dust or in bars, or after being shaped into discs, plaques, shields, diadems, &c. The Mexican hieroglyphic signs for gold were varieties of the swashtika which had origin in the Old World.

Gold, silver, pearls, precious stones, jade, and jadeite, &c., were thus as highly esteemed in the New World as in the Old. Withal, they were used in precisely the same way and connected with similar beliefs and practices. At the outset, therefore, the important question arises whether the habits of life and the habits of thought of the pre-Columbian treasure-seekers of the Americas were of spontaneous generation. Did their civilizations and their complex religious systems have independent origin in their homelands and develop there, entirely isolated from and uninfluenced by those of much greater antiquity in the Old World? Is it possible that the early

---

[1] Quoted by Saville in *The Goldsmith's Art in Ancient Mexico*, p. 115 (New York, 1920).

peoples who reached America from Asia carried no vestige of religious belief with them—that each migration, early and late, involved entire loss of memory, so that immemorial modes of thought, and immemorial customs and beliefs, were completely forgotten, and that after reaching the new land they set themselves to invent anew what their ancestors had invented before them, and to formulate religious ideas that had long been prevalent in the Old World whence they came?

CHAPTER II

Growth of New World Civilization

Distribution of Population—Attractions of Unhealthy Areas—Introduction of Complex Civilization—Aztecs as the Assyrians of America—How Spaniards discovered Gold-mines—Aztec Trade Wars—Aztec Control of Gold Supplies—Spaniards imitate Aztec Methods—Motives for Acquiring Wealth—The Æsthetic Theory—Jewels as "Tutelary Spirits"—Metal Symbolism—The "Golden Sun" and "Silver Moon" in Old and New Worlds—Jade and Jadeite—Psychological Motive for Search for Treasure—Theory of the Independent Origin of Complex Beliefs.

THE questions raised at the conclusion of the previous chapter are of vital importance in connection with the study of the religious systems of pre-Columbian America. As has been shown, gold and gems were searched for and found, and were utilized in much the same manner as in the Old World. This is a fact which no ingenious method of reasoning can well set aside. It is impossible to ignore it. We must deal with it and we must account for it. If it does not accord with any preconceived theory regarding the origin of New World civilization, then that theory must be readjusted or wholly abandoned. Solid structures of fact must replace the "hypothetical bridges" planned by those who had at their disposal much less evidence than is now available.

The necessity for this attitude is emphasized when we find that, owing to the religious value attached to precious metals and gems, the distribution and activities of the population were determined by the presence of these in different localities. Treasure-searchers were attracted to

the most unhealthy districts of Central America[1] and into
these carried the elements of a complex civilization, complex religious beliefs and symbols, and a highly developed
art, the histories of which must be sought for elsewhere.
The beginnings of Maya art and Maya religion cannot be
discovered in the Maya country.

The activities of the early searchers for substances of
religious value led to the opening up of trade routes,
and the struggle for the control of these caused rival
peoples to establish and build up political organizations
that exercised far and wide an overpowering influence.
The Aztecs, like the Assyrians of Western Asia, formed
a strong predatory state with purpose to enrich themselves
at the expense of their neighbours. Their accumulated
wealth had been won for them by military force and the
constant threat of military reprisals.

When Cortez, the Spanish conqueror of Mexico, found
that gold was so plentiful in the Aztec capital, he became
particulary anxious to discover the localities of the mines.
According to Bernal Diaz, Montezuma, the Aztec king,
informed Cortez that he was accustomed to receive gold
from three different places. The chief source of supply,
however, was the province of Zacatula (now called the
Rio Balsas in Guerrero) on the south coast, and situated
about a fortnight's journey from the city of Mexico.
There it was washed from the earth. Gold was obtained
also from the sands of two rivers on the north coast in
the province called Tustepec and from the countries
occupied by the Chinantec and Zapotec peoples.

---

[1] "The most inaccessible, unhealthful, and untillable lowlands . . . the densely-
forested, highly-feverish, and almost untillable lowlands of Peten and Eastern Gaute-
mala," as Professor Huntington puts it (*The Climate Factor*, Washington, D.C., 1914,
pp. 215, 223). It is of special importance to find, however, that Copan, the centre of
Maya culture, was situated on a tributary of the Motagua river, still famous as the
greatest gold-yielding Central American river. Maclaren, *Gold*, London, 1908, p. 608.

CHICHEN-ITZA: THE SO-CALLED CHURCH ("LA IGLESIA")

From a photograph by H. N. Sweet

REMAINS OF AN ANCIENT INCA SEAT OF JUSTICE,
NEAR LAKE TITICACA

Cortez arranged with Montezuma to send to the various gold-fields companies of Spaniards accompanied by escorts of Mexicans. In a letter to his king, Cortez wrote:

"For each of his (Montezuma's) own people I sent two Spaniards. Some went to a province called Cuzula, eighty leagues from the great city of Temixtitan, the natives of which are his vassals, and there they were shown three rivers, from each of which they brought me some specimens of gold of very good quality, although it was taken out with mean tools, as they had only those with which the Indians extract it. On the road they passed through three provinces, according to what the Spaniards said, of very fine land, and many hamlets and cities, and towns very populous, and containing buildings equal to any in Spain. They told me especially of a house and a fort, greater, stronger, and better built than the castle of Burgos, and that the people of this province, called Tamazulapa, were better dressed than any others we have seen, and, as it seemed to them, more intelligent."

The Spaniards were next taken to the province called Malinaltepeque, situated about seventy leagues distant from Temixtitan in the direction of the sea-coast. There they obtained samples of gold from a large river. Another party went to a mountainous country called Teniz, farther up the river. The people there were not subject to Montezuma and their king was named Coateli-camat. They spoke a distinct language, were very war-like and were armed with long lances. The king allowed the Spaniards to enter his country, but, because they were his enemies, refused that privilege to the Culúan vassals of Montezuma who accompanied them. The Spaniards were well received, and the people "showed them seven or eight mines where they took out gold". Samples were obtained for Cortez, to whom the native monarch sent presents of gold ornaments and of clothing.

Another Spanish party proceeded to the province of Tuchitepeque, twelve leagues farther on in the direction of the sea-coast, and were there shown one or two places in which gold was to be obtained. In some localities nuggets were found on the surface of the earth, but the chief sources were the river sands from which gold-dust was washed. The gold was carried from the workings in tubes of cane or melted in pots and cast in bars.[1]

In Tenochtitlan (city of Mexico) there was in these days a great market in which gold and precious stones were exposed for sale. According to the Anonymous Conqueror it was held every fifth day. "On one side of the plaza", he wrote, "are those who sell gold, and adjoining are those who sell stones of various classes set in gold, in the shapes of various birds and animals."[2]

Trading expeditions brought Mexico city into touch with the areas in which precious metals and gems were found. Trade followed the Aztec "flag" and the "flag followed trade". There appears to be little doubt that the chief motive for Aztec expansion was to secure control of trade. About a century and a half before the arrival of the Spaniards, Mayapan, the centre of Maya commerce and industry, was devastated by the Aztecs, and solely, it would appear, because it had been a dangerous trading rival to Mexico city. Other states were either over-run or wholly or partly brought under subjection. In some cases tribute was paid and collected at the point of the sword. Seler, dealing with this aspect of Mexican life, illustrates how Mexican trade was nursed into prosperity and protected by the Aztec kings, by relating the following tradition:

[1] Bernal Diaz, *The True History of the Conquest of Spain*, Vol. II, pp. 127-8; and Cortez, quoted by Marshall H. Saville, *The Goldsmith's Art in Ancient Mexico*, pp. 104-7.   [2] *Cortez Society Publications*, No. I, pp. 65-7.

"In the wild forests of Mictlanquauhtla some inhabitants of the city of Uaxyacac murderously attacked and plundered a Mexican caravan which was returning home from Tabasco with costly goods, the news of which did not reach the Mexicans until years later. The king who was then reigning, Motecuhzoma the elder, surnamed Ilhuicamina, equipped an expedition to avenge the dead, and the crime was atoned by the extermination of the entire tribe. A number of Mexican families and about 600 families from neighbouring cities situated in the valley of Mexico started out to settle the vacant lands of the exterminated tribe, under the leadership of four Mexican chieftains whom the king had chosen for his expedition. . . . Assault and assassination of Mexican merchants are almost always mentioned as the *casus belli* in the native records."

Wars were waged with purpose to compel independent states to grant special trading privileges. The Zapotecs, for instance, were forced "to allow Mexican merchants to pass through to the regions on the Pacific coast, and to grant them freedom of trade in their own territory".[1] The region over which the Aztecs extended their influence, or were in process of extending it when the Spaniards arrived, was that in which gold was used in greatest abundance. Where they did not obtain control of the gold-fields they were assured of supplies of gold not only by means of exchange but by payment of tribute. Montezuma, the Aztec king whose treasure was plundered by Cortez, received regularly every year rich tribute from the hot-land provinces. In Mexican documents "there are many pictures, in colours, of tributes of gold, jewels, feather ornaments and mantles, as well as portraits of the conquerors". The codex known as the "Tribute Roll of Montezuma" shows that tribute was paid also in gold-dust "kept in gourds or cane tubes and in bars", and the names of places from which tribute was received are

---

[1] *Bureau of American Ethnology*, Bulletin 28, pp. 258 *et seq.*

given.[1]   When the Spaniards obtained political control
of the Mexican plateau, they exacted tribute in precisely
the same manner as the Aztecs had previously done.
The only difference was that they were more tyrannical
and greedy.   At the Congress of Americanists in London
in 1912 very special interest was taken in " a memorial or
statement by the native inhabitants of Tepetlaoztoc (a
small hill-town between Tetzcoco and Otumba) of the
extortionate tribute exacted, and the ill-treatment suffered
under the Spanish masters to whom successively they had
been assigned by the King of Spain ".   The heavy tribute
demanded had, it would appear, brought about a condition
bordering on actual slavery.

When it is considered how the social, economic,
and religious life of pre-Columbian America, especially
in centres of civilization, was as strongly influenced,
as was the case in the civilizations of the Old World,
by the fictitious value attached to such a useless metal as
gold, it is difficult to believe that no cultural influences
ever " flowed " in ancient times across the Pacific.   Did
the Americans follow the promptings of some mysterious
human instinct when, to begin with, they set themselves
to search for gold by washing river mud ?   How did
they come to know of the existence of gold ; how was it
that they foresaw to what uses gold could be put ?   Was
it a mere coincidence that they invented a clay crucible
and a blow-pipe similar to the Egyptian crucible and
blow-pipe distributed throughout the Old World ?   Did
they search for gold, pearls, jewels, amber, and jade or
jadeite, which were all extremely difficult to find, simply
because it was " natural " for them so to do ?   Was it
because they were urged by that æsthetic sense supposed
to be dormant in man, that they were overcome with the

[1] Saville, *The Goldsmith's Art in Ancient Mexico*, pp. 108, 154, 158.

desire to ornament their bodies with jewels? Was it
their æsthetic sense that caused them to produce hideous,
grinning faces in gold, to disfigure their own ears, and to
thrust the so-called "ornaments" through their lips and
noses? Did they deposit their jewellery at temple foundations and bury them with their dead because they were
prompted by their innate sense of beauty? How came it
about that the ancient Americans, like the ancient Asiatics,
Europeans, and Egyptians, established a gold standard
and paid tribute in gold and jewels? Are we to regard
it as in no way surprising that they connected gold with
the sun and silver with the moon as did other ancient
peoples in the Old World, and that they should have
accumulated precious metals and jewels to increase
religious "merit" and the power of the ruling monarch
and to protect and stimulate themselves in this world and
the next?

It cannot be argued that the Maya people at Chichen
Itza, Yucatan, threw jewellery into lakes and rivers, as
did the Celts of Gaul, because they were overcome by an
overpowering sense of the beautiful: the jewels were
votive offerings as were likewise the jewels deposited by
pious natives at the foundations of their temple pyramid
in Mexico city. Dr. William Robertson, the eighteenth
century historian, recognized this when he referred to the
connection between deities and charms:

"The *manitous* or *okkis* of the North Americans were amulets
or charms which they imagined to be of such virtue as to preserve
the persons who reposed confidence in them from every disastrous
event, or they were considered as tutelary spirits whose aid they
might implore in circumstances of distress".[1]

In Japan the pearl (tama) might be a *shintai* ("god

[1] *History of America*, Book IV, Section 7.

body "); the soul of a god was a *mi-tama*, which as *mi* was an ancient name for a dragon-serpent, meant "dragon-pearl".

There is, it must be frankly recognized, a remarkable resemblance between the metal symbolism of pre-Columbian America and that of the Old World. One of the Peruvian creation myths sets forth that at the beginning three eggs fell from the sky, one of gold, one of silver, and one of copper. From the gold egg was hatched the curacas or chiefs, from the silver egg the nobles, and from the copper egg the common people. This connection between metals and castes is found in India; it is found also in the Indian and Greek doctrines of the world's Ages, which refer to races identified with the Gold Age, the Silver Age, the Copper Age, and the Iron Age.

In Mexico gold was given the same arbitrary connection with the sun and silver with the moon, as obtained in ancient Egypt and in ancient Asian and European civilizations. Among the gifts sent by King Montezuma to Cortez were two wheels, the one of gold and the other of silver, "each one", according to Captain Andrés de Tápia, "the size of a cart wheel". "Here", wrote Francisco de Aguilar, "they (the Spaniards) were given a present of a golden sun among some weapons and a moon of silver." Another writer refers to them as "two round discs, one of fine gold, the other of fine silver, finely worked with beautiful figures". This treasure was sent to Spain where it was seen by Oviedo who wrote of the great wheels, "The one of gold they had in reference to the sun and that of silver in the memory of the moon".[1]

[1] Authorities quoted by Saville in *The Goldsmith's Art in Ancient Mexico*, pp. 191 *et seq.*

It is difficult to believe that the same complex ideas connected with gold, silver, and copper, should have had independent origin in the New and Old Worlds. The problem involved is similar to that which presented itself to Mr. Berthold Laufer in his scholarly work on jade,[1] when dealing with the problem as to how it happened that the peoples of ancient America, Europe, and New Zealand attached, like the Chinese, a religious value to jade (nephrite) and jadeite. Heinrich Fischer[2] believed, when he wrote on the subject, that jade did not occur *in situ* either in Europe or America, and elaborated the theory that the mineral, or the objects worked from it, had been carried to both continents in ancient times by migrating peoples from Asia. Jade *in situ* was, however, subsequently discovered in different parts of Europe and in Alaska. Fischer's hypothesis could not, therefore, be upheld, but it would appear that the critics who destroyed it destroyed too much. They overlooked the fact that in Europe jade is scarce and difficult to find. Modern scientists searched for it for many years before they were able to locate it. As Laufer says, "it could not have been such an easy task for primitive man to hunt up these hidden places", unless we conclude that he was "much keener or more resourceful than our present scientists". The important aspect of the problem is not that early man in Europe succeeded in finding jade, but that he ever searched for it. Laufer writes in this connection :

"Nothing could induce me to the belief that primitive man of Central Europe incidentally and spontaneously embarked on the

[1] *Jade : a study in Chinese Archæology and Religion* (Field Museum of Natural History, Anthropological Series, Vol. X), Chicago, 1912.
[2] *Nephrit und Jadeit nach ihren mineralogischen Eigenschaften sowie nach ihrer urgeschichtlichen und ethnographischen Bedeutung.* Stuttgart, 1880 (second edition).

laborious task of quarrying and working jade. The psychological motive for this act must be supplied, and it can be deduced only from the source of historical facts. From the standpoint of the general development of culture in the Old World, there is absolutely no vestige of originality in the prehistoric cultures of Europe which appear as an appendix to Asia. Originality is certainly the rarest thing in this world, and in the history of mankind the original thoughts are appallingly sparse. There is, in the light of historical facts and experiences, no reason to credit the prehistoric and early historic populations of Europe with any spontaneous ideas relative to jade; they received these, as everything else, from an outside source; they gradually learned to appreciate the value of this tough and compact substance, and then set to hunting for natural supplies."[1]

In like manner the peoples of Europe and America searched for and found the peculiar clay from which fine porcelain is made; but they did not do so until after it was discovered how the Chinese made use of it. "The peoples of Europe and America", says Laufer, "could have made porcelain ages ago; the material was at their elbows, but the brutal fact remains that they did not, that they missed the opportunity, and that only the importation and investigation of Chinese porcelain were instrumental in hunting for and finding Kaolinic clay."[2]

Was then, it may be asked, the search for jade or jadeite, and for gold, silver, pearls, and precious stones, in pre-Columbian America quite spontaneous and incidental? Are the Mexicans, Mayans, Peruvians, &c., to be credited with spontaneous ideas relative to those things, which were indentical, or almost identical, with the ideas prevailing and pre-existing in ancient Asia and Europe? Are we to believe that certain religious conceptions—which were prevalent in Egypt, Babylonia, and Crete some twenty or

[1] *Jade*, p. 5.   [2] *Ibid.*, p. 4.

thirty centuries before the Christian era, and others that
were rooted and fostered in China and northern Siberia
in later times, before and after the dawn of Christianity—
sprang up in America and flourished there as a matter of
course a few centuries before the Spanish invasion?

The history of many complex beliefs that existed in
pre-Columbian America cannot be traced there, but they
can be traced elsewhere. Are we then to accept the
theory that, despite their complexity, they must have
been indigenous—that they were essentially the products
of natural laws and " well-known mental processes "?
" Great civilizations ", says a writer in this connection,
" like those whose ruins remain in Peru, Mexico, Egypt,
the Euphrates valley, India, and China . . . arose comparatively locally, comparatively recently, and comparatively suddenly. They seem to have been called forth
by new conditions, and to mark a new phase in the
history of the species." [1] The same view is taken by Sir
James Frazer in dealing with ancient religious phenomena.
He expresses the view that " recent researches into the
early history of man have revealed the essential similarity
with which, under many superficial differences, the human
mind has elaborated its first crude philosophy of life ", [2]
but he reminds us at the same time that " hypotheses are
necessary but often temporary bridges built to connect
isolated facts ", adding, " If my light bridges should sooner
or later break down, or be superseded by more solid
structures, I hope that my book may still have its utility
and its interest as a repertory of facts ".[3] The Marquis
de Naidaillac in his *L'Amérique Préhistorique* thinks it highly
probable that the same beliefs in the New and Old World
had independent origin. " From the nature of the human

---

[1] H. G. F. Spurrell, *Modern Man and His Forerunners*, p. 85 (London, 1917).
[2] *The Golden Bough* (3rd edition), Vol. I, p. 10.   [3] *Ibid.*, pp. xix, xx.

mind and the natural direction of its evolution follow,"
he writes, "very similar results up to a certain more or
less advanced stage in all parts of the world. . . . Attention
has frequently been called in the preceding pages to the
similar manner in which similar needs were met, similar
artistic ideas developed, and similar results obtained by
people in widely separated parts of the globe." He
thinks these "facts" testify to "the fundamental unity of
the human race".[1]

This theory, however, does not throw light on the
arbitrary connection between metals and the heavenly
bodies, and the fictitious value attached to gold and gems.

Those writers here quoted, and others like them who
favour the theory of the spontaneous generation of the
same complex beliefs in various parts of the world, follow
Dr. Robertson, the eighteenth century historian, who
wrote in this connection:

"Were we to trace back the ideas of other nations to that rude
state in which history first presents them to our view, we should
discover a surprising resemblance in their tenets and practices; and
should be convinced that, in similar circumstances, the faculties of
the human mind hold merely the same course in their progress,
and arrive at almost the same conclusions".[2]

The theory of independent origin is, however, after
all a theory. It cannot be justified merely as the confession
of a faith; it must be proved, and it cannot be proved
merely by drawing analogies from biological evolution.
Nor can it be proved by reference to the distinctive fauna
of the New World, because wild animals do not build and
navigate boats, erect monuments, invent systems of hiero
glyphic writing or formulate religious systems. The
association of man with wild animals has no connection

[1] English translation, *Prehistoric America*, London, 1885, pp. 524-5.
[2] *The History of America*, Book IV, Section VII.

with the progress of civilization except in so far as he may utilize them for his own purposes. The pre-Columbian Americans were not a pastoral people. They did not have domesticated cows, sheep, or horses. Wild animals, however, played a prominent part in their religious life, as did likewise reptiles and insects. American bees, scorpions, fish, frogs, snakes, lizards, crocodiles, turtles, herons, turkeys, vultures, eagles, owls, parrots, tapirs, armadillos, deer, hares, jaguars, pumas, coyotes, bears, dogs, bats, monkeys, &c., figure in their religious symbolism. If, however, it can be shown that the habits of a non-American animal have been transferred to an American animal in pre-Columbian mythology, the suspicion is at once aroused that culture contact existed at one time or other between the Old and New Worlds, and, if it can be proved that an Old World animal has been depicted, especially in association with beliefs similar to those prevailing in any part of the Old World, the suspicion is transformed into a certainty and the theory of independent origin and development breaks down.

In the next chapter it will be shown that the Indian elephant figures in the symbolism of the Maya civilization of Central America, and in the following chapter that the habits of the secretary-bird of Africa have been transferred in pre-Columbian mythology to the American eagle, and that the winged disk of Egypt, which was taken over and adjusted to local and national religious needs by the Assyrians, Persians, Phœnicians, and Polynesians, figures very prominently in the religious symbolism of pre-Columbian America.

CHAPTER III

The Indian Elephant in American Art

American Traces of Rhinoceros, Elephant, and Camel—Elephants on
Maya Stones—Indian Elephant connected with Sea God—Elephant and Snake
God—Elephant and Dragon—The Elephant of Indra—Elephant-headed God
—Buddha's Elephant Form—Controversy regarding American Representa-
tions of Elephant—The Macaw Theory—Macaw and Snake—Hindu Game
in Mexico—Buddhist Scene in Mexican Codex—The Central American
"Long-nosed God"—American "Elephant Mound" and "Elephant Pipes".

"THERE is not the slightest ground", wrote Bancroft in
his great work,[1] "for supposing that the Mexicans or
Peruvians were acquainted with any portion of the
Hindoo mythology; but since their knowledge of even
one species of animal peculiar to the Old Continent, and
not found in America, would, if distinctly proved, furnish
a convincing argument of a communication having taken
place in former ages between the people of the two hemis-
pheres, we cannot but think that the likeness to the head
of a rhinoceros, in the thirty-sixth page of the Mexican
painting preserved in the collection of Sir Thomas
Bodley; the figure of a trunk resembling that of an
elephant, in other Mexican paintings; and the fact,
recorded by Simon, that what resembled the rib of a
camel (*la costilla de un camello*) was kept for many ages
as a relic, and held in great reverence, in one of the
provinces of Bogota, are deserving of attention."

[1] *The Native Races of the Pacific States of North America*, London, 1876, Vol. V,
p. 43, Note 90.

The American writer and explorer, Mr. John L. Stephens, who, accompanied by Mr. Catherwood, an accomplished artist, visited the ruins of Maya civilization in Central America in the middle of last century, detected the elephant on a sculptured pillar at Copan, which he referred to as an "idol". "The front view", he wrote, "seems a portrait, probably of some deified king or hero. The two ornaments at the top appear like the trunk of an elephant, an animal unknown in that country."[1] A reproduction of one of the ornaments in question should leave no doubt as to the identity of the animal depicted by the ancient American sculptor. It is not only an elephant, but an Indian elephant (*Elephas Indicus*), a species found in India, Ceylon, Borneo, and Sumatra. The African elephant (*Elephas Africanus*) has larger ears, a less elevated head, and a bulging forehead without the indentation at the root of the trunk which is a characteristic of the Indian species. The African elephant has in the past been less made use of by man than the Indian, and has consequently not figured prominently in African religious life. In India the elephant was tamed during the Vedic period. It was called at first by the Aryo-Indians "the beast having a hand", and ultimately simply *Hastin* ("having a hand"). An elephant keeper was called *Hastipa*. Another name was *Vārana*, in which the root *vār* signifies water, as in the name of the sea god Varuna. Another name was *maha-nāga* ("great snake").[2] The elephant was thus connected with the *nāga* or snake deities which are mentioned in the Sutras. Nāgas were

[1] J. L. Stephens, *Incidents of Travel in Central America, Chiapas and Yucatan.* London edition, 1842, Vol. I, p. 156.

[2] Macdonell and Keith, *Vedic Index of Names and Subjects*, Vol. I, p. 440, and Vol. II, pp. 288 and 501. Macdonell, *Vedic Mythology*, p. 153.

rain gods; they were " wholly dependent on the presence of water and much afraid of fire, just like the dragons in many Chinese and Japanese legends. . . . The Indian serpent-shaped *Naga* ", says De Visser, from whom I quote, " was identified in China with the four-legged Chinese dragon, because both were divine inhabitants of seas and rivers, and givers of rain. It is no wonder that the Japanese in this blending of Chinese and Indian ideas recognized their own serpent, or dragon-shaped gods of rivers and mountains, to whom they used to pray for rain in times of drought. Thus the ancient legends of three countries were combined, and features of the one were used to adorn the other." The Nāgas were guardians of treasure and especially of pearls. They were taken over by the northern Buddhists, and northern Buddhism " adopted the gods of the countries where it introduced itself, and made them protectors of its doctrine instead of its antagonists ".[1]

The elephant was in Vedic times connected with the god Indra, who slew the drought demon, the serpent-shaped dragon Vritra, which caused the drought by confining the water supply in its coiled body. Indra rode on the elephant's back. In the Maya representation of the elephant are the figures of two men, one of whom is riding on its back while the other is grasping its head. Apparently the sculptor had never seen an elephant and had used as a model a manuscript picture or a carving in wood or ivory. That his elephant had, however, a religious significance there appears to be little doubt.

In India the connection between the Nāga and elephant was not merely a philological one. There was a blending of cults; Nāgas and elephants were associated

---

[1] Dr. M. W. De Visser, *The Dragon in China and Japan* (Amsterdam, 1913), pp. 5, 7, 13.

with the god Varuna, whose vehicle was the *makara*, a "wonder beast" of composite form like the Babylonian dragon and the "goat-fish" form of Ea, god of the deep. The *makara* like the *nāga* contributed to the complex dragons of China and Japan.

A later Indian form of Indra was the elephant-headed god Ganesha, the son of the god Shiva and Parvati. A Brahmanic legend was invented to connect the young god with the ancient Vedic rain-bringer who slew the water-confining serpent-dragon Vritra. In one of the Puranas it is told that Ganesha offended the planet Saturn who decapitated him. The god Vishnu came to the child-god's aid, and provided him with a new head by cutting off the head of Indra's elephant. At a later period Ganesha lost one of his tusks as a result of a conflict with a Deva-rishi. Ganesha was, in consequence, represented with one whole and one broken tusk.[1]

The Buddhists not only took over the "wonder beasts" with elephant and other parts and characteristics, but also adopted the white elephant, which was an emblem of the sun. According to one of their legends, Buddha entered his mother's womb in the form of a white elephant. This idea "seems", as Dr. T. W. Rhys Davis says, "a most grotesque folly, until the origin of the poetical figure has been . . . ascertained". The solar-elephant form "was deliberately chosen by the future Buddha, because it was the form indicated by a *deva* (god) who had in a previous birth been one of the Rishis, the mythical poets of the Rig Veda".[2] Rishis were learned priests who became demi-gods by performing religious ceremonies.

---

[1] *Indian Myth and Legend*, pp. 150–1. In like manner the Egyptian god Horus cuts off the head of Isis which Thoth replaces with the head of a cow.

[2] Rhys Davis, *Buddhism* (London, 1903), p. 148.

It will thus be seen that before the elephant, as a religious symbol, was carried from India to other countries, it was associated with complex beliefs as a result of Indian culture mixing. The history of the Maya elephant symbol cannot be traced in the New World. The view of Dr. W. Stempell[1] that the Copan and other elephants of America represent the early Pleistocene *Elephas columbi* has not met with acceptance. This elephant has not the peculiar characteristics of the Indian elephant as shown in the Copan stone, and it became extinct before the earliest representatives of modern man reached the New World.

Although, however, Dr. W. Stempell, reviewing the literature concerning the various representations of the elephant in pre-Columbian America, " vigorously protested against the idea that they were intended to be anything else than elephants ", certain Americanists have laboured to prove that they are either badly-drawn birds or tapirs. The Copan elephant, associated with the two human figures, has been identified with the blue macaw (see plate opposite) by Dr. Alfred M. Tozzer and Dr. Glover M. Allen.[2] In their reproduction of the Copan elephant, the one with human figures is not selected.

" There has hitherto ", write Tozzer and Allen, " been some question as to the identity of certain stone carvings, similar to that on Stela B from Copan of which a portion is shown in Plate 25, fig. 8. This has even been interpreted as the trunk of an elephant, but is unquestionably a macaw's beak." The unprejudiced reader will not be inclined to regard the macaw theory as finally

---

[1] *Nature* (" Pre-Columbian Representations of the Elephant in America "), November 25, 1915.

[2] *Animal Figures in the Mayan Codices* (Papers of the Peabody Museum of American Archæology and Ethnology, Harvard University, Vol. IV, No. 3), Cambridge, Mass., February, 1910, p. 343.

THE INDIAN ELEPHANT IN AMERICA

1, 2, and 4 are from Central American sculptured stones. The bottom figure (5) is the elephant mound in North America, and the one above (6) is "the elephant pipe" (North America). Near it is a sketch of a macaw's head (7), and at the top of the picture is the macaw on a sculptured stone (3). As will be seen from the elephant figure on right-hand top corner, the ancient Americans made a good shape at copying some picture or carving of an Indian elephant, but did not know it was so tall, as a man walks alongside with an arm over its head. The sitting man is the driver.

COPAN : STELA B

From a photograph by Alfred P. Mauaslay

settled, even although it finds support among not a few Americanists, and especially those determined to uphold "the ethnological 'Monroe Doctrine' which", as Professor Elliot Smith has written, "demands that everything American belongs to America, and must have been wholly invented there".

This extract is from a letter contributed to *Nature*, in which the various pre-Columbian representations have been discussed by Professor Elliot Smith, Professor Tozzer, and Dr. Spinden[1]. The first named holds that the Copan animals under discussion are Indian elephants. "Never having seen an elephant and not being aware of its size, no doubt", he says, "the Maya artist conceived it to be some kind of monstrous macaw; and his portraits of the two creatures mutually influenced one another." He points out, however, that in one of the figures the so-called macaw is given a mammalian ear from which an ear-ring is suspended, a characteristic Cambodian feature.

Professor Tozzer draws attention to the artistic treatment of both the macaw and elephant figures. In the "elephant" head "there is an ornamental scroll beneath the eye, which likewise is cross-hatched and surrounded by a ring of subcircular marks that continue to the base of the beak. The nostril is the large oval marking directly in front of the eye." He holds that a comparison of this "elephant" with that of the unmistakable macaw "shows that the two represent the same animal". Professor Elliot Smith writes on this point:

"This suggestion has served to direct attention to points of special interest and importance, viz. the striking influence exercised by the representatives of a well-known creature, the macaw, on the craftsmen who were set the task of modelling the elephant

[1] *Nature*, November 25, 1915; December 16, 1915; January 27, 1916.

which to them was an alien and wholly unknown animal. It explains how, in the case of the latter, the sculptor came to mistake the eye for the nostril and the auditory meatus for the eye, and also to employ a particular geometrical design for filling in the area of the auditory pinna. . . . The accurate representation of the Indian elephant's profile, its trunk, tusk, and lower lip, the form of its ear, as well as the turbaned rider and his implement, no less than the distinctively Hindu artistic feeling in the modelling are entirely fatal to the macaw hypothesis."

Professor Elliot Smith points out further that the "scroll" of which so much has been made was not borrowed from the macaw for the elephant, but from the elephant for the macaw.

"The scroll was an essential part of the elephant-design before it left Asia, and, in fact, is found in conventionalized drawings of the elephant in the Old World from Cambodia to Scotland."

Dr. Eduard Seler's view is that the objects under discussion are tortoises. Others have favoured the tapir. Dr. Spinden writes in the same connection:

"That the heads with projecting snouts used as architectural decoration are connected with the concept of the snake rather than the elephant is easily proven by a study of homologous parts in a series of designs."

As has been shown the elephant and the "nāga" (snake) cults and cult objects were fused in India. It should not surprise us therefore to find suggestions of Nāga-elephants in America, especially as other traces of Indian influence can be detected. As Chinese ethnological data prove, the cultural influence of India extended over wide areas as a result of Brahmanic and Buddhist missionary enterprise, just as Babylonian and Iranian influence flowed into India itself. Sir Edward Tylor has shown[1]

[1] *Journal of the Anthropological Institute*, 1879, p. 128.

that the pre-Columbian Mexicans acquired the Hindu game called *pachisi*, and that in their picture writing (Vatican Codex) there is a series of scenes taken from Japanese Buddhist temple scrolls.[1] "If", comments Professor Elliot Smith in this connection, "it has been possible for complicated games and a series of strange beliefs (and elaborate pictorial illustrations of them) to make their way to the other side of the Pacific, the much simpler design of an elephant's head could also have been transferred from India or the Far East to America."

The Maya "long-nosed god" is regarded by those who favour the hypothesis of direct or indirect Indian cultural influence in America as a form of the Indian elephant-headed god Ganesha, referred to above. This aspect of the problem will be dealt with in connection with the Aztec rain god Tlaloc.

Other traces of the elephant usually referred to are afforded by the "elephant mound" of Wisconsin and the "elephant pipes" of Iowa. It is held by Tozzer and others that the former is a bear, or some other local animal, and that the "trunk" does not belong to the original earthwork, and that the latter are "forgeries". The alleged maker of these forgeries must have been a very remarkable man indeed—"the most remarkable archæologist", says Professor Elliot Smith, "America has yet produced".

In the next chapter, it will be shown that even the culture influence of North Africa reached pre-Columbian America after drifting through various intervening areas.

---

[1] *British Association Report*, 1894, p. 774.

CHAPTER IV

Symbols with a History

Bird and Serpent Myths in Old and New Worlds—Theory of Indepen
dent Origin—Professor W. Robertson's Stratification Theory—Mental Habits
of Early Man—"Psychic Unity" and Instinct—Robertson's View adopted by
Miller, Wilson, Lang, &c.—Brinton on American Symbolism—The Mexican
"Feathered Serpent"—Origin of Bird and Serpent Combat—Homeric Version
—The Aztec Myth—Indian Garudas (Eagles) and Nagas (Serpents)—Wide-
spread Dragon, Tree, and Well Myths—Japanese Tengu and Elephant-headed
Gods—Thunder Birds and Thunder Dogs—American "Long-nosed" God—
Birds and Elephants as Thunder Gods—Mexican Cactus as Tree of Life—
Symbolism of Mexican Coat of Arms—Jewel-spitting Gods in India and
America—The Everlasting Combat—Origin of Water-confining Serpent.

In his treatise on the symbolism and mythology of the
"red race" of America,[1] Professor Daniel G. Brinton
deals at length with the symbols of the "Bird and Serpent", and shows that these are as prominent in the
mythologies of the New World as in the mythologies of
Asia and Europe. This fact does not surprise him, or even
arouse a suspicion that the associated beliefs of complex
character may have been due to culture contact or culture
drifting in ancient times. His book reveals him as a
believer in the spontaneous generation of similar religious
ideas and similar symbols among different peoples in
different parts of the world. He and certain other
Americanists hold that "there is", as Dr. Eduard Seler
puts it, "in all parts of the world a certain fundamental
uniformity in religious ideas, still more in religious

---

[1] *The Myths of the New World*, Philadelphia, 1905 (3rd edition), pp. 120 *et seq.*

practices, in spite of a wide difference in the details ".[1]
Here we meet with the theory of the "psychic unity of
mankind ".

This fashion of thinking—for there are fashions in
thinking as in other things—became prevalent in this
country during the late Victorian epoch. It was first
introduced, however, by Professor William Robertson
of the Edinburgh University, the eighteenth century
historian, whose ethnological speculations in his *The
History of America* (1777) have strongly influenced later
investigators in the same field of research.

Robertson advocated his theory of independent origin
with certain qualifications. He held, for instance,
that some peoples were capable of developing more
exalted ideas than others, although he did not inquire
into the reasons for their superior capabilities and attain-
ments; and expressed the belief that, even among the
most enlightened and civilized nations, the religious
opinions of persons in the inferior ranks of life are,
and ever have been, "derived from instruction, not
discovered by inquiry ".

Robertson was likewise the pioneer of the stratification theory which he advocated long before Darwinism
was heard of, and the habit became prevalent among
ethnologists of drawing analogies from biological evolution. He recognized a primary stage in human development—"the early and most rude periods of savage
life "—regarding which he wrote as follows :

"That numerous part of the human species, whose lot is
labour, whose principal and almost sole occupation is to secure
subsistence, views the arrangements and operations of nature with
little reflection, and has neither leisure nor capacity for entering

---

[1] *Mexican and Central American Antiquities* (Bureau of American Ethnology,
Bulletin 28), Washington, 1904, p. 275.

into that path of refined and intricate speculation which conducts
to the knowledge of the principles of natural religion.   When the
intellectual powers are just beginning to unfold, and their first
feeble exertions are directed towards a few objects of primary
necessity and use; when the faculties of the mind are so limited,
as not to have formed abstract or general ideas; when language is
so barren, as to be destitute of names to distinguish anything that
is not perceived by some of the senses; it is preposterous to expect
that man should be capable of tracing with accuracy the relation
between cause and effect; or to suppose that he should rise from
the contemplation of the one to the knowledge of the other, and
form just conceptions of a deity, as the Creator and the Governor
of the Universe.   The idea of creation is so familiar wherever the
mind is enlarged by science, and illuminated by revelation, that
we seldom reflect how profound and obtruse this idea is, or consider what progress man must have made in observation and
research, before he could arrive at any knowledge of this elementary principle in religion."

Robertson's view of early man is, so far, remarkably like
that of Professor G. Elliot Smith, who has written :

"The modern fallacy of supposing that he (early man) spent
his time in contemplation of the world around him, speculating
upon the nature of the stars above him, or devising theories of the
soul, is probably as far from the truth as it would be to assume
that the modern Englishman is absorbed in the problems of
zoology, astronomy, and metaphysics. . . . What the ethnologist
usually fails to recognize is that among primitive men, as amongst
modern scholars, before attempting to solve a problem, it is
essential to recognize that there is a problem to solve."[1]

Elliot Smith holds further that :

"The germs of civilization were planted when man's attention
first became fixed upon specific problems, which he was able to
deal with in an experimental manner, and, in co-operation with
other men, to solve in a way more or less satisfying to him and his

[1] *Primitive Man*, pp. 38 *et seq.*

contemporaries, and to hand on his solutions of them to those who came after them. Once this process began, a new era in the manifestation of the human spirit was inaugurated."

He emphasizes the "artificial character" and "the arbitrary nature" of the composition of the constituent elements of early civilization. "It bears the impress of its wholly accidental origin: it is equally alien to the instinctive tendencies of human beings."

Robertson accounted for the origin of progress in early religious thought by assuming that the human mind is "formed for religion", but he throws no light on the important problem as to why some people achieve more rapid progress than others—why some groups of people were "enlightened" while others remained in an "unenlightened" state, despite the fact that their minds were similarly "formed". He does no more than refer to the existence of the two well-defined groups of human beings, and proceeds to say that among unenlightened nations "the first rites and practices which bear any resemblance to acts of religion have it for their object to avert evils which men suffer or dread". Other peoples with more "enlarged" systems of thought had formed "some conception of benevolent beings as well as of malicious powers prone to inflict evil". But, although some people might not have arisen to the conception of a "Great Spirit", all peoples, and especially in America, were more united with regard to the doctrine of immortality.

"The human mind, even when least improved and invigorated by culture, shrinks from the thought of annihilation, and looks forward with hope and expectation to a state of future existence. This sentiment, resulting from a sacred consciousness of its own dignity, from an instinctive longing after immortality, is universal *and may be deemed natural.*"

Robertson's view regarding instinct is frankly adopted by Brinton, who has written :

"The universal belief in the sacredness of numbers is an instinctive perception of a fundamental fact, a recognition by the intellect of the method of its own action."[1]

Other modern "evolutionary" ethnologists "indignantly protest", however, "if", as Elliot Smith says, "a critic insists that the working of their brand of 'psychic unity' is indistinguishable from what the psychologist calls instinct".[2] Even those writers, however, who reject Robertson's theory regarding instinct, adopt his term "natural", and repeatedly apply it to the most complex religious phenomena.

The following passage from Robertson's *The History of America*, which sums up his view of ancient men, is of undoubted importance in the history of ethnological thought :

"Inattentive to that magnificent spectacle of beauty and order presented to their view, unaccustomed to reflect either upon what they themselves are, or to inquire who is the author of their existence, men, in their savage state, pass their days like the animals round them, without knowledge or veneration of any superior power".

Hugh Miller in his *Scenes and Legends*,[3] published fifty-eight years after Robertson's history made its appearance, applied the theory of spontaneous generation to folk-stories and flint-working, and wrote, remembering his Robertson :

"The most practised eye can hardly distinguish between the

[1] *Myths of the New World*, p. 119.
[2] "Primitive Man" (from the *Proceedings of the British Academy*, Vol. VII), London, 1917, p. 34. See also *Science*, October 13, 1916, Dr. Goldenweiser's letter.
[3] London, 1835 (first edition), pp. 31–2.

weapons of the old Scot and the New Zealander. . . . Man in
a savage state is the same animal everywhere, and his constructive
powers, whether employed in the formation of a legendary story
or of a battle-axe, seem to expatiate almost everywhere in the
same rugged track of invention. For even the traditions of this
first stage may be identified, like its weapons of war, all the world
over."

Dr. Daniel Wilson, writing twenty-eight years after
Miller,[1] followed him closely in the following extract
from his " Annals " :

"A singular unity of character pervades the primitive arts of
man, however widely separated alike by space and time. Placed
under the same conditions, the first efforts of his mechanical
instinct everywhere exhibit similar results. The ancient Stone
Period of Assyria and Egypt resembles that of its European
successor, and that again finds a nearly complete parallel among
the primitive remains of the valley of the Mississippi and in the
modern arts of the barbarous Polynesian."

Andrew Lang, in 1884, revived, in his *Custom and
Myth* (pp. 24–27), the same theory, remembering what
Hugh Miller, the Cromarty stone-mason geologist, a
self-educated man, had written under the influence of
Robertson :

"We may plausibly account for the similarity of myths, as we
accounted for the similarity of flint arrow-heads. The myths,
like the arrow-heads, resemble each other because they were
originally framed to meet the same needs out of the same material.
In the case of the arrow-heads, the need was for something hard,
heavy, and sharp—the material was flint. In the case of the
myths, the need was to explain certain phenomena—the material
(so to speak) was an early state of the human mind, to which all
objects seemed equally endowed with human personality, and to
which no metamorphosis appeared impossible."

[1] *Prehistoric Annals of Scotland*, London, 1863, p. 337.

Early man required implements. That he felt the same need for complex stories about birds and serpents and for connecting these with "certain phenomena" is very doubtful. He could not have been much concerned about the supply of rain before he domesticated cattle, and it is improbable that beliefs regarding the sun god and the rain and river god became stereotyped before the introduction of the agricultural mode of life. A considerable advance in civilization must have been achieved before the organization of society was reflected in religious systems, and man became capable "of tracing with accuracy", as Robertson put it, "the relation between cause and effect".

These extracts which have been given from the writings of Lang, Wilson, and Miller, are of special interest, because they show that the theory of independent origin has a definite history. Robertson introduced a formula which has provided a plausible and easy explanation for a very complex problem. It accounts for the numerous resemblances, but not for the numerous differences between the myths, symbols, and religious beliefs and customs of various ancient civilizations. Although it has helped to promote the comparative study of religious systems, it has, however, at the same time diverted attention from the process of culture drifting and of the fusions in various culture areas of imported ideas with those of local growth, reflecting local experiences.

Robertson's formula has been rigorously applied in America. His term "natural" is repeated again and again by writers who find themselves confronted with even the most complex religious phenomena. To Brinton it is "natural" that the bird and serpent symbols should have been linked in the pre-Columbian American mythologies, and he displays so much ingenuity in accounting for the various manifestations of the winged animal and reptile and for their arbitrary association, that one cannot help feeling that the early Red man must have been possessed of as subtle and resourceful a mind as himself. Brinton,[1] putting himself in the place of the early observers and thinkers, proceeds to say that the bird "floats in the atmosphere", "rides on the winds" and "soars towards heaven where dwell the gods". Early man conceived that "gods and angels must also have wings", an assumption which postulates the theory that he believed in gods and angels from the beginning. The bird was identified with the clouds, and it is "natural" therefore that thunder should have been regarded as "the sound of the cloud-bird flapping his wings".

Brinton then deals with the serpent. This reptile is "mysterious". We should not wonder therefore that "it possessed the fancy of the observant child of nature" whom Robertson has apparently slandered by asserting that he was "inattentive to that magnificent spectacle of beauty and order presented to his view". Brinton shows that early man saw serpents in the heavens and on the earth, and does not deal with the possibility that he may have deified the real serpent before he conceived of mythical ones. Lightning wriggles; so do serpents; therefore, argued early man, lightning is a serpent. The river has a "sinuous course"; it is "serpentine". "How easily", comments Brinton, "would savages, construing the figure literally, make the serpent a river or water god!" The serpent was certainly connected with water, but is Brinton's theory of how the connection was effected a very plausible one? It obtained in the Old World as well as in the New. That does not surprise him, nor is he surprised to find that in pre-Columbian America the

[1] *The Myths of the New World*, pp. 123 *et seq.*

serpent was depicted in religious symbolism "with its tail
in its mouth, eating itself", like the Scandinavian Midgard
serpent and other mythical serpents in other culture areas.
Among other "natural" conceptions, according to Brinton,
is that of the American "horned serpent", which is found
among the ancient Celtic symbols of Gaul and reminds us
of the horned serpent-dragons of China and Japan, the
horned dragon of Babylonia, &c. The American hero
who slays the horned serpent as Marduk, and St. George,
and others slew the serpentine dragon, is a god, and this
god was, Brinton explains, indentified with the "Thunder
Bird". It was "natural" therefore, he reasons, that the
serpent god and the bird god, as gods of rain, rivers, and
lightning, should have been closely associated, and that
early man in America should have evolved the idea of
a serpent bird or bird serpent and deified this monstrosity
as Quetzalcoatl, the "Feather Serpent", so as to "express
atmospheric phenomena" and recognize "divinity in natural occurrences". In other words the pre-Columbian
American genius, in his process of thinking, passed from
the abstract to the concrete and not from the concrete to
the abstract like the Chinese and other lesser breeds in
the Old World.

Despite the ingenuity and easy assurance of Brinton
and of other theorists, it is possible that, as the hypothesis
of independent origin has a history, the complex ideas
about birds and serpents in pre-Columbian America may
have had a history too. Those who remain unconvinced
that the arbitrary association of birds and serpents, and of
both with atmospheric phenomena, in the mythologies
of the New and Old Worlds should be regarded as
"natural", will maintain an open mind on the subject
and refuse to be caught in the glamour of a plausible
theory which accounts for far too much. It is frankly

unconceivable that early man should have connected
serpents and birds without a single hint from nature.
If we find that nature has in one part of the world
provided the plot for the mythological drama of the
everlasting battle between bird and serpent, it is not
surprising to learn that the combat should have been
introduced into a local or neighbouring pre-existing mythological system, which reflected not only natural
phenomena but even local political conditions. On the
other hand it cannot be regarded as other than astounding
to find in an area where no serpent-hunting bird exists
that such a bird should have been imagined, and that this
imaginary bird should have been utilized in precisely the
same way as in the area where the real bird has actual
existence. It is just as remarkable to find in pre-
Columbian mythological systems the bird and serpent
symbols as it is to find the Indian elephant represented
on a Maya stela.

There is only one bird in the world which is a persistent and successful hunter of serpents. This is the
well-known secretary-bird (*Serpentarius secretarius*) of
Africa. "In general appearance", writes a naturalist,
"it looks like a modified eagle mounted on stilts, and
may exceed four feet in height." It is heavy and powerful, with webbed feet and sharp talons. Verreaux gives
the following interesting description of the bird and of
its method of attacking snakes:

"As nature exhibits foresight in all she does, she has given to
each animal its means of preservation. Thus the Secretary Bird
has been modelled on a plan appropriate to its mode of life, and it
is therefore for this purpose that, owing to the length of its legs
and tarsi, its piercing eye is able to discover at a long distance the
prey which, in anticipation of its appearance, is stretched on the
sand or among the thick grass. The elegant and majestic form of

the bird becomes now even more graceful; it now brings into action all its cunning in order to surprise the snake which it is going to attack; therefore it approaches with the greatest caution. The elevation of the feathers of the neck and the back of the head shows when the moment for attack has arrived. It throws itself with such force on the reptile that very often the latter does not survive the first blow."

To avoid being bitten the bird, if the first attack is not successful, uses its wings as a kind of shield, flapping them vigorously; its powerful feet are " the chief weapons of offence ".[1]   No other bird has been so well equipped by nature for battling with snakes. Eagles and vulcans may have powerful talons and beaks, but they do not possess the long legs of the secretary-bird, which are absolutely necessary to ensure success when a serpent is attacked.

Stories regarding this strange bird appear to have been prevalent in Ancient Egypt. The priests and sea-men who visited Punt no doubt became familiar with its habits. It may well be that the secretary-bird suggested that form of the Horus myth in which the god as the falcon hawk attacks the serpent form of Set, the slayer of Osiris. The Set serpent took refuge in a hole in the ground, and above this hole was set a pole surmounted by the falcon head of Horus.[2]

The myth of the African serpent-slaying bird became widespread in the course of time. In Egypt the bird was identified with the hawk, and elsewhere it was supposed to be an eagle. An interesting reference to this myth is found in the *Iliad*. When the Trojans were attempting to reach the ships of their enemies and still stood outside the fosse, they beheld an eagle flying high above their heads.

---

[1] *The Natural History of Animals* (Gresham publication), Vol. II, 46–8.
[2] Budge, *The Gods of the Egyptians*, Vol. I, 481.

"In its talons it bore a blood-red monstrous snake, alive and struggling still; yea, not yet had it forgotten the joy of battle, but writhed backward and smote the bird that held it on the breast, beside the neck, and the bird cast it from him down to the earth in sore pain, and dropped it in the midst of the throng; then with a cry sped away down the gust of the wind. And the Trojans shuddered when they saw the gleaming snake lying in the midst of them; an omen of ægis-bearing Zeus." [1]

Polydamas regarded this omen as unfavourable and advised Hector, but in vain, not to continue the attack, believing that the Achæan snake would turn on and wound the Trojan eagle.

This eagle-serpent myth reached the New World. It is connected with the founding of the city of Mexico. The Aztecs had been wandering for many years and had reached the south-western border of a great lake in A.D. 1325:

"They there beheld, perched on the stem of a prickly pear, which shot out from the crevice of a rock that was washed by the waves, a royal eagle of extraordinary size and beauty, with a serpent in his talons, and his broad wings opened to the rising sun. They hailed the auspicious omen announced by the oracle, as indicating the site of their future city, and laid its foundations by sinking piles into the shallows; for the low marshes were half-buried under water. . . . The place was called Tenochtitlan,[2] in token of its miraculous origin, though only known to Europeans by its other name of Mexico. . . . The legend of its foundation is still further commemorated by the device of the eagle and the cactus which forms the arms of the modern Mexican republic."[3]

In Indian mythology the serpent-slaying bird is the Garuda. This monster, which does not resemble any eagle found in India, is the vehicle of the god Vishnu.

[1] *Iliad*, Book XII; translated by Lang, Leaf, and Myers, pp. 236-7.
[2] The name signifies " tunal (a cactus) on a stone ".
[3] Prescott (quoting authorities), *History of the Conquest of Mexico*, Vol. I, Chapter I.

The Garuda became the enemy of the snakes (nāgas) because his mother, Vinata, had been captured and enslaved by Kadrū, the mother of the Nāgas. Having enabled Indra to rob from the snakes the nectar of immortality, he is offered a boon, and he promptly asks Vishnu that the snakes should become his food. Thereafter Garuda swooped down and began to devour the snakes. Vasuki, King of the Nāgas, ultimately agreed to send daily to Garuda one snake to eat. "Garuda consented, and began to eat every day one snake sent by him (Vasuki)."[1]

Nāgas had three forms, viz. (1) fully human with snakes on their heads and emerging from their necks; (2) common serpents that guard treasure; and (3) with the upper half of the body of human shape and the lower part entirely snake-like. Garuda, or the Garudas, attacked Nāgas in each form they assumed. De Visser, dealing with Nāgas in Indian Buddhist art, refers to a relief in which

"a Garuda in the shape of an enormous eagle is flying upwards with a Nāgi (Nāga woman) in his claws, and biting the long snake which comes out of the woman's neck".[2]

The Nāgas had their abodes "at the bottom of the sea or in rivers or lakes. When leaving the Nāga world they are in constant danger of being grasped and killed by the gigantic semi-divine birds, the Garudas, which also change themselves into men. Buddhism has, in its usual way, declared both Nāgas and Garudas mighty figures of the Hindu world of gods and demons to be obedient servants of the Buddhas, Bodhisattvas, and saints, and to have an open ear for their teachings."[3] On those they favoured the Nāgas bestowed "super-

---

[1] Quoted in *The Dragon in China and Japan*, p. 19.   [2] *Ibid.*, p. 5.   [3] *Ibid.*, p. 7.

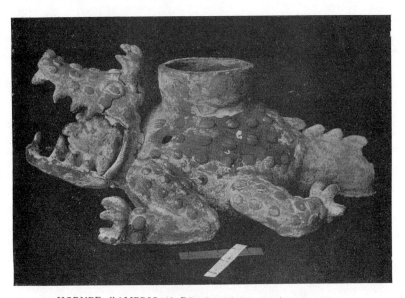

HORNED "AMERICAN DRAGON" FROM SANTA RITA
(Liverpool Museum)

In the mouth is head of rain-god Chac (Tlaloc). The body spots represent stars:
on the back is the "Mother Pot".

THE "GREAT TURTLE", QUIRIGUA
From a photograph by Alfred P. Maudslay

natural vision and hearing ".[1] Heroes and holy men
were received in their dwellings as guests. The Nāgas
were "gods of clouds and rain ".[2] "When ", says a
Buddhist text, "the great Nāga causes the rain to fall,
the ocean alone can receive the latter." Another characteristic text connects the Nāgas with dew: "when on
the mountains and valleys the Heavenly Dragons (the
Nāgas) cause the sweet dew to descend, this changes
into bubbling fire and spouts upon our bodies ".[3] A
legend connecting a Nāga with a sacred tree is of special
interest. Anyone who took a branch or leaf from the
tree was killed by the Nāga. The cutting of the tree,
even the taking of a single leaf, brought clouds and
caused thunder, manifestations of the Nāga's wrath. A
great Nāga king, named Pārāvatāksha, had his dwelling
under a lake which was overshadowed by a solitary
ashoka tree. He possessed "a matchless sword from
the war of the gods and the Asuras (demons) ", and
caused earthquakes and sent clouds. When he appeared
he resembled "the dense cloud of the day of doom ";
in his snake form he came "with flaming eyes, roaring
horribly ". De Visser's view is that "this is probably
thunder and lightning ".[4] A Chinese Buddhist text, from
a work in which the connection between Nāgas and
dragons is shown to be intimate, sets forth that there
are five sorts of dragons: (1) serpent-dragons; (2) lizard-
dragons; (3) fish-dragons; (4) elephant-dragons; (5)
toad-dragons.[5]

In Indian, Chinese, and Japanese stories the Nāga or
dragon dwells in a pool beneath a tree. The tree grows
on an island in a lake, or in the ocean. These lake
islands, with sacred trees and wells, are common in Gaelic

---

[1] Quoted in *The Dragon in China and Japan*, p. 9.   [2] *Ibid.*, p. 10.
[3] *Ibid.*, pp. 14–5.   [4] *Ibid.*, pp. 17–8.   [5] *Ibid.*, p. 23.

folk-lore. An island in Loch Maree has a wishing tree and curative well; once a year the fairies assemble on the island. A lake island was associated with the American jewel goddess Chalchiuhtlicue (see Chapter XII).

The well-known Gaelic legend of Fraoch resembles closely the Buddhist legend of Pārāvatāksha. A holly tree grows above a pool in which there is a dragon-like monster; this monster attacks anyone who plucks berries from the tree. In Gaelic lore the holly berries renew youth, promote longevity, and are the source of super-natural knowledge. The berries contain the "life sub-stance" of the tree-guardian which reposes in the well. This guardian, in one of the Indian Buddhist stories referred to above, gifts a favoured mortal with "super-natural vision and hearing"; he could understand ever afterwards "all sounds" and "the voices even of ants".[1] Siegfried was able, after eating the heart of the dragon, to understand the voices of birds. The birds revealed the secrets of the deities. Michael Scott acquired know-ledge of the future and of how to cure diseases by eating a portion of the white snake which, like the Indian Nāga, was connected with water; while Fionn,[2] the Gaelic hero, became a soothsayer after tasting of the juice of "the salmon of wisdom"; this salmon dwells in a pool and devours the berries of the holly tree, thus acquiring its red spots. The salmon is an avatar of the well or lake dragon and is a guardian of treasure like the Indian Nāga. A salmon form of a destroying dragon is, in Irish lore, associated with Loch Bél Séad ("the lake with the jewel mouth"), one of the lakes on the Galty Mountains.[3] Various cults favoured various trees.

---

[1] Quoted in *The Dragon in China and Japan*, p. 9.   [2] Pronounced *fewn*.

[3] O'Curry, *Lecture on Manuscript Materials*, p. 426; Joyce, *Irish Names of Places*, Vol. II, pp. 378–9.

Thus Thomas the Rhymer received the gift of prophecy by eating of an apple in the Fairyland Paradise. He then became "True Thomas"—that is, "Druid Thomas", "Sooth-saying Thomas". The goddess known as the Fairy Queen gave him the apple:

> Syne they came to garden green,
>   And she pu'd an apple frae a tree;
> Take this for wages, True Thomas,
>   It will give thee tongue that can never lie.

The connection between the soothsayer and the dragon can be traced in ancient Egyptian literature. Na-nefer-ka-ptah who slew "the deathless snake" obtained a magic book, and then "knew what the birds of the sky, the fish of the deep, and the beasts of the hills all said".[1] In the story of "The Shipwrecked Sailor", an Egyptian mariner tells of an island in the ocean inhabited by talking serpents. He describes the king serpent as follows:

"Suddenly I heard a noise as of thunder which I thought to be that of a wave of the sea. The trees shook, and the earth was moved. I uncovered my face and I saw that a serpent drew near. He was thirty cubits long and his beard greater than two cubits; his body was as overlayed with gold, and his colour as that of true lazuli. He coiled himself before me."

The serpent foretells that the sailor will return to his home. Like the dragon isles of China and Japan and the Celtic "Isles of the Blest" the Egyptian serpent island vanishes by sinking beneath the waves.[2]

In Japan the Tengu, originally a kite, was identified with the Garuda. A mythical story tells that once a dragon, having assumed the shape of a small snake, lay

---

[1] W. M. Flinders Petrie, *Egyptian Tales* (Second Series), London, 1895, p. 100.
[2] *Ibid.* (First Series), London, 1899, p. 81 *et seq.*

basking in the sun on the bank of a lake in which he lived. Suddenly a kite swooped down and carried it away.[1] Like other Japanese gods and demons, the Tengu was in the course of time clothed in Buddhist garb. It was likewise influenced by Chinese myths regarding the "Celestial Dog".

The Garuda was in Tibet similarly identified with another demon, and passed in its new form into Mongolia. De Visser, quoting Gruenwedel's *Mythologie des Buddhismus in Tibet und der Mongolei*, says that "the Garudas are described as represented in Lamaism with a fat (human) body, human arms to which wings are attached, and a horned bird's head. They are deadly enemies of the Nāgas (serpents identified with the Chinese dragons) and belong to the attendants of the dreadful gods." One illustration in Gruenwedel's work (p. 26) shows a Garuda "as an eagle or kite with a kind of head-dress and earrings, carrying away a Nāgi (serpent woman) and on the same page another figure of the same entirely human but with long wings at the back".[2] A characteristic of the Japanese Tengu, in its semi-human form, is its long nose. Grotesque stories are told of human beings making use of a Tengu's fan which promotes the growth of the nose. Of special interest, in this connection, is the fact that the *Shishishū*, a book of the Japanese Shin sect, identifies the Tengu with the elephant-headed Indian god Ganesha "on account of the human shape and the elephant's trunk". Although De Visser thinks this theory is wrong, because "there is no doubt as to the bird's shape of the Tengu",[3] it should not, however, surprise us to find that the kite demon, having been identified with the Chinese "celestial dog", should also be fused with the

---

[1] *Transactions of the Asiatic Society of Japan*, Vol. XXXVI, Part II, p. 41.
[2] *Ibid.*, Vol. XXXVI, Part II, pp. 88-9.   [3] *Ibid.*, p. 90.

Indian elephant. The Japanese Tengu, as a god of the mountains, was identified with the thunder god, and was consequently a rain-giver.

These references are of importance in dealing with the American culture complexes revealed by its mythological symbols. In the first place it will be seen that the attributes of one class of animals or reptiles pass freely, with drifting myths and doctrines, to another class—that birds, dogs, and even elephants may be fused and that bird-men, dog-men, and elephant-men may, as gods or demons, represent precisely the same idea, or a similar group of ideas. In one country the eagle or vulture, and in another the kite, took the place of the original secretary-bird as the destroyer of serpents. The serpent-slaying bird was depicted in a local natural form, or as a " composite wonder beast " or " wonder man ". The long-nosed Tengu of Japan, in semi-human shape, is a form of the original kite and possesses the attributes of the "celestial dog" of China, and of the elephant-headed deity Ganesha of India. It is possible therefore that " the long-nosed god " of America may be identified with an eagle, a macaw, or an elephant, or with a thunder god and a rain god. It may have been any of these or all of these in one.

The Buddhists made peace between the bird-men, the Garudas, and the snake-men and snake-women. Birds and serpents were united as allies and worshippers of Buddha. In the winged dragon, the Old World "feathered serpent", we have the union of these ancient enemies symbolized. A composite deity of partly human shape, as a wonder-beast, or as a long-nosed being, possessed the combined attributes of the original anthropomorphic deities and their animal symbols, and of the original enemies the secretary-bird and the snake—that is, of the Egyptian falcon god Horus and his enemy Set as "the roaring serpent".

The Mexican eagle with the snake caught in beak and talons is therefore like the Garuda-eagle of India which similarly preys on snakes. Both are mythical bird gods. Both have their history as mythological beings rooted in remote times in a distant area of origin.

As has been shown, the myth of the tree which grows over the pool or lake in some sacred spot, and especially on an island, is of complex character. The tree varies in different countries. It may be an oak, a rowan, a hazel, a palm, a vine, a sycamore, or, as we go eastward, a peach tree, plum tree, or cassia tree (China), or an orange tree (Japan). It is the tree or plant of life. In the Mexican national symbol a cactus stands for the tree or plant of life.

The oracle bird, in various mythologies, sits on the tree, and the serpent, as the guardian of the tree, lives in the pool as a fish or a serpent-dragon. Tree, bird, serpent, and fish (or toad) are avatars of the deity who dwells beneath the lake or pool as does the Nāga king in Indian myths. In Mexican mythology the gods of rain, the Tlalocs, have their dwelling beneath the cactus on the rocky island of the lake. They were consulted by the priests as the oracle bird was by the Celtic Druid. The Aztecs were advised by the Tlalocs to build their capital round the sacred lake.

The sacred island with its sacred tree or plant and sacred well, is found, as has been indicated, in many mythologies and in many folk-stories. It is the dragon island or fairy island, or an "Island of the Blest" in various countries from China to Scotland. The original, or at any rate the most ancient island with a life-giving well and tree, is referred to in the Egyptian Pyramid Texts. Beyond the eastern horizon the souls of Pharaohs were led by Horus in his form of a gorgeous green falcon, which was the Morning Star, to "the tree of life in the mysterious isle in the midst of the Field of Offerings". Above the island are the gods as swallows, the swallows being "the Imperishable Stars". Gods and Pharaohs are fed on the fruit of the tree, and drink of the water of life from the well, or receive food and water from the goddess in the tree, the goddess being the great mother (Hathor) of the sky and the sun.[1]

The mother goddess is the source of all life and the food-giver who sends the water of life as rain, dew, or river floods. The moisture comes from her sacred well. She is associated with the god who controls the water supply and the food supply—the god who instructs and guides mankind and leads the soul to the tree and well of life in his falcon form. The struggle between bird and reptile, which results in the production of fertilizing moisture, is the struggle of the forces that control the elements. When the moisture-retaining snake is slain, the water of life is released. The Mexican eagle-snake symbol of the Aztecs was a guarantee of an assured water supply. The moisture-retaining cactus is the plant from which the fertilizing moisture issues. One drop of the fertilizing moisture will produce a flood. The Egyptians believed that the Nile rose in flood after a tear fell from Sirius, the star of the mother goddess, on the "Night of the Drop". The same idea is found in the Japanese story already referred to of the Tengu carrying off the dragon in the shape of a small snake. The Tengu drops the snake "into a deep cleft in the rock . . . knowing well that the latter cannot take his own shape nor fly through the air without the aid of water, though even a single drop". A few days later the long-nosed Tengu carried off a priest

---

[1] Breasted, *Religion and Thought in Ancient Egypt*, pp. 133-4.

who was about to fill his pitcher at a well, and dropped him into the same cleft. There was, fortunately, a drop of water in the pitcher.

"The dragon, strengthened by the drop of water that is left in the pitcher, changes at once into a little boy, flies into the air amidst thunder and lightning with the priest on his back." [1]

Dragons, in Chinese and Japanese lore, frequently appear as little boys or little girls. The fact that children were sacrificed in Mexico to Tlaloc by being thrown into his lake is significant in this connection.

A single element in the Mexican symbol remains to be dealt with. This is the stone or rock from which the cactus springs. As a rule it is depicted in symbolic shape. Here we appear to have another form of a deity who may be shown as a standing stone, a pillar, or a mountain. The mountain splits to give birth to the sun: it is the "sun-egg"; in China stones split to give birth to dragons; in various countries influenced by drifting megalithic culture, stones from which moisture emanates are believed to be inhabited by spirits. The island and the stone are, like the tree or plant of life containing moisture, forms of the great mother of the god who, as the reincarnation of his father, is the "husband of his mother". Tlaloc is associated with the goddess Chalchihuitlicue, who, as will be shown, is an American Hathor connected with life-giving water, marsh plants, precious stones, and jadeite. The god and goddess are manifestations of the principle of life.

Both bird and serpent figure prominently in post-Columbian American mythologies. Bancroft [2] is another writer who regards this association as "natural". "As a

---

[1] *Transactions of the Asiatic Society of Japan*, Vol. XXXVI, Part II, p. 41.
[2] *The Native Races of the Pacific States of North America*, Vol. III, p. 134.

symbol, sign, or type of the supernatural ", he writes, "the serpent would *naturally* suggest itself at an early date to man." But allowing it to be natural—a mere coincidence—that the wriggling lightning and the wriggling river should suggest the wriggling serpent to the people of the Old World and the New, it is surely very remarkable that in pre-Columbian America as in India the serpent should be regarded as a demon which causes drought by confining the water supply, and that it should be regarded, too, as a producer and guardian of precious gems that bring "luck" to mankind, cure diseases, promote longevity, protect against injury in battle, promote birth, work charms, &c. There is nothing natural about the idea that the serpent must be slain so that the water supply may be assured and that the slayer should be a monstrous eagle or a god, and that the attributes of the slain serpent should be acquired by the bird or the deity of which the bird is a symbol or avatar. There must be surely some very special and definite reason for the widespread prevalence of such a conception. This "unnatural" religious complex has surely a history.

A reasonable explanation seems to be that the early people, who entertained such curious beliefs about a serpent-demon, or deity, were searchers for the gems that serpent gods were supposed to possess. In India the Garuda is a serpent-slayer, as has been shown. This mythical bird is evidently a memory of the African secretary-bird. The Indian enemy of the serpent is the mongoose. Its war against serpents is as constant and consistent in India as that of the secretary-bird's in Africa. If the original beliefs connected with the reptile-slaying animal had had spontaneous origin in India, the mongoose and not the mythical eagle would have been the aggressor. If, on the other hand, the importance attached to the combat and the complex beliefs regarding the treasure-possessing snake were introduced into India by searchers for treasure, who there localized their mythological system, we should expect to find in Indian mythology the mongoose taking the place of the secretary-bird and acquiring the attributes of the treasure-producing and treasure-guarding serpent it slays. As a matter of fact, this is exactly what we do find. Kubera, the Aryo-Indian god of the north, is the god of treasure. Laufer informs us that in Buddhist art Kubera is figured holding in his left hand a mongoose spitting jewels. By devouring snakes the mongoose "appropriates their jewels, and has hence developed into the attribute of Kubera".[1] The mongoose is here as a slayer not of ordinary snakes but of snake deities, a local substitute for the foreign secretary-bird in its mythological setting, as well as a form of a complex deity who had already been localized. That the treasure-seekers, who introduced into India the complex beliefs associated with the deity which guarded treasure and the deity which killed the treasure-producer to obtain gems, also reached Central America in the course of time is made evident by the fact that the Maya workers in jade and amethysts had a goddess named Ix Tub Tun, "she who spits out precious stones".[2]

Ix Tub Tun possesses the attributes of an Indian Nāgi (a female snake deity), of Kubera, the Indian god of treasure, and of his animal attribute, the snake-slaying mongoose. Before the treasure-seekers reached America from the Old World colonies which they had founded, the religious beliefs connected with gold, pearls, turquoises, lapis-lazuli, &c., had passed to jade, amethysts, &c. There

---

[1] *The Diamond* (Chicago, 1915), p. 7, Note 4.
[2] D. G. Brinton, *A Primer of Mayan Hieroglyphics.*

must therefore have existed in the Old World a set of highly complex ideas regarding jade and amethysts before the searchers for them crossed the Pacific. Can the view be reasonably entertained, especially in view of the Indian evidence, that among the pre-Columbian Americans there was not an imported psychological motive for the search for jade and amethysts as there was undoubtedly for the search for gold and silver? In the New as in the Old World the precious metals and gems were supposed to be possessed of "life substance" derived from supernatural beings. These objects brought luck (which meant everything mankind desired), protected warriors in battle, assisted birth, cured diseases, &c. The fact that the Maya had a god of medicine, named Cit Bolon Tun (the Nine Precious Stones) is of undoubted importance in this regard.[1]

The Mexican coat of arms, in which the eagle grasps in its talons and beak a wriggling snake, is a symbol, not only of an independent American nation, but of ancient American civilization which, like modern American civilization, had its origin in the Old World. The everlasting combat between bird and reptile is in the New World a mythical one, but in Africa it continues to be waged between two natural enemies. As it chanced, the bird and the serpent were incorporated at an early period into the complex mythology of that progressive people, the ancient Egyptians, whose seafarers reached and colonized distant lands and introduced into them the elements of their culture. The process of culture-mixing that resulted can still be traced in India, China, Indonesia, Polynesia, and in pre-Columbian America. The ancient colonies that were founded budded fresh colonies, and the original mythological system, in which the everlasting combat

[1] D. G. Brinton, *A Primer of Mayan Hieroglyphics*, p. 42.

between an animal and a reptile remained embedded like a fly in amber, was carried far and wide.

It may be noted here that the strange conception of a water-confining serpent has its history in Ancient Egypt. The two goddesses of Upper and Lower Egypt had vulture forms and snake forms. After the "two lands" were united these goddesses were regarded as the female counterparts of the Nile god Hapi and the one acquired the attributes of the other. They also became fused with the milk-yielding cow-form of Hathor, and were referred to in the Pyramid Texts as "two mothers, the two vultures with long hair and hanging breasts" (Breasted, *Religion and Thought*, p. 117). In the cavern source of the Nile the serpent-mother was the controller of the river, who sent the inundation once a year. It was because the Nile shrinks until June and then suddenly begins to flood, that the water-controlling deity was regarded as the confiner as well as the giver of water. The myth is in Egypt a record of natural phenomena. Bird and serpent were associated because in Egypt a political fusion brought about a fusion of cults. The secretary-bird illustration was superimposed on the Egyptian myth.

As will be shown in the next chapter, another complex symbol, which is closely associated with that of the secretary-bird and snake, was likewise carried to distant parts from the same area of origin, and it affords unmistakable proof of the far-spread and persisting influence of Egyptian culture in ancient times.

CHAPTER V

The Winged Disc and the World's Ages

Origin of the Winged Disc Symbol—Disc on Temple-door Lintels in Old and New Worlds—Symbolism of the Portals—Temple a Symbol of Mother Goddess—Doctrine of the World's Ages—Doctrine connected with Colour Symbolism and Metal Symbolism—The Greek, Celtic, Indian, Chinese, and Mexican Doctrines of the World's Ages—Mexican Sequence of Ages identical with Indian—First Age in Mexico and India of same Duration—Details of Mexican Ages—Babylonian System of Calculation in America—Points of Compass Coloured in Old and New Worlds—Gold Discs and Crosses in America—Symbolism of Coloured Garments—Ten Years' Cycle—Antiquity and Origin of Colour Symbolism—Blue Symbolism in Old and New Worlds—Alchemy and Colour Symbolism—Internal Organs coloured in Mexico, China, and Egypt—Complexity of American Ideas.

THE winged disc symbol of the sun god is found to have been distributed in ancient times over wide areas. It can be traced in Egypt, Phœnicia, Asia Minor, Mesopotamia, across the Iranian plateau, in Polynesia and in pre-Columbian America. This symbol had origin in ancient Egypt. Of that there can be no shadow of doubt. It was at once, in the Nile valley, a religious symbol and a political symbol. It is indeed as outstanding a symbol of ancient Egyptian civilization as is the Union Jack of the civilization of the British Isles. The Union Jack is made up of the crosses of England, Scotland, and Ireland: the winged disc is made up of the religious symbols of united Egypt. The disc represents the sun, the wings are those of the falcon god, Horus, the chief deity of the dynastic Egyptians who united by conquest Upper and Lower Egypt, and the two serpents that entwine the disc

61

and extend their bodies above the wings are the ancient
tutelary serpent goddesses of the two ancient divisions of
Egypt, namely Nekhebit and Uazit, called by the Greeks
Eileithyia and Buto.   Occasionally these serpents were
crowned with the diadems of Upper and Lower Egypt.
The ancient Egyptians placed the image of the winged disc
" over the entrances to the inner chambers of a temple,
as well as over its gates, and on stela and other objects ".
Sometimes the symbol is simply a winged disc without
the serpents.   " Although seldom represented in the Old
Kingdom, these winged discs were common in the New." [1]
It may be that in this complex we may trace the influence
of stories about the secretary-bird brought from East
Africa; as the winged disc, the god Horus pursues Set
and his companions in their various forms, including their
serpent forms.   The battle ends when Set " changed himself into a roaring serpent that hid itself in a hole ".[2]

In pre-Columbian America, as in Egypt, Phœnicia,
and Western Asia, the winged disc was placed on temple
door lintels.   It was utilized in like manner but in
modified form in India, Cambodia, Indonesia, Melanesia,
Polynesia, and in China and Japan.   Each ancient country
that adopted it added something of its own.   The Polynesian form is of special interest, because (1) it shows in
the disc the head of the bird-devouring serpent—the
secretary-bird of Africa with which seafarers had become
familiar, and (2) it is an interesting link between the
winged discs of the New World and the Old.   The
various representative examples of the disc (see Plate,
page 64) show how, as a giver and protector of life and
as a destroyer of the enemies of life, it was connected
with local symbols of the life-giver in different countries.

[1] Wiedemann, *Religion of the Ancient Egyptians*, London (trans.), 1897, pp. 77–8.
[2] *Ibid.*, 73.

There was a very special reason why in the Old World and the New the disc was placed above the entrances of temples. These entrances are the portals of the Artemis form of the ancient mother goddess. Elliot Smith has discussed in this connection " the remarkable feature of Egyptian architecture which is displayed in the tendency to exaggerate the door-posts and lintels, until in the New Empire the great temples become transformed into little more than monstrously overgrown doorways and pylons". He emphasizes " the profound influence exercised by this line of development upon the Dravidian temples of India and the symbolic gateways of China and Japan ".[1] The " gates " were of great significance because " they represented the means of communication between the living and the dead, and, symbolically, the portal by which the dead acquired a re-birth into a new form of existence. It was presumably for this reason that the winged disc, as a symbol of life-giving, was placed above the lintels of these doors."[2] The temple was in a sense a symbol of the mother goddess in which dwelt the god. The name Hathor signifies " house of Horus". The young god had origin in the " house ". He was " husband of his mother ", to use the Egyptian paradoxical term. As the symbol of the combined influence of the god and goddess, the winged disc was the " life giver " in the deepest and widest sense of the term. It gave rain which nourished vegetable life on which human beings fed, and in this sense symbolized the thunder-bird which slew the water-confining serpent-dragon; it ensured immortality or longevity as a temple symbol placed above the portals of birth; the dead were re-born so that they might enter the Otherworld. In pre-Columbian America, as in the Old

---

[1] *Journal of the Manchester Egyptian and Oriental Society*, 1916.
[2] *The Evolution of the Dragon*, pp. 184–5.

World, the winged disc with the feathered serpent and the snake-slaying eagle symbolized not only the powers that sent life-giving rain so that the food supply might be assured, but was likewise a guarantee of life after death; it was the guide, protector, and healer of the living and the dead.

When the winged disc, which originally flew from Upper to Lower Egypt, extended its flight until it ultimately crossed the Pacific, the ancient mariners and prospectors and traders, whose wanderings it followed, introduced the religious doctrines with which it had become associated in various areas of culture. The doctrine of the World's Ages is one of these. It is found in its most clearly-defined forms among Old World peoples in Greece and India, and in both countries it is associated with colour symbolism and metal symbolism. The Ages were coloured and each colour was symbolized by a metal. There is evidence, however, that before the metals were connected with colours, earth-colours were used. This, at anyrate, was the case with the colours black, white, red, and yellow. Black appears to have symbolized night and death; white symbolized daylight and life; red symbolized the life-blood, and yellow symbolized fire and heat; red speckled with yellow was the more elaborate symbol of life, while yellow speckled with red represented fire.

The Greek doctrine of the World's Ages has a different colour sequence from that of India. Hesiod gives in his *Work and Days* five Ages in all, but his fourth age is evidently a late interpolation. The first was the Golden Age when men lived like the gods under the rule of Kronos; they never grew old nor suffered pain or loss of strength, but feasted continually, enjoyed peace and security. This race became the beneficent spirits who

1

2

3

4

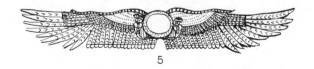

5

THE WINGED DISC

1, Assyrian. 2, American (Serpent Bird from Tikal). 3, Babylonian.
4, Polynesian. 5, Egyptian.

THE AZTEC CALENDAR STONE

Discovered in 1790. Now in the National Museum of Mexico.

watch over man and distribute riches. Men were inferior in the second or Silver Age. Children were reared up for a century and died soon afterwards. In the end Zeus, son of Kronos, destroyed this race. Then came the Bronze Age. Mankind sprang from the ash and had great strength, they worked in bronze and had bronze houses, but iron was unknown. As the Bronze Age men were violent, and deceitful, and takers of life, Zeus said to Hermes, " I will send a great rain such as hath not been since the making of the world, and the whole race of men shall perish. I am weary of their iniquity." Deucalion and his wife Pyrrha were, however, spared because they had received Zeus and Hermes, when these gods had assumed human shape, with hospitable warmth. Zeus instructed his host to build an ark of oak and store it with food. When this was done the couple entered the vessel and the door was shut. Then Zeus " broke up all the fountains of the deep, and opened the wellsprings of heaven, and 'it rained for forty days and forty nights continually ". The Bronze folk perished; even those who had fled to the hills were unable to escape. In time the ark rested on Parnassus, and when the waters ebbed the old couple descended the mountain and took refuge in a cave. The Fourth Age was the age of the Homeric heroes. When the heroes passed away they were transferred by Zeus to the Isles of the Blest. Then followed the Iron Age.

Jubainville has shown in his *Le Cycle Mythologique Irlandais et la Mythologie Celtique* that the doctrine of the World's Ages is embedded in Celtic mythology. The first Age, however, is the Silver which is followed by the Golden, the Bronze, and the Iron Ages in succession.

The colours of the four Indian Ages, called "Yugas",

are: (1) white, (2) red, (3) yellow, (4) black, and their names and lengths are as follows:

Krita Yuga,	4800	divine years.
Treta Yuga,	3600	,, ,,
Dwāpara Yuga,	2400	,, ,,
Kali Yuga,	1200	,, ,,
	12,000	

One year of mortals is equal to one day of the gods. The 12,000 divine years equal 4,320,000 years of mortals; each human year is made up of 360 days. A thousand of these periods of 4,320,000 years equals one day (Kalpa) of Brahma. A year of Brahma is composed of 360 Kalpas and he endures for 100 of these years.

Krita Yuga (Perfect Age) was so named because there was but one religion, and all men were so saintly that they did not require to perform religious ceremonies. No work was necessary; all men had need of was obtained by the power of will. Narayana, the Universal Soul, was white.

In the Treta Yuga sacrifices began; the World Soul was red and virtue lessened a quarter.

In the Dwāpara Yuga virtue lessened a half; the World Soul was yellow.

In the Kali Yuga men turned to wickedness and degenerated; the World Soul was black. This was " the Black or Iron Age ", according to the *Mahā-bhārata*.

The doctrine of the World's Ages can be traced in China. It is embedded in the works of Lao Tze the founder of Taoism, and of his follower Kwang Tze. " In the age of perfect virtue ", wrote the latter, " men attached no value to wisdom. . . . They were upright and correct, without knowing that to be so was Righteousness; they loved one another without knowing that to be so was Benevolence; they were honest and leal-hearted with-

out knowing that it was Loyalty; they fulfilled their en-
gagements without knowing that to do so was Good Faith;
in their simple movements they employed the services of
one another, without thinking that they were conferring
or receiving any gift. Therefore their actions left no trace,
and there was no record of their affairs."[1]   The reference
is quite clearly to the first Indian Age, Krita Yuga.

The doctrine of the World's Ages was imported into
pre-Columbian America. In Mexico these Ages were
coloured, (1) White, (2) Golden, (3) Red, and (4) Black.
As in other countries " golden" means "yellow", metal
symbolism having been closely connected with colour
symbolism. In the Japanese Ko-ji-ki yellow is the colour
of gold, white of silver, red of copper or bronze, and
black of iron. The following comparative table is of
special interest:

COLOURS OF THE MYTHICAL AGES

Greek—Yellow, White, Red, Black.
Indian I—White, Red, Yellow, Black.
Indian II—White, Yellow, Red, Black.
Celtic—White, Red, Yellow, Black.
Mexican—White, Yellow, Red, Black.

The Mexican sequence is identical with Indian II.
It may be noted that the White or Silver Age is the first
and most perfect in Indian, Celtic, and Mexican: Greece
alone begins with the Yellow or Golden Age of Perfec-
tion. The following comparative table shows the lengths
of the Indian and Mexican Ages:

Indian.	Mexican.
First Age, 4800 years.	4800 years.
Second Age, 3600 years.	4010 years.
Third Age, 2400 years.	4801 years.
Fourth Age, 1200 years.	5042 years of famine.

[1] *Myths of China and Japan*, Chapter XVI.

In both countries the First Age is of exactly the same duration. There were white, yellow, and red heavens in Mexico as in India. The Brahmanic Trinity, which in India was composed of Brahma, Vishnu, and Shiva, is found in Mexico too in association with the doctrine of the World's Ages. In the "Translation of the Explanation of the Mexican Paintings of the Codex Vaticanus", Kingsborough writes:[1]

"Plate I. *Homeyoco*, which signifies the place in which exists the Creator of the Universe, or the First Cause, to whom they gave the other name of Hometeuli, which means the God of three-fold dignity, or three gods the same as Olomris; they call this place Zivenavichnepaniucha, and by another name Homeiocan, that is to say the place of the holy Trinity, who, according to the opinion of many of their old men, begot, by their word, Cipatonal and a woman named Xumio; and these are the pair who existed before the deluge."

In the First Age of Mexico Water reigned till at length it destroyed the world. Men were changed into fish. A man and a woman escaped from this deluge by climbing a tree called Ahuehuete (the fir). Some believed that seven others who hid in a cave likewise saved their lives. During the First Age, which was called Coniztal ("the White Head") men ate no bread but only a certain kind of wild maize called Atzitziutil. The descendants of those who escaped the deluge repeopled the world. They worshipped their first founder whom they called "Heart of the People", to whom they made an idol which was preserved in a very secure place, covered with vestments.

"All their descendants deposited in that place rich jewels such as gold and precious stones. Before this idol, which they called their Heart, wood was always burning, with which they mixed copal or incense."

---

[1] Kingsborough, *Antiquities of Mexico*, Vol. VI, pp. 156 *et seq.*

One of the seven who sheltered in a cave and escaped the flood went to Chululan, "and there began to build a tower which is that of which the brick base is still visible. The name of that chief was Xelhua. He built it in order, should a deluge occur again, to escape it. . . . When it had already reached a great height, lightning from heaven fell and destroyed it." According to the Moslem version, the Tower of Babel was overthrown by a violent wind and earthquake sent by God.[1]

The Second Mexican mythical Age was named Coneuztuque (the Golden Age). Mankind ate no bread but only forest fruits called Acotzintli. This age was brought to an end by very violent winds, and all human beings were changed into apes with the exception of a man and a woman, who escaped change or destruction "within a stone" or sheltered in a cavern.

The Third Age was brought to an end by fire. During it men ate no bread and lived on the fruit of the Izlucoco.

The Fourth Age was, like the Kali Yuga of India, one of wickedness. It was called the "Age of Black Hair". The province of Tulan was destroyed on account of the vices of its inhabitants. A great famine prevailed. "Moreover it rained blood and many died of terror." All people were not, however, destroyed, "but only a considerable portion of them".

The rationalizing process can be traced in the Mexican as in the Greek doctrines of the World's Ages. Such traces of local influence and development are, however, of small account. The important fact remains that the Greek, Celtic, Indian, and Mexican doctrines are essentially the same and have evidently been derived from a common source. The Ages have their colours and, although the

[1] George Sale, *The Koran*, Chapter XVI.

colour sequence differs slightly, the symbolic colours or
metals are identical.   It would be ridiculous to assert that
such a strange doctrine was of spontaneous origin in
different parts of the Old and New Worlds.

It has been noted that the duration of the First Age
is the same in Mexico and India—namely 4800 years.
The Indian system gives the length of the four Yugas as
4,320,000 years of mortals which equal 12,000 divine
years.   That it is of Babylonian origin there can be no
doubt.   The Babylonians had ten antediluvian kings
who were reputed to have reigned for vast periods, the
total of which amounted to 120 saroi or 432,000 years.
Multiplied by ten this total gives the Indian Maha-yuga
of 4,320,000 years.   In Babylonia the measurements of
time and space were arrived at by utilizing the numerals
10 and 6.   The six parts of the body were multiplied by
the ten fingers.   This gave the basal 60, which multiplied
by the two hands gave the 120.   In measuring the
Zodiac the Babylonian mathematician fixed on 120
degrees.   The Zodiac was at first divided into 30 moon
chambers marked by the " Thirty Stars ".   The chiefs of
the " Thirty " numbered twelve.   Time was equalled with
space and 12 × 30 gave 360 days for the year.   In
Babylonia, Egypt, India, and Mexico the year was one
of 360 days to which 5 godless or unlucky days were
added, during which no laws obtained.   That the Mexicans should have originated this system quite independently is difficult to believe.

Another habit common to the New World and the
Old was that of colouring the points of the compass and
the four winds.   In this connection, as in that of the
doctrine of the Coloured Mythical Ages, the habit is of
more account than the actual details.   It is important, in
dealing with the question of culture drifting, to trace the

habit; it is astonishing to find that the details come so close to agreement in far-separated countries. The Indian doctrine of the Ages was better preserved in Mexico than in China.

It would be difficult to postulate a convincing reason why various peoples in different parts of the world should have simultaneously and independently "evolved" the habit of colouring the points of the compass. Nature affords no hint in this connection. "Red Land" was to the Aztec as to the ancient Egyptians a wholly mythical country — Paradise or a division of Paradise. The Egyptians had also a Red North and a White South, which were symbolized by the Red Crown of Lower Egypt and the White Crown of Upper Egypt; while their West, being the entrance to Dewat, the Underworld, was black speckled with red. Here, as in the doctrine of the World's Ages, the colours represent ideas, not natural phenomena. In India the north is white and the south, being Yama's gate and Yama the god of death, is coloured black. Southern India is no darker than the north. The Chinese coloured their north black, their south red, their east green or blue, and their west white. In Gaelic the north is black, the south white, the east purple-red, and the west dun or pale. This colour scheme obtained along the ancient sea and land routes, and in the East it seems to be intimately associated with Indian cultural influence. In Ceylon the north is yellow, the south blue, the east white, and the west red; in Java the north is black, the south red, the east white, and the west yellow. The same system can be traced in other parts of the Old World, including Japan, where the north is blue, the south white, the east green, and the west red. That the habit reached the New World by different routes across the Pacific is fully demonstrated by its prevalence among American peoples in various stages of culture. It is not a primitive habit, but one associated with complex rites that had become stereotyped before being disseminated far and wide, and with ideas closely connected with the symbolic colouring of lands, seas, rivers, mountains, races, mythical ages, and deities. In centres of ancient culture, whence the habit emanated, the symbolism of colour is closely associated with the symbolism of metals and with the ideas and practices of early alchemists. The early prospectors who searched for precious metals did so because a religious value had been attached to them. They identified the metals by their colours, and connected them with the elements. " Noble metals" like gold and silver were connected with the air and the sky, and with the heavenly deities. The colours revealed the attributes of sacred objects and of deities. Dyed cloths, precious stones, and feathers were likewise valued for their colours. What may be called a proto-alchemistic philosophy existed in early times among the people who had acquired from centres of complex religious culture fundamental ideas regarding the virtues of precious metals. These ideas were handed down from generation to generation as superstitions. The practice of wearing a gold talisman of symbolic shape, which Columbus found to be quite prevalent in the West Indies, had undoubtedly a history, although the wearers knew nothing of it and entertained as vague ideas regarding the significance of the practice as do modern dusky savages regarding the Christian cross symbol of which they make a fetish. Such savages know nothing of the history of Christianity, or its various sects and their theological systems. They wear the cross because they have been instructed by those to whom the symbol stands for much that unlettered peoples cannot comprehend. The habit of

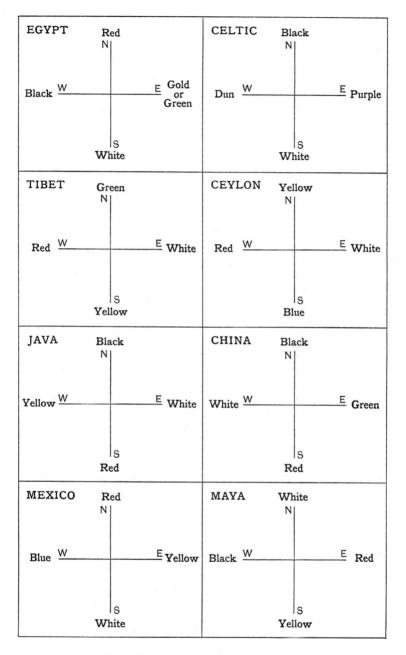

COLOURS OF THE CARDINAL POINTS

The habit of colouring the cardinal points was widespread in the Old and New Worlds. Some cults regarded one particular colour as peculiarly sacred. Thus the Buddhists favoured yellow, the Celts purple, and so on.

wearing it has become prevalent and widespread among certain peoples. In like manner the habit of attaching ideas of religious origin to colours was acquired by different peoples in ancient times. These people were unable to account for the origin of such ideas or to explain even the precise significance of their beliefs which had consequently passed to the stage known as "superstition". An interesting illustration of this fact is found in the account of the visit paid to Easter Island by the Spanish frigate *Santa Rosalia* in 1770. An officer wrote regarding the natives: "They are quite content with old rags, ribbons, coloured paper, playing cards and other bagatelles. *Everything of a bright red colour pleases them greatly, but they despise black.*" [1] The colour symbolism of the Easter Islanders had a history as had also their bird symbols and their habit of erecting stone images, but they knew nothing of that history, or of the ancient complex beliefs of which their superstitions were relics. These complex beliefs were originally associated with habits of life obtaining among peoples by whom their ancestors had been influenced either directly or indirectly. In the process of time the habits of life in question were either discarded or forgotten by the savages.[2]

When we find that among Red Indian tribes, as well as among the civilized peoples like the Aztecs and Maya, colour symbolism had wide applications and that colours were associated with the four cardinal points, it would be unreasonable to assert that the associated beliefs were either natural or necessarily of independent origin.

---

[1] Works issued by the Hakluyt Society, Second Series, No. XIII, p. 98.

[2] S. Routledge, *The Mystery of Easter Island*, London, 1920; W. H. R. Rivers, *The Disappearance of Useful Arts* (*Report, British Association*, 1912, p. 598); and *The History of Melanesian Society*, Cambridge, 1914.

Among the Navajo Indians the east is white, the south blue, the west yellow, and the north black. The southern and western colours are permanent, while those of the east and north are interchangeable. This fact is of undoubted importance. The colours of the cardinal points appear to have been influenced by the doctrines of the World's Ages, and by the custom of observing cycles or "sheafs" of years as constituting periods during which certain deities suffered loss of directing and stimulating power. One set of colours was favoured in one period and another set in another period. This practice obtained in connection with the king's attire in the country of Fu-sang described by an ancient Chinese writer. It is stated that:

"The colour of the King's garments is changed according to the mutations of the years. The first and second years (of a ten-year cycle) they are blue (or green); the third and fourth years they are red; the fifth and sixth years yellow; the seventh and eighth years white, and the ninth and tenth years black."

The custom of colouring the cardinal points was also closely connected with the custom of wearing coloured garments appropriate to certain ceremonies. A Chinese emperor, acting as high priest, wore azure robes when worshipping heaven, yellow robes when worshipping the earth, red robes when worshipping the sun, and white robes when worshipping the moon. In like manner the priestly robes in Salvador were coloured black, blue, green, red, and yellow.[1]

The Mongols, Tartars, and Tibetans observed the ten-years cycle, and the colours connected with the different periods of the cycle were represented in the robes of

[1] Bancroft, *The Native Races of the Pacific States of North America*, London, 1878, Vol. II, p. 728.

those who performed religious ceremonies.[1] Connected with the custom of colouring the cardinal points, cycles of years, and the robes of kings and priests, was the custom of associating certain colours with certain days. The Java peoples had a week of five days coloured (1) white, (2) red, (3) yellow, (4) black, (5) mixed colours. The first day was connected with the white east, the second with the red south, third with the yellow west, the fourth with the black north, while the mixed colours were symbolic of the centre of the cross of the four cardinal points.[2] There were lucky and unlucky days, as there were good and bad Ages according to the doctrine of the World's Ages.

The subject of colour symbolism is too complex a one to be dealt with at length here, but sufficient evidence has been cited to indicate that the post-Columbian habit of colouring the cardinal points was neither spontaneous nor natural, but was connected with doctrines either partially acquired to begin with, or partially retained by the descendants of those who had acquired them from centuries of ancient culture. In Tartary, Tibet, and Mongolia, the doctrines associated with an elaborate system of colour symbolism originally emanated from India and China, and both India and China had acquired the doctrines from older centres of civilization and developed them in the course of time. The habit of using colours symbolically is as old as civilization and can be traced in Babylonia and Egypt. Before the

---

[1] M. Huc, *Recollections of a Journey through Tartary, Tibet, and China*, London (Trans.), 1852.

H. de Charencey, *Des Couleurs considérées comme Symboles des Points de l'Horizon chez les Peuples du Nouveau-Monde*, Paris, 1877.

M. J. Klaproth, "Fragmens Bouddhiques" (extrait du *Nouveau Journal Asiatique*, Mars, 1831).

[2] J. Crawford, *History of the Indian Archipelago*, Edinburgh, 1820.

Egyptian system was disseminated in the ancient world it was closely associated with metal symbolism, and the symbolism of coloured garments worn by priests and gods, and the symbolism of body paint and coloured deities. Withal the colour scheme was applied to time and space and to the cardinal points.

We are therefore confronted with a very ancient habit and with relics of ancient and complex religious conception, when we find that in Dakota Red Indian rites white is a sign of consecration; blue is the colour of wind, of the west, of the moon, of water, of thunder, and sometimes of lightning even; while red symbolizes the sun, stone, various forms of animal and vegetable life; and yellow symbolizes the sunlight as distinguished from the fructifying power of the sun. The use of the colour blue is of marked significance, because the introduction of this colour is of comparatively recent origin in the history of civilization. It first came into prominence in Egypt where blue was manufactured by pouring molten copper on a local sandstone containing a blue-producing soda.[1] Egyptian blue became an important article in the trade of the ancient world, and was named by the Semitic traders after the Nile. In India it was known as *nil*, *nilam*, &c.[2] Blue was the colour sacred to the mother goddess Hathor, who had an intimate connection with water and the moon. In India the rain-giving god Indra is the patron of the east, and the Indra colour is *nila*. The Nāgas, however, live in the west, and in India, as in Dakota, the west is blue. Blue is the cardinal point from which the rain supply comes. In China the rain-makers

---

[1] Principal Laurie, Edinburgh, who has made this discovery, has succeeded in manufacturing Egyptian blue.

[2] After blue became a sacred colour it was obtained from vegetation, and Egyptian blue apparently became less valuable as an article of trade. Like murex purple it at first enriched the trade. Ultimately purple was also obtained from vegetation.

who face the east perpetuate a pre-Buddhistic rain ceremony in which Indra as the rain-giver is invoked in the
form of the Azure dragon.[1]

The Dakota custom had apparently origin among
a people who had been influenced by Buddhist ideas
regarding Nāgas (serpent gods) and the connection between Nāgas and water, thunder, and lightning. Red
symbolized the life-blood and the life-principle in the
sun, in the stone image, or habitation of the red sun god,
and the life-principle in vegetation and trees, the sap of
which was identified with blood. Yellow as sunlight is
evidently symbolic of fire and gold. In Ancient Egypt
the sun was red in one aspect and yellow or golden in
another. The Chinese coloured part of their summer red
and part of it yellow, and both colours were connected
with the south, red for the period of the red sun, and
yellow for the period of the yellow sun.

In Yucatan, according to Brinton, the north was
white, the south red, the west black, and the east yellow.
Other pre-Columbian American systems give the north as
black, the west as red, the east as white, and the south as
yellow, or the north as red, the south as white, the west
as green or blue, and the east as yellow. The Maya had
a white north, a yellow south, a red east, and a black
west. Green, blue, and black appear to have been interchangeable and to have symbolized the same influence.
The colour doctrine appears, too, to have been influenced
by local natural phenomena as well as by the system of
cycles.[2] But, as in other connections, the habit of colouring time, space, and localities is of more importance than

---

[1] De Visser, *The Dragon in China and Japan*, pp. 30–1.

[2] That is, if the north was the dry quarter as in China it was made black. In
Egypt the north was the source of the cool and reviving wind during the hot season,
and it was coloured red because it revived and stimulated.

the details of the colour system. That the habit was acquired in the New World the very complexity of the associated customs and beliefs, among unprogressive as among progressive peoples, demonstrates to the full. This is shown clearly by the Maya custom of associating colours with the internal organs of the human body. Yellow is the colour of the belly, red of the part named "serpent being", white of the "white being", while black is "disembowelled". This custom is in China connected with the belief that the elements and the cardinal points (and therefore the gods of the cardinal points) exercise an influence on bodily health and on the internal organs. The north which is black influences the kidneys and bladder; the south when red influences the heart and intestines, and when yellow the spleen; while the west, which is white, influences the lungs and small intestines; and the east, which is blue or green, influences the liver and gall. De Groot shows that the various cardinal points are in the complex Chinese religious system connected with the seasons, the elements, and the heavenly bodies.[1]

The east, controlled by the blue dragon, is connected with the spring, with wood, and the planet Jupiter; the south, controlled by the Red Bird, is connected with summer, fire, the sun, and the planet Mars; the west, controlled by the White Tiger, is connected with autumn, wind, metal, and the planet Venus; the north, controlled by the Black Tortoise, is connected with winter, cold, water, and the planet Mercury. Here the beliefs connected with alchemy and astrology are closely associated. The wind of the west gives birth to metal (noble metal) and enters the lungs, and Venus as the " Golden Aphrodite " or " Golden Hathor " is connected with metals,

[1] De Groot, *The Religious System of China*, Book I, Vol. III, 983.

while the sun heat of the red south which gives birth to fire is in the heart and the red planet Mars is controller.

In ancient Egypt red, which is the colour of the north, was connected with the small viscera; the south, which was white, with the stomach and large intestines; the west which was dark, with the liver and gall; and the east, apparently golden, with heart and lungs. This strange conception had origin in connection with mummification when the internal organs were placed in canopic jars dedicated to the Horuses of the cardinal points. It is quite evident that the Chinese system has a history outside China: it is interwoven not only with Buddhist ideas but has in weft and woof the intricate and far-carried conceptions of the ancient civilizations of Babylonia and Egypt. That the Maya system which survives in fragments which betoken its extreme complexity was of independent origin and perfectly natural, is a hypothesis that places a severe strain on credulity, especially as the internal organs of the dead were placed in jars dedicated, like the Horus jars of Egypt, to the four cardinal points. It involves not only a belief in the theory of " psychic unity", but necessitates the conclusion that the pre-Columbian Americans had precisely the same experiences and the same history in similar environments as the peoples of the Old World, and that the process of culture mixing was identical or almost so. Is it possible that widely separated peoples should have evolved the same arbitrary and artificial system of connecting colours with time and space, with the points of the compass and the gods of these points, and of connecting these colours and gods with wood, water, wind, and metal, and the internal organs of the body? It is not possible to account for such connections by American evidence alone. The history of the culture-mixing process cannot be traced in America. On the other hand the connections in China are most plausibly effected in the elaborate Fung-shui system, the history of which can be traced to India and beyond. It is quite inconceivable that the elaborate American system was not developed, as was the Chinese system, from imported complex ideas, originally based on experiences of the natural phenomena of a distant culture area, where a theorizing priesthood interpreted them in the light of their own particular traditions, experiences, and discoveries, and under pressure of distinctive political influences that necessitated a fusion of the ideas of rival cults. The pre-Columbian religious system is from the outset too complex and too artificial to have had independent origin. As its history cannot be traced in the New World, but can be in the Old World, the conclusion is inevitable that the influence of the Old World was at one time active and stimulating. The questions therefore arise: (1) whence the ancient influence or influences emanated? (2) what people or peoples reached America in pre-Columbian times? and (3) what route or routes did they follow?

CHAPTER VI

Semites, Celts, and Norsemen in America

Theory of Tertiary Man in America—Origin of American Civilization
—Race Question of Secondary Importance—Theories of American Origins—
Noah's Descendants—The Lost Ten Tribes—St. Thomas in America—The
Lost Atlantis Theory—Carthaginian Seafarers reached Sargasso Sea—Did
Phœnicians reach America?—American Legends of "White, Bearded Men"
—Welsh Legend of St. Madoc—Welsh-speaking Red Indians—Scottish Gaels
in America—An Irish Claim—Gaelic Numerals in Central America—Norse
Discovers of America—"White Man's Land"—Asiatic Links with America.

THE theory of the independent origin of American civilization and the pre-Columbian religious systems has so
obsessed the minds of some writers that they have set
back the migration of the Red Man from Asia to the
geological Tertiary epoch. It is asserted that the pioneer
settlers reached the American continent by a land-bridge
which formerly connected it with Asia. Later immigrants may, it is added, have arrived by way of Behring
Strait.

The theory that the ancestors of Modern Man were
already migrating in Tertiary times from the Old World
to the New is undoubtedly a staggering one. "Since
the Eocene period (of the Tertiary Age), which must
date back several millions of years, the whole mammalian
fauna", wrote Professor James Geikie in another connection, "has undergone manifold modifications and
changes, continuous evolution having resulted in the
more or less complete transformation of numerous types,

81

while many others have long been extinct." If the theory of man's existence in Eocene and Oligocene times is to be accepted, the view must obtain that, in his case alone, "evolution must have been at a standstill during a prodigiously extended period ".[1]

The Ice Age followed the Tertiary Age, and it was in its later phases and during what is known as post-Glacial times that Modern Man reached Western Europe. That he entered America at an earlier period has yet to be proved.

A fact that cannot be overlooked is that the so-called Red Man bears a striking family resemblance to certain inhabitants of north-eastern and central Asia, while other American peoples resemble Polynesian and Malayan types. But, at the same time, the race question is of secondary importance in dealing with the question of civilization. As language affords no certain proof of racial affinities, neither do racial affinities afford proof of the origin of a specific culture, and especially such a complex culture as is found among Maya and Aztec peoples. The possibility has always to be borne in mind that two sections of the same people may in separate areas be subjected to different cultural influences, and may embrace religions and be incorporated in social organizations that bear little or no resemblance one to another. The present-day Africans of the United States, for instance, are physically akin to the natives of West Africa, yet how deep and wide is the culture gulf that separates them!

When Columbus discovered the New World, he believed that San Salvador, the first island he reached, was situated in the Indian Ocean and not far distant from the famous island kingdom of Cipango (Japan). The natives were called "Indians", a name which has

---

[1] *Antiquity of Man in Europe* (Edin., 1914), pp. 4, 5.

clung to the Red Man. These islanders had canoes; they could not have reached San Salvador unless they had been seafarers. On another island, which Columbus name Fernandina, in honour of his king, he found that cotton was used for clothing, and that for beds the Indians had nets of cotton suspended from two posts and called "hamacs", another name which has been perpetuated.

After the Spaniards had conquered Mexico, the Old World theologians found it difficult to account for the peopling of America, and much speculation was indulged in as to whether Noah, one of his sons, or the immediate descendants of his sons, had selected that part of the world for settlement of a portion of the human race. It was urged that the crossing of the Pacific or Atlantic was unlikely to have presented difficulties to the descendants of a man who had the unique opportunity of solving the problems of navigation during his voyage in the ark.

Another theory was that the post-Columbian Americans were descended from the "lost ten tribes of Israel". It was first suggested by the Spanish monks who undertook the work of Christianizing the Red Man, and during the early part of the nineteenth century not a few writers set themselves to prove it. Chief among them was Lord Kingsborough who spent about £50,000 in publishing his great work *The Antiquities of Mexico* (London, 1830). The fact that the pre-Columbian Americans did not speak Hebrew was accounted for by some advocates of the Lost Ten Tribes theory by the suggestion that the devil had prompted them to learn new and various languages so that they might not be able to understand the language of the Christian faith. The devil never dreamed that the missionaries would cheat him by learning all these strange languages!

In conflict with this theory regarding the Satanic influence in the domain of languages, was the early monkish belief that St. Thomas had reached America and preached the gospel there. This mission was first suggested by the amazing discovery that the natives venerated the cross. Among the Mexican jewels sent to the King of Spain by Cortez were "a cross with a crucifix and its support", a coiled serpent symbol "with a cross on the back", "three little flowers of gold and greenstones, one with two beads and the other with a cross". Boturini relates that he discovered a cross, which was about a cubit in size and painted a beautiful blue colour, including five white balls on an azure shield, "without doubt emblems of the five precious wounds of our Saviour". Another cross was found in a cave in Lower Mixteca, and from this cave angelic music issued on every vigil of St. Thomas. The saint left marks of his feet in various parts of the New World as did Buddha in India. In like manner the Welsh were wont to point out the footprints of Arthur's horse which leapt the Bristol Channel when the romantic king pursued Morgan le Fay. The marks of the horse's hoofs of another hero who pursued the Cailleach are pointed out on the north shore of Loch Etive in Argyllshire. Wooden crosses were venerated in the state of Oaxaca and in Aguatolco among the Zapotecs. The Spaniards found crosses among the Maya in Central America, in Florida, in Paraguay, and among the Incas of Peru who venerated a jasper cross. As in the Old World, the cross symbol was connected with the gods of the four points of the compass who controlled the elements, and therefore with the doctrines referred to

"INCA INSCRIPTION STONE", TIAHUANACO, BOLIVIA

With petroglyphs similar to those found on megaliths and rocks in Western and Southern Europe

CARVED PANEL FROM THE TEMPLE OF THE FOLIATED CROSS,
PALENQUE, MEXICO

Maya worshipper presenting a symbolic figure to an anthropomorphic deity who stands on a shell.
In the shell is the "Long-nosed god" (Chac = Tlaloc) from whose hand a plant emerges and encloses
the head of the "maize god". The cross in the centre surmounted by the turkey (rain bird) represents
a deity from whom springs the maize.

Reproduced by permission from "A Glimpse at Guatemala", by A. P. and A. C. Maudslay

in the previous chapter, including that of the four ages of the world which were coloured like the cardinal points.

The Spaniards were so convinced, however, that the pre-Columbian cross was a Christian symbol that they examined Mexican mythology for traces of St. Thomas. Topiltzin Quetzalcoatl, the hero god, was regarded as a memory of the saint. "To" was an abbreviation of "Thomas", to which "pilcin" which means "son" or "disciple" was added. Topiltzin Quetzalcoatl closely resembled in sound and significance Thomas, surnamed Didymus. Some, on the other hand, regarded Quetzalcoatl as the Messiah[1] and this view found favour with Lord Kingsborough, who wrote:

"How truly surprising it is to find that the Mexicans should have believed in the incarnation of the only son of their supreme god Tonacatecutle. For Mexican mythology speaking of no other son of that god except Quetzalcoatl, who was born of Chimalman, the Virgin of Tula, without connection with man and by his breath alone . . . it must be presumed that Quetzalcoatl was his only son. Other arguments might be adduced to show that the Mexicans believed that Quetzalcoatl was both god and man, that he had, previously to his incarnation, existed from all eternity, that he had created both the world and man, that he descended from heaven to reform the world by penance, that he was born with the perfect use of reason, that he preached a new law, and, being King of Tula, was crucified for the sins of mankind. . . ."[2]

The "lost ten tribes" were supposed to have wandered eastward from Assyria and to have reached America by Behring Strait.

Another famous theory is that the pre-Columbian civilizations were established by colonists from the lost Island of Atlantis. Brasseur de Bourbourg has been its

[1] Bancroft, *The Native Races of the Pacific States of North America*, Vol. V, p. 25.
[2] *Mexican Antiquities*, Vol. VI, pp. 507-8.

chief exponent. He quotes Plato's record of the story that Solon when in Egypt was informed by the priests regarding the Lost Atlantis. It runs as follows:

"Among the great deeds of Athens of which recollection is preserved in our books, there is one which should be placed above all others. Our books tell that the Athenians destroyed an army which came across the Atlantic Sea and insolently invaded Europe and Asia; for the sea was then navigable, and beyond the strait where you place the Pillars of Hercules there was an island larger than Asia and Libya combined. From this island one could pass easily to the other islands, and from these to the continent which lies around the interior sea. The sea on this side of the strait (the Mediterranean), of which we speak, resembles a harbour with a narrow entrance; but there is a genuine sea, and the land which surrounds it is a veritable continent. In the island of Atlantis reigned three kings with great and marvellous power. They had under their dominion the whole of Atlantis, several other islands, and part of the Continent. At one time their power extended into Libya, and into Europe as far as Tyrrhenia; and, uniting their whole force, they sought to destroy our countries at a blow, but their defeat stopped the invasion and gave entire independence to all countries on this side of the Pillars of Hercules. Afterwards, in one day and one fatal night, there came mighty earthquakes and inundations, which engulfed that warlike people; Atlantis disappeared beneath the sea, and then that sea became inaccessible, so that navigation on it ceased on account of the quantity of mud which the engulfed island left in its place."

Proclus, quoting from a lost work, refers to islands in the exterior sea beyond the Pillars of Hercules and states that the inhabitants of one of these islands "preserved from their ancestors a remembrance of Atlantis, an extremely large island, which for a long time held dominion over all the islands of the Atlantic Ocean".

The Abbé Brasseur de Bourbourg, who has advocated the view that civilization had origin in America, found it necessary to assume that the American continent at one time extended as a great peninsula from the Gulf of Mexico and the Caribbean Sea to the Canary Islands or their immediate vicinity. This vast extension of land was submerged as a result of a great convulsion of nature. Yucatan, Honduras, and Guatemala sank too, but afterwards the land rose sufficiently high to restore these countries and the West Indian Islands. The Abbé, who was an accomplished American philologist, professed to have found records of this cataclysm in ancient American writings of which he gave a hypothetical interpretation. His philological argument in support of the view that his Atlantis had real existence runs as follows:

"The words *Atlas* and *Atlantic* have no satisfactory etymology in any language known to Europe. They are not Greek, and cannot be referred to any known language of the Old World. But in the Nahuatl language we find immediately the radical *a, atl*, which signifies water, war, and the top of the head. From this comes a series of words, such as *atlan*, 'on the border of', or 'amid the water', from which we have the adjective *Atlantic*. We have also *atlaça*, 'to combat', or 'be in agony'; it means likewise 'to hurl', or 'dart from water', and in the preterit makes *atlaz*. A city named *Atlan* existed when the continent was discovered by Columbus, at the entrance of the Gulf of Uraba, in Darien, with a good harbour; it is now reduced to an unimportant pueblo named *Acla*."

Those who have pinned their faith to Plato's account of the Lost Atlantis have overlooked two facts: (1) that the events related to Solon by the Egyptian priests took place " 9000 Egyptian years " earlier, and (2) that "navigation" on it (the Atlantic Ocean) ceased on account of the quantity of mud which the ingulfed island left in its place ". Geologists scoff at the idea that the Atlantic has ever been, since boats were invented, too shallow for safe navigation. " I know of no geological evidence ", wrote Professor James Geikie in this connection, "that puts it beyond doubt that the Atlantic basin is the site of a drowned continent. On the contrary, such evidence as we have leads rather to the belief that the Atlantic basin, like that of the Pacific, is of primeval origin." On the other hand Professor Edward Hull thought there was something in the tradition of the Lost Atlantis, but expressed the opinion that the submergence of the land or island took place during "the glacial period when much of Europe and the British Isles were covered by snow and ice". Hull dated the submergence at about 10,000 B.C., but others place the close of the Ice Age at from 20,000 to 30,000 B.C. Dr. Scharff, Dublin, has expressed the belief that the Atlantic land-bridge between Southern Europe and the West Indies was probably separated "in Miocene times"—that is millions of years ago and before the appearance of Modern Man on the globe. Recent discoveries in connection with the post-Glacial epoch have established a connection between Crô-Magnon man, the earliest representative of Modern Man in Western Europe, and North Africa. He imported Indian Ocean sea-shells from some centre in the East. These shells could not have been found nearer than Aden. The earlier Europeans of the Neanderthal species were on a low stage of civilization.

It has been found necessary on the part of those who favour the Lost Atlantis theory to assume that metals were first worked on the submerged sub-continent or island. Copper was in use in Egypt and Sumeria (the southern area of Babylonia) at about 3000 B.C. If they received their skill in metal-working from Atlantis, the pre-Columbian Americans should have known how to utilize copper at as remote, if not at an even more remote period. But, as a matter of fact, the introduction of metal-working in America is of comparatively recent date. "Most students of American archæology are agreed", writes Sir Hercules Read, "that the Mexican and Peruvian bronzes are not of any great antiquity, and that the Bronze Age must have been over in China long before it began in the New World." [1]

New light has been thrown of late on the movement of Eastern peoples towards the Atlantic, and of the exploration of the Atlantic coasts of Western Europe before the "Bronze Age", by discoveries of great importance made in Mesopotamia and Spain. Tablets found on the site of the ancient Assyrian capital of Asshur contain the statement that Sargon of Akkad, who reigned before 2500 B.C., occupied Caphtor (Crete) and tapped the trade from the Tin Land in the Upper Sea (the Mediterranean). In Spain M. Siret has found on sites earlier than the Bronze Age, cult objects called idols of Mesopotamian style, cut in hippopotamus ivory from Egypt, portions of ostrich eggs, alabaster perfume-flasks of Arabian pattern, Egyptian cups of marble and alabaster, painted vases of Oriental origin or style, mural painting on layers of plaster, religious objects of the Palm Tree cult, amber from the Baltic, jet from England (apparently from Whitby in Yorkshire), the green stone called *callaïs*, which is found in beds of tin, a diadem of gold belonging to the "Neolithic Age". A shell from the Red Sea (*Dentalium Elephantinum*), found by M. Bonsor, in a Neolithic or Eneolithic bed near Carmona, affords further proof of a racial and cultural drift from the East into Western Europe before the introduction of the manufacture of bronze. The Eastern traders and prospectors worked and exported metals and other substances, and had evidently coasted round to Britain and the Baltic. A canoe

[1] British Museum, *Guide to the Antiquities of the Bronze Age*, pp. 110–1.

found in Clyde silt, with a cork plug, evidently came from the Mediterranean and probably from Spain where cork trees grow.

These early navigators apparently found no difficulty in navigating the Atlantic. Did they visit any country which afterwards became submerged? An interesting fact in this connection is that the Clyde canoe was found embedded in silt twenty-five feet above the present sea-level. The land in Scotland has risen since it foundered. Now, when Scotland was rising, southern England and northern France were sinking. At Morbraz in Brittany there are megalithic monuments covered by several metres of water as a result of coast erosion and local land sinking after the last great land movement ceased. The Dogger Bank land-bridge or island and other North Sea islands were submerged about the same time. Clement Reid dates the beginning of the period of gradual land submergence at about 3000 B.C., and writes:

" We are dealing with times when the Egyptian, Babylonian, and Minoan civilizations flourished. Northern Europe was then probably barbarous, and metals had not come into use; but the amber trade of the Baltic was probably in full swing. Rumours of any great disaster, such as the submergence of thousands of square miles and the displacement of large populations, might spread far and wide along the trade routes. Is it possible that thus originated some of the stories of the deluge?"[1]

It is more possible that thus originated the legend of the Lost Atlantis and that the mud banks in the North Sea are those referred to in Plato's version of it. This view is rendered all the more plausible by the quotation from Timagenes given by Ammianus Marcellinus (XV, 9). Timagenes was informed by the Druids that a part of the inhabitants of Gaul was indigenous, that another part had

---

[1] *Submerged Forests*, Cambridge, 1913, p. 120.

come from the farthest shores and districts across the Rhine, expelled from their own lands by the frequent wars and the encroachments of ocean. This subsidence apparently occurred at the beginning of the Bronze Age,[1] which, so far as Western Europe is concerned, was evidently of earlier date than has hitherto been supposed. As much is indicated by the Asshur tablets referring to Sargon of Akkad's empire, and Siret's discoveries in Spain.

Among the believers that the Lost Atlantis was situated in the middle of the Atlantic was Dr. Schliemann, the famous pioneer of pre-Hellenic archæological excavations. He believed that the people of Atlantis had " a more advanced currency than we have at present ". Among his papers were found after his death one which states:

" I have come to the conclusion that Atlantis was not only a great territory between America and the West Coast of Africa and Europe, but the cradle of all our civilization as well. There has been much dispute among scientists on this matter. According to one group the tradition of Atlantis is purely fictional, founded upon fragmentary accounts of a deluge some thousands of years before the Christian era. Others declare the tradition wholly historical, but not capable of proof."

Schliemann's posthumous papers set forth that he found at Troy a bronze vase containing fragments of pottery, images and coins of " a peculiar metal ", and " objects made of fossilized bone ". On some of these relics are Phœnician hieroglyphics which he read as " from the King Chronos of Atlantis ". Subsequently he found among pre-Columbian relics from Central America, preserved in the Louvre, Paris, similar pieces of pottery

---

[1] These archæological " Ages " have served their day, and sooner or later must drop out of use. Apparently the " neolithic " industry was, as Siret's discoveries show, introduced by a sea-faring people who searched for metals.

and fossilized bone.   He asked that an "owl-headed"
vase should be broken open.   His grandson, Dr. Paul
Schliemann, announced in 1912 that he had found in
this pre-Columbian vase a coin or medal of "silver-like
metal" inscribed in Phœnician hieroglyphs that read,
"Issued in the Temple of Transparent Walls", and that
he had "reasons for saying that the strange medals were
used as money in Atlantis four thousand years ago".
His evidence, however, has not, so far, been accepted
by, or even submitted to, scientists capable of passing
judgment on it.

Schliemann's theory connects the Phœnicians with
Atlantis and pre-Columbian America.   Whether or not
these enterprising mariners, who, according to Herodotus,
circumnavigated Africa, crossed the Atlantic and discovered America is uncertain.   There are, however, vague
records of Carthaginian voyages which are of special interest in this connection.   The senate of Carthage, during
"the flourishing times" of that great trading city, dis-
patched two brothers, named Hanno and Himilco, to
found new trading stations of colonists on the Atlantic
sea-board.   Hanno's ships were steered to the south
beyond the Pillars of Hercules (Strait of Gibraltar), and
Himilco's to the north.   Accounts of their voyages were
inscribed on votive tablets which were preserved in the
temple of Moloch at Carthage.   These have long been
lost, but a Greek translation of Hanno's account has
survived and is known as the "Periplus of Hanno".
Himilco's account has survived in fragmentary form in
Pliny and in the *Book of Wonderful Stories*, ascribed to
Aristotle, while its substance is contained in the Latin
poem *Ora Maritima* of the Roman Consul Rufus Festus
Avienus (*c.* A.D. 350–400).   Himilco reached a group of
tin-bearing islands named the Œstrymnides, believed to

be identical with the Cassiterides. His fleet afterwards
ventured into the open sea and was driven southward.
The weather grew foggy, but in time the ships reached
a warmer sea and were becalmed in the vicinity of extensive masses of sea-weed, believed to be the Sargasso Sea.
On the homeward journey Himilco is believed to have
touched at the Azores and the island of Madeira. A description of a volcano suggests that Teneriffe was visited.
"The wonderful high crown of the mountain", says
Pliny, "reached above the clouds to the neighbourhood
of the circle of the moon, and appeared at night to be all
in flames, resounding far and wide with the noise of pipes,
trumpets, and cymbals."[1] This picture of "Mount Atlas"
was possibly derived from Carthaginian sources. Himilco
was prevented by the magicians who accompanied him
from continuing his voyage, and was thus apparently
robbed of the glory that some 2000 years later fell to
Columbus.

It would appear, however, that other Phœnician
voyagers subsequently ventured across the Atlantic. The
sailors of Gades (the Phœnician colony of Cadiz) were
wont to describe "the deserted track in the ocean four
days' sail to the south-west", in which shoals of tunny-
fish of "wonderful size and fatness" were found. In the
Book of Wonderful Stories, ascribed to Aristotle, it is stated:

"In the waters of the Atlantic, four days' sail from Gades
(Cadiz), the marine plants on which they (the tunny-fish) feed
grew to unusual size, and the tunnies and congers of this coast
were delicacies sought after in Athens and Carthage; the latter
city, after she obtained possession of the south of Spain, forbade
their export to any other place ".

When Columbus sighted on the Atlantic vast fields
of weed, resembling sunken islands, among which were

[1] *Hist. Nat.*, V, I.

tunny-fish, he remembered the account given in the
work ascribed to Aristotle of the weedy sea. The sea-
animals crept upon the tangled weed. The Sargasso Sea,
apparently the " sea-weed meadows " of Oviedo, " are the
habitation ", says Humboldt, " of a countless number of
small marine animals ". The glowing accounts of the
islands in the Atlantic alarmed the senate of Carthage,
which feared an exodus to them, and visits were forbidden
on pain of death.

Some writers are inclined to identify the " Fortunate
Isles " with the West Indies, and to regard vague references to a " great Saturnian continent " beyond the
Atlantic as indicating a traditional knowledge of the
existence of America emanating from Carthage. Diodorus Siculus, who states that the Phœnicians discovered
a large island in the Atlantic in which the inhabitants had
magnificent houses and gardens, explains that the Carthaginians wished to use it as a place of refuge in case of
necessity.

One of the most prominent advocates of the theory
that the Phœnicians crossed the Atlantic and founded
settlements in America has been Mr. George Jones, the
author of a *History of Ancient America*. He has dealt
with the similarities between American and Egyptian
pyramids, the Greek style of certain American ruins,
and other Old World resemblances in the New World.
His view is that after Alexander the Great captured
Tyre a remnant of the conquered people fled to the
Fortunate Isles, and afterwards reached the American
continent; they founded their first city at Copan. Pre-
Columbian American legends regarding " bearded white
men ", who " came from the East in ships ", have been
cited by Jones and others in support of the theory that
the " Colhuas " of America were the Phœnicians.

A Celtic claim of having discovered America has been urged on behalf of the North Welsh prince Madoc, who, in the twelfth century of our era, set out on a voyage across the Atlantic to find peace from family bickerings. He discovered a land that pleased him, and leaving there 120 of his people returned to Wales. There he gathered together a band of adventurers and then set sail with ten ships. He was never heard of again. The land reached by Madoc "must needs be", wrote Hakluyt in his *English Voyages*, "some part of that country which the Spaniards affirme themselves to be the first finders since Hanno's time ".

It has been suggested that Madoc settled "somewhere in the Carolinas ", and that his people were subsequently "destroyed or absorbed by some powerful tribe of Indians ". In the preface to Southey's " Madoc " epic, the poet says that about the same time as the Welsh prince settled in America, the Aztecs migrated into Mexico. He considered that their emigration was connected with the adventures of Madoc.

In 1660, the Rev. Morgan Jones, a Welsh chaplain, discovered traces of Welsh influence in South Carolina. He and others were captured by Tuscarora Indians and they were condemned to die. Mr. Jones exclaimed in Welsh, " Have I escaped so many dangers and must I now be knocked on the head like a dog? " An Indian who overheard and understood what he said, spoke in Welsh too, and said that he should not die.

In the account of his experiences, written in 1686, and published in *The Gentleman's Magazine* in 1740, Mr. Jones relates that he and his party were welcomed by the Indians to their town. They " entertained us very civilly and cordially for four months, during which time I had the opportunity of conversing with them familiarly in the

British (Welsh) language, and did preach to them in the same language three times a week. . . . They are settled upon Pontigo River, not far from Cape Atros."

It has been claimed too that America was reached by Gaelic-speaking adventurers, and that vague memories of these settlements are preserved in the legends regarding St. Brandan's Islands, the Isles of the West, &c. In this connection reference may be made to traces of the Gaelic language on the isthmus of Darien. Wafer in his *New Voyages* gives, among the vocabularies of the tribes in this area, the following numerals which, excepting "div", are Gaelic:[1]

> hean,
> div,
> tree,
> caher,
> cooig,
> deh.

The fact that Scotland was responsible for a Darien expedition may not be unconnected with this discovery.

Lord Monboddo, a patriotic seventeenth century Scotsman, was a believer in the Welsh colonization of America and urged a claim on behalf of his own country. He found traces of the Gaelic language in different districts. A Highlander who took part in a polar expedition found that after a few days contact with an Eskimo he was able to converse with him by using Gaelic. "The Celtic language", wrote his lordship, "was spoken by many of the tribes of Florida, which is situated at the north end of the Gulf of Mexico." A Highland gentleman who had resided in Florida for several years informed him that the languages of some of the tribes "had the greatest

---

[1] pp. 185–8; see also Cullen's *Darien*, pp. 99-102, and Bancroft, *The Native Races of the Pacific States of North America*, Vol. III, p. 795.

affinity with the Celtic". The native names "of several
of the streams, brooks, mountains, and rocks, of Florida,
are also the same which are given to similar objects in
the Highlands of Scotland. .... But what is more remarkable, in their war-song, not only the sentiments, but
several lines, the very same words are used in Ossian's
celebrated majestic poem of the wars of his ancestors who
flourished about thirteen hundred years ago." [1]

Irish claims have likewise been made. The needs of
the "Isles of America" were thoughtfully remembered by
St. Patrick, who sent missionaries thither. Some have
expressed the belief that one of these missionaries was
remembered in Mexico as the god Quetzalcoatl. [2]

There appears to be no doubt that America was
reached by the Norsemen in the eleventh century. The
two chief records are *Hauk's Book*, a collection of early
fourteenth century manuscripts, and the *Flatey Book* which
was written about 1380. In the tenth century there
were settlements of Norsemen, and of the mixed population of Norsemen and Celtic peoples, in Iceland. Erik
the Red, the son of a Norse nobleman who became
involved in a feud that compelled him to seek refuge
in Iceland, left that island and sailing westward discovered
Greenland. He spent a winter there, and returning to
Iceland sailed again to Greenland with twenty-five ships
for the purpose of establishing a colony. Biarni, son
of one of the colonists, was in Norway when his father
left Iceland for Greenland. He resolved to follow him.
Soon after he set sail the weather grew very stormy and
he was driven across the Atlantic until he sighted low-
lying land which may have been Cape Cod. The
weather moderated and he sailed for two days towards

[1] Quoted in Priest's *American Antiquities*, p. 230.
[2] References in De Costa's *Pre-Columbian Discoveries of America*, p. xviii.

the north-east, and again sighted land which may have been Nova Scotia. Three days later a mountainous land, which may have been Newfoundland, was reached. The voyage was continued until at length the Greenland colony was discovered.

About fourteen years later the unknown country sighted by Biarni was visited by Leif, the son of Brattahlid, after whom the Greenland colony had been named. Leif was a contemporary of Olaf Tryggvason, who had been converted to Christianity in Britain, and at the instigation of that hero promoted the new faith in Greenland. In 1002 Leif set out in his ship to sail to Norway. He lost his course and was drifted towards a strange land covered with glaciers. As the foreground resembled a flat rock, he called it Helluland (the land of flat stone). Sailing southward, Leif in time sighted a low-lying wooded country with stretches of white sand which he named Markland (land of woods). After landing, the voyage was resumed towards the south. In two days an island was discovered. It lay opposite the north-east part of the mainland. Leif directed his course between the island and a cape, and passed up a river into a bay. A safe landing was effected. The season was mid autumn and, as wild grapes were found, Leif called the country Vinland (wineland). Huts were erected so that the winter might be passed in this locality, where the climate was mild and the soil excellent.

There can be no doubt that America was reached by both Biarni and Leif. Helluland may have been the coast of Labrador, but some incline to favour Newfoundland, and Markland may have been in Nova Scotia.

Leif returned to Greenland with a cargo of timber.

His father, Erik the Red, had died, and he succeeded to his estate and responsibilities. Next year his brother Thorvald visited Vinland and wintered there. In the summer he explored the coast westward and southward. He was killed by natives whom the Norsemen called "skrœlinger". Some think these were Eskimos and others that they were Red Indians. The skrœlinger had skin canoes and slept under them.

In 1020 Thorfinn Karlsefni fitted out an expedition and set out in search of Vinland. In one of his ships were two Scots, named Hake and Hekia, who were very swift of foot. Thorfinn wintered in Vinland, and his wife gave birth to a son from whom was descended Thorvaldsen the Danish sculptor. In the spring Thorfinn explored the coast farther west and south, and, according to some writers, went south of Nantucket in Long Island Sound which he named Straumsfjord. He stayed for some months with his party at a place he named Hop, which Mr. Gathorne Hardy identifies with the creek at the extreme western end of Long Island Sound close to New York.[1] After spending three winters in America, Thorfinn, with part of his company, returned to Greenland.

Another colonizing party was led to Vinland by Leif's sister Freydis, a blood-thirsty woman, who killed several men and women because they annoyed her. She returned to Greenland.

A trading station appears to have been founded in Vinland. The colonists are said to have been visited by a Christian priest named Jon or John who settled in Iceland. He was "murdered by the heathen".

The story is told of an Icelandic nobleman named Biorn Asbrandson, who set out for Vinland but was

[1] *The Norse Discoveries of America*, London, 1921.

driven south of it to the region called by Norsemen Hvitramannaland (land of the white men). There he became a chief of a Red Indian tribe. The crew of a Norse vessel were captured by the Indians some years later, and were released by Biorn who knew one of them. He spoke freely regarding his Icelandic friends, but decided to remain in the new land.

An interesting reference to the Norse colonists in America is contained in a letter from New England published in 1787 by Michael Lort, vice-president of the London Antiquary Society. It was written half a century earlier and states:

" There was a tradition current with the oldest Indians in these parts that there came a wooden house, and men of another country in it, swimming up the Assoonet, as this (Taunton) river was then called, who fought the Indians with mighty success ".[1]

How far south the Norse adventurers penetrated it is difficult to say. Some think " white man's land " extended to Florida. Brasseur de Bourbourg considered that he found traces of Scandinavian influence in the languages of Central America, and draws attention in this connection to the traditions of the Central American nations that point to a north-east origin.[2]

There seems to be no doubt that the Atlantic was crossed by Norse explorers about two centuries before Columbus discovered America. It is possible, too, that Welsh, Irish, and Scottish mariners may have found their way to the New World when they set out, as did the Chinese, to search for the " Isles of the Blest ". The Phœnicians, who circumnavigated Africa and traded on the Indian Ocean, may have likewise penetrated beyond

[1] Quoted by Baldwin in *Ancient America*, London, 1872, pp. 283-4.
[2] *Nouvelles Annales.*

the Sargasso Sea with which they appear to have been familiar. But the civilization of pre-Columbian America contains elements that point to a process of culture-drifting not across the Atlantic but across the Pacific. The dragon of America is more like the " wonder beast " of China and Japan than that of Western Europe or North Africa; the American "winged disc" resembles the Polynesian, while the elephant symbols of Copan are not of African but of Indian origin. Withal, there is no evidence that the Atlantic adventurers opened up trade routes, and maintained constant trading relations with the New World. The Norse trade between Green-land and Nova Scotia was never a very important one, and it was certainly not from Norway, Iceland, or the Norse settlements in the British Isles that the beliefs and customs of Mexicans, Mayans, or Peruvians were derived.

In the next chapter, it will be shown that there were in earlier times than those to which Norse and Celtic sea-faring activities can be ascribed far eastern "Vikings" of the Pacific, who are known to have been traders for about 1500 years, and that migrations from south-eastern Asia into Polynesia and beyond were in progress for many centuries.

CHAPTER VII

American-Asiatic Relations

Huron Woman in Tartary—Evidence of Mummification—Geographical Distribution of Mummification—American Mummies—Torres Straits Mummy —Traces of Egyptian Surgery—" Culture Drifts "—Evidence of Plate Armour —Western-Asiatic Armour in America—American Influence in North-eastern Asia—Koryak Boats of Egypto-Asiatic Type—Evidence of Ivy and Mugwort Cults—The Sacred Pillar and Fish Goddess—The "Vikings of the East"— Stone-using Seafarers—Jade Beliefs in Asia and America—Head-flattening Custom—"Stone-men" in Korea, Indonesia, and Eastern Islands—Cultures spread by Seafarers.

THAT cultural influences reached pre-Columbian America from Asia there can now be very little doubt. It would appear, too, that American cultural influences " drifted " into a part of Asia. The theory of American isolation breaks down completely when these facts are established.

Interesting evidence regarding ancient trading relations between the Old and New World was forthcoming many years ago, but has been obscured by the once fashionable doctrine of independent origin. "Charlevoix, in his essay on the origin of the Indians, states", as Dr. Daniel Wilson has noted,[1] " that Père Grellon, one of the French Jesuit Fathers, met a Huron woman on the plains of Tartary, who had been sold from tribe to tribe, until she passed from the Behring Straits into Central Asia. By such intercourse as this incident illustrates, it is not difficult," comments Wilson, " to conceive of some intermixture of vocabularies; and that such migration has

[1] *Prehistoric Man*, p. 599 (London, 1865).

taken place to a considerable extent is proved by the intimate affinities between the tribes on both sides of the (Behring) Straits."

An important link between the north-eastern Asiatic littoral and the Aleutian Islands and between these and America is afforded by the practice of mummification. The evidence in this connection has been closely examined by Professor G. Elliot Smith, the chief authority on the subject. During over nine years residence in Egypt he had unique opportunities, as Professor of Anatomy in the Government School of Medicine in Cairo, for studying the ancient practice of mummification. He has since extended his investigations to all parts of the world, and has found that "the practice of mummification has a geographical distribution exactly corresponding to the area occupied by the curious assortment of other practices just enumerated". These practices include:

"The building of megalithic monuments, the worship of the sun and serpent, the custom of piercing the ears, the practice of circumcision, the curious custom known as couvade, the practice of massage, the complex story of the creation, the deluge, the petri-faction of human beings, the divine origin of Kings and a chosen people sprung from an incestuous union, the use of the swastika-symbol, the practice of cranial deformation, &c." [1]

Elliot Smith shows that the Eastern Asiatics, the Aleutian Islanders, and certain Red Indian tribes practised the same method of mummification. He deals as an anatomist with the evidence provided by H. C. Yarrow in his authoritative article, "A further Contribution to the Study of the North American Indians",[2] and with the able summary by L. Reutter,[3] with regard to the practice

---

[1] *The Migrations of Early Culture*, p. 3 (London, 1915).

[2] *First Report, Bureau of American Ethnology*, Washington, 1881.

[3] *De l'embaumement avant et après Jésus-Christ*, Paris, 1912.

of embalming among the Incas and other peoples of the New World. In addition he writes regarding Peruvian mummies he has himself examined. The following extracts regarding embalming in the New World are of special interest:

"The custom of preserving the body was not general in every case, for amongst certain peoples only the bodies of Kings and chiefs were embalmed. The Indian tribes of Virginia, of North Carolina, the Congarees of South Carolina, the Indians of the North-west coast of Central America and those of Florida practised this custom as well as the Incas."

Details are given regarding the methods of embalming practised by various tribes. In Kentucky, for instance, the body was dried and filled with fine sand, wrapped in skins or matting and buried either in a cave or hut.

"In Columbia the inhabitants of Darien used to remove the viscera and fill the body cavity with resin, afterwards they smoked the body and preserved it in their houses. . . . The Muiscas, the Aleutians, the inhabitants of Yucatan and Chiapa also embalmed the bodies of their kings, of their chiefs, and of their priests by methods similar to those described, with modifications varying from tribe to tribe. . . . Alone amongst the people of the New World who practised embalming the Incas employed it not only for their kings, chiefs, and priests, but also for the population in general. These people were not confined to Peru, but dwelt also in Bolivia, in Equador, as well as in a part of Chili and of the Argentine."

The Virginian Indians removed the whole skin and afterwards fitted it on to the skeleton again.

"Great care and skill had to be used to prevent the skin shrinking. Apparently the difficulties of this procedure led certain Indian tribes to give up the attempt to prevent the skin shrinking. Thus the Jivaro Indians of Ecuador, as well as certain tribes in the Western Amazon area, make a practice of preserving the head only, and, after removing the skull, allowing the softer tissues to shrink to a size not much bigger than a cricket-ball."

REPRESENTATION OF A BLOOD-LETTING CEREMONY
(British Museum)

This sculptured panel was originally carved on the under side of a door lintel in one of the temples of the great Maya city of Yaxchilan, in southern Mexico. A priest with a ceremonial staff is shown at the left, supervising a blood-letting ceremony, possibly by a neophyte, who is kneeling at the right. Note the gorgeous details of the priest's costume. The neophyte, scarcely less handsomely garbed, is engaged in drawing blood from himself by passing through a slit in his tongue a long piece of rope with sharp thorns fastened to it. A basin on the ground catches the drops of blood as they fall.

Elliot Smith shows that the practice of mummification had its origin in ancient Egypt and spread over a great part of the ancient world. In reply to the suggestions of those who believe it is "natural" that people should want to preserve their dead in this way, he deals at some length with a Torres Straits mummy he examined in an Australian museum. It yielded evidence of surgery of Egyptian origin, and especially " new methods introduced in Egypt in the XXIst Dynasty " (1090–945 B.C.). The eastern practitioners wholly misunderstood "an elaborate technical operation ", and could not have invented it.[1] In ancient Egypt " it took more than seventeen centuries of constant practice and experimentation to acquire the methods exemplified in the Torres Straits mummies ". Associated with the practice of mummification in this and other areas are many distinctive ceremonies and practices " as well as traditions relating to the people who introduced the custom of mummification ". Dr. Haddon, writing on " funeral ceremonies " in the Torres Straits area,[2] says:

" A hero-cult, with masked performers and elaborate dances, spread from the mainland of New Guinea to the adjacent islands: part of this movement seems to have been associated with a funeral ritual that emphasized a life after death. . . . Most of the funeral ceremonies and many sacred songs admittedly came from the west."

The evidence regarding embalming in East and West Africa and in the Canary Islands is similar to that obtained at various points between the Red Sea and Torres Straits. " The technical procedures " in these African areas " were not adopted in Egypt until the time of the XXIst Dynasty " (p. 63). Langdon states with regard to em-

---

[1] Elliot Smith, *The Migrations of Early Culture*, pp. 21 *et seq.*
[2] *Reports of the Cambridge Anthropological Expedition to Torres Straits*, Vol. VI, p. 45 (Cambridge, 1908).

balming in Babylonia[1] that it "is not characteristic of Babylonian burials and the custom may be due to Egyptian influence". In India the ancient Aryans, who did not burn their dead, disembowelled the corpse and filled the cavity with *ghee*.[2] Interesting evidence regarding methods of mummification has been gleaned from Burmah, Ceylon, south-eastern India, Tibet, Polynesia, &c., which will be found in Professor Elliot Smith's book.[3] He holds that the complex culture associated with mummification was carried from Indonesia "far out into the Pacific and eventually reached the American coast, where it bore fruit in the development of the great civilizations on the Pacific littoral and isthmus, whence it gradually leavened the bulk of the vast aboriginal population of the Americas".

Pursuing his researches in quite another field Mr. Berthold Laufer, the well-known American Oriental scholar, dealing with the problem of plate armour in Ancient China, writes, after reviewing the evidence:

"Altogether the impression remains that plate armour, the last offshoots of which we encounter in the farthest north-east corner of Asia and the farthest north-west of America, took its origin from Western Asia."[4]

As this conclusion is of far-reaching importance, it is necessary to review the evidence on which it is based. "The American savages", writes O. T. Mason,[5] "were acquainted with body armour when they were first encountered. Wherever the elk, the moose, the buffalo,

---

[1] Hastings, *Dictionary of Religion and Ethics.*

[2] Mitra, *Indo-Aryans,* Vol. I, p. 135, London, 1881.

[3] *The Migrations of Early Culture: A Study of the Significance of the Geographical Distribution of the Practice of Mummification as Evidence of the Migrations of Peoples and the Spread of Certain Customs and Beliefs* (London, 1915).

[4] *Chinese Clay Figures,* Vol. I, p. 291 (Chicago, 1914).

[5] *The Origins of Invention,* p. 390.

and other great land mammals abounded, there it was possible to cover the body with an impervious suit of raw hide." Hide armour appears to have been "nearly everywhere in North America, even in the eastern area", as Laufer says, "the oldest form of body protection in war". As in the case of mummification, customs varied between tribes. The Thompson River Indians, for instance, had "the wooden cuirass covered with elk hide". Some Indians strengthened their armour with wooden slats, or reeds, or bone-plates. "No fundamental difference", comments Laufer, "can be found in the employment of wood, and bone or ivory, which simply present purely technical changes of material."

Plate armour was known to the Chinese and the Japanese, but there is evidence to show that it was used in America in pre-Japanese times. The Eskimo people used plate armour as did also the Su-shên, an ancient people of north-eastern Asia. Here we touch on the relations between the inhabitants of the latter area and America. Laufer accepts and emphasizes the view that the culture types of north-eastern Asia

"have strong and pronounced characteristics which have hardly any parallels in the rest of the Asiatic World, and that owing to geographical conditions the entire area has remained purer and more intact from outside currents than any other culture group in Asia. The profound researches of Bogoras and Jochelson have shown us that in language, folk-lore, religion and material culture, the affinities of the Chukchi, Koryak, Yukagir, and Kamchatdal, go with Americans, not with Asiatics" (p. 267).

This view is of special interest in so far as it establishes the fact that there was culture contact in ancient times between north-east Asia and America. The evidence afforded by mummification cannot, however, be overlooked. Withal, there is other evidence of far-reach-

ing importance.   Mr. E. Keble Chatterton[1] refers to Mr.
Jochelson's account of Koryak boats which they use on
the Sea of Okhotsk in the north-west Pacific, and shows
that their craft retain remarkable similarities to those of
Ancient Egypt:

"Thus, besides copying the ancients in steering with an oar,
the fore-end of the prow of their sailing-boats terminates in a fork
through which the harpoon-line is passed, this fork being sometimes
carved with a human face which they believe will serve as a protector of the boat.   Instead of rowlocks they have, like the early
Egyptians thong-loops, through which the oar or paddle is inserted.
Their sail, too, is a rectangular shape of dressed reindeer skins
sewed together.   But it is their mast that is especially like the
Egyptians and Burmese. . . . Possibly it came from Egypt to
India and China and so further north to the Sea of Okhotsk."

Dr. Rendel Harris, working in another sphere, has
accumulated much important evidence to show that beliefs
connected with ivy and mugwort, and the deities associated
with these plants, drifted eastward through Siberia and
reached the Kamchatdal.   Krasheninnikoff, one of the
first Russian explorers in Siberia, wrote an account of
his travels during the years 1733–43.   A French translation of this work entitled, *Voyage en Sibérie, contenant la
description de Kamtchatka,* was published in Paris in 1768.
Dr. Rendel Harris, referring to it,[2] says that "there are
two idols in the underground Kamchatadal dwelling, one
of which is in the shape of a woman, with her lower half
in the shape of a fish; the other is a herm or pillar with
a carved head".   He compares the idols of the Kam-
chatkans to "the lovely pair of Dionysiac herms in the
House of the Vettii at Pompeii", and continues:

"Hardly less interesting than the ivy-clad pillar and the

---

[1] *Sailing Ships and their Story,* pp. 32 *et seq.*
[2] *The Ascent of Olympus,* pp. 98 *et seq.*

associated herm is the female goddess with fish termination. Archæologists will at once begin to recall the various fish forms of Greek and Oriental religions, the Dagon and Derceto of the Philistines, the Oannes of the Assyrians, Eurynome of the Greek legends and the like. . . . The discovery of the primitive sanctity of ivy, and mugwort, and mistletoe, makes a strong link between the early Greek and other early peoples, both East and West."

As we shall find, the mugwort goddess reached Mexico.

The ebb and flow of cultural influences between America and north-eastern Asia have yet to be fully investigated. There can be little doubt, however, that seafarers were active in ancient times and absolutely none that the vessels they used were of Egypto-Asiatic origin. The sea-boat was an Egyptian invention, and was passed on from people to people, and country to country, until it ultimately reached America.[1]

Evidence has been forthcoming from China to throw light on the activities of at least one active and influential seafaring people in the area under consideration. They were known to the ancient Chinese as the Su-shên and the Yi-lou. It is of importance to note that the Su-shên used hide armour and bone armour. "It is a remarkable fact", says Laufer, "that the Chinese do not ascribe bone armour to any other of the numerous tribes, with whom they became familiar during their long history, and whose culture they have described to us." The characteristic arms of the tribe were "wooden bows, stone crossbows, hide and bone armour". They had withal, "stone axes which played a rôle in their religious worship".[2]

Laufer refers to the Su-shên as the "Vikings of the East". They occupied an area to the north-east of China, "beyond the boundaries of Korea". The northern

[1] See for evidence, *Myths of China and Japan*, Chapter II.
[2] *Chinese Clay Figures*, pp. 262–3.

limit of their country is unknown. In the seventh century of our era their sea-raids and sea-battles made them notorious in Japan and China. "For a thousand years prior to that time", says Laufer, "the Chinese were acquainted with this tribe and its peculiar culture. . . . From Chinese records we can establish the fact that the Su-shên lived through a stone age for at least fifteen hundred years down to the Middle Ages, when they became merged in the great flood of roaming Tungusian tribes."

The Su-shên were traders as well as pirates. In the third century of our era they carried iron armour as tribute to the Chinese. Laufer writes in this connection:

"As the Su-shên were not able to make iron armour, not being acquainted with the technique of smelting and forging iron, they consequently must have received it in the channel of trade from an iron-producing region, such as we find in ancient times in the interior of Siberia, in Central Asia, and, in the beginning of our era, also in Korea." [1]

Laufer emphasizes this aspect of the problem in opposition to the view that American cultures ever had any relation with Japan, and continues:

"The threads of historical connection running from America into Asia do not terminate in Japan, but first of all, as far as the times of antiquity are concerned, in a territory which may be defined as the northern parts of modern Manchuria and Korea. From ancient times the varied population of this region has shared to some extent in the cultural elements which go to make up the characteristics of the North Pacific culture-province. It does not suffice for the study of American-Asiatic relations to take into consideration only the present ethnological conditions, as has been done, but the ancient ethnology of that region must first be reconstructed."

[1] *Chinese Clay Figures*, pp. 271–2.

The bone armour evidence is of undoubted importance in establishing the existence of culture contact between the New and Old Worlds.   This is brought out clearly when we find Laufer writing:

"Bone-plate armour anciently existed in the western part of the Old World among Scythian tribes; and this case shows that, in regard to north-east Asiatic and American bone-plate armour, we need not resort to the theory of explaining it as an imitation of iron in bone."

An important discussion on the Su-shên will be found in the *Transactions of the Asiatic Society of Japan*.[1]   Parker shows that the Su-shên "inhabited holes dug in the ground, depth marking high status in the occupant". They had thus habits of life similar to the mysterious Koro-pok-guru of Japan.   Their arrow-heads were "made of green stone".   Red and green jade were valued by them, and they occasionally sent their jade to China. This fact should be borne in mind when we find that jadeite was so highly prized by the Mexicans and was associated with Chalchilcuitlicue, the goddess consort of the rain god Tlaloc, whose mountain-seat was "Mugwort Mountain".   The Su-shên sacrificed "to the spiritual powers, the gods of the land and the stars.   They worshipped Heaven in the tenth moon. . . . In the east of their state there was a great cave called *Sui-shên*, to which they all went on a pilgrimage also in the tenth moon."   Of an East-Korean people it was recorded by the Chinese that "they knew how to observe the stars, and could prophesy the abundance or scarcity of the year. They always sacrificed to Heaven in the tenth moon, when they drank wine, sang, and danced night and day; this was called 'dancing to Heaven'.   They also sacrificed

[1] Vol. XVIII, pp. 157 *et seq*, "On Race Struggles in Corea", by E. H. Parker.

to the tiger, which they considered a spiritual power."

Another group of ancient people in Southern Korea "esteemed pebbles and pearls" but did not value gold. References are made to tattooing in this area and to a custom well known in America, which is referred to as follows: "When a son was born they liked to flatten his head and always pressed it with stones". Boats were used "for immigration" in this area. There are references to "stone men" in Korea. The *Shih-i-ki* (a Chinese work) speaks of human stone statuary in the "Dark Sea". The *Yu-yang Tsah-tsu* speaks of a stone man fifteen feet in height in the *Lai-tsz* state, and of a stone man which used to frighten tigers away on a mountain called *Sün-yang*.

The Japanese sacred writings echo "in a bewildering medley", as Laufer says, "continental-Asiatic and Malayo-Polynesian traditions".[1] In like manner we find a medley of imported customs and beliefs in Korea and the area to the north and north-east of it, in which traces of Asiatic and American influences have been found. The seafaring Su-shêns traded with Siberia, and their bone armour passed into America where it was imitated by Red Indian tribes. Boats of Egyptian type were in use in the North Pacific. In Korea the custom prevailing in Easter Island of erecting stone men was introduced, apparently by early seafarers. The same custom obtained in Indonesia. Single menhirs (standing stones) associated with Dolmens at Kopa had each "the form of a man". The faces "resembled slightly those of the images on Easter Island".[2]

We cannot fail to recognize the immense and widespread influence exercised in ancient times by seafaring peoples, who went far and wide in search of precious

[1] *Chinese Clay Figures*, p. 272.
[2] Perry, *The Megalithic Culture of Indonesia*, p. 19.

things, and introduced new modes of life and thought in various isolated regions.   In north-eastern Asia their culture met and mingled with the cultures that drifted from Siberia.   That the Su-shên and other peoples like them carried cultural elements into America, the evidence afforded by bone-plate armour and mummification leaves little doubt.   But it was not in this area alone that a connection between the New and Old World can be traced.   In the next chapter it will be shown that other routes were available for the drift of Asiatic influences into America, and that the cumulative evidence in this connection is of a striking character.

CHAPTER VIII

Sea Routes of Ancient Pacific Mariners

The Chinese Hypothesis—"Blood Bag" Myth in China and America—
Migrations across Behring Strait—Asiatic Homeland of the Red Indians—
Black Current Route across Pacific—Similar Buddhist Myths and Pictures in
Japan and Mexico—Polynesian Route to America—Similar Boats in Polynesia
and America—Phœnician Traces in Polynesia—Solomon's Sea Trade—Im-
ports from Malay State of Pahang—Ancient Colonies in Far East—Armenoids
reached Polynesia—Pearl and Shell Beliefs and Customs in Old and New
Worlds—Polynesians and Americans searched for Well of Life and Earthly
Paradise—Search for the "Plant of Life".

It has been urged by some writers that China was the
chief source of pre-Columbian civilization in America.
A number of interesting links have been detailed to support this hypothesis. One, which has not hitherto been
noted, may here be referred to. In the half-mythical
Chinese annals it is told of Wu-yih, one of the last kings
of the Dynasty of Shang, who is supposed to have ruled
from 1198 till 1194 B.C., that he made an image of a man,
which he called "the Spirit of Heaven" and "gamed
with it"—that is, he played dice or some game resembling chess with the image or its priest. When the
image was unsuccessful, Wu-yih "disgraced it", and
made a leather bag which he filled with blood. He had
the bag "placed aloft" and shot at it, and he called this
"shooting at Heaven". One day he was killed by
lightning, and the people regarded the tragic event as the
just and appropriate vengeance of Heaven.[1]

[1] Legge, *The Shu King*, p. 269, Note 5.

It would appear that Wu favoured some old heretical cult which had been introduced into China and was ultimately suppressed and forgotten. Herodotus (Book II, Chapter 122) tells that Pharaoh Rhampsinitus of Egypt played dice with the goddess Ceres, "sometimes winning and sometimes suffering defeat": the event led to the founding of a special festival, the significance of which is obscure.

The shooting at gods for the purpose of subduing them is referred to in the Hindu classic, the *Mahá-bhárata*. A king shot hundreds of arrows into the ocean, the god of which rose and exclaimed, "Do not, O hero, shoot thy shafts (at me)! Say, what shall I do to thee. With these mighty arrows shot by thee those creatures which have taken shelter in me are being killed, O tiger among Kings. Do thou, O lord, grant them security."[1] The ancient Celts likewise cast weapons into the sea. Evidently the shooting at the blood bag had a ritualistic significance.

It is of special interest to find the blood bag among the Indians of Nicaragua who had emigrated from Mexico. When they sacrificed to the deities of the deer and rabbit, they collected the clotted blood of a slaughtered animal and wrapped it in a cloth, which was placed in a basket and suspended in the air. A ceremony of this kind is not likely to have been of independent origin in China and America. But it does not follow that it passed into America from China. The Chinese and the Indians of Nicaragua in all probability received it and the associated beliefs from the carriers of ancient culture, who followed various routes across the Old World and towards the New. In China the blood-bag offering was connected with a custom that obtained in India,

[1] *Açwameda Parva*, Section XXIX, slokas 1-5.

and was acquired by the Celts from some unidentified source.

The Chinese were an agrarian people. They did not take to the sea before the earliest elements of pre-Columbian civilization had taken root in America. Before they began to build junks, their coasts had been visited by maritime peoples who likewise visited Japan, where the pre-Ainu culture of the Koro-pok-guru flourished for a time; these maritime peoples also settled around the Sea of Okhotsk, where the Koryaks still have boats resembling those invented by the Ancient Egyptians. Chatterton, as has been noted, thinks that these Koryak vessels passed originally " from Egypt to India and China, and so farther north to the Sea of Okhotsk ".[1] Apparently the ancestors of the Koryaks acquired their knowledge of boat-building and navigation from more highly civilized peoples, who in ancient times were attracted to their gold-yielding area.

As we have seen, the evidence afforded by mummification, bone-protected armour, &c., indicates that there were racial and cultural drifts across the Behring Strait and by the Aleutian Islands route to the New World. These commenced at an early period and apparently were connected with racial movements in Central Asia and Siberia. Professor Elliot Smith has traced the Red Indians to their original homeland in the Trans-Caspian area. " Not far from the head-waters of the Yenesie", he writes, " their kinsmen still persist."[2] This area was reached at an early period by prospectors from centres of ancient civilization in quest of precious metals and gems. Their operations had far-reaching results. Apparently their influence was felt in the Shensi province of China as far

---

[1] *Sailing Ships and their Story*, pp. 32–3.
[2] *Journal of the Manchester Geographical Society*, Vol. XXXIII (1917), p. 21.

back as 1700 B.C.   It appears to have permeated north-
eastern Asia too, and set in motion race movements that
remain exceedingly obscure.

The northern racial drift from Asia to America appears
to have been constant and steady.   It has left its impress
on the physical characters of the vast majority of the
aboriginal inhabitants of the New World.   But, from
a cultural point of view, the more important intrusions
were those of the seafarers who crossed the Pacific by
way of Oceania and the Black Current route from Japan.
Like intruding minorities elsewhere, these mariners and
prospectors appear to have revolutionized the social life
of the people among whom they settled, although their
physical impress may have been slight and less permanent.
"Immigrant peoples", writes Dr. Haddon, "may bring
a culture and a language permanently affecting the
conquered peoples, yet the aboriginal population, if
allowed to survive in sufficient numbers, will eventually
impair the racial purity of the new-comers, and there is
a tendency for the indigenous racial type to reassert itself
and become predominant once more." [1]

The "Black Current" or "Black Stream" (*Kuro
Siwo*) flows steadily in a northerly direction along the
eastern coast of Japan, and then sweeps in a curve towards
the west coast of North America.   Japanese vessels have
frequently been carried along this current.   "The January
monsoons from the north-east", writes Bancroft, "are apt
to blow any unlucky coaster which happens to be out
straight into the *Kuro Siwo*."   The vessels are drifted
either to the Sandwich Islands or to North America,
"where they scatter along the coast from Alaska to
California".   Cases have been recorded of Japanese junks
being carried by the Black Current to America in his-

[1] *The Wanderings of Peoples*, pp. 4, 5.

torical times. Bancroft, summarizing the evidence of Brooks and others in this connection, writes:

" In a majority of cases the survivors remained permanently at the place where the waves had brought them. . . . A great many Japanese words are to be found in the Chinook jargon, but in all cases abbreviated, as if coming from a foreign source. . . . How many years this has been going on can only be left to conjecture."

Bancroft inclines to attach importance to the views of Mr. Brooks, who accounts for the similarities existing between the Californian Indians and the Japanese " by a constant infusion of Japanese blood and customs, through a series of years, sufficient to modify the original stock wherever that came from ".[1]

Japan itself was subjected to several racial intrusions before its historical period opened. The Koro-pok-guru, a seafaring people, were earlier settlers than the Ainu, and the Ainu were followed by Koreans and Malayans. It may well be that a proportion of the early navigators, who were bound for Japan from the south or from the Chinese coasts, were carried to America by the Black Current. Bancroft writes further on this aspect of the problem:

" Viollet-le-Duc points out some striking resemblances between the temples of Japan and Central America. It is asserted that the people of Japan had a knowledge of the American continent and that it was marked down on their maps. Montanus tells us that three ship captains, named Henrik Corneliszoon, Schaep, and Wilhelm Byleveld, were taken prisoners by the Japanese and carried to Jeddo, where they were shown a sea-chart on which America was drawn as a mountainous country adjoining Tartary on the north. Of course the natives (of north-western America) have the usual tradition that strangers came among them long before the advent of the Europeans. There were in California at

[1] Bancroft, *The Native Races of the Pacific States of North America*, Vol. V, pp. 52–3.

the time of the (Spanish) conquest Indians of various races, some of the Japanese type." [1]

In a lecture delivered before the British Association in 1894, Professor E. B. Tylor dealt with an important link between Japan and Mexico.[2]   This distinguished anthropologist showed that the conception of weighing the heart of the dead in the Judgment Hall of Osiris made its earliest appearance in Ancient Egypt.   It could be traced thence "into a series of variants, serving to draw lines of intercourse through the Vedic and Zoro-astrian religions extending from Eastern Buddhism to Western Christendom".   Tylor continued:

"The associated doctrine of the Bridge of the Dead, which separates the good, who pass over, from the wicked, who fall into the abyss, appears first in Ancient Persian religion, reaching in like manner to the extremities of Asia and Europe.   By these mythical beliefs historical ties are practically constituted, connecting the great religions of the world, and serving as lines along which their interdependence is to be followed out."

Tylor then dealt with the Asiatic influences "under which the pre-Columbian culture of America took shape", and showed that

"In the religion of old Mexico four great scenes in the journey of the soul in the land of the dead are mentioned by early Spanish writers after the conquest, and are depicted in a group in the Aztec picture-writing known as the Vatican Codex. The four scenes are, first, the crossing of the river; second, the fearful passage of the soul between the two mountains which clash together; third, the soul's climbing up the mountain set with sharp obsidian knives; fourth, the dangers of the wind carrying such knives on its blast."

---

[1] Bancroft, *op. cit.*, pp. 53, 54, and Note 114.
[2] "On the Diffusion of Mythical Beliefs as Evidence in the History of Culture" (*Report of the British Association*, 1894, p. 774).

Professor Tylor showed these four Mexican pictures, and also more or less closely-corresponding pictures of Buddhist hells or purgatories from Japanese temple scrolls. In the latter:

"First, the river of death is shown, where the souls wade across; second, the souls have to pass between two huge iron mountains, which are pushed together by two demons; third, the guilty souls climb the mountain of knives, whose blades cut their hands and feet; fourth, fierce blasts of wind drive against their lacerated forms the blades of knives flying through the air".

Tylor argued that "the appearance of analogues so close and complex of Buddhist ideas in Mexico constituted a correspondence of so high an order as to preclude any explanation except direct transmission from one religion to another".

It does not necessarily follow that the Japanese carried the doctrines illustrated by the Mexican pictures to the New World. Both Japan and Mexico may have received them from a common source.

The Oceanic or Polynesian route to America appears to have been one along which profound cultural influences were carried. Among the Polynesians have been detected physical traits that connect them with the natives of India and the Malay Peninsula, and even with the Armenoids of Western Asia and with the Mediterranean race. Their legends are full of accounts of their long sea voyages, and there is much evidence to show that they originally passed from Indonesia to their coral islands. They reached Easter Island on the east and Madagascar on the west.

William Ellis, the well-known missionary and author of *Polynesian Researches*,[1] has commented on the coincidences in language, mythology, &c., of the Polynesians

[1] London (1st edition), 1829, Vol. II, pp. 37 *et seq.*

A MEGALITHIC GATEWAY, TIAHUANACO, BOLIVIA

TRILITHON MONUMENT AT NUKUALOFA, TONGA ISLANDS,
POLYNESIA

with those of the Hindus, the natives of Madagascar, and the Americans. He mentions a tradition that

"the first inhabitants of the South Sea Islands originally came from a country in the direction of the setting sun, to which they say several names were given, though none of them are remembered by the present inhabitants",

and notes that Bishop Heber, an authority on the Hindus, stated "that many things which he saw among the inhabitants of India reminded him of the plates in *Cook's Voyages*". Ellis considered, however, that "the points of resemblance between the Polynesians and the Malayan inhabitants of Java, Sumatra, and Borneo, and the Ladrone, Caroline, and Philippine Islands are still greater", and wrote further in this connection:

"There are also many points of resemblance in language, manners, and customs between the South Sea Islanders and the inhabitants of Madagascar in the west; the inhabitants of the Aleutian and Kurile Islands in the north, . . . and also between the Polynesians and the inhabitants of Mexico and some parts of South America. The general cast of feature, and frequent shade of complexion, the practice of tatooing which prevails among the Aleutians and some tribes of America, the process of embalming the dead bodies of their chiefs and preserving them uninterred, the game of chess among the Araucanians, the word for God being *tew* or *tev*, the exposure of children, their games, their mode of dressing hair, ornamenting it with feathers; the numerous words in their language resembling those of Tahiti, &c.; their dress, especially the poncho; and even the legend of the origin of the Incas, bear no small resemblance to that of Tü, who was also descended from the sun."[1]

The Polynesians were in the habit of making long sea voyages. Even in Ellis's time voyages of from 400

[1] Ellis, *op. cit.*, Vol. II, p. 46.

to 700 miles were not uncommon, as he records. Mr. Elsdon Best[1] has shown "how the Maori explored the Pacific Ocean and laid down the sea roads for all time". In his important monograph he deals at length with their vessels, their methods of navigation, their stores of food and water, and the reasons why they went on voyages of exploration. From the Samoan Islands, one of which was apparently the Hawaiki of their legends, the Polynesians reached and peopled New Zealand to the south and Hawaii to the north.[2] A section of the inhabitants of Easter Island came from the Solomon Islands.[3] Indeed, within the area covered by the South Sea Islands, the Polynesians voyaged more than twice the distance that separates their islands from the American continent. Is it possible that, having reached Hawaii, the Marquesas, and Easter Island, they could have missed the Galapagos Islands off the coast of South America and the mountainous land beyond? When we find that the pre-Columbian Americans had so many customs and beliefs in common with the Polynesians, and that they used similar boats, in which they reached and peopled the West Indies, the theory that they never discovered or could have discovered America seems hazardous and unconvincing.

Dr. D. Macdonald of the New Hebrides mission, who has found traces of Phœnician influence in the Oceanic languages, writes regarding the South Sea mariners:

"From whatever point the Oceanic race migrated into the Island world, they did so in sea-going vessels, and we may reasonably infer that before doing so they were habitually in possession

---

[1] "Maori Voyages and their Vessels" (*Transactions and Proceedings of the New Zealand Institute*, Vol. XLVIII (1916), p. 447.

[2] Westervelt, *Legends of Old Honolulu*, 1915, pp. 12, 13.

[3] Routledge, *The Mystery of Easter Island*, pp. 296–8.

of such vessels, or were a sea-going, commercial people, as for the most part they are to-day ".[1]

He refers to the fleets of Solomon, which were manned by Phœnicians, and, according to Josephus, reached the Malay Peninsula. The reason why Solomon went into the shipping trade, which had been established before his time, is revealed by the Biblical details of the things he imported. From Ophir his Phœnician mariners fetched gold (*1 Kings*, ix, 28), and "algum-trees and precious stones" (*2 Chronicles*, ix, 10). They made long voyages:

"For the king's ships went to Tarshish with the servants of Hiram; every three years once came the ships of Tarshish, bringing gold, and silver, ivory, and apes, and peacocks" (*2 Chronicles*, ix, 21).

It has been suggested that Tarshish was in Spain, but that country does not possess apes and peacocks. The peacocks and apes and ivory appear to have come from the east, and apparently from the land referred to by Josephus as *Aurea Chersonesus*, "which", as he noted, "belongs to India". It is of special interest, therefore, to find Sir Hugh Clifford[2] referring to "the recent discovery in the Malayan state of Pahang—the home of apes and ivory and peafowl—of immense gold-mines of very ancient date, and of a workmanship that has no counterpart in South-eastern Asia". He considers that this discovery "supplies an ample reason for the designation 'golden' so long applied to the Chersonese".

Ophir appears to have been a market or trading port in Arabia to which the wealth of the countries yielding precious metals and stones, pearls, &c., was carried in ancient times by enterprising mariners. These mariners

[1] *The Oceanic Languages* (London, 1907), pp. 4 *et seq.*
[2] *Further India* (1904), p. 13.

searched for metals, jewels, herbs, incense-yielding trees,
&c., that had a religious value and therefore a commercial
value.   They founded colonies that became centres from
which the elements of ancient civilization radiated.   Their
arts and crafts and their religious beliefs and customs were
acquired by various alien peoples, and from the different
centres of civilization that were established the colonists
and their mixed descendants went on voyages of exploration, and reached Sumatra, Java, Borneo, the Philippines,
Formosa, Japan, the coasts of China, and even as far north
as the Koryak country round the sea of Okhotsk; they
also passed by way of the Celebes towards New Guinea
and the South Sea Islands.   India was permeated by their
influence long before it was invaded by Aryans.   After
the Aryans came into touch with the Dravidian civilization they passed from their Vedic to their Brahmanic stage
of religious culture.

Professor Elliot Smith, who notes that in the course
of their wanderings the ancient mariners " became inter-
mingled with Ethiopians and Arabs and Indians and
Malays ", draws attention to the fact, already referred to,
that " the substratum of the original stock that populated
Polynesia was composed of sailors from the Mediterranean
and the Persian Gulf, into whose constitution the enterprising southern branch of the Armenoid race entered so
largely ", and writes:

" The wandering mariners were themselves the colonizers of
Polynesia, which therefore became the most exclusively maritime
population in the history of the world ".

A proportion of the wanderers were induced, like the
lotus-eaters of Homeric legend, to settle on coral islands,
but, says Professor Elliot Smith, referring to the main
" wave " of prospecting mariners:

" If we can judge of their behaviour elsewhere, we may assume that, as they visited island after island of Polynesia, without discovering either gold or pearls, they did not stay, but pushed on farther in the quest of such riches. . . . The more energetic and enterprising of the wanderers . . . pushed on until they got their reward as the pioneers of the civilization of the Old World in America."[1]

Traces of the ancient pearl-searchers survive in Hawaiian traditions, place-names, and religious beliefs. The natives have their dragons with pearls, their " Pearl Harbour ", their dragon-stones, and even their Nāga-like reptile goddess who lives in a "large deep pool". Hawaiian dragon-lore closely resembles that of China and Japan, and the Nāga-lore of India.[2]

Mr. Wilfrid Jackson has shown[3] that the ancient mariners who searched for pearls and pearl-shell, which had a religious value, reached America, and that the shell and pearl beliefs and customs in the New World were identical with those of the Old World. In my first chapter of this book the identity of the New and Old World beliefs and customs connected with gold is dealt with in detail. Professor Elliot Smith, the greatest living authority on mummification, affords proof, as has been shown, in his *The Migrations of Early Culture*,[4] that the mummification customs and beliefs in different parts of the Old World provide important evidence regarding the spreading of these into America.

In the next chapter the water-burial customs of the Old and New Worlds are dealt with. These, it would appear, were connected with the search for the Well of

[1] *Journal of the Manchester Geographical Society*, Vol. XXXIII (1917), pp. 19-20.
[2] See my *Myths of China and Japan* (" Dragons " in Index).
[3] *Shells as Evidence of the Migrations of Early Culture*, London, 1917.
[4] London, 1915.

Life and the Earthly Paradise.[1]   The Polynesians pro-
secuted this immemorial search.   Ellis refers in this
connection to " the Hawaiian account of the voyage of
Kampapiikai to the land where the inhabitants enjoyed
perpetual health and youthful beauty, where the *wai ora*
(life-giving fountain) removed every internal malady, and
every external deformity or paralysed decrepitude, from
all those who were plunged beneath its salutary waters ".
He notes that the expedition, "which led to the discovery
of Florida, was undertaken not so much from a desire to
explore unknown countries, as to find an equally celebrated fountain, described in a tradition prevailing among
the inhabitants of Puerto Rico, as existing in Binini, one
of the Lucayo Islands.   It was said to possess such
restorative powers as to renew the youth and vigour of
every person who bathed in its waters." [2]

Sahagun relates an American tradition that the ancestors of the Nahua, who founded pre-Columbian civilization
in Mexico, crossed the seas in vessels searching for the
Earthly Paradise.   " In coming south to seek the Earthly
Paradise ", we read, " these men certainly did not deceive
themselves, for it is the opinion of those that know that
it is under the equinoctial line: and in thinking that it
ought to be a high mountain they are also not mistaken,
for, so say the writers, the Earthly Paradise is under the
equinoctial line, and it is a very high mountain whose
summit almost touches the moon.   It appears that these
men or their ancestors had consulted an oracle on this
matter, either a god or a demon, or they possessed an
ancient tradition that had been handed down." [3]

As in the Old World, the peoples who reached

---

[1] See my *Myths of China and Japan* (Index under " Well of Life ").
[2] Ellis, *Polynesian Researches*, Vol. II, pp. 47–8.
[3] Quoted in *Folk-lore*, Vol. XXXII, No. 3, p. 174.

America searched also for the "Plant of Life", as did Gilgamesh in the Babylonian epic, including, as will be shown, the milk-yielding plant and the mugwort of the mother goddess.

These and other links between the pre-Columbian Americans and the peoples of Asia, North Africa, and Europe, cannot be ignored. The cumulative effect of the evidence is to support the view that New World civilization was not of spontaneous generation.

CHAPTER IX

Water Burials and the Ship of Death

Races and Customs—Cultures changed by Intruding Minorities—Red Indian Well and River Burials—The Voyage to Paradise—Cradle-boats in New and Old Worlds—Water Burials in Oceania—Life renewed by Water—The Lunar Well of Life—Persian Gulf Water Burials—African and European Customs—Guatemala Lake Burials—Canoe Burials—Canoe as Bird Form of Mother Goddess—Bird-shaped Ship of Death in Borneo and America—Ship of Death in Egypt and Europe—History of Bird-shaped Ship.

EVIDENCE of ancient race and culture "drifting" is obtained from the burial customs of pre-Columbian America. These would appear to show that there were various drifts at various periods from Asiatic culture areas. It does not follow that each particular custom was introduced by a different people. Religious beliefs, like languages, cannot be regarded as sure indications of racial affinities. "Red", "Yellow", "Black", and "White" men do not change their skins when they change their beliefs. The carriers of a particular culture may bear little physical resemblance to the people among whom it originated. Nor need they constitute a majority in the area in which the imported culture is adopted. Intruding minorities have, in various parts of the world, changed languages at one time or another; intruding minorities have in like manner changed religious beliefs, as did the Buddhists who reached China and Japan. In some cases it is found that a particular burial custom is confined to the ruling class or to the chief and his family. An intruding minority clung to their custom of mummifying or burning their dead, but the con- quered continued to perpetuate the custom favoured by their ancestors. In some cases the imported custom is found to have been influenced by the local custom. A people who buried their dead in a crouched position adopted mummification, but, instead of laying out the bodies as did the Ancient Egyptians, tied them up in a crouching position as they did before mummification was introduced. In other cases it will be found that after being embalmed the body was cremated.

One of the interesting burial customs found among the North American Indians is the " water burial ". The dead were " disposed of by sinking in springs or water courses, by throwing into the sea, or by setting afloat in canoes ". Water burial was, like other burial customs, an expression of a religious system of which other traces survive, and, like mummification, was not peculiar to pre-Columbian America.

The Red Indian tribe of Goshutes in the Great Salt Lake Valley, favoured water burial. Captain J. H. Simpson has provided interesting evidence in this con- nection: [1]

" Skull Valley, which is part of the Great Salt Lake Desert, and which we have crossed to-day, Mr. George W. Bean, my guide over this route last fall, says, derives its name from the number of skulls which have been found in it, and which have arisen from the custom of the Goshute Indians burying their dead in springs, which they sink with stones or keep down with sticks. He says he has actually seen the Indians bury their dead in this way near the town of Provo, where he resides."

Captain Simpson himself found a skeleton at the bottom

[1] *Exploration Great Salt Lake Valley, Utah*, 1859, p. 48, quoted in *First Annual Report of the Bureau of Ethnology*, Washington, 1881, p. 181.

of a spring. It had to be dug out of the mud before the water could be used. This proceeding was rendered necessary because in that country water is scarce, and Indians took care not to pollute the wells they used for ordinary purposes. It cannot be held therefore that in their case water burial resulted from indolence or carelessness, or because water was plentiful. They were evidently perpetuating a custom that had arisen elsewhere, and did so in response to the inexorable dictates of a religious system that involved serious inconvenience to themselves; indeed, by limiting the number of wells that could be used, a real sacrifice was involved.

The Chinook custom is of special interest. It is given by Mr. George Catlin,[1] who saw a woman launching a "burial canoe", which was a little cradle containing the body of a baby.

"This little cradle has a strap which passes over the woman's forehead whilst the cradle rides on her back, and if the child dies during its subjection to this rigid mode, its cradle becomes its coffin, forming a little canoe, in which it lies floating on the water in some sacred pool, where they are often in the habit of fastening their canoes containing the dead bodies of the old and young, or, which is often the case, elevated into the branches of trees, where their bodies are left to decay and their bones to dry whilst they are bandaged in many skins and curiously packed in their canoes, with paddles to propel and ladles to bale them out, and provisions to last and pipes to smoke as they are performing their 'long journey after death to their contemplated hunting grounds', which these people think is to be performed in their canoes."

In this form of water burial the body of the dead is supposed to be carried in a canoe to Paradise. A similar custom is found in the early English epic *Beowulf*. Scyld of the Sheaf, a "culture hero", came to the Danes across

1 *History of the North American Indians,* 1844, Vol. II, p. 141.

the sea as a baby foundling who lay in a boat with his head pillowed on a sheaf of corn. He became the king of the tribe, and when he died his body, according to his last request, was sent to sea in a ship.

"They, his fast friends, carried him to the water's edge, as he himself had asked when he, protector of the Scyldings, still wielded his words. . . . They laid then the beloved chieftain, giver out of (money) rings, on the ship's bosom. . . . Their soul was sad, their spirit sorrowful. Who received that load, men, chiefs of councils, heroes under heaven, cannot for certain tell!"

They (the mourners) "furnished him with no less of gifts, of tribal treasures, than those had done who, in his early days, started him over the sea alone, child as he was".[1] Scyld symbolized a set of intruders who had introduced the agricultural mode of life into the homeland of the Danes. His body was disposed of in accordance with the custom of the intruders. The god Balder was disposed of after death like Scyld of the Sheaf. His body was laid in a vessel called Ring-horn, which was launched. The ship was, however, set on fire. In this case the water-burial custom is combined with the cremation custom.

The earliest reference to setting a child adrift on a river is found in the legend of Sargon of Akkad, a great Mesopotamian monarch who lived before 2500 B.C. Sargon's mother was a vestal virgin of the sun god cult, and Sargon is made to say in the ancient story:

"When my mother had conceived me, she bare me in a hidden place. She laid me in a vessel of rushes, stopped the door thereof with pitch, and cast me adrift on the river. . . . The river floated me to Akki, the water drawer, who, in drawing water, drew me forth. Akki, the water drawer, educated me as his son, and made me his gardener. As a gardener, I was beloved by the goddess Ishtar."

[1] *Beowulf*, translated by J. R. Clarke Hall (London, 1911), pp. 10, 11.

This myth resembles the one of Scyld who was set adrift as a living child. It was known in India, and attached there to the memory of the legendary hero Karna, son of the princess Pritha and the sun god Surya. The birth was concealed, and, according to the *Mahâ-bhârata* version of the legend, the mother placed her babe in a basket of wicker-work which was set adrift on a river. It was carried by the river Aswa to the river Jumna, and by the Jumna to the Ganges, and by the Ganges to the country of Anga, where a charioteer rescued the child and reared him as his own son.[1]

That the legend originally attached to a god is shown by the fact that the god Heimdal, like Scyld, was as Scef (Sheaf) the original "culture hero" in northern mythology. He represented the god of the people who introduced the agricultural mode of life.[2] The Babylonian god Tammuz came as a child. A Sumerian hymn contains a significant reference in this connection:

> In his infancy in a sunken boat he lay.
> In his manhood in the submerged grain he lay.[3]

Tammuz was the "true son of the deep water", according to O. Jensen and H. Zimmern. The goddess Aphrodite concealed Adonis in a "chest" and confided him to the care of Persephone, queen of Hades. In Ancient Egypt the god Horus was in one of his phases a living or dead child floating in a chest or boat. He was placed in this form in the constellation Argo, the chief star of which is Canopus. Orion, the constellation above Argo, was connected with Osiris.

It would appear that the legends of living and dead

---

[1] *Indian Myth and Legend*, pp. 173-4.   [2] *Ibid.*, p. 21.
[3] Langdon, *Sumerian and Babylonian Psalms*, London, 1909.

children drifting in a chest or cradle had a mythological origin, and that the custom of setting adrift the bodies of children or adults on a river or on the ocean had origin in the belief that the dead were carried in a boat to Paradise. The Ancient Egyptian Pharaohs of the sun cult were supposed to enter the boat of the sun god Ra. The Chinese believed in a Celestial Yellow River, which was the " Milky Way ", as the Indians believed in a Celestial Ganges, and the Egyptians in a Celestial Nile. A Chinese story tells that a sage sailed up the Yellow River and found himself at length drifting across the sky. An oar of his boat fell from heaven and was preserved in the Royal palace. Apparently the American Chinook custom of setting the dead adrift on a river was imported from the Old World. The Paradise with jewel-laden trees was forgotten, and the Happy Hunting Grounds Paradise retained and connected with the imported belief in the celestial origin of rivers.

Water burials were not common in America. The two examples given are the only ones that Dr. Yarrow could find. It is of special interest therefore to ascertain that they were better known in Oceania. The evidence obtained from that area seems to indicate that the custom was imported into Polynesia and Melanesia, just as it evidently was into America, by a people who had adopted complex beliefs regarding water as a source of life. One of the burial customs in the Shortlands group of islands was to convey a corpse to the sea and drop it overboard. " The usual mode of burial on Duke of York Island ", writes Dr. George Brown, " was at sea, generally in some deep part of the lagoon. Large stones were fastened to the toes, so that the body remained in a standing position in the water. . . . On New Ireland the dead were rolled up in coverings made from leaves of *pandanus* sewn together, then weighted with stones and buried at sea. In some places they were placed in deep underground water-courses or caves."[1] The Rev. George Turner tells that on Aneiteum in the New Hebrides two native members of the mission party died.

"On the death of these two the natives wished their bodies thrown into the sea according to custom. . . . When they cast a dead body into the sea, if it is the body of a man, they do not wrap it up in anything, but paint the face red, and sink it not far from the shore by tying stones to the feet. If it is the body of a woman, they wrap it up in the leaf girdles worn by the women."[2]

The following extract, which also refers to Aneiteum, is of very special interest, because it indicates how burial customs were changed by the introduction of new religious beliefs, and further because it shows that the custom of widow-burning which prevailed among the cremating people was adopted by those who favoured water burial:

"A commencement was made some years ago to bury the dead, instead of throwing them into the sea; but the teachers found out that a notion was spreading that all who were buried went to heaven, and all who were cast into the sea went to hell, and there-fore gave up saying much about it, that the people may understand it is a matter of no moment, as regards his eternal interests, where the body of a man is disposed of after death. A man died lately who regularly attended the services, and of whom the teachers have some hope. After his death they succeeded in saving his widow from being strangled. They had all but a fight over it, as her brother insisted on carrying out the old custom."[3]

Instances of widow strangling and sea burials are given by the Rev. A. W. Murray, who was for forty years a missionary in Polynesia and New Guinea. Sick and insane people were put to death. A young man who had

---

[1] *Melanesians and Polynesians* (London, 1910), pp. 211–2, 386, and 390.
[2] *Nineteen Years in Polynesia* (London, 1861), p. 365.   [3] *Ibid.*, p. 434.

become delirious was carried to a river and thrown in and drowned.[1]

Behind the water-burial custom, as has been indicated, lay the fundamental belief in "water of life". "Some of the South Sea Islanders", writes Turner, "have a tradition of a river in their imaginary world of spirits, called 'water of life'. It was supposed that if the aged, when they died, went and bathed there they became young, and returned to earth to live another life over again."[2] This conception originally drifted into Polynesia from the Indian culture area. The Indian dead were supposed to bathe in the Celestial Ganges. Yudhishthira, the Panadava elder brother, in the Sanskrit epic the *Mahd-bhdrata*, is not cremated, nor does he die. He and his brothers set out to walk to heaven, first going eastwards towards the "Red Sea", then southward, and then by the west towards the white sacred north. All the brothers fall dead on the way except Yudhishthira. After reaching heaven and visiting hell, Yudhishthira is taken to the celestial river. His guide says:

"'Here is the celestial river, sacred and sanctifying the three worlds. It is called Heavenly Ganga. Plunging into it, thou wilt go to thine own regions. Having bathed in this stream thou wilt be divested of thy human nature. Indeed, thy grief dispelled, thine ailments conquered, thou wilt be freed from all enmities.' . . . Having bathed in the celestial river Ganga, sacred and sanctifying and ever adored by the Rishis, he (Yudhishthira) cast off his human body. Assuming then a celestial form, King Yudhishthira the Just, in consequence of that bath, became divested of all his enmities and grief."[3]

The Maori of New Zealand believed that the moon was being consumed by a disease when on the wane:

---

[1] Murray, *Wonders in the Western Isles* (London, 1874), p. 113.
[2] *Nineteen Years in Polynesia*, p. 353.
[3] *Mahá-bhárata* (*Swargaohanika Parva*, Section III, Roy's translation, pp. 9–10).

"When she is excessively weak she goes and bathes in the Wai-ora-a-tane (the living water of Tane), which gradually restores her strength until she is as great in power and life as when first created; but again the disease consumes her, and again she bathes in the water."

Another version is:

"When the moon dies she goes to the living water of Tane—to the great lake of A-ewa (lake of god let loose from a bond)—to the water which can restore all, even the moon to its path in the sky ".[1]

It is quite evident that the water-burial customs in America and Polynesia were connected with a great body of imported complex beliefs. Water burial had a history, the origin of which cannot be traced either in America or Polynesia. No one can assert that the custom and the associated beliefs had origin in Polynesia. The onus of proof lies with those who assume that the custom and beliefs had spontaneous origin in America.

Dr. H. C. Yarrow in his "A Further Contribution to the Study of the Mortuary Customs of the North American Indians", reminds us that "the Ichthyophagi, or fish eaters, mentioned by Ptolemy, living in the region bordering on the Persian Gulf, invariably committed their dead to the sea, thus repaying the obligations they had incurred to its inhabitants. The Lotophagians did the same, and the Hyperboreans, with a commendable degree of forethought for the survivors, when ill or about to die, threw themselves into the sea."

The ancient custom was likewise known in Africa. Dr. Yarrow refers to the evidence of the Rev. J. G. Wood,[2] who states that the Obongo "take the body to

---

[1] John White, *The Ancient History of the Maori*, Vol. I, pp. 141-2.
[2] *Uncivilized Races of the World*, 1870, Vol. I, p. 483.

XOLOTL AS A DOG GOD

The god Xolotl (pronounced *shol-ot'l*) in *Codex Vaticanus A*, with part of Italian priest's interpretation received from the Aztecs. This deity was in one of his aspects a "dog of Hades", and, like the dog-headed Egyptian god Anubis, a guide of souls. The Indian death-god Yama had a dog form. The Aztecs sacrificed a dog to lead the dead to the Otherworld. Xolotl is here a complex deity. He was connected with fire, lightning, and the sun, and also with fertility, the earth, and sacrifices. Here he is shown with penitential and other symbols on his head, a solar symbol below ear, a life-giving shell necklace, and the Quetzalcoatl shell symbol on his breast. (See pp. 232, 233.)

some running stream, the course of which has been previously diverted. A deep grave is dug in the bed of the stream, the body placed in it, and covered over carefully. Lastly the stream is restored to its original course, so that all traces of the grave are soon lost."

Reference has been made to the water burials of Scyld and Balder. In the early part of the fifth century the Goths in Calabria diverted the course of the River Vasento, and "having made a grave in the midst of its bed, where its course was most rapid, they interred their king with a prodigious amount of wealth and riches. They then caused the river to resume its regular course, and destroyed all persons who had been concerned in preparing this romantic grave."

Bancroft states that the Itzas of Guatemala, who inhabited the islands of Lake Peten, threw their dead into the lake. The theory that they did so "for want of room" is not convincing. "The Indians of Nootka Sound and the Chinooks", says Yarrow, "were in the habit of thus getting rid of their dead slaves, and, according to Timberlake, the Cherokees of Tennessee 'seldom bury their dead, but throw them into the river'."

Closely related to water burial was the American custom of placing the dead in canoes, which were either raised on a platform or buried in the ground. According to Mr. George Gibbs, who has dealt with the burial customs of the Red Indians of Oregon and Washington Territory,[1] "the common mode of disposing of the dead among the fishing tribes was in canoes. These were generally drawn into the woods at some prominent point a short distance from the village, and sometimes placed between the forks of trees, or raised from the ground on posts." Dr. Yarrow says that this mode of burial "is

[1] *North American Ethnology*, 1877, I, p. 200.

common only to the tribes inhabiting the north-west coast ", and he gives a few examples.

The canoe was a symbol of the goddess who had had her origin in water. Like the pot in Egyptian mythology, the canoe symbolized her womb from which the soul was reborn in the after life. It also symbolized the bird form of the deity that was supposed to carry souls to Paradise, either through the air or along the mythical river to the Celestial regions. In short, the bird-shaped boat was the " ship of the dead "—the carrier of the dead as it was of the living. The Dyaks of Borneo, who received with boats the complex culture associated with the seafaring mode of life, had a ship of the dead in the form of a bird, the head and beak forming the raised stem, and the outspread tail the raised stern, while the sails were the wings. The raised prow of the American burial canoe retained the shape of the raised head of the bird favoured by the Dyaks, which was the *buceros* or rhinoceros hornbill. This bird was supposed by reason of the weight and strength of its beak to " disperse the dense clouds enveloping the sun ". " The ship itself ", says Frobenius, " was a bird."

" In the ship, in this wonderful structure, the souls go in quest of the hereafter; and not only the souls themselves, but with them all the stores which are laid out at the tiwah, all the food and drink that are consumed at the tiwah, all the slaves and other poor wretches who, on the occasion of this tiwah, are openly or stealthily murdered and deprived of their heads." [1]

The North American Indians who favoured canoe-burial similarly provided the dead with all that was required for the last journey. The Chinook custom is described as follows :

[1] Leo Frobenius, *The Childhood of Man* (translated by A. H. Keane, London, 1909), p. 262–3.

"When the canoe was ready, the corpse, wrapped in blankets, was brought out, and laid in it on mats previously spread. All the wearing apparel was next put in beside the body, together with her trinkets, beads, little baskets, and various trifles she had prized. More blankets were then covered over the body, and mats smoothed over all. Next, a small canoe, which fitted into a large one, was placed, bottom up, over the corpse, and the whole then covered with mats. The canoe was then raised up, and placed on two parallel bars, elevated four or five feet from the ground, and supported by being inserted through holes mortised at the top of four stout posts previously firmly planted in the earth. Around these holes were then hung blankets, and all the cooking utensils of the deceased, pots, kettles, and pans, each with a hole punched through it, and all her crockery ware, every piece of which was first cracked or broken, to render it useless; and then, when all was done, they left her to remain for one year, when the bones would be buried in a box in the earth directly under the canoe; but that, with all its appendages, would never be molested, but left to go to gradual decay."[1]

The Dyaks did not provide a boat coffin, but set up a big panel on which the bird-ship of the dead was depicted. They believed that the vessel carrying the soul, &c., passed through great perils. It had to cross the "fire sea" or the "fiery whirlpool" before reaching "the golden fields of the after life". After living in this region for a long period, the soul returned to earth, and cropped up as "a fungus, a fruit, a leaf, grass, and the like". A human being eats the fruit or fungus, and the soul is reborn as a little child.[2]

The ancient seafarers, whose vessels were the prototypes of all the ships of the world's oceans, appear to have been the introducers of the ship-burial customs. Reference has been made to the Scandinavian custom of

---

[1] Quoted from Swan's *Northwest Coast* (1857), p. 185, in *First Annual Report of the Bureau of Ethnology*, Washington, 1881, p. 171.
[2] Frobenius, *The Childhood of Man*, pp. 262-4.

sending the dead adrift in a boat. Another custom was
to drag ashore a big ship, and lay the dead Viking in it.
Over the boat a sepulchral chamber was erected. If a
ship was not used, a ship-shaped grave was constructed
with stones. Of these "one of the most interesting",
writes Du Chaillu,[1] "is that where the rowers' seats are
marked, and even a stone placed in the position of the
mast". Stone-shaped graves, named *naus* or *navetas* by
archæologists, have been found in the Balearic Islands in
association with the towers called *talayots*, resembling the
muraghi of Sardinia and the *brochs* of Scotland, which
were erected by ancient seafarers.[2] The ancient Egyptians placed models of boats in tombs. Their sun god
sailed daily across the heavens in a boat which was a symbol
of the mother goddess ; it was the Pharaoh's "ship of
death". In time, when the belief obtained that nobles
and priests could enter the Paradise of the solar cult,
models of boats manned by their servants were placed in
their tombs. The earlier custom was to place in graves
implements and ornament-charms for the use of the dead.
When the Osirian and solar conceptions of the Otherworld were fused, it was believed that the dead crossed
a river in a boat in which the four Horuses formed the
crew. Another conception was that the dead on reaching
the solar Paradise to the east of the sky had to cross the
long, winding "Lily-lake" to the island on which grew
the Tree of Life (the goddess Hathor's sycamore). Like
the swan-boat of Lohengrin, the ferryboat moved of its
own accord, and could speak. "All was alive, whether
it was the seat into which the king dropped, or the steer-
ing-oar to which he reached out his hand, or the barque
into which he stepped, or the gates through which he
passed. To all these, or to anything which he found, he

---

[1] *The Viking Age*, Vol. I, p. 309.   [2] T. Eric Peet, *Rough Stone Monuments*, p. 73.

might speak; and these uncanny things might speak to him." The surly ferryman, "Face-behind" or "Look-behind", rarely opened his lips, however. Appeals and threats had to be made so that he might ferry over the dead. The sun god's aid was asked for as in the Pyramid text:

"O Ra! Commend King Teti to 'Look-behind', ferryman of the Lily-lake, that he may bring that ferryboat of the Lily-lake, for King Teti, in which he ferries the gods to yonder side of the Lily-lake, that he may ferry King Teti to yonder side of the Lily-lake to the east of the sky".

If the ferryman refused to hear, another boat called "Eye of Khnum" was summoned. This "Eye" is parallel with the designation "Eye of Horus", which may also be applied to the boat. The "Imperishable Stars", or the "two sycamores in the east", would ferry the Pharaoh if the ferryman failed him. "The son of Atum is not without a boat", a Pyramid text protests. If there is, after all, no boat, the Horus falcon will carry the Pharaoh to the celestial regions. "This King Pepi", a text says, "flies as a cloud to the sky, like a masthead bird . . .", or "King Unis flaps his wings like a zeret-bird", or "King Unis goes to the sky! On the wind! On the wind!" He might even ascend on smoke as in the Pyramid text which says, "He ascends upon the smoke of the great incense-burning".[1]

In the Egyptian texts can be traced the history of the bird-ship of death, and even of ideas regarding the passing of the soul favoured by cults that had no ship of death. The belief that one can reach the celestial regions by ascending in smoke is found in Polynesia. As will be shown in the next chapter, it also lies behind the custom of cremating the dead.

[1] Breasted, *Development of Religion and Thought in Ancient Egypt*, pp. 105–10.

The ship of death is in Babylonian literature used by Gilgamesh to reach the island of his ancestor, the survivor of the deluge. Ea, god of the deep, had a ship with a crew, including In-ab, the pilot. A description of the vessel in a Sumerian text ends with the lines:

> May the ship before thee bring fertility,
> May the ship after thee bring joy,
> In thy heart may it make joy of heart.

Ea was the god of Eridu, the Sumerian seaport and the "cradle" of Sumerian culture. It would appear that the conception of the "ship of death", which was the ship of the gods, like the Egyptian ferryboat on the Lily-lake, was carried far and wide by ancient mariners until it reached Borneo, Polynesia, China, and America, on the one hand, and as far west and north as Scandinavia on the other. The bird-boats of death of the Dyaks and Red Indians have a history rooted in the land in which boats were invented. Closely related to these boats of death (as goddess-womb symbols) are the boats used by the favoured few who escaped death during the flood.

CHAPTER X

Cremation and Other Burial Customs

Why Bodies were burned—Fire God as Guide of Souls—Grave Fires in Old and New Worlds—Fire and Sun as Life-givers—Mexican Fire Doctrine —Red Indian Customs—Fire Baptism in Old and New Worlds—Descriptions of Red Indian Cremations—Widows' Ordeal—Cremation as Privilege of Select Few — Old World Analogies — Head-burning Custom — Erect Burials in Oceania and America—Widows strangled by Melanesians and Red Indians —Exposure of Dead in America and Asia—Platform Burials—Burials in Trees, Mounds, and Crevices of Mountains—Indonesian Customs—Theory of " Similar Psychology "—Significance of Culture Complexes.

THE origin of the cremation custom is wrapped in obscurity. In the New and Old Worlds it was practised by peoples who regarded it as absolutely necessary so as to ensure the happiness of the dead. It was supposed to be impossible for souls to reach, or at anyrate to enter, the Celestial Paradise until their bodies were consumed by fire. This belief is brought out very clearly in the *Iliad*. The ghost of the hapless Patroklos appears to Achilles in a dream and says:

" Thou sleepest, and hast forgotten me, O Achilles. Not in my life wast thou ever unmindful of me, but in my death. Bury me with all speed, that I pass the gates of Hades. Far off the spirits banish me, the phantoms of men outworn, nor suffer me to mingle with them beyond the River, but vainly I wander along the wide-gated dwelling of Hades. Now give me, I pray pitifully of thee, thy hand, for never more again shall I come back from Hades, when ye have given me my due of fire." [1]

---

[1] *Iliad*, Book XXII (Leaf, Lang, and Myers' translation), p. 452, London, 1914 edition.

In the *Odyssey* the soul of the sailor Elpenor makes a similar appeal to Odysseus:

"Leave me not unwept and unburied as thou goest hence, nor turn thy back upon me, lest haply I bring on thee the anger of the gods. Nay, burn me there mine armour, all that is mine, and pile me a barrow on the shore of the grey sea, the grave of luckless man, that even men unborn may hear my story. Fulfil me this and plant upon the barrow mine oar, wherewith I rowed in the days of my life, while yet I was among my fellows."[1]

Homer's Achæans, who burned their dead, appear to have represented a religious cult that had origin in Asia or Europe — probably in the former continent — and became influential in ancient times. The early exponents of it swept through Europe after bronze-working had been introduced. They appear to have been conquerors who formed military aristocracies. In Sweden the upper classes alone were cremated. In Britain cremation and inhumation were practised simultaneously in some areas, and only one member of a family—perhaps the chief— might be cremated, while the others were buried in the ancient way. The Central European evidence is of like character. The cremated burials near Salzburg, in Upper Austria, "were those of the wealthier class, or of the dominant race"; at Hallstatt "the bodies of the wealthier class were reduced to ashes", but at Watsch and St. Margaret in Carniola "the unburnt burials" were "the richer and more numerous", the earlier people having apparently maintained their supremacy.

The two customs, cremations and unburnt burials, obtained among the Aryan invaders of India; an un-cremated body might be either buried in the ground or exposed, perhaps on a raised platform. Those who burned their dead became politically predominant. They

[1] *Odyssey*, XI (Butcher and Lang's translation), London, 1913, p. 174.

were worshippers of the fire god Agni. The Vedic epithet *agni-dagdha* applied to the dead who were cremated, and *an-agnidagdhāh* ("not burnt with fire") to those who were buried, while *paroptāh* ("casting out") and *uddhitāh* ("exposure" of the dead) referred to other customs.[1] The cult of the god Varuna appears to have favoured burial in the ground. A Varuna Vedic hymn makes reference to the dead's "house of clay". "Burial was", we are told, "not rare in the Rigvedic period: a whole hymn (x, 18) describes the ritual attending it. The dead man was buried apparently in full attire, with his bow in his hand." The widow was led away from her dead husband's grave by his brother or nearest kinsman.[2] If all the Aryans who entered India were of the same racial stock and came from the same culture area, it is evident that they were divided into different religious cults. That the fusion of cults was in progress during the Vedic period is made evident by the fact that Varuna and Mitra were worshipped as well as Agni and Surya.

There can be no doubt as to why the Agni worshippers burned their dead. The god of fire was prayed to so that he might convey to the "fathers" (ancestors) the mortal "presented to him as an offering". The soul was supposed to pass to "realms of eternal light in a car or on wings", and to recover there "its ancient body in a complete and glorified form".[3] "It was expected that the dead", write Macdonell and Keith, "would revive with his whole body and all his limbs", although it is also said (*Rigveda*, x, 16, 3) that the eye goes to the sun, the breath to the wind, and so forth.[4]

Some writers have attempted to connect the cremation

[1] Macdonell and Keith, *Vedic Index of Names and Subjects*, Vol. I, pp. 8–9.
[2] *Ibid.*, p. 8.
[3] Muir, *Original Sanskrit Texts*, V, 302.   [4] *Vedic Index*, p. 9.

custom with the custom of burning fires in or near graves, and as both customs are found in America, it would be well to deal with them before citing the American evidence.

Dr. Dorpfeld[1] has suggested that the Achæan invaders of Greece burned their dead only when engaged in distant wars, and that they practised inhumation in their homeland. He thinks, too, that cremation arose from the custom of scorching bodies prior to burial for hygienic reasons. This view is not supported by the Indian evidence. The dead who were unburned were supposed to walk to Paradise and cross a river on their way, while the dead who were burned were transported to Paradise by the fire god. In Southern and Central Europe, as well as in the British Isles, the custom of cremation succeeded the earlier one, and was mainly confined to the upper classes—the descendants of the conquerors who had introduced new religious beliefs and customs.

Dr. Dorpfeld refers, in support of his theory, to what he regards as " partial burnings " in tombs at Mycenæ. The charred fragments of bones may have, as Burrows suggests, been due partly to sacrifices and partly to " charcoal brought in to comfort and warm the dead ". Burrows notes, in this connection, that " clay chafing-pans filled with charcoal are actually found in several of the Zafer Papoura graves (Crete). In one of them, and also in the Royal Tomb at Isopata, the charcoal is in a plaster tripod that forms a regular portable hearth." [2]   Charcoal deposits are often found in early European graves, usually referred to as " Bronze Age graves ", and it has been suggested that they are remains of fires used to cook food for the dead. It may be, however, that the fires were of

---

[1] *Mélanges Nicole* (in honour of Jules Nicole), 1905, Geneva, pp. 95 *et seq.*
[2] Ronald Burrows, *The Discoveries in Crete*, London, 1907, pp. 211–2.

a more ceremonial character. Early burials took place at night, and it may be that the torches used were thrown into the grave. Grave fires may have been lit in as well as near the graves.

The Polynesians and Melanesians lit fires when a death occurred. Dr. George Brown says that in Samoa "large fires were lighted in front of the house. They were kept burning all night until the body was buried, and sometimes for a week and ten days afterwards." Those who favoured water burial also lit fires. "In ordinary cases of burying at sea", writes Dr. Brown, "a fire was lit on the beach so that the spirit of the departed might come and warm himself if he felt so inclined." [1]

The Rev. George Turner, referring to the burial of the embalmed Polynesian chiefs " on a platform raised on a double canoe ", writes :

"On the evening after burial of any important chief, his friends kindled a number of fires at distances of some twenty feet from each other, near the grave; and there they sat and kept them burning till morning light. This was continued sometimes for ten days after the funeral; it was also done before burial. In the house where the body lay, or out in front of it, fires were kept burning all night by the immediate relatives of the departed. The common people had a similar custom. After burial they kept a fire blazing in the house all night, and had the space between the house and the grave so cleared as that a stream of light went forth all night from the fire to the grave. . . . At Aneiteum, of the New Hebrides, they also kindled fires, saying that it was that the spirit of the departed might come and warm itself." [2]

Turner refers to the Jewish custom of lighting grave fires. When King Asa died his body was laid in " the bed, which was filled with sweet odours and divers kinds of spices prepared by the apothecaries' art; and they

[1] George Brown, *Melanesians and Polynesians*, London, 1910, pp. 396 and 402.
[2] Rev. George Turner, *Nineteen Years in Polynesia*, pp. 232, 315.

made a very great burning for him ".[1] The wicked King Jehoram, who departed from the faith and " made high places in the mountains of Judah", and like his father favoured false prophets, was not similarly honoured after he died : " his people made no burning for him like the burning of his fathers ".[2]

Traces of " burnings " have been found in the ruins of Sumerian towns in Mesopotamia. Writing on burial customs, and the early graves beneath houses, King says :

" From the quantity of ashes, and from the fact that some of the bodies appeared to have been partially burnt, Dr. Koldeway erroneously concluded that the mounds marked the sites of ' fire-necropoles', where he imagined the early Babylonians burnt their dead, and the houses he regarded as tombs. But in no period of Sumerian or Babylonian history was this practice in vogue. The dead were always buried, and any appearance of burning must have been produced during the destruction of the cities by fire." [3]

It may be that the burnings similar to those that obtained among the Jews were not unknown in Babylonia, and that all traces of fire in graves were not due alone to the burning of houses by enemies.

The Dyaks of Borneo believed, like the Indians, that the soul hovered beside the body until the funeral ceremony was completed. The soul had itself a body and soul. " The soul's soul shivers until it can gaze in the glowing eyes of Tempon-telon. So they fear lest the soul's soul rob them of their fire." [4] The custom of lighting funeral fires may have originated therefore in the belief that, if fires were not provided for the dead, household fires would be taken away by them, just as " the substance " of food is supposed to be taken away

---

[1] 2 *Chronicles*, xvi, 14.   [2] *Ibid.*, xxi, 19.
[3] *A History of Sumer and Akkad*, p. 21.
[4] Leo Frobenius, *The Childhood of Man*, pp. 265-6.

by the fairies to whom offerings of food had to be made
in ancient times. The dead required fire just as the
fairies required food. In the *Odyssey* the dead require
blood—the blood which is life. They drink the blood,
are animated by it, and are then able to converse with
the living as they do with Odysseus. In Polynesia the
soul of the dead required fire, and might appear " with
a flame, fire being the agent employed in the incantation
of the sorcerers ".[1] When the gods were invoked fires
were extinguished.[2] Here we have another reason for
lighting fires at funerals. The living were protected by
fire against the attacks of the dead. But the fundamental
idea in the funeral fire custom appears to be that the
dead are animated by fire—the " vital spark ". The
Indian belief that fire was life is found in the *Mahá-
bhárata* :

> " Mudita, the favourite wife of the fire Saha, used to live in
> water.[3] And Saha, who was the regent of the earth and sky, begot
> in that wife of his a highly sacred fire called Advuta. There is
> a tradition amongst learned Brahmanas that this fire is the ruler
> and inner soul of all creatures."

Another passage states :

> " That other fire which has its seat in the vital airs of all
> creatures, and animates their bodies, is called Sannihita. It is the
> cause of our perceptions of sound and form."

There are various kinds of fires. The fire " called
Bharata " vouchsafes " development " to all creatures,
" and for this reason is called Bharata (the Cherisher) ".
" The fire that gives strength to the weak is called Valada
(' the giver of strength ')."[4] A Babylonian fire hymn

---

[1] Ellis, *Polynesian Researches* (1st Edition), Vol. I, p. 518.
[2] *Ibid.*, Vol. I, pp. 120–1.
[3] Here the fire as "life substance" links with the pearl, gold, &c., taken from
water. See below.   [4] *Vana Parva*, Sections CCXX–CCXXIII.

declares that " of all things that can be named thou (fire) dost form the fabric ".[1]   The post-Columbian Americans identified fire with the sun, and regarded both as givers of life.   The Algonkin word for the sun is *Kesuk*, which means " to give life ".[2]   In Zunian mythology " the sun formed the seed-stuff of the world ".[3]   " Know that the life in your body and the fire on your hearth are one and the same thing, and that both proceed from one source ", a Shawnee sage declared.[4]   The word for sun is derived from the word for fire in some South American dialects. In many American languages the words for fire, blood, and the colour red are closely connected.   Brinton gives the following examples :

" Algonkin : *skoda*, fire, *mi-skoda*, red; Kolosch : *kan*, fire, *kan*, red; Ugalentz : *takak*, fire, *takak-uete*, red; Tahkali : *cun*, fire; *tenil-cun*, red; Quiche : *cak*, fire, *cak*, red, &c.   From the adjective *red* comes often the word for *blood*, as Iroquois : *onekwensa*, blood, *onekwentara*, red; Algonkin : *miskwi*, blood, *miskoda*, red, &c., and in symbolism the colour red may refer to either of these ideas." [5]

The Nahuas of Mexico regarded fire as " the father and mother of all things and the author of nature ".   To them " fire was the active generator, the life-giver, the source of animate existence ".   The Aryo-Indian wor-shippers of the fire god Agni connected him with the sun; a Vedic hymn declares that " the sun has the nature of Agni ".   In Brahmanic mythology the Creator existed in the form of Agni before the worlds were formed.

In Mexico the god of fire was " the father and mother of all the gods ".   Fire was named Tota, our Father, and Huehueteotl, Oldest of the Gods.   When a child was born a fire was lighted, and was kept burning " to nourish

[1] *Records of the Past*, III, 137.   [2] Roger Williams, *Language of America*, p. 104.
[3] Cushing, *Zunian Creation Myths*, p. 379.   [4] *Narrative of John Tanner*, p. 161.
[5] Brinton, *The Myths of the New World*, p. 163, *n*.

its life " for four days. " The infant passed through a baptism of fire on the fourth day of its life." [1]

There can be little doubt that the custom of lighting funeral fires, which, as we have seen, prevailed in Polynesia, and was known also in America, is closely connected with the belief that fire is an animating force. Bodily heat and sun heat were regarded as being identical with fire. Dr. Yarrow, in his exhaustive article on the mortuary customs of the North American Indians, quotes from a writer on the Algonkins:

" The Algonkins believed that the fire lighted nightly on the grave was to light the spirit on its journey. By a coincidence to be explained by the universal sacredness of the number, the Algonkins and Mexicans maintained it for four nights consecutively. The former related the tradition that one of their ancestors returned from the spirit land and informed their nation that the journey thither consumed just four days, and that collecting fuel every night added much to the toil and fatigue the soul encountered, all of which could be spared it."

A tradition current among the Yurok of California regarding the use of fires is given by Stephen Powers [2]:

" After death they kept a fire burning certain nights in the vicinity of the grave. They hold as I believe, at least the ' Big Indians' do, that the spirits of the departed are compelled to cross an extremely greasy pole, which bridges over the chasm of the debatable land, and that they require .the fire to light them on their darksome journey. A righteous soul traverses the pole quicker than a wicked one, hence they regulate the number of nights for burning a light according to the character for goodness or the opposite which the deceased possessed in this world."

Dr. Yarrow adds: " Dr. Emil Bessels, of the Polaris expedition, informs the writer that a somewhat similar belief obtains among the Esquimaux ".

[1] Brinton, *op. cit.*, p. 169 and p. 198.
[2] *Contribution to North American Ethnology*, Vol. II, p. 58.

The animating fire gave light as well as heat, and because it animated it purified. Light came also from jewels buried with the dead; they shone in darkness. In China jade, gold, pearls, coral, &c., shone by night because they were impregnated with Yang (life substance) which was concentrated in the sun. It is impossible to trace in America the origin of the various fire customs and the beliefs connected with fire. These were evidently imported, as they were into Polynesia, by a people or by peoples who had acquired the fire doctrines that prevailed in Asia. Similar customs and beliefs were distributed throughout Europe. In Scotland "new fires" or "friction fires" were lit, as in Mexico, with ceremony. Martin and Pennant testify as to the existence in the Highlands of the custom of fire baptism. "It has happened", writes the latter, "that, after baptism, the child is thrice handed across the fire, with the design to frustrate all attempts of evil spirits or evil eyes", and he suggests that the rite was originally one of purification. Fire was carried round a mother morning and evening until a child was baptized, according to Martin. Fire was connected with the sun, as in America. The Gaelic sayings, "Evil never came from the east", and "No evil comes from fire", testify as to this, as well as the custom of passing children through a circle of fire to remove the effects of evil eye. The worshippers of the goddess Bride (Brigit) kept perpetual fires burning, as did American worshippers of fire deities. These and other similar beliefs and customs can be traced throughout Europe. They were not necessarily connected with the custom of cremating the dead. The Persian fire-worshippers, for instance, did not approve of cremation.

In America the cremation custom was well known. Dr. Yarrow says it was practised especially by the tribes

FUNERARY VASES, ZAPOTEC PEOPLE, OAJACA, MEXICO

(British Museum)

THE GREAT PYRAMID-TEMPLE AT CHICHEN-ITZA, YUCATAN

"living on the western slope of the Rocky Mountains, although we have undoubted evidence that it was also practised among the more eastern ones". An interesting account of a cremation burial, as practised by the Tolkotins of Oregon, is given by Ross Cox.[1] He tells that the corpse was kept for nine days, so that the friends and relatives might have an opportunity of coming from distances to verify the death. The pyre was about seven feet long and of split cypress with a quantity of gummy wood in the interstices. When it was lit to burn the corpse, the bystanders appeared to be "in a high state of merriment". The widow was subjected to a trying ordeal. She slept beside the corpse until the day of burial. She also lay beside the body on the pyre, and was not allowed to rise from it after the fire was kindled until her body was covered with blisters. The narrative continues:

"When the friends of the deceased observe the sinews of the legs and arms beginning to contract, they compel the unfortunate widow to go again on the pile, and by dint of hard pressing to straighten those members".

If the widow had been unfaithful to her husband, or had neglected her duties, she was flung on the pyre and had to be rescued by friends. When the burning was over she collected the bones and had to carry them about with her until they were finally interred. During this period she was treated as a slave.

Stephen Powers, describing a cremation ceremony of the Se-nél of California, writes:

"The corpse was that of a wealthy chieftain, and as he lay upon the funeral pyre, they placed in his mouth two gold twenties, and other smaller coins in his ears and hands, on his breast, &c.,

[1] *Contribution to North American Ethnology*, 1877, Vol. III, p. 341.

besides all his finery, his feather mantles, plumes, clothing, shell money, his fancy bows, painted arrows, &c ".

Gifts were thrown on the blazing pyre by the mourners.

Traces of cremation have been found in the pre-Columbian cemeteries of North America. In some cases the customs of inhumation and cremation were, as in Europe, practised in the same area simultaneously. Brinton shows, in this connection, that among some peoples cremation was " a privilege usually confined to a select few ", and writes:

" Among the Algonkin-Ottawas only those of the distinguished totem of the Great Hare, among the Nicaraguans none but the caciques, among the Caribs exclusively the priestly caste were entitled to this peculiar honour.

" The first gave as a reason for such an exceptional custom, that the members of so illustrious a clan as that of Michabo, the Great Hare, should not rot in the ground as common folks, but rise to the heavens on the flames and smoke. Those of Nicaragua seemed to think it the sole path to immortality, holding that only such as offered themselves on the pyre of their chieftain would escape annihilation at death; and the tribes of Upper California were persuaded that such as were not burned at death were liable to be transferred into the lower orders of brutes." [1]

The descendants of the introducers of new cultures, and of chieftains or conquerors, were buried according to their own ancestral or tribal rites, while the masses of the people perpetuated their own peculiar customs. A similar explanation is suggested by the custom of mummifying chiefs or high-priests only. In Tibet, as L. A. Waddell informs us, " the bodies of the Grand Lamas and a few other high-priests are embalmed and enshrined within gilded tombs (chortens), and the remains of the more wealthy priests are sometimes cremated. . . . The usual

---

[1] Brinton, The Myths of the New World, pp. 169–70.

method of disposing of the bodies, however, is by cutting off the flesh from the bones and throwing the pieces to dogs and vultures to be consumed. . . . The corpses of poor people, criminals, those killed by accident, lepers, and sometimes barren women, are dragged by a rope, like a dead beast, and thrown into rivers and lakes." [1] Tibet was a meeting-ground of cultures from various areas of origin, and the customs of the higher classes were those of the culture or cultures politically in the ascendant.

Oceanic customs reveal similar evidence. "In the Shortlands group", writes Dr. George Brown, "the dead, if common people, are buried, but the ordinary mode of burial is to wrap the body up in mats weighted with heavy stones and then convey it to certain places where it is dropped overboard. The bodies of chiefs, however, and people of some importance are cremated." On New Ireland the cremation custom was confined to the north end of the island: in other parts water burial was favoured. [2] Here the custom is a tribal one and not confined to a class. Elsewhere mummification was favoured by the ruling caste. "Embalming", wrote Turner, "is known and practised with surprising skill in one particular family of chiefs. Unlike the Egyptian method, as described by Herodotus, it is performed in Samoa exclusively by women." [3] Like the Egyptian Pharaohs the Polynesian priests "were supposed to have a separate place (in the after life) allotted to them". [4] In Indonesia Perry has found evidence that certain burial customs were associated chiefly with the ruling class, the descendants of intruders. [5]

Not only were certain burial customs confined to tribes or families in America; there is also evidence of

[1] *Customs of the World*, Vol. I, pp. 573–4.
[2] George Brown, *Melanesians and Polynesians* (London, 1910), pp. 386, 390.
[3] *Nineteen Years in Polynesia*, p. 231.　　[4] *Ibid.*, p. 237.
[5] *Megalithic Culture in Indonesia*, pp. 26, 168–9, 179 *et seq.*

culture-mixing in some of these customs. Dr. Yarrow quotes from General Tompkins of the United States Army, an account of a curious burial custom favoured by the Achomawi Red Indians of California. The General tells that it is the custom of these people to

"bury the body in a ground in a standing position, the shoulders nearly even with the ground. The grave is prepared by digging a hole of sufficient depth and circumference to admit the body, the head being cut off. In the grave are placed the bows and arrows, bead-work, trappings, &c., belonging to the deceased; quantities of food, consisting of dried fish, roots, herbs, &c., were placed with the body also. The grave was then filled up, covering the headless body; then a bundle of faggots was brought and placed on the grave by the different members of the tribe, and on these faggots the head was placed, the pile fired, and the head consumed to ashes. . . . I noticed while the head was burning, the old women of the tribe sat on the ground, forming a large circle, inside of which another circle of young girls were formed standing and swaying their bodies to and fro, and singing a mournful ditty. This was the only burial of a male I witnessed. The custom of burying females is very different, their bodies being wrapped or bundled up in skins and laid away in caves, with their valuables, and in some cases food being placed with them in their mouths. Occasionally money is left to pay for food in the spirit land." [1]

Heads were mummified, instead of being burned, by some Red Indians, Polynesians, &c. That the head-burning custom did not originate in America is evident when we find it was practised in Melanesia. In the Solomons " some tribes bury a chief with his head near to the surface, and over the grave light a fire, which burns away the flesh from the head; the skull is afterwards dug up for preservation. In some of the Western

---

[1] Dr. Yarrow, " A Further Contribution to the Study of the Mortuary Customs of the North American Indians ", p. 151. The Chinese custom of placing jade, gold, pearls, &c., in the mouths of the dead suggests another reason for the Red Indian custom of placing coins, &c., in the mouths of the dead.

Solomons the bodies of chiefs and members of their families are usually burnt, and the ashes and skulls and some other bones are preserved." [1]

The erect posture is, as we have seen, associated with water-burial on Duke of York Island. It was also favoured by some who buried their dead in the ground. "In some cases", writes Dr. Brown, "but very rarely, I believe, a chief was buried in an upright position. This grave was called *tung na tauba*; but I cannot tell what this means, the real interpretation of the words being the hole or pit of the large snake (*tauba*)." [2] Some Red Indians like the Algonquins and Dakotas believed that the " Brig o' Dread " (the Scottish name) across the river of death was formed by a snake; others, like the Hurons and Iroquois, believed the bridge was formed by a tree.

Erect burial was practised in Ireland. Joyce writes in this connection :

"Occasionally the bodies of kings and chieftains were buried in a standing posture, arrayed in full battle costume, with the face turned towards the territories of their enemies."

In the *Book of the Dun Cow* a hero is buried "with the face turned southwards upon the Lagenians, [as it were] fighting with them, for he was the enemy of the Lagenians in his lifetime". Of another hero it is told : " He was killed in that battle and buried standing up in that place ". Skeletons standing up in graves have been found in a tumulus in County Meath and in a cairn in County Mayo. [3]

An interesting case of erect burial in America has been described by E. A. Barber, who writes : [4]

[1] *Customs of the World*, p. 42.   [2] *Melanesians and Polynesians*, p. 386.
[3] P. W. Joyce, *A Smaller Social History of Ireland*, p. 536.
[4] *American Naturalist*, 1878, p. 629.

"On the New Jersey bank of the Delaware River, a short distance below Gloucester City, the skeleton of a man was found buried in a standing position ".

The skull was wanting.

"A careful exhumation and critical examination by Mr. Klingbeil disclosed the fact that around the lower extremities of the body had been placed a number of large stones, which revealed traces of fire, in conjunction with charred wood, and the bones of the feet had undoubtedly been consumed."

In Polynesia foot burning was resorted to so that the sick might be animated. "I have seen ", writes Turner, "a poor fellow dying from an arrow-wound in the neck, and the sole of his foot just burned to a mass of raw flesh." [1]   In cases of cremation-burials in Oregon the doctor, who had attended the man who lies on a pyre, "for the last time tries his skill in restoring the defunct to animation " before the fire is kindled.[2]

Red Indian widows were not burned with the dead as in India. As in Indian Vedic times they might be led from the grave by relatives, or compelled to endure indignities and even torture. Some widows committed suicide, while widowers fled "to distant quarters to avoid the brutal treatment which custom has established as a kind of religious rite ".[3]

Women were strangled by some Red Indian tribes when husbands or relatives died. The Natchez of Louisiana practised this custom.

"A cord is fastened round their necks with a slip-knot, and eight men of their relations strangle them by drawing, four one way and four the other."[4]

---

[1] *Nineteen Years in Polynesia*, p. 92

[2] Dr. Yarrow, "A Further Contribution to the Study of the Mortuary Customs of the North American Indians" (*First Annual Report of the Bureau of Ethnology*, Washington, 1881, p. 145).

[3] Dr. Yarrow, *op. cit.*, pp. 145–6.   [4] Dr. Yarrow, *op. cit.*, p. 187.

The Melanesians similarly strangled widows. Turner informs us that, on the island of Aneiteum,

"it was common, on the death of a chief, to strangle his wives, that they might accompany him to the regions of the departed. The custom has been found in various parts of the Pacific."[1]

Some American burial customs are confined to particular tribes. It does not follow, however, that they are of independent origin. Indeed, when it is found that identical customs prevailed in Asia, and were exceedingly prevalent in some areas, the suspicion arises that they were imported into America at some period or another. This suspicion hardens to a certainty when it is shown that a particular custom has a history in Asia, and is rooted in a body of definite beliefs, and it is without a history in America, and perpetuated there merely as a traditional usage on special occasions. A case in point is the custom of offering the dead to birds and beasts. In Tibet, as we have seen, the bodies of the common people were thus disposed of, while priests were either cremated or embalmed. The Caddoes or " Timber Indians " neither mummified nor cremated their great men. Common people were buried, and those worthy of the highest honour were treated like the commoners of Tibet. Yarrow gives the following quotation in this connection :

"If a Caddo is killed in battle, the body is never buried, but is left to be devoured by beasts or birds of prey, and the condition of such individuals in the other world is considered to be far better than that of persons dying a natural death ".[2]

The custom was an expression of religious ideas, and confined to warriors. Apparently it was introduced by a people who either effected settlement by conquest, or

<hr />

[1] *Nineteen Years in Polynesia*, p. 93.   [2] *Op. cit.*, p. 103.

came from an area outside America, where warriors, as the descendants of the fighting caste, were honoured after death in accordance with the beliefs prevailing in the area of origin whence the original conquerors came.

The custom of exposing the dead had, so far as our knowledge goes, its origin in Irania. Some of the pastoral fighting peoples who entered India in early Vedic times exposed their dead, as has been indicated. They appear to have been more numerous, or at any rate more influential in Tibet before cremation and mummification were introduced by religious teachers, and confined to them and their successors. In Persia, however, the custom of exposing the dead to birds and beasts of prey was very prevalent. When the corpses were devoured "their joy was very great", writes M. Pierre Muret;[1] "they enlarged themselves in praises of the deceased, every one esteeming them undoubtedly happy, and came to congratulate their relations on that account. For as they believed assuredly, that they were entered into the Elysian fields, so they were persuaded, that they would procure the same bliss for all those of their family." The Parthians, Medes, and Caspians favoured the custom. Dogs, called *canes sepulchrales*, were trained and kept by the Bactrians and Hircanians to devour dead bodies. " It was deemed proper ", says Yarrow, quoting Bruhier and Muret, " that the souls of the deceased should have strong and lusty frames to dwell in." The Parsees (descendants of Persians) in India still expose their dead on their " towers of silence ", so that they may be devoured by vultures. Monier Williams, who wrote regarding the Parsee custom in the *Times* (January 28, 1876), was informed as follows by a Parsee regarding the beliefs connected with it :

[1] *Rites of Funeral Ancient and Modern* (1683), p. 45.

"Our prophet Zoroaster, who lived 6000 years ago, taught us to regard the elements as symbols of the deity. Earth, fire, water, he said, ought never, under any circumstances, to be defiled by contact with putrefying flesh. Naked, he said, came we into the world, and naked we ought to leave it. But the decaying particles of our bodies should be dissipated as rapidly as possible, and in such a way that neither Mother Earth nor the beings she supports should be contaminated in the slightest degree. . . . God, indeed, sends the vultures."

Originally the vultures were themselves forms of the deity. As Agni, the fire god, consumed bodies and transported souls in smoke to the Celestial regions, so, apparently, did the birds or dogs who devoured the dead carry the souls to another world.

Platform burials are in some lands connected with beliefs similar to those of the ancient Persians. In America, however, the dead who are thus disposed of are protected in canoes or boxes, or carefully wrapped up on flat boards. The "platform" tombs are common in Asia. As in America they are found to be supported by Y-formed stakes. They are also placed in the forks of trees. The Y symbol is in ancient Egypt associated with the god Shu who supports the firmament. Four Y symbols represent the sky pillars of the four cardinal points.[1] Platforms supported on Y-formed stakes appear to have been symbols of heaven; the corpse laid on the platform was thus offered to heaven; the canoe, supported on Y-formed stakes, was evidently symbolic of the sun boat that sailed across the sky, and was entered by the soul of the dead Pharaoh. The fork of a tree was, it would appear, favoured because the pillars of the four cardinal points were often represented as trees. They were also represented as mountains. The custom of

---

[1] See illustration in Breasted, *A History of Egypt*, opposite p. 54.

burying the dead in trees, or in coffins made from sacred trees, and that of burying in mountain fissures, which were known in America and Asia, may have been connected with the belief that the dead were returned to the tree or mountain form of the Great Mother. Pyramids and cairns were symbols of the world pillars too. They were specially connected with the sun cult, which regarded the sun as the child of the Mother Goddess. The sun emerged from the " Mount of Dawn ", and returned to the " Mount of Sunset ", or it emerged from the Tree of Life that supported the world. Burial mounds in America and Asia were like the Babylonian temples, sacred " mountains "—symbols of the deity, who was the giver of life at the beginning, and who animated the body after death.

Dr. O. G. Given, an American physician, provides the following notes regarding the burial customs of the Kiowas, Comanches, and Apaches.

"They bury in the ground or in crevices of rocks. . . . I was present at the burial of Black Hawk, an Apache chief, some two years ago, and took the body in my light wagon up the side of a mountain to the place of burial. They found a crevice in the rocks about four feet wide and three feet deep." [1]

In this crevice they buried the chief, filling up the grave with loose rocks. Perry has recorded this burial custom in Indonesia. " The custom of placing the dead in clefts of the rocks is found among the people of the Simbuang-Mapak Valley." The Kabui Naga sometimes " place the dead in an excavation in the side of a hill, and close up the opening with stones ".[2] Indeed the jumble of burial customs in Indonesia is repeated in America. It may be therefore that the culture-mixing involved took place in Asia, and that the migrating people who reached

[1] Yarrow, *op. cit.*, p. 142.   [2] *Megalithic Culture of Indonesia*, pp. 22–23.

Oceania and America were carriers of a variety of customs and beliefs. No doubt fresh culture-mixing took place in new countries. The burial customs of the pre-Columbian Americans were of complex character from the very beginning. As has been shown from the examples given, each custom was rooted in religious beliefs that are not peculiar to America and cannot be proved to have originated there. Some believe that similar burial customs in Polynesia, America, and Asia were of independent origin. Such a theory is difficult to entertain and is unsupported by positive evidence. "It is an evident fact", writes Mr. Thomas A. Joyce, "that the Americans physically stand in comparatively close relation to the Asiatics. That being so, a somewhat similar psychology is natural, and this would lead, subject to modifications produced by environment, to the evolution of culture and art in which certain analogies might be expected to appear." [1] Here a theory rests on a theory, and Robertson's term "natural" is once again repeated. If a "similar psychology" depends on race, how are we to explain the existence of the same burial customs among Mongols, Papuans, Dravidians, Aryo-Indians, and Egyptians? If it was "natural" for one Red Indian tribe to burn their dead, as did certain Polynesian, Melanesian, and Aryo-Indian peoples, was it "natural", too, that other Red Indians should have embalmed their dead, as did the ancient Egyptians, certain Polynesian and Melanesian peoples, &c.? If mummification has a definite history in one part of the world, has it no history in other parts? If cremation is associated with a definite body of beliefs in India, and with the same complex body of beliefs in the New World, are we justified in assuming that the origin of the American custom was natural and

[1] *Mexican Archæology*, p. 371.

spontaneous, especially when we find that migrating peoples in Asia and Europe distributed the cremating custom far and wide? The theory of "similar psychology" breaks down when we find such a great variety of burial customs among tribes physically akin. Nor can it be urged when consideration is given to the fact that certain customs were confined to the priestly or ruling classes and other customs prevailed among the commoners. The priests and chiefs of a particular tribe had not necessarily different minds from their kinsmen. "A somewhat similar psychology" is surely "natural" among members of the same nomadic tribe.

Cultures like languages afford no sure indication of racial affinities. The carriers of a particular culture were not necessarily the originators of it. They may have formed a small minority in a community, although the influence exercised by them may have been very great. In some instances they appear to have changed the burial customs of a whole tribe: in other instances they appear to have done no more than establish a burial custom for the family they founded. The chief and his family might be mummified or cremated, while the common people perpetuated their own ancient burial customs. A special heaven was reserved for chief, priest, or warrior: it was the heaven of the imported religion; the common people continued to believe they would share in the after life the fate of their ancestors in the heaven of the ancestral faith. In almost every country of the world it is found that the division of society into classes as a result of conquest was in ancient times accompanied by culture complexes in religious life. The fusion of the older faith with the new had a political aspect that was reflected in the various burial customs of a single people. Among peoples like the Red Indians of America, who were mainly in the hunting stage of civilization, the existence of mummification, cremation, and water-burial customs cannot be explained by appeal to the psychological theory. They should all have buried their dead as did hunters elsewhere, and all hunters should have displayed in this connection a "similar psychology". The fact that they did not emphasizes the argument that the great variety of customs that obtained in disposing of the dead was due to the introduction from time to time of a variety of religious systems of which burial customs were expressions, remaining as historical records. The Red Indians, the Aleutian islanders, the Indonesians, and the Polynesians mummified the dead, and in doing so displayed surgical skill they never originated but had acquired. The methods they adopted had a history, but the history cannot be traced in the New World; it is found only in the Old.

CHAPTER XI

The Milk Goddess and her Pot Symbol

Ancient Theories regarding Origins—Foam as Milk—The Cow Mother
—Milk Pot and Water Pot—Milk in Rivers, Vegetation, and the Sky—
Pot Symbol in Old and New Worlds—The Holy Grail and the Pot of Plenty
—Indian Milk Goddess and "Milky Ocean"—Holy Men as "Foam
Drinkers"—Cow Mother as Grandmother of Horses, Milk-yielding Trees,
and Parrots—Earth Mother in India and America—Zuni World-pot Myth—
The Churning of Ocean—Twins spring from Ocean Foam—The Under-
world—Separation of Sky and Earth—Mexican Many-breasted Milk Goddess
—Pulque-yielding Agave Plant—Agave Sap as Milk and Nectar—Pulque
Jug as "Mother Pot"—Twins spring from Pulque Froth—Mayauel, the
Agave Goddess, and the Ephesian Artemis—Artemis as the Fig Tree—Milk
Elixir in Mexico, India, Greece, and Scotland—Milk-yielding Trees in
Different Lands—Roman Milk Goddess and River Milk—Ocean-churning
Myths in Old and New Worlds—Agave as "Tree of Life"—Fish Links
between Mayauel and Artemis—Pulque Gods of War, Death, and Harvest.

In various ancient countries the mother goddess was the
source of all life—celestial, human, animal, vegetable, and
mineral.[1]   The cosmic goddess of ancient Egypt was
Hathor.   She was regarded by the theorizing priests as
"the personification of the great power of nature, which
was perpetually conceiving and creating, and bringing
forth and rearing, and maintaining all things, both great
and small".[2]   Various theories were entertained regarding
her origin.   According to Plutarch, Isis (who ultimately
absorbed the attributes of Hathor) was often called by
the name of Athene, which signifies "I have come from
myself".[3]

[1] It was believed that minerals grew like plants.
[2] Budge, *Gods of the Egyptians*, Vol. I, p. 431.   [3] *De Iside et Osiris*, Chapter IX.

In the early period, however, the goddess was simply the gigantic mother who had existed from the beginning —the first being of whom nothing was known, the personification of the principle of life. One of her ancient symbols was the water pot. This pot was at once the primeval deep and the inexhaustible womb of nature. Out of the world pot came the gods, human beings, the heavenly bodies, the water that fertilized the land and caused vegetation to spring up, the gems, &c., containing life substance, and so on.

The priests puzzled their minds to discover how life originated inside the world pot. One of their theories was that the water was set in motion by the wind, and began to bubble and foam. From the foam sprang the first god and goddess, or the multiplying lotus bloom, out of which the sun god emerged. The mother goddess herself was supposed by some to have arisen from the foam, as did Aphrodite from the froth of the breaking waves.

In the myths that survive to us the simple conceptions of the early people are found to be fused with the accumulated theories of centuries. It was long after the idea of a mother goddess had had origin that the problem of how she came into existence occupied the minds of thinking men.

According to the evidence provided by various ancient mythologies, the foam in the pot, or on the primeval ocean symbolized by the pot, was identified with body moisture—perspiration, saliva, tears, semen, or milk.

The theory that the life principle was in milk has an interesting history. At a remote period the Egyptian domesticated the cow, and regarded the cow-mother as the originator of all life. Her milk fed her children, and in her milk were " the seeds of life ". The milk pot was identified with the water pot after the theories of those who had conceived of a cow mother were fused with the theories of those who had conceived of a world pot.

The idea of the primeval cow mother is found in Northern mythology, which preserves not a few archaic conceptions. Ymir, the cosmic world giant, came into existence where the warm wind from the fiery south caused the icy vapours of the dark frozen north to melt and form living drops of moisture. Simultaneously the cosmic cow Audhumla had origin. From her teats ran four streams of milk—the four primeval rivers of the cardinal points—and " thus ", says the *Prose Edda*, " fed she Ymir ". The body of Ymir was used to make the world :

> From the flesh of Ymir the world was formed,
> From his bones were mountains made,
> And Heaven from the skull of that frost-cold giant,
> From his blood the billows of the sea.[1]

Here rocks, earth, the sky, and the sea have origin from air, heat, and moisture, and the sea is identified with blood—the fluid of life. The fluid had its origin in moisture, and the first man was sustained by milk.

The clay pot of the early worshippers of the cow mother was the earliest churn. It was observed that cream rose to the surface of milk as did foam to the surface of the sea. A pestle was used to churn the cream, and butter was produced. Butter was identified with fat; both were solidified liquids that could be melted when subjected to heat.

The discovery that a fluid like milk solidified when churned is reflected in the Indian myth of the " Churning

---

[1] O. Bray, *The Elder Edda*, p. 47.

POTTERY VASES. PROTO-CHIMU PERIOD, TRUXILLO REGION, PERU

(British Museum)

of the Ocean ". As will be shown, this churning myth was adopted by peoples who had no domesticated milk-yielding animals.

The offspring of the mother goddess included, as has been indicated, the various forms of vegetation which had had origin from her tears, or from those of her divine sons. Vegetation was nourished by the milk of the goddess, which came down flooding rivers as foam, or as whitish or yellowish clay, and certain trees and herbs yielded a milk-like sap, which was regarded as an elixir and was supposed to be the goddess's milk. The "Milky Way" in the night sky was similarly supposed to be the milk of the goddess.

As the cosmic cow goddess, the Egyptian Hathor was depicted with a star-spangled body; her limbs were the four supporting pillars of the world. In her human form as the goddess Nut she bent over the earth, her legs and arms forming the pillars of the cardinal points; her body, like that of the cow, was also star-spangled. In one interesting representation of the goddess[1] the moon emerges from her breasts, into the palm of the god Shu, as a pool of milk; the sun, as other illustrations indicate, emerged from her womb.

In the ancient Egyptian system of hieroglyphs a bowl of water stands for the female principle. Its phonetic value is "nu". The male principle in the cosmic waters ("nu") is Nun and the female Nut.[2] As the sky goddess, Nut personified the waters above the firmament; she was also the goddess of the primeval deep.

In Babylonia the symbolic pot is held by a god who pours out the fertilizing water, that is, the rivers

---

[1] Breasted, *A History of Egypt*, p. 55.

[2] F. Ll. Griffith, *Archæological Survey of Egypt* (1898), p. 3, and Elliot Smith, *The Evolution of the Dragon* (1919), p. 178.

Euphrates and Tigris.   Hapi, the Nile god, is similarly
depicted as a man with a water pot or vase.

The Indian "water pot" was essentially a sacred
object.   Each ascetic had one.   When it was taken from
him, he was unable to purify himself and could then be
attacked and slain by demons.   A famous ascetic had
a son who emerged from a saint's water pot into which
the seed of life had fallen, and was called Drona ("pot
born ").   "The foremost of all wielders of weapons—the
preceptor Drona—hath ", a text states, "been born in
a water pot ".[1]

The symbolic pot and the doctrines associated with it,
reached the New World.   As Brinton states, "the vase
or the gourd as a symbol of water, the source and pre-
server of life, is a conspicuous figure in the myths and in
the art of Ancient America.   As Akbal or Huecomitl,
the great or original vase, in Aztec and Maya legends it
plays important parts in the drama of creation; as Tici
(Ticcu) in Peru it is the symbol of the rains, and as
a gourd it is often mentioned by the Caribs and Tupis
as the parent of the atmospheric waters.   Large reclining
images, bearing vases, have been exhumed in the valley
of Mexico, in Tlascala, in Yucatan, and elsewhere.   They
represent the rain god, the water-bearer, the patron of
agriculture."[2]

The symbolic pot is an inexhaustible food-supplier,
because it contains the fluid from which all things have
come—the water and its foam and blood-red clay that
fertilizes parched land when rivers rise and overflow, or
when, after a period of drought, rain falls from heaven.
It figures as the symbol of life in myth, ritual, and
romance.   Men searched for it as, in the Old and New

---

[1] *The Mahá-bhárata* (*Adi Parva*), Sections CXXXI, CXXXIX, and CLXVIII.
[2] Brinton, *The Myths of the New World*, p. 152.

Worlds, they searched for the Well of Life—that earthly
"pot" in which the life-giving water collected. The
memory of the pot lingered for centuries in Western
Europe after Christianity became widespread. In Arthurian romance it is Christianized as the "Holy Grail".
When Galahad and his fellows found the Grail, they

"saw angels, and two bare candles of wax, and a third a towel,
and the fourth a spear which bled marvellously, that three drops
fell within a box which he held with his other hand.[1] And they
set the candles upon the table and the third the towel upon the
vessel, and the fourth the holy spear even upright upon the vessel."

From the Grail emerged a child whose visage "was
as red and bright as any fire". This child entered a
portion of bread so that "the bread was formed of a
fleshly man". The knights were fed from the Grail with
"sweet meats".[2]

The earlier Pagan "Pot of Plenty" is found in Gaelic
and Welsh folk-literature. In the Hindu *Mahá-bhárata*,
the sun god sends a copper pot to the chief of the Pan-
davas, from which could be obtained an inexhaustible
supply of "fruits, and roots, and meat, and vegetables".
The sun was, in India, regarded, like the "water suns"
of America, as the source of food and water,

"converting the effects of the solar heat (vapours) into clouds
and pouring them down in the shape of water, causing plants to
spring up. . . . Thus it is the sun himself who, drenched by lunar
influence, is transformed, upon the sprouting of seeds, into holy
vegetables."[3]

In both the Old and New Worlds the ancient complex
ideas regarding the pot, the star-spangled mother goddess
and her animals, can be traced in myths, and in the arts

---

[1] Here blood is the fertilizing fluid of life. Light (fire) is symbolized by the candles.
[2] Malory, *Morte Darthur*, Book XVII, Chapter XX.
[3] The *Vana Parva* of the *Mahá-bhárata* (Roy's translation), pp. 11 *et seq*.

and crafts. Interesting evidence in this connection is provided for America by pottery vessels recently found in Honduras.[1]

In India the Hathor cow is Surabhi, "the mother of all kine", whose daughters bring forth not only calves, but horses, long-feathered birds, Nāgas (snakes), milk-yielding trees, &c.

Surabhi is located in *Rasā-tala*, "the seventh stratum below the earth". The milk she yields "is the essence of all the best things of the earth". It contains Amrita (soma); Surabhi herself "sprang in days of old from the mouth of the Grandsire gratified with drinking the Amrita and vomiting the best of things".[2]

It is told in the *Mahá-bhárata*[3] that:

"A single jet only of her milk falling on the earth, created what is known as the sacred and the excellent 'Milky Ocean'. The verge of that ocean all round is always covered with white foam resembling a belt of flowers. Those best of ascetics that are known by the name of the *Foam-drinkers* dwell around this ocean, subsisting on that foam only. They are called *Foam-drinkers* because they live on nothing else save that foam."

From the "Milky Sea" came "Amrita" (the elixir or nectar of the gods), the goddess Lakshmi, the prince of steeds, the best of gems, and the wine called "Vāruni".

"Those waters that yielded these precious things had all been mixed with the milk."

The Celestial milk "becometh *sudha* (food of the Nāgas, the serpent gods) unto those who live on *sudha*, *swadhū* (food of the *Pitris*, the souls of ancestors) to those that

---

[1] *Man* ("An American Dragon"), November, 1918; Elliot Smith, *The Evolution of the Dragon*, p. 182.

[2] The cow and the Brahmans.

[3] *The Udyoga Parva* (Roy's translation), pp. 309 *et seq.*

live on *swadhā*, and *Amrita* (food of the gods) to those that live on *Amrita* ".[1]

In a *Mahá-bhárata* description of the regions of the four cardinal points, Surabhi is placed in the west:

"It is in this region that Surabhi, repairing to the shores of the extensive lake adorned with golden lotuses, poureth forth her milk".

The west is the region where "the rivers which always feed the ocean have their sources. Here in the abode of Varuna are the waters of the three worlds ".[2]

Surabhi, "the mother of all kine ", has, as has been indicated, several daughters, including Rohina from whom "have sprung all kine ", Gandharvi from whom have sprung "all animals of the horse species ", and Analā who "begat the seven kinds of trees yielding pulpy fruits ". The tree children of Analā are

"the date, the palm, the hintala, the tali, the little date, the nut, and the coco-nut ".

Surabhi's daughter Shuki is "the mother of the parrot species ".[3]

Here we have not only horses and kine, but also parrots and milk-yielding trees connected with the Indian Hathor cow.

As we have seen, Surabhi is located in the Underworld. She may be referred to as an "Earth goddess " (that is, a "world goddess "). In *Bhishma Parva* of the *Mahá-bhárata* we read:

"Earth, if its resources are properly developed according to its qualities and prowess, is like an ever-yielding cow, from which the three-fold fruits of virtue, profit, and pleasure may be milked ".

---

[1] *Vana Parva* of the *Mahá-bhárata*, Section CI.

[2] *Udyoga Parva* (Roy's translation), pp. 328–9. The "three worlds " are (1) the celestial, (2) the earthly, and (3) the underworld.

[3] *Adi Parva* of the *Mahá-bhárata* (Roy's translation), p. 163.

Roy notes that Nilakantha explains this passage as follows:

"The gods depend on sacrifice performed by human beings; and as regards human beings, their food is supplied by the Earth. The superior and inferior creatures, therefore, are all supported by the Earth; the Earth then is their refuge. The word Earth . . . is sometimes used to signify the world and sometimes the element of that name." [1]

The famous Rishi Vashishta had a cow named Nandini which yielded "everything that was desired of her".

"When she was addressed 'O give!' she ever yielded the article that was sought. And she yielded various fruits and corn both wild and grown in gardens and fields, and milk, and many excellent nutritive viands filled with the six different kinds of juice, and like unto nectar itself, and various other kinds of enjoyable things of ambrosial taste, for drinking and eating, and for lapping and sucking, and also many precious gems [2] and robes of various kinds."

This wonderful cow had "eyes prominent like those of the frog", and could speak and weep, "crying so piteously"; when enraged her eyes became red, and she was "terrible to behold, like unto the sun in his mid-day glory". She then attacked an army. From her tail came fire and demons; then demons and savages came from other parts of her body, many having existence "from the froth of her mouth". [3] Here we have the Hathor cow connected with the sun, fire, the frog, jewels, vegetation, &c.

These extracts from the *Mahá-bhárata* throw considerable light on the religious ideas and myths of the

---

[1] Roy's translation of *Bhishma Parva*, pp. 33-4.

[2] The connection between gems, milk, and water is further brought out in the references to the goddess Lakshmi, "who wears a necklace of a thousand streams and a girdle of the milky sea" (*Dasakumára*).

[3] *Adi Parva* of the *Mahá-bhárata* (Roy's translation), pp. 501-4.

pre-Columbian Americans. The Earth mother (or "world mother") of the Zuni Red Indians has a "terraced bowl" which is simply the "mother pot" with the stepped symbol of Isis multiplied upon it. She uses her bowl as a churn. It is told of her:

"She took a great terraced bowl into which she poured water; upon the water she spat, and whipping it rapidly with her fingers, it was soon beaten into foam as froths the soap-weed, and the foam rose high up around the rim of the bowl. The Earth mother blew the foam.[1] Flake after flake broke off, and, bursting, cast spray downward into the bowl. 'See', said she, 'this bowl is, as it were, the world, the rim its farthest limits, and the foam-bounded terraces round about, my features, which they shall call mountains . . . whence white clouds shall rise, float away, and, bursting, shed spray, that my children may drink the water of life, and from my substances add unto the flesh of their being." [2]

The Zuni comment on the bowl shows how closely it resembles the solar copper pot in the Indian *Mahá-bhárata* and the Hathor pot of Egypt:

"Is not the bowl the emblem of the Earth, our mother? From it we draw both food and drink, as a babe draws nourishment from the breast of its mother." [3]

The foam provided by the mother goddess was transformed by the Zuni sun god into gods who were intended to serve the human beings in the dark cave-wombs of the goddess of earth:

[1] Here we meet with the wind and water idea which is the germ of the Chinese *Fung-shui* (wind and water) doctrine, the white tiger god of the west being the source of wind, and the green dragon god of the east the source of water. At the Aztec baptism ceremony the midwife blew on the water before sprinkling it on the infant. The wind is the "breath of life", the "water" (as foam, milk, or blood) contains the substance of life. In Japan the mountains, rivers, &c., are *kami* as well as are divine beings. The Hindu Vedic hymns connect mountains and clouds and cows. Indra drives "cloud cows" and smites "cloud-rocks".

[2] Cushing, "Zuni Breadstuff" (*Indian Notes and Monographs*, Vol. VIII, New York, 1920, pp. 23–4). [3] *Ibid.*, p. 24.

"The Ancient Sun pitied the children of Earth. That they might speedily see his light, he cast a glance upon a foam-cap floating abroad on the great waters. Forthwith the foam-cap became instilled with life and bore twin children."

Their shield was "spun and woven" from the clouds so that it might "darken the earth with raindrops", their bow was the rainbow which "clears away the storm shadows", and their "arrows" the thunderbolts that "rive open mountains".[1] With the bow "they lifted from his embraces the sky father from the bosom of the earth mother", and with their arrows they broke open the mountains to release human beings from "the cave-wombs of the earth mother".[2]

The wolf, the dog, or the coyote is the friendly god who "opens the way" in some tribal myths. According to the Lenni Lenape Red Indians the primeval race was released from the Underworld by a wolf which scratched away the soil; the burrowing rabbit, a holy animal, may have been connected with the mother goddess for a similar reason. Other Red Indian tribes like the Mandans and Minnetarres on the Missouri River believed their ancestors emerged from a mountain, climbing upwards. Caves and fissures in rocks were supposed by not a few peoples to lead to the Underworld. The South American tribes had, like those of North America, myths about the Underworld in which their ancestors dwelt in happiness before coming to the surface of the earth.[3] After death the souls of the dead returned to the land of ancestors below mountains, and rivers, and ocean. This belief is found reflected in burial customs. The dead

[1] In the *Mahá-bhárata* Indra slays his powerful rival, Vritra, with the aid of froth. He found "in the sea a mass of froth as large as a hill. . . . And he threw at Vritra that mass of froth blended with the thunderbolt. And Vishnu, having entered within that froth, put an end to the life of Vritra." (*Udyoga Parva*, Roy's translation, p. 25.)
[2] *Ibid.*, pp. 24, 25.   [3] Brinton, *Myths of the New World*, pp. 257 *et seq.*

"MILKING" THE MAGUEY PLANT FOR THE PREPARATION OF
PULQUE, THE MEXICAN NATIONAL BEVERAGE

The maguey, or agave plant (*Agave americana*), is a species of prickly cactus with "fleshy"
stems and a generous supply of milky juice, which, when fermented, is called "pulque".

THE MEXICAN MILK-TREE GODDESS

1, The milk-yielding tree (*chichiual quauitl*) which nourished children in the "Children's Paradise" (*Codex Vaticanus A*). 2, Mayauel, goddess of the agave plant, suckling a fish (*Codex Borgia*). 3, Agave plant as tree of life, with fish in the "mother pot" (*Codex Vaticanus B*). 4, Conventionalized Assyrian date tree of life. 5, Mayauel rising from agave plant (*Codex Vaticanus A*). 6, One of the four trees of life of the cardinal points (*Fejérváry Codex*). 7, Babylonian tree of life.

were deposited in caves, in the fissures of mountains, in stone-lined graves, or in wells and in the sea, so that they might reach the earth mother's land of bliss. In China and Japan, in Polynesia, Indonesia, and India, and as far westward as the British Isles, traces remain of the ancient conception of an Underworld paradise resembling that of Osiris in Egypt.

It may also be noted in passing that the myth about the separation of heaven and earth which was known to the Zuni Indians is found also in Polynesia, where Rangi is separated from Pappa, and in Ancient Egypt where Shu separates Nut from Seb.

Another form of the world goddess—the many-wombed one of the Zuni Indians—is the many-mouthed earth goddess of the Mexicans, who was sometimes depicted as a frog with a blood-stained mouth in every joint of her body. The mother goddess gave birth to mankind; after death she "devoured" the dead; she was also the devourer of sacrifices.

The habit of multiplying the organs of the deities was prevalent among the Hindus and other peoples of the Old World. It is usually regarded as an expression of "great powers in any given direction". At the same time, however, it had a history, as we shall find in dealing with the many-breasted mother goddess.

The Mexican mother goddess of this order was Mayauel. "They feign", writes Kingsborough,[1] quoting his authorities, "that Mayauel was a woman with four hundred breasts, and that the gods, on account of her fruitfulness, changed her into the maguey, which is the vine of that country (Mexico) from which they make wine. . . . They manufactured so many things from this plant called the maguey, and it is so very useful in that country, that

[1] *Mexican Antiquities*, Vol. V, pp. 179–80.

the devil took occasion to induce them to believe that it
was a god and to worship and offer sacrifices to it."

It is obvious that, in the first place, the many-breasted
goddess is a milk-provider who suckles her human offspring. Before, however, we consider her in that aspect,
it would be well to deal with the maguey plant with
which she was closely associated.

The maguey, or agave plant (*Agave americana*), is
a species of prickly cactus with "fleshy" stems and a
generous supply of milky juice. It is of slow growth.
The fable that it takes a hundred years to come to
maturity has given origin to its name of "the Century
Plant". In Mexico, where it has long been cultivated, it
is a deep green shrub with hard prickly or pointed leaves,
somewhat resembling those of the iris, grouped in a large
rosette. At the end of about eight years, a long stem
arises from the centre of the rosette, and is ultimately
crowned with a voluminous inflorescence. The agave
blossoms once only. After the fruit forms and ripens
and the seeds escape the whole plant dies down.

The agave is cultivated chiefly for its sap. As soon
as the Mexican perceives that it is beginning to throw
up the central stem he hollows out the central bole. Into
the cavity, which is big enough to hold a pail, the milky
juice of the plant flows freely for three or four months.
It has to be emptied once or twice daily. The juice is
carried away in skins, or poured into jars and barrels.
In a few days it ferments and acquires a strong taste and
very disagreeable odour.

The fermented juice is called "pulque". "It is the
people's chief beverage", writes an American traveller.[1]
"It tastes like sour and bad-smelling buttermilk, is white
like that, but thin. They crowd around the cars with it,

[1] *A Winter in Mexico*, by Gilbert Haven, New York, 1875, p. 81.

selling a pint measure for three cents. . . . It ferments fiercely, and the barrels are left uncorked and the pigs' (skin bags') noses unmuzzled to prevent explosion. You will see the natives sticking their noses into the hog's nose and drinking the milk of this swinish coco-nut, even as they are dumping it on the platform."

A very intoxicating liquor distilled from pulque is called *mexical* or *aguardiente de maguey*. A part of the plant is used medicinally and sweetmeats are made from the root, while the fibres of the maguey supply hemp and paper, and the prickles can be used for pins and nails.

"The abundance of the juice produced by a maguey of scarcely five feet in height", writes a compiler,[1] "is the more astonishing, as the plantations are in the most arid ground, frequently on rocks scarcely covered with earth. The plant is not affected either by drought, hail, or cold. The vinous beverage is said to resemble cyder; its odour is that of putrid meat; but even Europeans, when they have been able to conquer the aversion inspired by the fetid smell, prefer the pulque to every other liquor."

The name "pulque" has been derived from the language of the natives of Chile. In ancient Mexico the intoxicating plant juice was called "octli" and the agave plant itself the "metl".

According to Sahagun,[2] the goddess Mayauel was simply the discoverer of the agave plant. But all deities figure as the "discoverers" of the medicinal herbs, precious stones, elixirs, &c., which were supposed to contain their own "life substance", and to which they gave origin by weeping fertilizing tears or shedding their blood. As the goddess with four hundred breasts, mentioned in

[1] *The Modern Traveller* (London, 1825), Vol. I, p. 178, quoting Bullock and Humboldt.
[2] X, XXIX.

Codex Vaticanus A, Mayauel was undoubtedly in Mexico regarded as a personification of the agave plant.

"The goddess", writes Seler, "is everywhere figured seated before or on the agave plant, which the artists of the picture-writings always understand how to reproduce tolerably true to nature, with its stiff leaves curved slightly outwards, and furnished with spines at the tips and along the edges, and with its tall spike of bloom." Seler then proceeds to give further important details regarding the pictorial representations of the interesting many-breasted Mexican goddess:

"On sheet 31 of our manuscript above the root of the plant is further seen a snake, while in *Codex Laud* 9 (Kingsborough's notation) the plant rises above a turtle which rests on a dragon designed in the form of a coral snake. The goddess herself is here in *Codex Borgia* pictured with a white garment, but which is edged with a broad band painted in the colour of the green jewel (chalchiuitl), hence to a certain extent resembles that of the Water goddess. In her nose she wears a blue plate which tapers step-fashion and resembles *Xochiquetzal's yacapapalotl*. As with the Sun God, her flame-coloured hair is bound up with a jewelled chain which bears a conventional bird's head on the frontal side. The tuft of feathers also (*iuitemalli*) on the head of the goddess is like that worn by the Sun God on sheet 14 of *Codex Borgia*. Doubtless by this device it was intended to give expression to the 'fiery drink'. . . . On sheet 89 of our manuscript the goddess holds in one hand a bowl from which the flower-studded liquor foams out, in the other a dish full of stone knives, for pulque is the 'sharp' drink." (*Codex Vaticanus B*, p. 152.)

Sometimes the bulging pulque jug is shown pierced by an arrow with blood issuing from the "wound". Seler continues:

"A noteworthy peculiarity is shown by sheet 31 of our manuscript, where the heads of a little man and of a little woman are seen in the pulque protruding from the mouth of the jug. The face of the first is painted red, the colour of men; that of the woman has a yellow colour, and below the nose hangs the blue step-shaped nasal plate *yacapapalotl* of the goddess *Xochiquetzal*.[1] Obviously by this picture, as doubtless also by the *tlaitzcopiutli* figures decorating the pulque jug, wine and woman are brought into relation. Even now, for instance, amongst the Indians of Vera Paz, the marriage ceremony is officially concluded by the bridegroom handing the brandy-bottle to the bride."

A white animal was associated with the goddess of the agave plant. The head may be compared to that of a fox or coyote; the tail is long. On one of the sheets of *Codex Vaticanus B* (No. 31) this animal " holds in one hand a pulque bowl" and in the other a fan, or a bell-studded ring. Seler notes that the same animal is to be recognized in " the animal-headed priest, who, on the famous sheets 25 and 28 of the Dresden Maya manu-script, introduces the representative of the new year ".

It may be remarked here that our admiration for Seler's profound researches need not blind us to the fact that some of his conclusions are unconvincing. It is dif-ficult, for instance, to believe that the goddess of the agave plant was given a hair tuft of the same feathers as the sun god simply because pulque is a " fiery drink ", that a dish of stones knives was placed beside the bowl because pulque is " the sharp drink ", and that " wine and woman are brought into relation " by the figures " decor-ating " the pulque bowl. The feathers, knives, and figures had evidently a much more profound significance than Seler's comments would lead us to suppose. As much is indicated by the knife-pierced pot from which blood issues.

Mayauel, the goddess with four hundred breasts, appears, as has been stated, to be in the first place a milk-

---

[1] The love and flower goddess.

provider, a sustainer of life.   She recalls the four hundred
breasted Artemis of Ephesus, better known by her Roman
name of " Diana of the Ephesians . . . whom ", as Paul
knew well, " all Asia and the world worshippeth ".[1]   Like
other ancient deities Artemis had many forms.   She was
shown in association with various animals, including the
lion, the bear, the ram, the bull, the roe-deer, the stag, the
boar, the hare, &c., which were forms of herself.[2]   She
was essentially a fosterer of life, and she loathed the eagle
because it devoured " the pregnant hare " as Aeschylus
informs us.   Farnell notes that she was in one of her
forms a serpent goddess and a tree goddess.   A coin of
Myra " shows her in the midst of a cleft trunk from
which two serpents are starting.   Her trees include
myrtle and pine.[3]   Of special interest is the form of
Artemis " on a vase published by Gerhard, where she
stands in a rigid and hieratic pose, with her forearms held
out parallel from her body and a torch in each hand;
above her is a wild fig tree, from which a sort of game
bag containing a hare is hung as a votive offering ".[4]

It was evidently as the fig-tree goddess that Artemis
was depicted with many breasts.   Figs were in ancient
times referred to as " teats ".   Some hold that this name
was suggested by their shape, but Siret[5] has pointed out
that the true reason was because the green parts of the
fig tree, including the fruit, distil a white milk-like juice
in abundance.   " For that reason we call it lactescent.
The ancients said ' lactiferous ' or ' ruminal '.   They
believed, not without reason, that the vegetable milk filled
with regard to the young parts of the plant the same
service that animals do to their young."

---

[1] *The Acts of the Apostles*, xix.
[2] Farnell, *Cults of the Greek States*, Vol. II, p. 435.   [3] *Ibid.*, Vol. II, p. 523.
[4] *Ibid.*, Vol. II, pp. 523–4.
[5] *L'Anthropologie*, Tome XXX, pp. 235 *et seq.*

An interesting fact about the fig tree is that it never blossoms. The fruit is an undeveloped flower. Canon Tristram has reminded us in this connection that "the fruit of the fig . . . is an enlarged, succulent, hollow receptacle containing the imperfect flowers in the interior. Hence the flowers of the fig tree are not visible until the receptacle has been cut open."[1] As the fruits (teats) appear before the leaves, the tree was personified as a goddess with many breasts.

The prototype of Artemis and other fig-tree goddesses was the mother goddess Hathor of Egypt, whose tree (the "Tree of Life") was the sycamore fig. "The peculiarity of the sycamore", writes Dr. Inglis, "is this: the fruit all adheres to the stock of the tree, and not, as in the common fig tree, to the extremity of the branches".[2]

Hathor, the sycamore goddess, was connected with the sky and the sun; as a solar deity she was the "Eye of Ra", and here, perhaps, we should find the solar connection of the Mexican goddess Mayauel with the sun god whose feathers (rays) she wore in her hair. In her form of Nut, goddess of the sky, or in her cow form, Hathor was depicted with star-spangled body. Her milk, as stated, formed the "Milky Way", which was known as "Hera's Milk" to the Greeks and "Juno's Milk" to the Romans. The souls of the dead Pharaohs were suckled by the goddesses and fed on the milk and food of the sycamore fig tree of Life in the Egyptian paradise.[3]

The milk elixir from the sacred milk-yielding trees or plants was known in several ancient countries. It was supposed to be specially efficacious to children. In Mexico the agave plant's fluid appears to have been regarded as milk, as is indicated by the fact that Mayauel who personified it

---

[1] Quoted by Inglis, *Bible Illustrations from the New Hebrides* (Edinburgh, 1890), p. 81.
[2] *Ibid.*, p. 83.   [3] Breasted, *Religion and Thought in Ancient Egypt*, p. 137.

was, in one of her forms, a many-breasted woman. Mendieta tells us that the Mexicans had " a sort of baptism " and, " when the child was a few days old, an old woman was called in, who took the child out into the court of the house where it was born, and washed it a certain number of times with the wine of the country (pulque), and as many times again with water; then she put a name on it, and performed certain ceremonies with the umbilical cord ". Another ceremony took place at the end of every fourth year, when godparents were selected for those born during the preceding three years. Children were passed over a fire and their ears were bored. Then a ceremony was performed " to make them grow", and " they finished by giving the little things pulque in tiny cups, and for this the feast was called ' the Drunkenness of Children ' ".[1]

It is evident that these elaborate ceremonies had a history. We cannot, however, trace that history in America. Children were not given pulque simply because it intoxicated them. As an elixir for children pulque was, in the first place, regarded as milk from the goddess-plant — the milk of the goddess herself. This habit had origin in the Old World, and probably in Ancient Egypt, when the " milk " of the sycamore fig was an elixir. In Greece the non-intoxicating " milk " of the fig was given to newly born children. A similar custom appears to have obtained in Ancient Britain. The Highlanders of Scotland regarded the hazel as a " milk-tree "; the " milk " is the white juice of the green nut. A traditional recipe for a tonic for weakly children is " comb of honey and milk of the nut " (in Gaelic, *cìr na meala 'is bainne nan cnò*). The honey

---

[1] Bancroft, *The Native Races of the Pacific States of North America*, Vol. III, p. 376, note 27, quoting Sahagun, &c.

is of special importance, because in Gaelic the bee is one of the forms assumed by the soul. Farnell reminds us that the bee was one of the symbols of Artemis.[1]

In their "sober sacrifices", from which wine was excluded, the Greeks offered four libations. These were τὰ ὑδρόσπονδα, "libations of water", τὰ μελίσπονδα, "of honey", τὰ γαλαχτόσπονδα, "of milk", and τὰ ἐλαιόσπονδα, "of oil". These were sometimes mixed together.

The milk elixir was known in India, as has been shown. Soma (Amrita) resembled pulque. It was prepared from a plant. It was mixed with milk, and "in some cases honey was mixed with Soma". There are references in Aryo-Indian religious literature to its "pungent" flavour. "The effects of Soma in exhilarating and exciting the drinkers are often alluded to." There are "many references to sickness caused by it".[2] A Soma river (Su-soma) is mentioned in the Rig-veda.[3] "Madhu" (mead) sometimes "denotes either 'Soma' or 'milk', or less often 'honey'. . . . Taboos against the use of honey are recorded."[4]

Milk-yielding trees were the "grandchildren" of the cow mother. We find very definite evidence regarding the beliefs associated with these trees in the *Bhishma Parva* of the *Mahá-bhárata*, which throws light not only on the American custom of giving pulque to infants, but on the custom of depicting in the froth of pulque, as in sheet 31 of *Codex Vaticanus B*, "a little man and woman", or twin children. These children are either the first man and woman, or twin deities like those who have their origin in foam in the Zuni myth.

---

[1] *Cults of the Greek States*, Vol. II, p. 481.
[2] Macdonell and Keith, *Vedic Index*, Vol. II, pp. 474 *et seq.*
[3] *Ibid.*, p. 460. [4] *Ibid.*, pp. 123-4.

It is told in the *Mahá-bhárata*[1] that in the country of the northern Kurus "there are some trees that are called 'milk-yielding trees'. These always yield milk, and the six different kinds of food of the taste of Amrita (soma) itself. Those trees also yield cloths, and in their fruits are ornaments (for the use of man). . . . There twins (of opposite sexes) are born. . . . They drink the milk, sweet as Amrita, of those 'milk-yielding' trees. And the twins born there (of opposite sexes) grow up equally."

In India the intoxicating Amrita (soma) was obtained from a "milk-yielding" plant, and milk and nectar were regarded as being identical. The "fig milk" of Greece and the "nut milk" of Britain were not fermented before being given to children. When the custom first arose of giving infants the milk-like sap of trees, it was believed that the white fluid was identical with that which came from the breasts of the goddess who personified the tree. It was celestial milk, and like the milk of the cow mother Surabhi, the Hathor of India, "the essence of all the best things of the earth". The pre-Columbian Americans entertained and perpetuated the Old World ideas in this connection. In *Codex Vaticanus A* an illustration depicts a group of children getting milk from the branches of a tree. Here the tree is undoubtedly a form of the complex mother goddess, the Hathor of America. In an Aztec creation myth[2] the first parents of mankind are "pot born". Fragments of bone are placed in a pot, and the blood of the gods is sprinkled on them. A boy and girl emerge, and they are fed by the god Xolotl on the "milk" of the maguey. The Spaniards called the maguey a "thistle", and they translated the Aztec name

---

[1] *Bhishma Parva*, Roy's translation, pp. 24 *et seq.*
[2] Bancroft, *The Native Races*, Vol. III, p. 59 and note 17.

of the elixir as "the milk of the thistle" (*la leche de cardo*).

An interesting variant of the mother milk-tree myth is found in the Chinese account of the mythical islands associated with Fu-sang, one of the Far Eastern " Islands of the Blest". The island in question lay to the east of Fu-sang. It is told that the women there have hairy bodies. They enter a river in spring, and when they bathe become pregnant. Instead of breasts they have white locks at the back of their heads (or hairy organs at the nape of the neck) from which comes a liquor (milk) that nourishes children. Here we have the " tree women ", fertilized by water, whose hair (branches) yield milk as do the branches of milk-yielding trees.

The celestial milk of the mother goddess, who was depicted as a milk-yielding tree, an animal, or a many-breasted woman, was supposed, as has been stated, to nourish all life. It came down in rivers like the Nile, the Ganges,[1] or the Yellow River of China, which was supposed to flow from the Milky Way. Siret[2] reminds us that the ancient name of the Tiber was Rumon, a word derived from Ruma and Rumen, signifying milk and the teat that produces it. The water of the river had been assimilated with the terrestrial milk of the old Latin goddess Deva Rumina, the divine nurse to whom milk was offered instead of wine. On earth the goddess was represented by the ruminal, or milk-yielding fig tree, under which the shepherd found the twins Romulus and Remus, who were suckled by the she-wolf form of the mother deity, as the Cretan Zeus was suckled by

---

[1] The confluence of rivers is sacred in India. At the point of the confluence of the dark waters of the River Jumna with those of the Ganges, the waters of the latter " are so white from the diffusion of earthy particles that, according to the creed of the natives, the river flows with milk ". (H. H. Wilson, *Essays on Sanskrit Literature*, Vol. II, p. 361, note 358.)

[2] *L'Anthropologie*, Tome XXX, pp. 235 *et seq*.

the horned sheep of one cult and the sow of another, and the Chinese royal foundling was suckled by a tigress. The Haidas Red Indians of the north-west coast of America had a "bear-mother". She was a chief's daughter who married the king of bears, and bore him a chief who was half human, half bear.

In India, as we have seen, the milk of the goddess in cow form was mixed with the waters of the " Milky Sea " and was identified with foam. The same ancient doctrine is met with in Egypt, where the Nile god Hapi was sometimes depicted with female breasts from which milk issued forth. The vulture goddesses of Upper and Lower Egypt, who were the female counterparts of Hapi, suckled the souls of Pharaohs in Paradise.[1]

These traces of an ancient cult that believed in universal milk as the early nutrition of all forms of life are of undoubted importance in dealing with the more or less obscure survivals in pre-Columbian religion in America. The beliefs connected with the milk elixir had been fused with those connected with other elixirs before the custom arose of making children drunk with pulque. At first milk from a tree or a cult animal was given to the young in accordance with a very ancient conception of Nature, personified as a mother or wet-nurse. This fact was recognized by Plutarch[2] when discussing the problem as to why milk and not wine was offered to Bona Dea (Deva Rumina); he expresses the belief that, as the protectress of children, she "accepted no wine because it would be harmful to these small beings ".

As we find in the *Mahá-bhárata* myth of the Milky Ocean, however, milk and wine were assimilated after fermented liquors came into use. The vine became a

---

[1] Breasted, *Religion and Thought in Ancient Egypt*, p. 130. (All vultures were supposed to be females.)   [2] *Quest. Rom.*, c. 57.

rival Tree of Life to the fig tree. Other plants yielding
a fluid that was fermented like grape juice were likewise
regarded as sources of the elixir of life. In India, Amrita
(soma) was manufactured from the sap of some unidentified plant. This sap was regarded as the active principle in
all life. The Indian cow mother Surabhi sprang from the
saliva of the Creator when he was drinking Amrita. She
had her origin from Amrita, and her milk, when churned,
yielded Amrita, the wine called Vāruni, the gem containing her "life substance", &c.

It was long after the original conception of the All-
mother had become obscure, and the doctrines regarding
the milk elixir had been fused with those regarding intoxicating elixirs, that the myths and customs associated with
Mayauel and the agave plant were established in America.
The beliefs were localized in Mexico as they were elsewhere. It had been forgotten that the original elixir was
simply vegetable milk, and that an intoxicating liquor
should not be given to children or offered to the goddess
who protected children. The children were given the
juice of the agave plant because the custom had been
perpetuated of giving them vegetable "milk". If the
custom had had origin in America, we should be able to
trace its history in that country. It would be possible to
show that a people who domesticated the cow or the goat
or the sheep had a goddess who had a cow, goat, or sheep
form, and had been connected with a tree like the fig
whose fruits were called "teats" and was personified by
a human deity with four hundred teats. Instead, we find
the many-breasted Artemis of the Old World identified
with a cactus, which has no resemblance to a fig tree
except in so far as it yields a milky fluid.

It would be, further, possible to account for the
mother-pot symbol associated with Mayauel. That her

pulque jar is the symbolic pot there can be little doubt. It bleeds when the stone knife pierces it, and in its foam appear the twins who similarly spring from the foam of the ocean in the Zuni myth. The foam is the milk elixir and was drunk, because it was Amrita, by the Indian ascetics who were called "foam-drinkers". It was the food and drink of the gods, the Nāgas, and the souls of the dead.

Still further proof that the complex doctrines associated with milk-yielding plants and the mother pot did not originate in America is afforded by the traces that survive of the Old World churning myth. The Mexicans, who did not keep domesticated animals, knew nothing about the butter-churn. Yet we find that both they and the Zuni Indians had received and adopted the churning myth.

In Indian mythology the Milky Sea is churned so that Amrita, the goddess Lakshmi, the best of gems, and certain cult animals, may be brought into existence. This myth was evidently the original creation myth of the ancient folk who regarded milk as the source of all life. In India the myth survives in highly complex form. The churn pestle is Mount Meru on which the supreme god sits. It is placed on the back of a tortoise, an avatar of the blue Indo-Egyptian god Vishnu. A Nāga (serpent deity) is used as a churning rope. The gods grasp its head, and the Asuras (demons) its tail, and churn the Milky Ocean.

The Indian form of the myth reached Japan. In a Japanese illustration of it the mountain rests on a tortoise, and the supreme god sits on the summit, grasping in one of his hands a water vase similar to that of the Babylonian god Ea and that of the Egyptian Nile god Hapi. The sun rises from the churned

ocean.[1]   The Japanese Shinto myth of creation, as related
in the *Ko-ji-ki* and *Nihon-gi*, is likewise a churning myth.
Twin deities, Izanagi, the god, and Izanami, the goddess,
stand on " the floating bridge of heaven " and thrust into
the ocean beneath the " Jewel Spear of Heaven ".   With
this pestle they churn the primeval waters until they
curdle and form land.[2]

This complex churning myth reached America.   In
Codex Cortes (sheet 19 B) there is a grotesque but recog-
nizable Maya representation of the ocean churning.   The
tortoise is, however, on the summit of the mountain-
pestle instead of being beneath it, and the other form of
the serpent god appears above his avatar.   Round the
mountain-pestle is twisted a snake, called "a rope" by
Seler.   Two dark gods, evidently demoniac forms of
deities, like the Indian Asuras, hold one end of the snake-
rope while the other end is grasped by the elephant-
headed god.   To the rope is attached a symbol of the
sun (*Kin*).[3]

In the Zuni myth the world mother churns the ocean
with her hand.   But then Mount Meru was a form of
the goddess, while the milk of " Milky Ocean " was her
" life substance ".   The Zuni mother spits in her bowl;
her saliva was life substance.   Saliva, like milk, blood,
&c., was life-giving body moisture.

Like the mountain, the milk-yielding plant or tree
was a form of the goddess.   The agave plant of the
many-breasted Mexican goddess Mayauel was identified
with the mountain used to churn the ocean.   On sheet 31
of *Codex Vaticanus B* there is a snake " above the root of
the plant", and in *Codex Laud* 9 " the plant rises above

---

[1] See illustration in Jackson's *Shells as Evidence of the Migrations of Early Culture*,
p. 62.   [2] *Myths of China and Japan*, pp. 347–50.
[3] Seler, *Zeit. für Ethnol.*, 42, p. 48, fig. 724.

a turtle which rests on a dragon designed in the form of a coral snake ".[1]

The agave plant was also regarded by the Mexicans and other Nahua peoples as the Tree of Life, just as was the sycamore fig of the goddess Hathor in Egypt, and as were the vine, the date tree, and the pomegranate tree in Assyria. In *Codex Vaticanus B*[2] the agave is depicted in as highly conventionalized a form as were the Assyrian, Hindu, and other cosmic trees. The double spike of the bloom rises in the centre, and the massive stem (which is more like the trunk of a tree) is adorned with significant spiral symbols similar to those on the trunks of the Assyrian Trees of Life, while the blooms are treated in a manner which is markedly Assyrian. At the lower part of the plant, which has four conventionalized leaves, evidently representing the four cardinal points, the pulque-storing central bulb " forms ", as Seler puts it, " a kind of cave ". It is full of liquid. " From the roof of the cave hangs a kind of peg at which a fish is sucking." This " peg " is evidently a teat. Seler, however, sees in it only a tube which was really a symbol of a teat. " We know ", he writes, " that in the hole cut out of the heart of the agave plant is collected the clear sweet sap, which is drawn off by means of a suction tube (a longish gourd) and after fermentation yields the pulque." Seler over-looks the fact that the gourd was a form of the " mother pot ".

It is of importance to note that the so-called " cave " of the agave plant (as the " plant of life ") is formed by a reversed U symbol—one of the forms of the symbolic pots of the Old World mother goddess. The " cave " is evidently, like the Zuni world goddess's bowl, the " pot "

[1] Seler, *Codex Vaticanus B*, p. 152 (Berlin and London, 1902–3).
[2] Seler, *op. cit.*, p. 196, fig. 410.

POPOCATEPETL, "THE SMOKING MOUNTAIN", VIEWED FROM TLAMACAS

filled with the water of the primeval ocean—the " Milky Sea ". The fish is drinking Amrita milk—the milk elixir of life.

That Mayauel, as the life-sustaining goddess, provided milk not only for human beings and animals, but also for fish, is shown clearly in *Codex Borgia*[1]. "Whereas", says Seler, "the other goddesses, and even Mayauel of *Codex Fejérváry*, have a child at the breast, this Mayauel of *Codex Borgia* is suckling a fish."

It may seem absurd that a fish should be placed at the breast of a goddess in human form. But this absurdity has a history. The goddess Neith of Egypt, who is generally regarded as having been originally a Libyan deity, was in one of her forms depicted as a woman "with a crocodile sucking at each breast".[2] The crocodile was a form of the god Sebek who was called the "son of Neith" as far back as the Pyramid Age.[3] Neith, as the Great Mother, was a milk-providing deity and the crocodiles were her twins.

Artemis was like Mayauel, connected with the fish. She was a goddess of lakes, marshes, and streams, as well as of mountains, trees, and herbs. Farnell[4] draws attention to an interesting archaic representation of Artemis as a "fish goddess" on a strange vase found in Bœotia. On either side of her are snarling beasts, regarded as lions, and two water birds heraldically opposed like the lions. A bull's head appears below one of her extended arms. On the lower part of the goddess's gown is a fish with its head pointed upwards as in the "cave" of the agave plant of the American goddess Mayauel.

---

[1] See illustration reproduced in Seler's *Codex Vaticanus B*, fig. 409, p. 196.
[2] Budge, *Gods of the Egyptians*, Vol. I, p. 451; Lanzone, *Dizionario*, plate 175, No. 3.
[3] Budge, *op. cit.*, Vol. I, p. 32, Note 1.
[4] *Cults of the Greek States*, Vol. II, p. 522, and plate XXIXa.

Farnell, dealing with this connection between Artemis and the fish, refers to the half-fish, half-woman form of that goddess which Pausanias saw at Phigaleia.[1] Deities with fish terminations were depicted in Babylonian art. It is of special interest to find that the seafaring Kamschatdales had a goddess with fish termination[2]. India has a fish avatar of Vishnu, and the god was depicted issuing from the mouth of a fish. The Japanese have the latter form of the sea god, and also the Indian Nāgas in their half-human, half-reptile forms. In Polynesia the god of the Underworld had a human head and body "reclining in a great house in company with spirits of departed chiefs", while "the extremity of his body was said to stretch away into the sea, in the shape of an eel or serpent".[3]

The Kamschatdales and other Siberian tribes, who worshipped the half-fish form of the Far Eastern Artemis, manufactured for themselves intoxicating and stupefying drinks which had a religious value like the pulque of the Mexicans. An intoxicating fungus was eaten and also made into a drink in order to produce prophetic states of inspiration.[4]

According to Mexican tradition, the art of making pulque was first discovered on "the mountain called thereafter Popoconaltepetl, 'mountain of foam'". Sahagun tells that "all the principal old men and old women were invited, and before each guest were placed four cups of new wine". One of the guests drank a fifth cup and disgraced himself. He was forced by shame to flee with his followers to the region of Pànuco, and founded the

---

[1] *Cults of the Greek States*, Vol. II, p. 522.
[2] Rendel Harris, *The Ascent of Olympus*, p. 98.
[3] Turner, *Nineteen Years in Polynesia*, p. 237.
[4] Rendel Harris, *The Ascent of Olympus*, p. 100.

nation afterwards known as the Huastecs.[1] The four
cups were evidently dedicated to the four gods of the
cardinal points and the offence of the guest was no doubt
of religious significance. Unlawful pulque tipplers were
beaten to death in ancient Mexico.[2]

The agave plant (metl) was connected with the moon
(metztli) in which was a rabbit, and the moon was
enclosed in the same U symbol that enclosed the cave
of the agave plant with its fish. There were four
hundred pulque gods who were known as the " Four
Hundred Rabbits ".[3] They were harvest gods. Mayauel,
as the milk-provider, nourished the crops like the milk
goddess of the Old World. According to Sahagun, one
of the pulque gods was supposed to have " found the stalks
and roots of which pulque is made "—that is, he found,
according to Seler, " what was added to the pulque to
enhance its intoxicating narcotic strength ". These roots
were called oc-patli, " pulque physic ". The god who
discovered them was named Pàtecatl (" he from the land
of the [pulque] medicine ").[4] The U symbol is worn as
a nose ornament by pulque gods, and figures on pulque
vessels.

Pulque was drunk to celebrate the new harvest, and
other auspicious events. It not only inspired men to
prophesy but to perform deeds of valour; warriors drank
pulque, and pulque gods were sometimes depicted as war
gods. Pulque was also an elixir which promoted longevity
in this world and the next. A curious myth tells that
the pulque god Ometochtli was killed by the god Tezcatlipoca, " because if he did not die all persons drinking
pulque must die ". It is explained, however, that " the

---

[1] Bancroft, *The Native Races of the Pacific States of North America*, Vol. V, pp. 207–8.
[2] Seler, *Codex Vaticanus B*, p. 262.
[3] *Ibid.*, p. 152.   [4] *Ibid.*, p. 168.

death of Ometochtli was only like the sleep of one drunk, and that he afterwards recovered and again became fresh and well ".[1]

The connection of pulque and the pulque deities with death and life is indicated by sheet 31 of *Codex Vaticanus B*. A red man and a blue skeleton, each holding a vessel with protruding snakes' heads, are shown in front of a pulque vessel.[2] Here apparently the vessel is the pot of the mother goddess who provides the milk elixir in this world and the next.

Just as many ancient myths and practices can be traced in ancient Mexican religion, so do we find survivals in Christianized Mexico. Brinton in his *Nagualism* (Philadelphia, 1894) quotes Father Vetancurt's statement regarding the Mexican custom of circulating fires and throwing new pulque into the flames. In ancient Mexico pulque (octli) was always offered to the god of fire, as was soma in India. "Let us pour forth soma to Jatavedas (fire)", says a Vedic hymn (Muir's *Sanskrit Texts*, Vol. IV, p. 499).

Another survival is referred to by Gilbert Haven in his *A Winter in Mexico* (1875, p. 136); he tells that the Mexicans associate with the maguey a white rat, a white worm, and a brown worm, which they eat. These are forms of the dragon referred to on p. 180. In China and Japan the dragon had white rat and worm forms, as De Visser has shown.

[1] Seler, *op. cit.*, p. 167.   [2] Seler, *ibid.*, p. 153.

CHAPTER XII

The Jewel-Water and Mugwort Goddess

A Virgin-mother Goddess—Her Connection with Water and Precious Stones—A Lunar and Sky Deity—Goddess of Birth—Her Herb Medicines for Women and Children—Remover of Original Sin—Priests were Celibates—Names of Goddess—Her Idols and Symbols—The Mother-pot—The Mugwort Mountain—Links with Artemis as Herb, Mountain, and Water Deity—Mugwort Beliefs in Greece, Siberia, China, and Japan—Old and New World Symbolism of Shells, Jade, and Herbs—"Jewel Water" as Life Blood—Green Stones as Funerary Amulets—Goddesses in Old and New World Deluge Legends—The American "Lady of the Lake"—Links with Syrian Goddess—American Goddess of Marriage—Baptism Ceremonies—Lustration by Fire—The Butterfly connected with Fire in Scotland and Mexico—The Butterfly Soul in Old and New Worlds.

AMONG the American goddesses, Chalchiuhtlicue,[1] "she whose gown consists of green jewels" (*chalchiuitl*), is of outstanding interest. She is a virgin-mother, who is sometimes depicted suckling a child. In this and certain other respects she links with Mayauel, as both do with Artemis and that great prototype of so many goddesses, the Egyptian Hathor. Mayauel, however, as has been shown, is fundamentally the milk-provider; Chalchiuhtlicue is more intimately connected with water and marsh plants, and especially with the green jewel containing "life substance"—the "jewel water" ("life blood") of the Mexican texts, and, indeed, with all precious stones worn as talismans. As a water goddess she is a "Lady of the Lake", a goddess of streams and of the sea, and as such she was

---

[1] Pronounced Chal'chi-oot'-lick-way.

adored by water-sellers, fishermen, and seafarers in general; she is a weather controller who can raise tempests and still the storms.   Her snake form and frog form emphasize her connection with water; like her brothers, the Tlaloque, and her spouse, the god Tlaloc, she sends rain to give sustenance to crops.   Like Artemis she is connected with high mountains as well as with lakes, marshes, and streams; and like other water goddesses she is connected with the waters "above the firmament", and is therefore a sky goddess.   In the latter connection she is a lunar deity and the mother of the stars of the northern hemisphere (*Centzon Mimixcoa*).   Her cardinal point is the west, as it is that of the mother goddess of China.   The Chinese god of the west is the tiger, and Chalchiuhtlicue is associated with the jaguar (the American tiger).

As a mother goddess she presides at birth, and prayers are offered to her to assist birth.   Like Artemis she provides herb medicines, and especially those required by women and young children.   Children are baptized with water to secure protection from her, and she protects the dead on whom holy water is sprinkled.   As a compassionate and beneficent goddess she washes away sin, including original sin, "the filth" an infant inherits from its parents. As a "culture deity" she gives the shield and the bow with arrows to male children, and the spindle, distaff, and weaving implements to female children.   Her priests, like those of the great mother goddess of Western Asia, are celibates, and greatly given to fasting and penance and solemn meditation, and they enter her temples barefooted and in silence, clad in long, sombre-coloured robes. Like Mayauel, the Zuni mother goddess, and other world goddesses in the New and Old Worlds, she is connected with the symbolic pot—the ancient "water pot" whence all life was supposed to emerge at the beginning.

The attributes of this complex goddess are revealed by her names, her idol-forms, and the pictures of her in the Codices. As Apoçonallotl she is "foam of water", a name of special significance, seeing that foam was connected with milk and, as in the Zuni myth, with saliva; as Acuecueyotl she is "water-making-waves"; as Ahuic she is "motion of water" (the swelling and fluctuation of water); as Xixiquipilihui she is "rising-and-falling-of-waves" (the ebb and flow of tides, &c.); as Atlacamani she is "sea-storm", and as Aiauh she is "mist" (and also apparently "spray"). All these names connect her with the "water-pot" myth. Life had origin when the water in the "pot" began to move and foam and rise, producing spray and mist and rain-dropping clouds. The goddess controls the pot-water in all its manifestations.

Among the Tlascaltecs our "jewel-water" goddess was known as Matlalcueje ("clothed in a green robe"), and her mountain is the highest in Tlascala; it attracts the stormy clouds that "generally", as has been recalled by various writers, "burst over the city of Puebla". On the summit of this mountain the goddess was in Pagan times worshipped and sacrificed to, as was the Cretan mountain-goddess who, as Sir Arthur Evans has shown, had an intimate connection with the sea, being the Minoan Aphrodite, a dove-and-serpent goddess.

The Aztecs of Mexico generally depicted Chalchiuht-licue as a woman with a blue forehead and the rest of her face yellow. Turquoise ear-rings dangle from her ears. She had therefore a solar connection, as had the Egyptian Hathor, who was likewise connected with turquoise, for ear ornaments are solar symbols. On her head is a blue cap with plumes of green feathers. Her clothing consists of a blouse and a blue skirt fringed with marine shells—another link with Hathor. She wears white sandals. In her left hand she grasps a shield and a white water-lily, and in her right hand a vessel shaped like a cross, evidently a symbol of the four cardinal points.

In *Codex Borgia* (fig. 292) she wears a helmet mask formed by a snake's throat, the face being painted yellow, "the colour of women", says Seler,[1] "but with two short broad bands of a deep black colour on the lower edge of the cheek, which are also met with on Mexican stone effigies of this goddess, indicated by sharply rectangular curvings."

These face lines are of special interest; no doubt they had a very special significance. It may be that they had some such meaning as had similar symbols, interpreted as the written character *wang* ("king") on the forehead of jade representations of the Chinese tiger god of the west, and on shields, on soldiers' buttons, and on amulets. Laufer shows that the simple stroke-symbols appear on "a strongly conventionalized figure of the tiger, with an arrangement of spiral ornaments on the body such as is met with also on other jade pieces connected with the symbolism of the quarters".[2]   As Chalchiuhtlicue was a jade or jadeite deity, it would not be surprising if her symbols are found to have a similar significance to those connected with jade or jadeite in the Old World.

In the *Codex Borgia*, Chalchiuhtlicue wears the well-known nose U symbol, as also do the pulque deities. This symbol is widely distributed in the Old World, and is associated with the mother goddess and with the four quarters.   It appears to be connected with the pot of the Great Mother ; sometimes it is shown with serpent-heads at either end or with the "stepped" ornament—a world-symbol connected with Isis and Osiris ; in Egypt women's wigs were given the U shape, with spiral termina-

[1] *Codex Vaticanus B*, p. 99.   [2] Laufer, *Jade*, pp. 176-177.

STONE FIGURE OF THE WATER GODDESS, CHALCHIUHTLICUE
Front and back views

(British Museum)

THE LIFE-GIVERS

1, Male form of goddess Chalchiuhtlicue (Altcanals), a blue god with yellow hair or wig, and purple face with Tlaloc eye, teeth, and blue serpent nose and lips, surrounded by green marsh plants with red stalks. There are shells and jewels in blue water below red roots (*Codex Vaticanus A*). **2,** Chalchiuhtlicue suckling child. In front of her is the Plant of Life (the Babylonian *nig-gil-ma*) growing up from jewelled pot with blood and heart symbols (*Codex Fejérváry-Mayer*). **3,** Chalchiuhtlicue as fish goddess in water descending to first man and woman, survivors of a deluge (*Codex Vaticanus A*).

tions enclosing solar symbols; the boat of the sun god is sometimes depicted as a U with a dot inside it. The mother goddess was the boat, and the boat was, apparently, her womb—"the house of Horus", which is what Hathor's name happens to signify. As the ear-ring was a solar symbol, the nose ornament was evidently connected with the "breath of life" as well as with "the moisture of life".

An interesting illustration in *Codex Borgia* (fig. 539) connects Chalchiuhtlicue with the symbolic pot and the pot-twins. Tlaloc is the central figure. A stream of water issuing from his body falls into a green vessel—a water pot—in which are seated two images of Chalchiuhtlicue, one painted green and the other painted blue, with shell discs in their hair.[1]

One of the most pleasing of all the representations of the goddess is a stone figure in the British Museum, which shows her on her knees, apparently in a religious pose, with lips apart as if repeating a formula and an earnest expression on her frank, maidenly face.

The goddess's connection with marsh plants, including grasses, reeds, the white water lily, and especially the mugwort or wormwood (*Artemisia*), is of far-reaching importance. In *Codex Borgia* she is shown in association with a bunch of dried herbs, an indication that she was in the "herbal profession", as Dr. Rendel Harris puts it in another connection. Seler suggests that she is a provider of "healing draughts of physic". Her mountain near Mexico was called Yauhqueme, which signifies "covered with mugwort". She dwelt on that mountain. In like manner Artemis dwelt on Mount Taygetus, and her herb *Artemisia* grew there. "The presence of Artemis in the mountain", writes Dr. Rendel Harris, is "due to the plant, and Artemis is the plant", one of the names of

---

[1] *Codex Vaticanus B*, p. 284.

which is "taygetes". This name "can only refer to the mountain in Laconia (Mt. Taygetus), which is, more than any other district, sacred to Artemis".[1]

Dr. Rendel Harris goes on to show that "the plant (*Artemisia*) is Artemis and Artemis is the plant. Artemis is a woman's goddess and a maid's goddess, because she was a woman's medicine and a maid's medicine. If the medicine is good at child-birth, then the witch-doctress who uses it becomes the priestess of a goddess, and the plant is projected into a deity."

Artemis, like Chalchiuhtlicue, assisted at birth and in the rearing of children; her herb was a child's medicine as well as a woman's medicine. It protected people magically, and was carried by travellers, and was hung over doors to keep houses safe from attacks by demons. The expression "Artemis of the Harbour" connects the goddess with seafarers; like Chalchiuhtlicue she sent winds, and her herb was supposed to protect mariners against tempests.

Other links between the American and Greek goddesses are brought out in the following passages from Dr. Rendel Harris's book :[2]

"The herbalists tell us to look for the plant by runnels and ditches, and some add (perhaps with Mt. Taygetus in mind) in stony places. We must try and find what the earliest of them say as to the habitat of the plant. If they mention marshes or lakes, then *Artemis Limnæa* is only another name for the Artemisia, or for some other plant in her herb garden.

"It is agreed on all hands that Artemis, in her earliest forms, is a goddess of streams and marshes; sometimes she is called the River Artemis, or Artemis Potamia, and sometimes she is named after swamps generally as Limnæa, the Lady of the Lake (Miss Lake), or Heleia, the marsh maiden (Miss Marsh), or from some particular marsh as Stymphalos, or special river as the Alpheios.

[1] *The Ascent of Olympus*, p. 75.   [2] *Ibid.*, pp. 85-86.

It seems to me probable that this is to be explained by the existence of some river or marsh plant which has passed into the medical use of the early Greek physicians."

Dr. Harris tells that the goddess was also given names after the diseases cured by her herbs.   There are traces of an "Artemis Podagra, the herb that cures gout, and Artemis Chelytis, which seems to be a cough mixture". The mugwort gout cure was famous enough to be imported into China.   Professor Giles writes in this connection to Dr. Harris:

"There is quite a literature about *Artemisia vulgaris*, L., which has been used in China from time immemorial for cauterizing as a counter-irritant, especially in cases of gout.   Other species of Artemisia are also found in China."[1]

As has been indicated, the mugwort cure and the goddess associated with the plant reached Siberia, and were acquired by the seafaring Kamschatkans, who had a goddess with fish termination and a herm-god.   "The discovery of the primitive sanctity of ivy and mugwort and mistletoe (in North-eastern Asia) makes", says Harris, "a strong link between the early Greek and other peoples both East and West, and it is probable that we shall find many other contacts between peoples that, so far as geography and culture go, are altogether remote." [2]

An immortal lady, known in Chinese lore as Ho Sien Ku and in Japanese as Kasenko, is said to have fed on mother-of-pearl, which made her move swiftly as a bird. She is usually depicted by Japanese artists "as a young woman clothed in mugwort, holding a lotus stem and flower and talking to a phœnix", or "depicted carrying a basket of loquat fruits which she gathered for her sick mother".[3]

---

[1] *The Ascent of Olympus*, pp. 85-87, and p. 86, Note 1.
[2] *Ibid.*, pp. 99-100.   [3] Joly, *Legend in Japanese Art*, p. 163.

Here we have the mugwort connected with pearl-shell and the lotus. This lotus is a cult symbol, just as the white water-lily is a cult symbol in America, and is associated with Chalchiuhtlicue. The pearl-shell, like the mugwort, ensures longevity. Both are depositories of " life substance ". Chalchiuhtlicue, as has been shown, is associated with shells; she wears them in her hair and on the fringes of her skirt. She is also the goddess of precious stones, and especially of jadeite. In China the symbolism of shells is identical with that of jade or jadeite. The shells, jade, jadeite, &c., the mugwort, the " fungus of immortality ", &c., cure diseases, prolong life in this world and in the next, assist birth, and so on. In short, the symbolism of the American variety of mugwort (*Artemisia*), jadeite, and shells, is identical to that of the Chinese. Is it possible that the complex beliefs involved were of independent origin in the New and Old Worlds? There is nothing " natural " in the idea that shells, herbs, and minerals contain " life substance " which cure disease, ease pain, and prolong life, or in the arbitrary association of herbs with jadeite and shells. As we can trace the history of the complexes in the Old World and cannot do so in the New World, the only reasonable conclusion that can be drawn is that the hotch-potch of quackery associated with Chalchiuhtlicue was imported into China and into America by a people who have left no written records of their activities. The modern explorer who, when cutting his way through a trackless African forest, picks up a box of pills manufactured in his native land, does not assume that the natives have invented them; he never doubts that the pills were either dropped by a white man who has preceded him or by natives who obtained them from a white man. Just as the pills and the belief in their virtues were trans-

ported from a distant area of origin, so, apparently, were
the medicines of the American goddess, Chalchiuhtlicue,
carried across the Pacific.

The association of this American deity with jadeite
was apparently in no way accidental. There is nothing
about a green mineral or a green stone to suggest that
it can impart vitality to human beings. In America it
was connected with life-giving water and with life blood.
In *Codex Borgia* (fig. 19)[1] is a picture of a priest gouging
out his eye, "that is", says Seler, "sacrificing himself,
drawing blood from incisions in his own body to bring
it as an offering to the gods".[2] Another picture (fig.
392, *Codex Vaticanus B*) shows a young warrior offering
blood by piercing one of his ears, and carrying in his
right hand a winged-disc symbol marked with the cross
of the four quarters and a sea shell. In the picture of
the priest is found "the hieroglyph *chalchiuitl* ('green
jewel'), and the hieroglyph *atl* ('water'), which", says
Seler, "combined yield *chalchiuhatl* ('jewel water'). . . .
This 'jewel water' is meant to denote blood", which is
"the precious water of mortification".[3]

The "jewel water" is not only "the blood drawn
from the penitent", but "the precious moisture that
drops from heaven". It is life-giving water—water
impregnated with "life substance"; the blood offered
by the priest or warrior "was intended to bring down
the rain on the fields".[4]

Those who have urged the view that the green stone
symbolized green water, and that the green stone also
symbolized the green corn or young grass, find their

---

[1] Reproduced in *Codex Vaticanus B*, p. 184, fig. 390.

[2] The eye-offering was of Egyptian origin. Horus offered one of his eyes to Osiris
so that he might become an immortal. The "little man in the eye" was the soul.

[3] *Codex Vaticanus B*, p. 184.   [4] *Ibid.*, p. 75.

theory put to a severe test by the discovery that Crô-Magnon man, when in the Aurignacian stage of culture, made use of green stone amulets. Small green pebbles are found between the teeth of some of the Crô-Magnon skeletons in the Grimaldi caves near Mentone. Crô-Magnon man did not practise agriculture; he was a hunter. The Mexicans and other pre-Columbian Americans were in the habit of placing a *chalchiuitl* (a green stone amulet) "between the lips of the deceased".[1] As Brinton puts it, "they interred with the bones of the dead a small green stone which was called 'the principle of life'".[2] Lip ornaments were connected with the heart, as ear ornaments were with the eye and soul ("the little man in the eye"). In one of the Mexican creation myths the gods sacrificed themselves to the sun so as to give it power to rise :

"So they died like gods; and each left to the sad and wondering men who were his servants his garments for a memorial. And the servants made up, each party, a bundle of the raiment that had been left to them, binding it about a stick into which they had bedded *a small green stone* to serve as a heart. These bundles were called *tlaquimilloli*, and each bore the name of that god whose memorial it was; and these things were more reverenced than the ordinary gods of stone and wood of the country. Fray Andres de Olmos found one of these relics in Tlalmanalco, wrapped up in many cloths, and half rotten with being kept hid so long."[3]

The Quiches in like manner worshipped a great bundle left by one of their divine ancestors, and burned incense before it. They called it "the Majesty Enveloped". A sacred "bundle" was given up to the Spanish Christians by a Tlascaltec some time after the conquest. It was

[1] Bancroft, *The Native Races*, Vol. III, p. 454.
[2] *The Myths of the New World*, p. 294.
[3] Bancroft, *op. cit.*, Vol. III, pp. 61-2.

supposed to contain the remains of Camaxtli, the chief god of Tlascala.[1]

The habit of wrapping sacred stones in cloth was known in the Scottish Highlands. Green stones were worn as amulets by the Hebrideans.[2]

The Crô-Magnon and Mexican custom of placing a green stone in the mouth of the dead was known in China. The Chinese placed jade amulets in the mouth to preserve the body from decay and stimulate the soul to ascend to the celestial regions. These amulets were shaped to imitate the cicada. The cicada, creeping out of the earth, changes its form, spreads its wings and soars into the air.[3]

The Ancient Egyptians regarded the green scarab, which was interred with the dead, as a life prolonger; it was addressed, "My heart, my mother—my heart whereby I came into being".[4]

In China gold, pearls, or cowries might be substituted for jade as a mouth amulet. "If", runs a Chinese text, "there is gold and jade in the nine apertures of the corpse it will preserve the body from putrefaction."[5] Another text states: "On stuffing the mouth of the Son of Heaven (the Emperor) with rice they put jade therein; in the case of a feudal lord they introduce pearls; in that of a great officer, and so downwards, as also in that of ordinary officials, cowries are used." De Groot comments in this connection, "The same reasons why gold and jade were used for stuffing the mouth of the dead hold good for the use of pearls", and he notes that pearls were regarded as "depositories of *yang* matter"; that medical works

---

[1] Bancroft, *op. cit.*, Vol. III, p. 54 and Note 9, for authorities.

[2] Dalzell, *The Darker Superstitions*, p. 140.

[3] Laufer, *Jade*, pp. 299-301, and my *Myths of China and Japan*, Index, under *Jade* and *Cicada*. [4] Budge, *Gods of the Egyptians*, Vol. I, p. 358.

[5] Laufer, *Jade*, p. 299.

declare "they can further and facilitate the procreation of children", and that they are useful "for recalling to life those who have expired or are at the point of dying".[1]

There is much evidence in the Old World to show that the early searchers for the elixir of life connected precious stones with herbs; they sought for shells, and when they found pearl-yielding shells they regarded the pearl as the very "life of life"; the symbolism of shells and pearls was imparted to green stones, to green malachite, to gold and other metals, to jade, to amber, to coral, to jet, in different parts of the ancient world. Jade was found in Chinese Turkestan and imported into Mesopotamia during the Sumerian period. It was imported into Europe by the carriers of bronze. Laufer has emphasized in this connection (Chapter II) that there must have been a psychological motive for the search for jade, and he refuses to believe that the early Europeans "incidentally and spontaneously embarked on the laborious task of quarrying and working jade". He finds "no vestige of originality in the pre-historic cultures of Europe". The same can be said of the cultures of pre-Columbian America. There must have been a psychological motive for the search for the jadeite and the mugwort with which Chalchiuhtlicue was so intimately associated.

The more closely the character of this Mexican goddess is investigated, the more abundant become the links between her and certain Old World deities. In *Codex Borgia* (sheet 57) she is shown in association with the god Tlaloc. Between the pair is a *chalchiuitl* jewel, shaped like a two-handed pitcher, from which a naked human being emerges. This pitcher is evidently a form of the symbolic mother-pot. Both deities have strings of jewels coloured green, blue, and red. In the Far East red

---

[1] De Groot, *The Religious System of China*, Book I, pp. 274 *et seq.*

pearls were supposed to be depositories of life substance—the fire and blood of life.

There is in *Codex Laud* a picture of a man wearing a jewel (*chalchiuitl*) over his heart and presenting a bird as an offering to his goddess. The goddess offers him a pot and a *cozcatl* (chain of beads). Seler ascribes to this scene the meaning of sexual intercourse.[1] Other illustrations show chains of beads held in the mouths of opposed deities, such as the god and goddess of love, in the form of quetzal birds (*Codex Laud*, 36, and *Codex Borgia*, 58), the descent of a jewel between a male and female as the descent of a child (*Codex Laud*, 35), and a god drawing a chain of jewels from between the breasts of a goddess, symbolizing the birth of a child or children (*Codex Laud*, 36). Seler, discussing these and other pictures, writes: "The jewel (*chalchiuitl*), the neck ornament, the chain of beads (*cozcatl*), the feather adornment (*quetzalli*), all this is still the child—*nopilhtze, nocuzque, noquetzale*, 'my child, my chain of beads, my feather ornament'".[2] The bird, as a symbol of fecundity, figures in *Mahá-bhárata* myths.

In Japanese mythology (*Kojiki* and *Nihongi*) we have the god Susa-no-wo and the goddess Amaterásu producing children by standing on either side of the "celestial river" (the "Milky Way") and crunching jewels; they blow away the fragments and these take human form.[3] The Mexican love and flower god (*Xochipilli*), who in *Codex Laud* and *Codex Borgia* acts a part as a gem cruncher similar to that of Susa-no-wo, is also like that god connected with the lower regions as well as with the heavens.

Chalchiuhtlicue was, like the goddess Ishtar, connected with the deluge. According to the interpreter of *Codex*

[1] *Codex Vaticanus B*, p. 225, fig. 465.   [2] Seler, *Codex Vaticanus B*, pp. 233-235.
[3] See my *Myths of China and Japan*, under *Susa-no-wo* in Index.

Telleriano-Remensis she saved herself, and was the woman who survived the deluge. It is also shown that she was represented holding in one hand a spinning-wheel and in the other a weaving implement. In *Codex Vaticanus* she stands on foaming water on which a burnt-offering of firewood and rubber[1] is seen floating. She grasps a bone dagger and an agave spike used for ceremonial blood-shedding.

The mythical Chinese Empress, Nu Kwa, similarly figures as the "Royal Lady of the West", taking the place of Ishtar, the friend of mankind, who, in the Babylonian deluge myth, lifted up her "great jewels" and cried:

"What gods these are! By the jewels of *lapis lazuli* which are upon my neck, I will not forget! . . .
Let the gods come to the offering."

She was wroth because the gods had drowned her people. The "offering" was in seven vessels, under which were "reed and cedar wood and incense".[2]

The Chinese Nu Kwa[3] waged war against the giants and demons who caused the deluge; she stemmed the rising waters by means of charred reeds. Thereafter she created dragons and set the world in order. She also created jade for the benefit of mankind. In Japan Nu Kwa is known as Jokwa.

The burnt offering on foaming water associated with the American Chalchiuhtlicue appears to be similar to the offering of burnt reeds associated with the Chinese Nu Kwa.

According to Boturini,[4] Chalchiuhtlicue—"the goddess

---

[1] The rubber tree being a "milk-yielding tree", rubber on water symbolizes milk in its foam form.   [2] King, *Babylonian Religion*, p. 136.
[3] See my *Myths of China and Japan*, Chapter X.
[4] Quoted by Bancroft, *op. cit.*, Vol. III, pp. 367-8.

of the skirt of precious stones"—was "symbolized by certain reeds that grow in moist places". She was often represented "with large pools at her feet". The "precious stones" included green quartz, jade or jadeite, and the stone known as *madre de Esmeralda*. The city of Tlaxcalla was often called *Chalchuihapan*, from a "beautiful fountain of water near it" which appears to have been associated with the goddess. Squier in *Palacio, Carta,* refers to an idol of the goddess in her character as the "Lady of the Lake"—the lake being near the village of Coatan :

"Its water is bad; it is deep, and full of caymans. In its middle there are two small islands. The Indians regard the lake as an oracle of much authority. . . . I learned that certain negroes and mulattos of an adjacent estate had been there (on the islands), and had found a great idol of stone, in the form of a woman, and some objects which had been offered in sacrifice. Near by were found some stones called *chalchibites*."[1]

Lucian's Syrian goddess was connected with a sacred lake which was situated to the west of the temple. "In the midst of the lake", he says, "stands an altar of stone. . . . It is always decked with ribbons, and spices are therein, and many every day swim in the lake with crowns on their heads performing their acts of adoration." Sacred fish were reared and kept in this lake. The deity was in one of her aspects a "fish goddess".[2] Chalchiuht-licue was also a "fish goddess".

The spinning and weaving implements favoured by Chalchiuhtlicue are of special interest. Neith, the Egyptian-Libyan goddess, has a shuttle for one of her symbols. Lucian tells of the Syrian goddess who "in one of her

[1] Quoted by Bancroft, *op. cit.,* Vol. III, p. 368, Note 20.
[2] Lucian, *De Dea Syria,* chapters 45-47 ; translation, *The Syrian Goddess,* by H. A Strong, with Notes by J. Garstang, London, 1913, pp. 81-82.

hands holds a sceptre and in the other a distaff".[1]   He calls her Hera, but says she has "something of the attributes of Athene, Aphrodite, Silene, Rhea, Artemis, Nemesis, and the Fates.   Gems of great price adorn her, some white, some sea-green, others wine-dark, others flashing like fire".   Lucian would have been interested in the American goddess of water and jewels and curative herbs, and he would have connected her with as many goddesses as he connected the Syrian Hera, for she was similarly a highly complex deity with a long pedigree.

As the goddess of marriage, Chalchiuhtlicue was adored by great ladies who "were accustomed", according to Boturini, "to dedicate to her their nuptials".   As has been stated, she presided at birth like Artemis, Astarte of Phœnicia, and Mylitta, whose name is said to be derived from *mu'allidatu* ("The Giver of Birth" or "The Helper of Birth").   Various forms of the birth deity are found throughout Asia.[2]

As a goddess of young children, Chalchiuhtlicue was the deity presiding over baptism.   The midwife who performed the ceremony appealed to the goddess at length, and the following is an extract from the prayer:

"Purge it (the infant) from the filthiness it inherits from its father and its mother, all spot and defilement let the water carry away and undo.   See good, O our lady, to cleanse and purify its heart and life that it may lead a quiet and peaceable life in this world; for indeed we leave this creature in thine hands, who art mother and lady of the gods, and alone worthy of the gift of cleansing that thou hast held from before the beginning of the world."

During the ceremony the midwife "took water and blew her breath upon it,[3] and gave to taste of it to the babe,

---

[1] *De Dea Syria*, chapter 32.
[2] Herodotus (I, 131, 199).   *The Syrian Goddess*, p. 16, note 48.
[3] Here we meet with the wind-and-water idea, as in the Chinese *fung-shui* doctrine.

and touched the babe with it on the breast and on the top of the head". Then she dipped the child in the water.[1]

A ceremony of like character was until recently performed by midwives in the Scottish Highlands. The writer was once an eye-witness of it. At the second Mexican ceremony of baptism or lustration "the midwife", according to Bancroft, "gave the child to taste of the water". The Highland midwife dipped her finger in the water in which the babe was first washed and touched the babe's lips and forehead. When the Mexican midwife touched the babe's lips she said, "Take this; by this thou hast to live on the earth, to grow and to flourish; through this we get all things that support existence on the earth; receive it". Then she poured water on the child's head, saying:

"Take this water of the Lord of the World, which is thy life, invigorating, refreshing, washing and cleansing. I pray that this celestial water, blue and light blue, may enter into thy body and there live. . . . Into thine hand, O goddess of water, are all mankind put, because thou are our mother Chalchiuhtlicue."[2]

Some writers tell that this baptism was "supplemented by passing the child through fire". Bancroft shows, however, that this ceremony took place on "the last night of every fourth year, before the five unlucky days". It was then that parents chose godparents for their children; they "passed the children over, or near to, or about the flame of a prepared fire". They also bored the children's ears. . . . "They clasped the children by the temples and lifted them up 'to make them grow'; wherefore they called the feast *izcalli* (growing)."[3] Reference has already

---

[1] Bancroft, *op. cit.*, Vol. III, pp. 372-3.
[2] Bancroft, *op. cit.*, Vol. III, pp. 370 *et seq.*
[3] A similar custom obtained in the Scottish Highlands.

been made to this feast, at which, as stated, the children were given pulque to drink.

Fire also played its part in the water-baptism, a "great torch of candlewood" being kept burning. The candle-burning was known in ancient Britain. Women were, after birth, "unclean" until they attended church, and the Manx term for this church ceremony was *lostey-chainley* ("candle-burning"). Candles were kept burning in the room in which a birth took place, in various parts of Britain. A similar custom is known among the Albanians and in the Cyclades.[1] The ancient Greeks had "a ritual at which the new-born child was solemnly carried round the hearth-fire and named in the presence of the kinsmen".[2] Children were "passed through the fire" in Scotland to remove the influence of "evil eye". The late Rev. Dr. A. Stewart, Nether Lochaber, has described the ceremony. Four women performed it, while a fifth, the mother, looked on. An iron hoop was used. Round it a rope of straw had been twisted and set on fire. The child was passed and re-passed eighteen times through the hoop, being eighteen months old.[3] This rite was practised in the south-west Lowlands within living memory. Biblical references to the Pagan custom of passing children "through the fire" indicate how widespread was the custom in ancient times. King Manasseh, who worshipped Baal and "made a grove" and "worshipped all the host of heaven", "made his son pass through the fire".[4] The Phœnicians passed their children through the fire, and the custom, which was known in India, apparently reached America, with much else besides.

---

[1] Frazer, *On Certain Burial Customs*, p. 85, note.

[2] *Anthropological Essays* (presented to E. B. Tylor), Oxford 1907, p. 82.

[3] *Proceedings of the Society of Antiquaries of Scotland*, March 10, 1890.

[4] *2 Kings*, xxi, verses 3-6. See also *Deuteronomy*, xviii, verse 10, &c.

It may not be possible to trace, step by step, the migration of a set of complex beliefs from the area of origin to outlying parts, but when we find the same complexes preserved in far-separated countries which were never in touch with one another, and find also here and there over the wide intervening area scattered traces of their existence at one time or other, only one conclusion can be drawn, and that is that the complexes were distributed by ancient carriers of culture. The fire customs referred to above may be taken as an instance. That these could not have been of spontaneous and independent origin both in the Old and New Worlds is shown clearly by the existence of similar fire-and-butterfly beliefs in Mexico and Scotland. The Mexicans regarded the butterfly as a form of fire and of the soul.[1] In Scottish Gaelic one of the names of the butterfly is *teine-dé* ("fire of God"); another is *dealan-dé* ("brightness of God"), *dealan* referring to lightning, burning coal, the brightness of the starry sky, &c. *Dealan-dé* was also the name of the burning stick taken from a ceremonial fire, and twirled round to keep it alight while it was being carried to a house with purpose to re-kindle an extinguished fire. The ceremonial fire had been lit by friction. In the Mexican *Codex Bologna* a butterfly figure, issuing from the lower end of a fire drill, symbolizes the fluttering flame.[2] "All men know that butterflies are the souls of the dead" is a significant statement in an Irish folk-story related by Lady Wilde.[3] The butterfly soul issued from the mouth of a dead Irishman. In *Codex Remensis* is an anthropomorphic butterfly from whose great mouth a human face issues, showing the teeth, and a skull is

---

[1] *Codex Vaticanus B*, pp. 29, 254.

[2] *Codex Vaticanus B*, fig. 72. It was one of the forms assumed by the god of fire.

[3] *Ancient Legends*, Vol. I, pp. 66-7.

attached to the plumage. Greek artists frequently depicted the soul as a butterfly, and especially the particular butterfly called ψυχή ("the soul"). From the open mouth of a death mask engraved on a tomb in Italy a butterfly issues. The Serbians believed that witches had butterfly souls, and in Burmah ceremonies were performed to prevent the butterfly soul of a baby following that of a dead mother to the Otherworld. Among antique Chinese jade objects is found the butterfly soul which was associated with the Plum Tree of Life.[1] The fire vessel (*tlecuilli*) was in Mexico associated with the south.[2] Among the Chippeways a symbol of the south was the butterfly.[3] The white butterfly was also associated with the Mexican flower and love god Xochipilli.[4]

At the Mexican baptism ceremony an old woman "performed certain ceremonies with the umbilical cord". These were of similar character to the umbilical cord ceremonies performed generally in the New and Old Worlds.

[1] E. R. Emerson, *Masks, Heads and Faces*, p. 77; W. R. S. Ralston, *Songs of the Russian People*, pp. 117 *et seq.*; Laufer, *Jade*, p. 310; *Journal of the Anthropological Institute*, XXVI (1897), p. 23.

[2] *Codex Vaticanus B*, p. 310.   [3] Brinton, *The Myths of the New World*, p. 182.

[4] *Codex Vaticanus B*, pp. 159, 195, 328.

BUTTERFLY DEITIES

1, Itzpapalotl, the Obsidian-knife Butterfly (Chichimec goddess) with symbols (*Codex Borgia*). 2 and 3, Warrior's Device—(2) Fire Butterfly and (3) in shield with eagle's foot (*Codex Mendoza*). 4, Butterfly form of Xochiquetzal, the love goddess. 5, Butterfly from *Aubin Codex* (Maya). 6, Butterfly or Moth from *Nuttall Codex* (Maya). 7, Butterfly form of Quetzalcoatl.

CHAPTER XIII

Goddesses of Love and Food

Gardens and Trees of Life of Old and New Worlds' Goddesses—Mexican and Chinese Paradises of the West—Mexican Love Goddesses' Garden and Attendants—Weaving Goddesses of Mexico, China, Japan, &c.—Love-inspiring Flowers—Love Goddess as First Woman—The Yáppan Temptation Myth—Hindu Myths of similar Character—Echoes of Hindu Controversies in America—American Brahmans—Hindu Asceticism in America—The Sin Eater—Confession and Absolution—The Grandmother Deity—Maize God and Goddess—The Snake Mother—The Pot Myth—Xolotl's Flight from Hades—Similar Japanese Myth—First Parents are Pot-born—Mexican Xolotl and Egyptian Bes—Goddess of the Snake Skirt and Snake Mountain.

The Aztec goddess of love had several names, including Tlaçolteotl, Ixquina, and Tlaelquani. In Tlascala she was known as Xochiquetzal, and was supposed to dwell in the Celestial region of the ninth heaven. Like Si Wang Mu (the Japanese Seiobo), the Goddess of the West, she had a beautiful garden. In the Chinese garden is the Peach Tree of Life and in the American garden the Tree of Flowers, Xochitlalpan ("where the flowers are").[1] Another name for the American garden is Tamoanchan, the Paradise of the West. In this garden the goddess of love is associated with Xochipilli, whom Seler calls the "god of flowers and food supplies". In *Codex Borgia* (fig. 51) he appears in jaguar form, embracing the Tree of the West (the tree form of the goddess). The West is "the home of the maize plant". It is also

[1] In the wonderful rose garden of Laurin is the linden Tree of Life; see my *Teutonic Myth and Legend*, pp. 424 *et seq.*

the quarter of the humming-bird which gives the western tree its name *uitzitzilquauitl* (" Humming-bird Tree ").

The Chinese animal god of the West is the White Tiger. The Chinese colour of this quarter and of its season, which is autumn, is white. It is of interest therefore to find that in *Codex Vaticanus B*, the Mexican western tree " is painted white with red stripes, and seems to bear fruits instead of blossom at the tips of the branches "—a suggestion of the fig tree. In the *Fejér-váry Codex*, " the tree is given in a white colour ". The flower god is also associated with the planet Venus and the lower regions.[1]

The flower goddess of the West was of unequalled beauty. It was told, according to Camargo, that[2]

" she dwells above the nine heavens in a very pleasant and delectable place, accompanied and guarded by many people, and waited on by other women of the rank of goddesses, where are many delights in fountains, brooks, flower gardens, and without her wanting for anything, and that where she sojourned she was guarded and sheltered from the gaze of the people, and that in her retinue she had a great many dwarfs and hunchbacks, jesters and buffoons, who entertained her with music and dancing, and whom she sent as her confidants and messengers to the other gods, and that their chief occupation was the spinning and weaving of sumptuous, artistic fabrics, and that they were painted so beautifully and elegantly that nothing finer could be found amongst mortals. But the place where she dwelt was called *Tamohuan ichan, Xochitl ihcacan, Chicuhnauh-nepaniuhcan, Itzehecayan*, that is, the House of the Descent or of Birth, the place where are the flowers, the ninefold enchained, the place of the fresh cool winds. And every year she was honoured with a great feast, to which many people from all parts were gathered in her temple." [3]

In Japan the festival named *Tanabata* is connected

[1] Seler, *Codex Vaticanus B*, pp. 80 and 116.
[2] *Historia de Tlaxcala*, Tome I, Chap. XIX.
[3] Quoted by Seler in *Codex Vaticanus B*, p. 188.

with a pair of star deities who dwell on opposite sides of the Celestial River (the " Milky Way "). The goddess, who seems to link with the American love goddess in one of her aspects, is the " Weaving Girl " whose star is Vega. Her lover, the Herdsman, is associated with the star Aquila. The fable, which is of Chinese origin, tells that the " Weaving Girl " goddess

" was so constantly kept employed in making garments for the offspring of the Emperor of Heaven—in other words, God—that she had no leisure to attend to the adornment of her person. At last, however, God, taking compassion on her loneliness, gave her in marriage to the Herdsman who dwelt on the opposite bank of the River. Hereupon the woman began to grow remiss in her work. God, in his anger, then made her recross the river, at the same time forbidding her husband to visit her oftener than once a year." [1]

The festival was celebrated on this day of re-union. Susa-no-wo and Amaterásu (the sun goddess) create children, as has been stated, when standing on the opposite sides of the Celestial River. Afterwards Susa-no-wo breaks through the roof of the hall in Heaven where Amaterásu is sitting at work with her " Celestial weaving maidens ".[2] Is it a mere coincidence that the American, Chinese, and Japanese love goddesses should be spinners and weavers? As we have seen, the Egyptian goddess Neith had a shuttle, and the Syrian goddess a distaff.

The flowers in the American garden of the West had love-inspiring qualities as had the flowers and peaches in the Chinese Paradise of the West. According to Camargo, the individual who touched a flower from the garden of the American love goddess became an ardent and constant lover. The flowers were evidently impreg-

---

[1] Chamberlain, *Things Japanese*, pp. 327–328.
[2] See my *Myths of China and Japan*, under Index.

nated with the attributes of the goddess. As will be found in a previous chapter, flowers were forms assumed by foam (milk) in Hindu and American Zuni myths. Flowers therefore contained " life substance ".

Seler writes in this connection :

" The flower was for the Mexicans an emblem of the beautiful and of enjoyment. Everything that was beautiful and contributed to the enjoyment of life—colour, fragrance, taste, art, and artistic skill, music, and sport, but above all love, and even sexual indulgence—all was in the imagination of the Mexicans associated with the picture of the flower." [1]

The connection between flowers, love, &c., appears, however, to have been of more fundamental character than Seler supposes.

Flower garlands are still worn in India and Polynesia. In Sanskrit literature flowers fall from heaven when the gods honour a hero or heroine, approving of him or her. Not only the Indian gods, but mortals wore flower garlands and used ointments and scents, but these were of symbolic significance just as were the colours. Like the colours and scents, flowers revealed the attributes of deities. Aphrodite had her flowers. The Chinese and Japanese still make symbolic use of flowers at weddings, &c. In Ancient Egypt the lotus, a symbol of the mother goddess, was in high favour. Its scent was life-inspiring.

Camargo tells that the American love goddess " had formerly been the spouse of the rain god Tlaloc, but that Tezcatlipoca had abducted her and brought her to the nine heavens, and made her the Goddess of Love ". She was the patroness of courtezans, and her feast was in certain communities of somewhat obscene character. The Mexicans had a myth which represented the love

[1] *Codex Vaticanus B*, p. 186.

goddess and the sun god (as a "Lord of the Night") as the divine pair of lovers. These appear to have been identical with the first human pair—the Heavenly Twins. In *Codex Borbonicus* (fig. 19) the goddess and the sun god are shown wrapped in a coverlet in quite the fashion favoured by Maori lovers. The enclosure, however, is evidently symbolic of the mother pot and the pulque pot from which the twins emerge as the first man and woman. It would appear that the pair are also identical with "the goddess of the starry robe", and "the stellar sun god" of one of the Mexican hymns.

"In the concept of this (love) goddess", Seler writes, "the dominant notion was that of the young goddess, the beloved of the Sun God (*Piltzintecutli*), or of the Maize God (*Cinteotl*), this being doubtless conditioned by the *Xochitl* occurring in her name."

The following extract is from a song referring to her:

> Out of the water and mist I come, Xochiquetzal, the Goddess of Love.
> Out of the land where (the Sun) enters the house, out of Tamoanchan.
> Weepeth the pious Piltzintecutli—
> He seeketh Xochiquetzal.
> Dark it is, ah, whither I must go.

"She was regarded as the first woman", says Seler, who adds that she was identified with the consort of Tonacatecutli, Lord of Life, God of Procreation, who dwells in the uppermost thirteenth heaven.[1]

That the American love goddess did not have origin in America is suggested not only by her close resemblance to the Chinese and Japanese goddesses, but also by a myth in which she figures prominently in the character of a Hindu Apsara (a voluptuous Celestial nymph).

[1] *Codex Vaticanus B*, pp. 133 and 188.

There are several legends in the *Mahá-bhárata* of ascetics who engage themselves in accumulating religious merit and spiritual power by practising austere penances. One ascetic, for instance, "had set his heart upon the destruction of the world".[1] That famous rishi Viswamitra was originally a Kshtatriya (military aristocrat), but determined to become a Brahman. "I see", he said, "that asceticism is true strength."

"And saying this, the monarch, abandoning his large domains and regal splendour and turning his back upon all pleasures, set his mind on asceticism. And crowned with success in asceticism and filling the three worlds with the heat of his ascetic penances, he afflicted all creatures and finally became a Brahman. And the son of Kushika at last drank *Soma* with Indra himself (in the heavens)." [2]

The gods sometimes found it necessary to intervene and disturb the minds of the brooding ascetics, lest they should acquire too great power. They usually sent an Apsara to tempt a sage and thus reduce his stock of merit. The famous Drona (the " Pot-born ") owed his origin to a happening of this character. Sometimes, however, an ascetic successfully resisted the lures of the Celestial nymph. One of these had "Desire and Wrath" so much at his command that they washed his feet.[3]

Boturini relates a story of the American love goddess and an American ascetic which might have been taken from an ancient Hindu religious book. The name of the ascetic is Yáppan. Like a pious Hindu who resolves to turn his back on the world's pleasures, he leaves his wife and relatives, to lead a chaste and religious life as a hermit in a desert place, so that he may win the regard of the gods. Bancroft's rendering of the narrative proceeds :

[1] *Adi Parva* (Roy's translation, p. 512).
[2] *Ibid.* (Roy's translation, p. 504).   [3] *Ibid.*, pp. 381, 382, 476, 500.

"In that desert was a great stone or rock, called Tehuehuetl, dedicated to penitential acts; which rock Yáppan ascended and took his abode upon like a western Simeon Stylites. The gods observed all this with attention, but doubtful of the firmness of purpose of the new recluse, they set a spy upon him in the person of an enemy of his, named Yáotl, the word *yáotl* indeed signifying 'enemy'. Yet not even the sharpened eye of hate and envy could find any spot in the austere continent life of the anchorite, and the many women sent by the gods to tempt him to pleasure were repulsed and baffled. In heaven itself the chaste victories of the lonely saint were applauded, and it began to be thought that he was worthy to be transformed into some higher form of life. Then Tlazolteotl (goddess of love), feeling herself slighted and held for nought, rose up in her evil beauty, wrathful, contemptuous, and said: 'Think not, ye high and immortal gods, that this hero of yours has the force to preserve his resolution before me, or that he is worthy of any very sublime transportation; I descend to earth, behold now how strong is the vow of your devotee, how unfeigned his continence!'"

The goddess left her wonderful flower garden, and that day the lean, penance-withered man on the rock beheld the fairest of women. "My brother, Yáppan", she said, "I, the goddess Tlazolteotl, amazed at thy constancy, and commiserating thy hardships, come to comfort thee; what way shall I take or what path, that I may get up to speak with thee?"

Yáppan was caught in her spell and, descending, helped the goddess to climb the rock. She tempted him and he fell. After the goddess left him he was slain by Yáotl, the enemy.

"The gods transformed the dead man into a scorpion, with the forearms fixed lifted up as when he deprecated the blow of his murderer; and he crawled under the stone upon which he had his abode."

Yáotl then went in search of Yáppan's wife, who was

named Tlahuitzin. Having found her he led her to the place of her husband's shame and slew her.

"The gods transformed the poor woman into that species of scorpion called the *alacran encendido*, and she crawled under the stone and found her husband. And so it came that the tradition says that all reddish-coloured scorpions are descended from Tlahuitzin, and all dusky or ash-coloured scorpions from Yáppan, while both keep hidden under the stones and flee the light of shame for their disgrace and punishment. Last of all the wrath of the gods fell on Yáotl for his cruelty and presumption in exceeding their commands; he was transformed into a sort of locust that the Mexicans called *ahuacacha-pullin*." [1]

It has been suggested that this story was invented in America to account for the habits of the scorpion (*colotl*). The scorpion was, like the rattlesnake, associated with deities such as the fire god, the god of flowers, and Tezcatlipoca, and according to Seler denoted mortification and the time of mortification (midnight). There were likewise four scorpions of the four cardinal points.[2]

That the myth of Yáppan was, however, imported and localized by being connected with the scorpion is suggested by a close parallel from the *Mahá-bhárata*. The legend is related by Calya to Yudhishthira, the Pandava monarch, and begins:

"Listen, O king, to me as I relate this ancient story of the events of former days,—how, O descendant of Bhárata, misery befell Indra and his wife!"

As Yáppan and his wife became scorpions, Indra and his wife became insects or grubs. The story proceeds:

"Once Twashtri, the lord of creatures and the foremost of celestials, was engaged in practising rigid austerities. And it is

<hr/>

[1] Boturini, *Idéa*, pp. 15, 63–6. Bancroft, *The Native Races of the Pacific States,* Vol. III, pp. 378–80.   [2] *Codex Vaticanus B*, pp. 155, 256, 327.

said that from antipathy to Indra he created a son having three heads. And that being of universal form possessed of great lustre hankered after Indra's seat. And possessed of those three awful faces resembling the sun, the moon and the fire, he read the *Vedas* with one mouth, drank wine with another, and looked with the third as if he would absorb all the cardinal points.

"And given to the practice of austerities, and mild, and self-controlled, he was intent upon a life of religious practices and austerities. And his practice of austerities, O subduer of foes, was rigid and terrible and of an exceedingly severe character. And beholding the austerities, courage and truthfulness of this one possessed of immeasurable energy, Indra became anxious, fearing lest that being should take his place. And Indra reflected,—How may he be made to addict himself to sensual enjoyment; how may he be made to cease his practice of such rigid austerities? For were the three-headed being to wax strong, he would absorb the whole universe!—And it was this that Indra pondered in his mind; and, O best of Bhárata's race, endued with intelligence, he ordered the celestial nymphs[1] to tempt the son of Twashtri. And he commanded them, saying, 'Be quick, and go without delay, and so tempt him that the three-headed being may plunge himself into sensual enjoyments to the utmost extent. Furnished with captivating hips, array yourselves in voluptuous attires, and decking yourselves in charming necklaces, do ye display gestures and blandishments of love. Endued with loveliness, do ye, good betide ye, tempt him and alleviate my dread. I feel restless in my heart, O lovely damsels. Avert, ye ladies, this awful peril that hangs over me!'"

The nymphs promised to allure the ascetic and bring him under their control. On reaching Indra's enemy

"those lovely damsels tempted him with various gestures of love, displaying their fine figures".

The ascetic was able, however, to resist them, as Yáppan resisted the women who visited him before the goddess of love herself paid him a visit. "Although he looked at

---

[1] Apsaras.

them", as it is told, "yet he was not influenced by desire." The Apsaras returned to Indra and said, "O lord, that unapproachable being is incapable of being disturbed by us".

The story then proceeds to tell that Indra slew his enemy with his thunderbolt, and prevailed upon a carpenter to cut off the three heads. Having, however, slain a Brahman, he was "overpowered by the sin of Brahmanicide". He fled "to the confines of the world" and hid himself. For a time he lay concealed in water as a writhing snake. Then he hid as a small creature inside a lotus. His wife set out in search of him, guided by the goddess of Divination. Assuming Indra's form, she crept into the stalk of a white lotus in the middle of a beautiful lake on an island:

"And penetrating into the lotus stalk, along with Cachi, she saw Indra there who had entered into its fibres. And seeing her lord lying there in minute form, Cachi also assumed a minute form, as did the goddess of Divination too. And Indra's queen began to glorify him by reciting his celebrated deeds of yore."

Indra was subsequently purified of his sin and resumed his wonted form.[1]

In this story, Indra is the enemy of the ascetic, and is punished for his sin of slaying him. Although the holy man resists temptation, there are other Hindu narratives of like character in which the Apsara succeeds as does the goddess of love in the American story. One of these refers to the ascetic, Bharadwaja, "ceaselessly observing the most rigid vows". On a day when he intended to celebrate the *Agnihotra* sacrifice he was tempted by Gritachi, "that Apsara endued with youth and beauty". She had arrived to interfere with the sacrifice.

---

[1] *Udoga Parva* of the *Mahá-bhárata* (Roy's translation, pp. 18 *et seq.*).

"With an expression of pride in her countenance, mixed with a voluptuous languor of attitude, the damsel rose from the water after her ablutions were over. And as she was gently treading on the bank, her attire was loose and disordered. Seeing her attire disordered, the sage was smitten with burning desire." [1]

Another *Mahá-bhárata* story tells of two young men, named Sunda and Upasunda, of the Asura race. They became ascetics, and their austerities were very severe, as they were intended for "the subjection of the three worlds".

"The celestials became alarmed. And the gods began to offer numerous obstructions for impeding the progress of their asceticism. And the celestials repeatedly tempted the brothers by means of every precious possession and the most beautiful girls." [2]

The brothers resisted the Apsaras and ultimately became very powerful. In the end the Grandsire (Brahma) created with the aid of gems a celestial damsel of great beauty, who was "unrivalled among the women of the three worlds".

"And because she had been created with portions of every gem taken in minute measures, the Grandsire bestowed upon her the name of Tilottamā."

When the brothers saw her they fell in love. Each claimed her for his wife. "And maddened by the beauty of the damsel, they soon forgot their love and affection for each other." They fought and slew each other.

"The Grandsire was pleased and said to Tilottamā, 'O beautiful damsel, thou shalt roam in the region of the Adityas. And thy splendour shall be so great that nobody will be able to look at thee for any length of time.'" [3]

Here we have the love goddess connected with precious stones.

---

[1] *Adi Parva* of the *Mahá-bhárata* (Roy's translation, pp. 382–383).
[2] *Ibid.* (Roy's translation, pp. 580–583).   [3] *Ibid.* (Roy's translation, pp. 583–590).

The Hindu stories of which a selection has been given are found in post-Vedic literature. After the Aryan peoples had settled in India a great deal of culture mixing took place. Colonies of seafarers, who searched for precious metals and precious stones and pearls, had settled in India, and their mythology and religious rites were mingled with those of the Aryans. In the *Mahábhárata* there are many stories and long theological arguments to justify the elevation of the local deities above those imported by the peoples of Aryan speech, who came from the Iranian plateau. The story of Indra's sin and transformation is one of the stories in question. Even he, the great thunder god, the Aryan Zeus, could not slay a Brahman without paying the penalty. The gods of the military aristocrats were subdued by the ascetics who performed penances and accumulated religious merit. It was possible for these ascetics themselves to become gods.

The searchers for gold and gems, which contained " life substance " and therefore spiritual power, passed beyond India and reached America. They imported, as it would appear, into the New World not only their own religious ideas connected with gold and gems, but also the myths framed in India to justify the elevation of the priests above the gods. The story of Yáppan appears to be of Indian origin—an echo of the religious struggle which took place on that sub-continent in post-Vedic times, when the Aryan gods were represented as being afraid of the ascetics who set themselves to accumulate religious merit and spiritual power. The story of the temptation and fall of Yáppan is too like that of the temptation and fall of his Indian prototypes to be of spontaneous origin in the New World.

In one of the Hindu versions the enemy of the ascetic

Panquetzaliztli Al primo di decembre

e interpretato esaltatione de insegne perche al primo y aua sopra la sua casa una Insegna picola di Carta per e e li capitani e gente di guerra sacrificauano delli uigione in guerra li q̃ primo de sacrificiuli melcua me uguali accio che se deffendessino denouo e con con Centeuano e amalauano e cose li sacrificauano in n̄

A LIFE-GIVING AND WAR GODDESS

The goddess Pan-quetzal-itztli as a day goddess (connected with winter solstice), from *Codex Vaticanus A*, with part of Italian priest's interpretation recéived from the Aztecs. In her hand she carries a war banner surmounted by the "mother pot" in which grows the cotton plant (here the "Plant of Life" like the Babylonian *nig-gil-ma*). On her head is the symbol of the cotton plant and the jewel (*chalchiuitl*), a life-giving symbol. The shell symbol is on her breast and beneath it are lunar symbols. She carries the banner, arrows, and shield of a war deity, having been associated with the god Huitzilopochtli, as well as with the goddess Chalchiuhtlicue whose nose-plug she wears. "Quetzalitztli" connects her with the quetzal bird and obsidian symbolism.

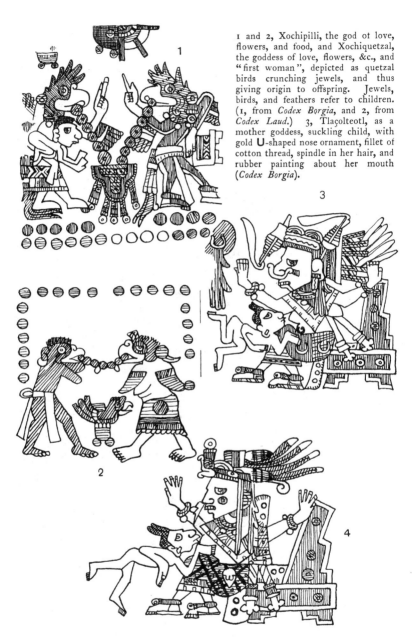

1 and 2, Xochipilli, the god of love, flowers, and food, and Xochiquetzal, the goddess of love, flowers, &c., and "first woman", depicted as quetzal birds crunching jewels, and thus giving origin to offspring. Jewels, birds, and feathers refer to children. (1, from *Codex Borgia*, and 2, from *Codex Laud*.) 3, Tlaçolteotl, as a mother goddess, suckling child, with gold U-shaped nose ornament, fillet of cotton thread, spindle in her hair, and rubber painting about her mouth (*Codex Borgia*).

LOVE AND MOTHER DEITIES

4, Xochiquetzal, the goddess, as mother suckling child, adorned with the fillet and the eagle-feather head-dress which has a solar significance. On her cheek is a black rubber circular patch, and from her nose is suspended a tapering and stepped yellow (gold) plate. She wears blue garments. Her seat, like that of Tlaçolteotl (3), is stepped and has stellar symbols (*Codex Borgia*).

is, as we have seen, the god Indra. That the Mexican Yáppan's " enemy " was likewise a god is suggested by his name Taotl which was one of the names of Tezcatlipoca, " the only deity ", says Bancroft, " that can be fairly compared with the fitful Zeus of Homer—now moved with extreme passion, now governed by a noble impulse, now swayed by brutal lust, now drawn on by a vein of humour ".[1] Indra was the Hindu Zeus.

The conclusion drawn from the evidence of the Yáppan myth that Hindu cultural influence reached America is greatly strengthened when we find Acosta informing us that certain Mexican ascetics, who assisted the priests, " dressed in white robes and lived by begging ".[2] The wandering Brahman and Buddhist pilgrims in India similarly begged their food. Like the Hindu ascetics, those in Mexico " went out into the mountains to sacrifice or do penance ", engaged in hymn-chanting and incense burning; while some abstained from meat, tortured themselves, smeared their bodies with various substances, allowed their hair to grow long and never combed or cleansed it; others carried pans of fire on their heads, and so on. Torquemada tells of priests who became saints by undergoing a four years' penance, thinly clad, sleeping on the bare ground, eating little food, watching and praying, and drawing blood from their bodies. " Blood drawing was the favourite and most common mode of expiating sin and showing devotion " in America as in India, while " fasting was observed as an atonement for sin ".[3]

Although the Aztec goddess of love and flowers was associated with carnality, she was also as Tlaelquani the " sin eater ", or " eater of filthy things ". She pardoned

---

[1] *The Pacific States*, Vol. III, p. 444.   [2] Bancroft, *op. cit.*, pp. 436–7.
[3] Authorities quoted by Bancroft in *The Pacific States*, Vol. III, pp. 435 *et seq.*

sins; the penitent confessed to her priests, first taking an oath to tell the truth by touching the ground with his hand, licking the dust that adhered to it, and throwing copal on a fire. After confession the sinner might have to pierce his tongue or ears with maguey thorns or undergo a long and painful fast. The priest gave absolution.[1]

The love goddess was, as Tlalli iyollo, the "earth goddess", or "world goddess". Seler inclines to identify her, too, with the earthquake goddess who was called Toci, "our grandmother" (as the Indian Brahma was "grandsire"), and Teteo innan, "mother of the gods"— the "All-begetter, mother of gods and men", who "appears to have had her home amongst the tribes of the Atlantic sea-board".[2]

Seler writes as follows regarding this deity:

"In the songs the goddess is hailed as *coçauic xochitla*, 'the yellow Bloom', and *iztac xochitla*, 'the white Bloom', the *tonana teumechaue*, 'our Mother, the goddess of the thigh-skin-face-painting', or as the *ti noci teumechaue*, 'thou my Grandmother, thou goddess of the thigh-skin-face-painting', she who dwelleth in the Tamoanchan, 'the House of the Descent', which, perhaps, properly means 'the House of Birth', the *Xochitl icacan*, 'the place where are the flowers', that is, the paradise of food supplies, the home of maize, the West, where of her was born the Maize God (Cinteotl), the god Ce xochitl, 'one flower'".

The following song or hymn is translated by Seler:

Our Mother, the goddess Tlaçolteotl, did arrive.
The Maize god is born in the House of the Descent, in the place
    where are the flowers, the god "One Flower".
The Maize god is born in the place of water and of mist where
    the children of men are made, in the Jewel-Michuacan.

As the earth goddess, this deity was the goddess of

---

[1] Seler, *Codex Vaticanus B*, pp. 100–101. Bancroft, *The Native States*, Vol. III, pp. 380 *et seq.*   [2] Sahagun in Book VI, Chapter VII.

death who took "the dead to her bosom", as Seler puts it.[1] She was also as Cinteotl[2] the goddess of maize, which she protected and nourished. In this aspect she was the "mother". "The force", as Müller puts it, "which sustains life must also have created it. Cinteotl was therefore considered as bringing children to light and is represented with an infant in her arms. . . . Cinteotl is the great producer, not of children merely; she is the great goddess, the most ancient goddess."[3] Her names include Tonacajohua ("she who sustains us") and Tzinteotl ("the original goddess").

Closely connected with Cinteotl was the goddess Xilonen, whose name is derived from *xilotl* ("young ear of maize"). A woman impersonated her at her festival and was sacrificed. This victim wore strings of gems round her neck and over her breasts, and above these a solar symbol of gold, indicating a connection between her and Chalchiuhtlicue.

Another form of the divine mother was Ciuateotl ("snake woman"), who was also called Tonantzin ("our mother"). She was a royal lady in rich attire who carried a cradle on her shoulders, but in it, instead of a child, was a stone knife used for sacrificing human victims. She was in one of her aspects a goddess of toil, poverty, and adversity.

The flint knife (*tecpatl*) was not only connected with sacrifice, which was made to prolong the life of the gods, but also with birth. Like the *chicauaztli* (rattle-stick) it symbolized fecundity. Both were shown between the first human pair.[4]

---

[1] *Codex Vaticanus B*, pp. 100–102. The dead were likewise to the Greeks "Demeter's folk". [2] And the god of the same name.

[3] Müller, *Amerikanische Urreligionen*, p. 493.

[4] Seler, *Codex Vaticanus B*, pp. 83, 84, 133, 134.

The goddess Citlalinicue (or Omeciuatl), spouse of the god Citlallatonac (or Ometecutli), dwelt in the thirteenth heaven. Before the world was peopled she gave birth to a stone knife which her sons threw down to earth. At the place where it fell 1600 earth gods came into being.[1] To these gods she made the request that a bone should be brought from Hades. They delegated Xolotl ("servant") to obtain it. He like the Japanese Ohonamochi,[2] who was similarly the "servant" of his numerous brethren, obtained a great bone but had to run away with it at high speed, for he was chased by the Lord of Hades as was the young Japanese god by Susa-no-wo.

On his return to earth the bone was broken into fragments and placed in a pot. The gods who had sprung from the flint knife drew blood from their bodies and sprinkled it over the bone. On the fourth day after this ceremony was performed a boy emerged from the pot. More blood was sprinkled and then a girl emerged. The children were nursed by Xolotl, who fed them on the "milk of the maguey", and they became the first man and woman from whom the human race is descended.[3]

Xolotl bears some resemblance to the grotesque dwarf god Bes of the Ancient Egyptians. Bes had long arms, large ears, a big mouth, and crooked legs, and was connected with birth, and beloved by children whom he amused with his dances. He had an animal form. In Mexico the god Xolotl has a dog form and appears to have attended on the dead. He was in human form misshapen in body and limbs. Like the Ancient Egyptians, the Mexican nobles kept dwarfs and hunchbacks to amuse them. They were called *xolomê*, a word derived from

---

[1] See my *Myths of China and Japan*, under *Izanami* in Index.

[2] See my *Myths of China and Japan*, under Index.

[3] Bancroft, *The Native Races*, Vol. III, pp. 58–60.

xolotl. Xolotl was a god of a ball game. Bes, the grotesque merry-making dwarf god of the Egyptians, was in the underworld a gigantic deity who "menaced the wicked with his knife, threatening to tear out their hearts ".[1]

Couatlicue was an earth goddess, a goddess of death and a goddess of war. Her name signifies "snake skirt". She was connected with the mountain Coatepec ("mountain of the snake") near the city of Tulla. Sahagun notes that she was greatly reverenced by the dealers in flowers, and this fact suggests that she may have been a form of the love goddess. At an annual festival she received offerings of the new flowers of the year. As will be shown she was the mother of the great war god of Mexico.

---

[1] Wiedemann, *Religion of the Ancient Egyptians*, p. 168. Seler, *Codex Vaticanus*, p. 181–3.

CHAPTER XIV

Tlaloc and the Dragon

Old and New World Thunder Gods—The "Feathered Serpent"—
"Wonder Beasts" and Culture Mixing—Culture Mixing in Europe and
Asia—Chinese and Indian Rain Gods—The "Drift" to America—Chinese
and American Rain Gods of the East—Tlaloc as a Nāga—Tlaloc on Back of
Crocodile—Tlaloc's Thunderbolt—Indra and the Maruts—Tlaloc and the
Tlaloque—Chac and the Chacs—The Chacs, Bacabs, Horuses, and Ptahs—
The Maya God B—Hindu Myths in America—Thunder Dog in India,
China, Japan, and America—Buddhist Dragons—Bad and Good Rain from
Tlaloc and Nāgas—Dragons of Four Quarters—Tlaloc and the Deer—The
Old World Deer God—Prayers and Sacrifices to Tlaloc—American Paradises.

THE American thunder and rain god was evidently not of
spontaneous generation. He presents several phases that
are quite familiar to students of Old World mythologies.
In the first place he wields an axe or hammer, or throws
the mythical thunderbolt—"the all-dreaded thunderstone"
of Shakespeare—like Zeus, Thor, Indra, &c., and in the
second place he is a dragon-slayer. He is also a complex
deity who now figures as a bird which preys on serpents,
and anon as a bird-serpent or winged dragon—that is, the
bird and serpent in one, like the Chinese and Japanese
dragon. Sometimes, too, we find that the American
serpent swallows the god and afterwards disgorges him, as
happens in the Old World myths. Not less striking is
the fact that Tlaloc, the Mexican thunder and rain god, is,
like the god Indra and the Chinese azure or green dragon,
associated with the East. If, one may comment here in
passing, it is held that these complexes are "natural",

one wonders what some theorists are really prepared to regard as "unnatural".

The idea that thunder is caused by a giant god who pounds the sky or the mountains with a hammer or bolt, or cleaves them with an axe (the Greek *astropeléki*), may not be a great effort of the human imagination, but it is something definite and concrete. It does not follow that it was first suggested by an early blacksmith or copper-smith, or even by a primitive flint chipper. The axe was in ancient Egypt a symbol of a deity who had no particular connection with thunder, while two arrows and a shield symbolized a goddess. It is possible that the axe, as a symbol of divinity, has a long history, and that, simple as such a symbol may now seem to be, it really represents a group of complex ideas. If, however, it is assumed that the axe is an axe and nothing more, and that the axe-wielding god was suggested to different peoples widely separated by time and space when they saw axe-wielding savages chopping wood or cutting up animals, is it con-ceivable that the different peoples should have "quite naturally" connected or identified the axe god with a bird? Granting, however, that the bird connection was suggested because the thunder-cloud might have been thought of as a bird, is it probable that widely-separated peoples should have unanimously assumed that the mythical bird was a destroyer of mythical serpents? Further, can we regard as convincing the theory that in the New World, as in the Old, the thunder-bird should have been confused with the serpent "as a matter of course", and, in addition, that the "wonder beast" should have been given horns, and especially the horns of a stag, gazelle, or antelope? The mythical serpent, it must be borne in mind, is, in America as in India, a water confiner—a "drought demon", and the bird or the axe-wielding god, who slays it, does so to release the water and bring the season of drought to an end. Is it "natural" that such an idea should have cropped up spontaneously in Mexico, China, and India, seeing that no bird wages war on serpents in any of these countries, and that no serpent really confines water? The rattlesnake of America, which is the symbol of water, has in its natural state no particular connection with water. If, as has been assumed, the rattlesnake suggested water "by its sinuous movements", it was not surely confined water, but rather flowing water that it suggested. The rattlesnake has not, of course, any particular connection with a deer. It is difficult to understand, therefore, why widely separated peoples should have connected in their religious symbolism the deer and the serpent, or have found it necessary to give horns to even a mythical water-confining reptile.

The conception of a horned serpent furnished with wings, or plumes, or ornamented with green feathers, which withholds or controls the water supply, and has to be slain by a bird, or by a big man wielding a thunder-axe, is too complex a one to be dismissed as "natural". That the "wonder beast" (dragon) should be found in America may not be "surprising", seeing that American religious symbolism is on the whole of highly complex character; but it is, if not surprising, at any rate, from the historian's point of view, interesting and suggestive to discover that the American complex bears so close a resemblance to the Asiatic. The Asiatic "wonder beast", known as the dragon, was undoubtedly the product of "culture mixing". That culture mixing had in India not only a religious but a political significance.

Each part of the anatomy of the symbolic "wonder beast" has a history in Asia. Is it possible or probable that the "wonder beast" of America simply "grew up" because, as it chanced, precisely the same historical happenings took place there as in Asia, and because precisely the same religious rivalries existing there produced precisely the same results in the social and religious life of the people? In these days, when so much more is known than was the case a generation ago about the mythologies of great culture centres like India and China, and much evidence has been accumulated to place beyond the shadow of doubt that "culture-drifting" was in ancient times a reality, the theory that the same particular set of complex beliefs had spontaneous origin in different parts of the world can no longer be maintained.

The discoveries in Crete and Spain have demonstrated that the impress of ancient Egyptian religious beliefs can be detected in more than one European area. India has yielded much evidence of culture-drifting from the Iranian plateau which had been influenced by Babylonia, and of culture-drifting across the Indian Ocean, which was crossed and re-crossed by ancient mariners who founded colonies and engaged in trade. Even China has been shown to have been, before Buddhist missionary enterprise became active and widespread, a debtor to other civilizations. Its culture-historical development did not take place in complete isolation. Laufer writes in this regard:

"In opposition to the prevalent opinion of the day, it cannot be emphasized strongly enough on every occasion that Chinese civilization, as it appears now, is not a unit and not the exclusive production of the Chinese, but the final result of the cultural efforts of a vast conglomeration of the most varied tribes, an amalgamation of ideas accumulated from manifold quarters and widely differentiated in space and time. . . . No graver error can hence be committed than to attribute any culture idea at the outset to the Chinese for no other reason than because it appears within the precincts of their empire." [1]

In another work the same distinguished scholar has shown, not only by the comparative study of certain beliefs and customs but by the evidence of ancient Chinese writings, that certain fundamental religious ideas reached China from "Fu-lin" (Syria and Byzantium). [2] De Visser, in his important work *The Dragon in China and Japan*, has shown that the composite "wonder beast" of the Far East owes much to the Indian Nāgas. [3] The whole subject has been reviewed by Professor Elliot Smith in his epoch-making work *The Evolution of the Dragon*. [4] He dissects the "wonder beast", and traces each part to its area of origin. Withal, he follows the flight of the winged serpent through Asia and across the Pacific to America. He finds America "a rich storehouse of historical data" and "a museum of the cultural history of the Old World", and writes:

"The original immigrants into America brought from North-Eastern Asia such cultural equipment as had reached the area east of the Yenesei at the time when Europe was in the Neolithic phase of culture. Then when ancient mariners began to coast along the Eastern Asiatic littoral and make their way to America by the Aleutian route there was a further infiltration of new ideas. But when more venturesome sailors began to navigate the open seas and exploit Polynesia, for centuries there was a more or less constant influx of customs and beliefs, which were drawn from Egypt and Babylonia, from the Mediterranean and East Africa, from India and Indonesia, China and Japan, Cambodia and Oceania. One and the same fundamental idea, such as the attributes of the

1 *Jade : A Study in Chinese Archæology and Religion*, Chicago, U.S.A., 1912, p. 57.
2 *The Diamond : A Study in Chinese and Hellenistic Folklore*, Chicago, 1915.
3 Dr. M. W. De Visser, *The Dragon in China and Japan*, Amsterdam, 1913.
4 London and Manchester, 1919.

serpent as a water god, reached America in an infinite variety of guises, Egyptian, Babylonian, Indian, Indonesian, Chinese, and Japanese, and from this amazing jumble of confusion the local priesthood of Central America built up a system of beliefs which is distinctively American, though most of the ingredients and principles of synthetic composition was borrowed from the Old World." [1]

Tlaloc and other deities of a like character betray their Old World affinities, now as dragon-slayers and anon as feathered serpents with horns and crests.

The Chinese dragons sleep all winter and awake in the spring, when they fight and thunder, and thus cause rain to fall. In the Eastern quarter is the green or azure dragon—sometimes it is green and sometimes it is blue. It is essentially the water controller. The opposing deity, the white tiger god of the west, is the wind controller.[2] De Visser writes regarding these deities of China:

"The so-called *fung-shui* ('wind and water') is a geomantical system, prevalent throughout China from olden time down to the present age. The tiger and the dragon, the gods of wind and water, are the keystone of this doctrine. . . . De Groot has given already a full account of its origin, elements, meaning, and influence. 'It is', says he, 'a quasi-scientific system, supposed to teach men where and how to build graves, temples, and dwellings, in order that the dead, the gods, and the living, may be located therein exclusively, or as far as possible, under the auspicious influences of nature.' The dragon plays a most important part in this system, being 'the chief spirit of water and rain', and at the same time representing one of the four quarters of heaven (i.e. the East, called the Azure Dragon, and the first of the seasons, Spring). *'The word Dragon comprises the high grounds in*

[1] *The Evolution of the Dragon*, p. 87.
[2] The god Quexalcoatl, as wind god of the west, is similarly opposed to Tlaloc, as rain god of the east, while Tezcatlipoca, as wind god of the north, is opposed to Huitzilopochtli, as rain god of the south.

general, and the water-streams which have their sources therein or wind their way through them.' Hence it is that books on *fung-shui* commonly commence with a bulky set of dissertations, comprised under the heading *Rules Concerning the Dragon*, in reality dealing with the doctrines about the situation and contours of mountains and hills and the direction of watercourses." [1]

We seem still to be in China when we find Seler writing of the Mexican Tlaloc and the Tlaxcaltec goddess of rain in *Codex Vaticanus B*, pp. 106 *et seq.*:

"The beautiful cone-shaped mountain rising in the east of their territory, and draped to the summit with vegetation, was regarded by the Tlaxcaltecs as the seat and embodiment of the rain deity, whom they thought of as a female deity and designated Matlalcueye, 'the Lady of the Blue Robe'. But for the inhabitants of the Mexican tableland the same part was played by the lofty ridges which separate their domain on the east from that of the neighbouring Tlaxcaltecs, and above which farther south the two giants *Iztac ciuatl*, 'the White Woman', and *Popocatepetl*, 'the Smoking Mountain', rise far into the region of everlasting snow. To this ridge, over which the way led from *Tetzcoco* to *Uexotzinco* and *Tlaxcallan*, was specially appropriate the name of *Tlaloc* or *Tlalocan*."

On this upland seat of the god was an idol of white lava which faced the east. Into a vessel on its head edible seeds were poured from priestly hands on occasions of annual ceremonies. "The name *Poyauhtlan*", says Seler, "which frequently occurs in songs to Tlaloc and in the worship of the Mexican rain god, appears to have been merely *another name for the same upland region*."

The Indian serpent deities called Nãgas, who were rain gods, sometimes appeared in human form with snakes on their heads or round their necks. "They

---

[1] De Visser, *The Dragon in China and Japan*, pp. 55-60. De Groot, *The Religious System of China*, Vol. III, Chap. XII, pp. 935-1056.

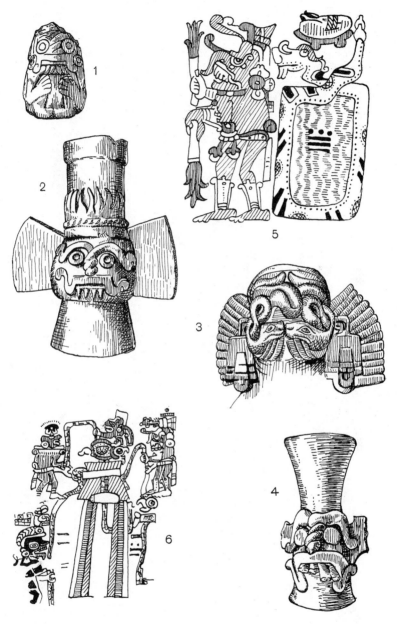

THE WATER CONTROLLER

1, 2, 3, 4, Figures of the American rain god as serpent dragon.   5, The elephant-headed god and the water-confining serpent.   6, The Churning of the Ocean (in *Codex Cortes*). On the summit of the "churn" is a tortoise, and round the "churn" is a snake which is grasped by deities.   On the back of the tortoise is a god holding another snake. (See p. 191.)

are water spirits", writes Kern,[1] "represented as a rule
in human shapes with a crown of serpents on their
heads." Tlaloc was sometimes depicted, as in a stone
image preserved in the Royal Ethnological Museum,
Berlin, with a face formed by the coils of two snakes,
and sometimes with snakes forming eyebrows and nose
and also the mouth from which four long teeth project
downwards.[2]   In a significant illustration in *Codex
Fejérváry-Mayer 4* (*Codex Vaticanus B*, fig. 309), Tlaloc
stands on the back of a crocodile-like dragon[3] in water.
A streak of wriggling fire issuing from Tlaloc's mouth
and grasped in his right hand, enters the jaws of the
reptile.   The Indian Nāgas and Chinese dragons lived
in pools and arose to cause thunder and lightning, and
to assemble clouds and send rain. Offerings were made
to Tlaloc not only on the mountains but also in the lake
at Mexico, in which there is a whirlpool caused by an
underground outlet. Artificial ponds were consecrated
to the deity.   In *Codex Borgia* (fig. 14) he is shown
facing a pool of water in which there is a fish rising
towards a floating offering of firewood and rubber.[4] Fish,
snails, and frogs were connected with Tlaloc.

In his anthropomorphic form Tlaloc was the wielder
of the thunderbolt, and resembled the Hindu Indra, who
was likewise a god of the East. "The Indra colour",
says De Visser, "is *nila*, dark blue, or rather blue-black,
the regular epitheton of the rain clouds."[5] Tlaloc was
invariably depicted with a blue ring encircling the whole
eye, and often with a blue ribbon round the mouth. In
some of his forms he had a dragon-shaped axe and a

---

[1] *Histoire du Bouddhisme dans l'Inde*, Vol. I, p. 310.
[2] *Codex Vaticanus B*, pp. 106 *et seq.*   [3] The Japanese *Wani*.
[4] The fish of Mayauel drinks milk. Here rubber is a form of milk.
[5] *The Dragon in China and Japan*, p. 31.

serpentine thunderbolt. In *Codex Borgia* and *Codex Vaticanus B* appear interesting forms of Tlaloc in green and black. Above or before him is a burning house "on which lies a flaming axe (symbol of lightning?), and beside or below it a stream of water with snails or fishes". Inside the house in *Codex Vaticanus B* is "a tailed animal armed with the claws of beasts of prey".[1] This may refer to some obscure ceremony. Fire was used in Buddhist ceremonies to control dragons. De Visser writes in this connection:

"An exorcist of Nāgas went with his pitcher full of water to the pond of such a being and by his magic formulæ surrounded the Nāga with fire. As the water of the pitcher was the only refuge the serpent could find, it changed into a very small animal and entered the pitcher."[2]

The nāgas, like the Chinese and Japanese dragons, were much afraid of fire. It may be that Tlaloc, as the American Indra, takes the place of the exorcist who compelled the nāga-dragon to ascend to the sky from his pitcher and send rain, or to prevent the nāga-dragon from sending too much rain. Seler sees in the burning house episode a reference to "fiery rain" (*tlequiauitl*). Evil or sick nāgas and dragons sent "calamity rain".

The Hindu Indra was assisted by a group of subsidiary beings called the Maruts, who were sons of Rudra. These "youths" had chariots drawn by spotted deer, and were armed with bows and arrows, spears and axes. They were "cloud shakers", and were wont to cleave "cloud rocks" so as to drench the earth with quickening showers. When following the storm god, Rudra, these assistants were called "Rudras". The "hastening Maruts" accom-

---

[1] *Codex Vaticanus B*, p. 151.
[2] *The Dragon in China and Japan*, p. 13.

panied Indra when he came to a place of sacrifice and accepted offerings.[1]

Tlaloc was, in like manner, assisted by the Tlaloque, who distributed rain from pitchers which he smote with serpentine rods, or carried symbols of thunder and lightning.

The god Chac of Yucatan, who links with Tlaloc and Indra, was likewise assisted by subsidiary beings known as the Chacs. According to Brinton, "Chacs" signifies "the red ones"; the Indian group were the "red Rudras". These assistants of Chac carried axes (thunder axes) like the Mexican Tlaloc and some, if not all, of the Tlaloque. They appear to have been forms of the Bacabs, the gods of the four quarters, like the Egyptian Horuses, or "four sons of Horus". Ptah, the Egyptian god of Memphis, who carried a hammer (a thunder hammer?), had eight dwarfish assistants closely resembling the *pataikoi*, the dwarf gods adored by Phœnician mariners. The Maruts, the Rudras, the Tlaloque, the Chacs, and the Bacabs, appear to have been all water bringers, as were the Horuses and the Ptahs of Egypt. In the *Mahá-bhárata* the East is the quarter which was regarded as "the foremost or first born", and "the source of all the prosperity of the gods, for it was there that Cakra (Indra) was first anointed as the king of the celestials".[2] The four quarters were controlled by the king god of the East. This belief may be the germ of the conception of the four rain gods of the four quarters. There were four Tlalocs and four Chacs, as there were four Nāgas as well as groups of Tlalocs, Chacs, and Nāgas, associated with the "first born" king god of the East.

---

[1] My *Indian Myth and Legend*, pp. 5, 6, 25, 26, 58, 377.

[2] *Açwamedha Parva* (Roy's translation, p. 106), and *Udyoga Parva* (Roy's translation, p. 323).

As we have seen, the Bacabs, like the Horuses, protected the jars containing the internal organs of the mummies. The same doctrine, without the practice of mummification, however, is found in the *fung-shui* system of China, where the liver and gall are associated with the east, the heart and intestines with the south, the lungs and small intestines with the west, and the kidney and bladder with the north. The Maya, as has been shown, connected the Bacab of the south with the belly, the "serpent being" organ with the east, the "white being" organ with the north, and "disembowelled" with the west. In Egypt the order of the internal organs in their relation to the cardinal points was altered in the course of time.[1]

These notes are given at this point to indicate the far-reaching complexity of the doctrines associated with the American and Old World gods of the East and their connections with the other quarters.

The key to the Chac-Tlaloc problem appears to be provided by the god lettered B in the Maya manuscripts. Schellhas notes that he is the "most common figure in the codices". Those who regard him as being related to "Itzamna, the serpent god of the East", and "Chac, the rain god of the four quarters and the equivalent of Tlaloc of the Mexicans",[2] are supported by the comparative evidence collected by Professor Elliot Smith.[3] The god B—the "long-nosed" god—has a head which has puzzled many Americanists. Some regard the head as that of a tapir. Elliot Smith calls him "the elephant-headed rain god".

In India, as has been shown, Indra's place was taken

---

[1] See Budge, *Gods of the Egyptians*, Vol. I, p. 492, and Elliot Smith and others in "The Heart and Reins" (*Journal of the Manchester Oriental Society*, 1911, pp. 41 *et seq.*).

[2] Spinden, *Maya Art*, p. 62.   [3] *The Evolution of the Dragon*, pp. 84 *et seq.*

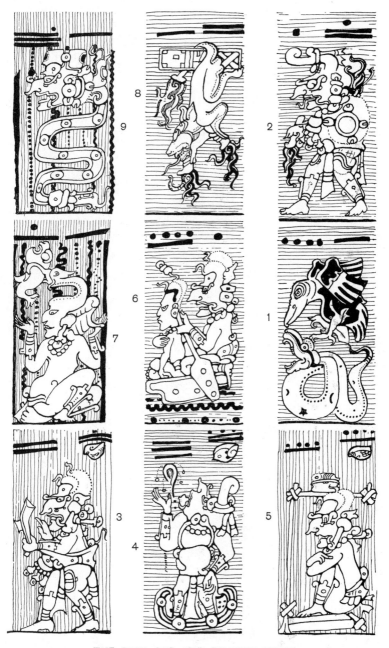

THE RAIN GOD AND DRAGON MYTH
(*From the Dresden Codex*)

The numbers refer to the order in which the pictures are described in the text
(pp. 245, 246).

in Brahmanic times by his son, Ganesha, a young god with an elephant's head. The younger god was invested with the attributes of the elder. Indra, in the Vedic hymns, slays Vritra, the "drought demon"—a serpent-dragon which confines the waters. When the demon is slain the rains are released. The priest then sang:

I will extol the manly deeds of Indra:
The first was when the thunder stone he wielded
And smote the dragon ; he released the waters,
He oped the channels of the breasted mountains.[1]

In the *Codex Cortes* the American elephant-headed god, who is decorated with the characteristic Cambodian ear ornament, is shown with a thunderbolt in each hand standing beside a bearded rattlesnake, whose body forms an enclosure full of water. Another picture in *Codex Troano* shows the serpent-dragon after the enclosure formed by its body has been opened. On its head stands the elephant-headed god, Chac, pouring the rain from a jar, while a goddess, similarly employed, stands on the tail.

Elliot Smith draws attention to page 36 of the *Dresden Codex* of the Maya, in which the complex rain god and dragon myth appears to be represented in several of its phases. There are nine pictures in all. One depicts the American black vulture attacking a living snake with jaws a-gape and the body curved to form two enclosures. Here the vulture acts the part of the African secretary-bird, and also that of the mythical garuda bird of India which wages constant war on the nāgas (snakes). A second picture shows the elephant-headed, or "long-nosed", god in human form carrying a lightning torch, while, in a third, he carries the "thunder axe". The

---

[1] *Rig Veda*, 1, 32; my *Indian Myth and Legend*, pp. 6–7.

god, in a fourth picture, stands on water, looking upward towards a rain cloud, and, in a fifth, he is crouched inside his house either resting or accumulating spiritual strength in contemplation. A sixth picture shows him coming from the east in a boat with a goddess, in ceremonial pose, seated in front of him. This may be the same goddess who, in the seventh picture, sits in the rain with her hair in the form of a long-necked bird (a heron) which grasps a fish in its beak. The thunder god is, in the eighth picture, a dog descending from the sky bearing firebrands. In the ninth picture the god is combined with the serpent as a long-nosed human-headed serpent which gives forth rain, the enclosures formed by the curving body having been opened.

Now, the dog was in India associated with Indra. In times of drought the hill tribes still torture dogs so that the "big dog" may hear and thunder and thus send rain. The Chinese "celestial dog" is similarly a thunder and lightning deity, and there are many references to it in the Chinese books, including the following:

"When dark clouds covered the sky everywhere at night, a noise of thunder was heard in the north. . . . This was what people call a descent of the celestial dog. . . ."

"It has a shape of a large moving star, and produces a noise. When it descends and reaches the earth it resembles a dog. Whatever it falls upon becomes a flaming fire; it looks like a fiery light, like flames flaming up to heaven. . . ."

"Thunder resounded in the north-west in a cloudless sky, and this was called a descent of the celestial dog. . . ."

"The celestial dogs live on the top of high mountains. . . . Their colour resembles that of the wan-i (crocodile dragon)."

The dogs are mentioned "as a kind of badgers living in the mountains, or as birds or plants (the *ginseng* = man-drake), or dragons". In Japan the celestial dog became confused with the long-nosed Tengu, and both were identified with the India Garuda and with Ganesha.[1]

It is apparent from the evidence of the *Dresden Codex* that the thunder dog was added with the elephant-headed god of India to the American "mythological museum". Indeed, in the Maya codices, the dog (*pek*) "is", as Brinton notes, "most conspicuous". It is associated with the sign for night, with the god of death, and with storm and lightning. Brinton writes:

" Dr. Schellhas and Dr. Seler regard him (the dog) as a symbol of lightning. But I am persuaded that, while not disconnected with this, the dog represents primarily some star or constellation. At times he is dotted with spots to represent stars. . . . His body is often in human form, carrying a torch in each hand (*Dresden Codex*, p. 39). . . . In *Cod. Dres.*, p. 40, he falls from the sky. . . . He plays on the medicine drum (*Cod. Tro.*, p. 20), and is associated with the rains." [2]

The resemblance to the Chinese celestial dog is undoubtedly very close.

The human-headed or elephant-headed snake is another form of the "feathered serpent"—a combination of the thunder bird (Garuda) or thunder god (with long nose or elephant's trunk) with the nāga. This union took place in India. The northern Buddhists "declared both the Nāgas and Garudas, mighty figures of the Hindu world of gods and demons, to be the obedient servants of Buddhas. . . . In the same way northern Buddhism adopted the gods of the countries where it introduced itself and made them protectors of its doctrine instead of its antagonists."[3]   In China the combined thunder god and water god is represented by the winged dragon, as

---

[1] De Visser on "The Tengu" (*Transactions of the Asiatic Society of Japan*, Vol. XXXVI, Part II, pp. 25 *et seq.*).   [2] *Mayan Hieroglyphics*, pp. 71–72.

[3] De Visser, *The Dragon in China and Japan*, p. 7.

it is in America by the feathered snake and the elephant-headed snake. In India the elephant was a "Nāga", as has been already shown.

"Every possible phase of the early history of the dragon story and all the ingredients which in the Old World went to the making of it, has," comments Elliot Smith, "been preserved in American pictures and legends in a bewildering variety of forms and with an amazing luxuriance of complicated symbolism and picturesque variety."[1] The rain god is sometimes the dragon-slayer, sometimes the dragon in his "vehicle", like the *makara* of the Indian god Vishnu, and sometimes the god and the dragon are one. Among the Maya the elephant and shark were forms of the *makara*, or sea-dragon, as in China and Polynesia.

As the controller of the cardinal points, the Maya Chac and the Mexican Tlaloc have, as has been indicated, four forms. In Egypt the four Horuses who supported the sky at the four quarters were sometimes represented by their symbols. Tlaloc's axe plays a similar part in America. Seler refers to a symbolic axe with "sharp edge upwards and above it the sun, from which a stream of blood flows down and along the haft of the axe, and bears in the middle a reeking human heart pierced by a dart. The axe with its upturned cutting side recalls", he adds, "the Mixtec saga of the copper axe on the mountain of Apoala, on whose edge the sky rests".[2]

Tlaloc supports not only the four quarters, but figures in the fifth quarter, which is the centre "from above downwards".[3] There were also four Tlaloc "rooms" in the middle of a large court in which stood four vessels of water.[4]

---

[1] *The Evolution of the Dragon*, pp. 87–88.   [2] *Codex Vaticanus B*, p. 27.
[3] *Ibid.*, pp. 281-4.   [4] *Ibid.*, pp. 295-6.

"The first water is very good, and from it comes the rain when the maize-ears and the field-fruits thrive, and when the rain comes at the right time. The second water is bad when it rains, and with the rain on the maize-ears grow cobwebs (fungus smut) and they become black. The third water is when it rains and the maize-ears freeze. The fourth when it rains and the maize-ears put out no grains and wither up. The description of the various kinds of water corresponds . . . to the four quarters of the heavens, east, west, north, south."

The Nāgas of the Buddhists likewise sent good and bad rain.

"Whenever men obey the law, and cherish their parents and support and feed the Shamans, then the good Nāga-rajas are able to acquire increased power, so that they can cause a small fertilizing rain to fall, by which the five sorts of grain are perfected in colour, scent, and taste. . . . If, on the contrary, men are disobedient to the law . . . then the power of the wicked dragon increases, and just the opposite effects follow; every calamity happens to the fruits of the earth and to the lives of men."[1]

Nāgas injuring crops are referred to in various texts.[2] The good rains "cause all plants and trees to shoot up and grow". It is of interest to note in this connection that good rain "does not come forth from his (the Nāga's) body but from his heart".[3]

The Mexican four dragons of the cardinal points are in *Codex Borgia*, 72 (*Codex Vaticanus B*, fig. 550) shown in their rooms, which are so arranged as to form a swashtika symbol which revolves, each "room" being connected with a season-controlling cardinal point.

In Mexico, as in China, Japan, and India, the dragons were adjusted to reflect local phenomena, and were connected with local fauna and flora. The American turkey appears to have taken the place of the Indian

---

[1] *The Dragon in China and Japan*, p. 23.   [2] *Ibid.*, 18.   [3] *Ibid.*, p. 24.

peacock as a rain bird, and symbolized "jewel water" (good rain and life blood). It is of special importance, however, to find that the deer remained associated with the rain-giver in America. Tlaloc is depicted in human form with a deer in front of him. There was also a deer god of the east and a deer god of the north. The eastern deer was white and the northern one brown. According to Seler the brown deer of the north signified drought— the north being in Mexico, as in China, the quarter of drought. He thinks that the white deer, which is dead, was connected with the foam on white incense vessels, and denoted the fire of the incense which means "plenty of food supplies", and indicates the east as "a region of fertility and increase".[1] The dragons, however, were sometimes depicted with the horns of deer. This trait is a feature of the dragon on the rocks at Piasa, Illinois. Brinton refers to the "fabulous horned snake", which was a famous "war physic" and gave protection.[2] Similar beliefs regarding dragon's horns obtained in China.

It would appear that the arbitrary connection between the water snake and the antelope, gazelle, and deer first took place in Southern Babylonia. Ea, originally a river god, was connected with the snake and afterwards with the antelope, gazelle, and stag. As has been shown, the Maruts of India had deer-drawn chariots. In China the dragon had deer's horns and was sometimes called "the celestial stag".[3]

As is shown in a Tlaloc prayer, given by Sahagun, the god was addressed as "giver and lord of verdure and coolness" who controlled "the gods of water, thy subjects". The prayer continues:

---

[1] *Codex Vaticanus B*, pp. 302–3.　　[2] *The Myths of the New World*, pp. 136 *et seq.*

[3] De Groot, J. de Morgan, Sayce, &c., quoted by Elliot Smith in *The Evolution of the Dragon*, pp. 130 *et seq.*

"It is woeful, O our Lord, to see all the face of the earth dry, so that it cannot produce the herbs nor the trees, nor anything to sustain us,—the earth that used to be as a father and mother to us, giving us milk and all nourishment, herbs and fruit that therein grew. Now is all dry, all lost; it is evident that the Tlaloc gods have carried all away with them, and hid in their retreat, which is their terrestrial paradise. . . . Give succour, O Lord, to our lord, the god of the earth, at least with one shower of water, for when he has water he creates and sustains us." [1]

Tlaloc is called "Lord of green things and gums, of herbs odorous and virtuous". In Pyramid Text No. 699 Osiris is "Lord of green fields". He was identified with the waters, the soil, and vegetation.[2]

According to Camargo, Tlaloc was greatly feared. "Whoever dared to blaspheme against him was supposed to die suddenly or to be stricken of thunder; the thunderbolt, instrument of his vengeance, flashed from the sky even at the moment it was clearest".[3] The Homeric Zeus and the Hindu Indra smote their enemies in like manner.

Dogs and human beings were sacrificed to the god, their hearts being torn out and burned, while incense was made to darken the faces of idols.

Children were sacrificed to Tlaloc, some being butchered and others drowned in the lake of Mexico. Those drowned were called *Epcoatl*. If the children wept, it was taken as a sign that rain would fall.

A similar diabolical custom obtained in Ireland, where children were sacrificed to Crom Cruach so that the people might be assured of supplies of "milk and corn".

The children offered to Tlaloc and to Chalchiuhtlicue were "bedecked with precious stones and rich feathers". Their blood was "jewel water" and was supposed, like

---

[1] Bancroft, *The Pacific States*, Vol. III, pp. 325 *et seq.*
[2] Breasted, *Religion and Thought in Ancient Egypt*, pp. 22, 23.   [3] *Ibid.*, p. 331.

that of other victims, to revive the god and assist him to provide life-giving moisture.

Jadeite images of Tlaloc were greatly favoured. At one of the god's festivals the priests and people entered a lake and swallowed live water-snakes and frogs. Chalchiuhtlicue was sometimes depicted as a frog, and jadeite frogs were favoured amulets.

The thunder deities of the various American peoples were all rain-bringers and associated with the bird and serpent. Sometimes the dragons assumed human shape. Bancroft[1] refers to a Honduras myth which tells of a beautiful white woman called Comizahual ("flying tigress"), a reputed sorceress. She introduced civilization and gave birth to three sons who ruled her kingdom. When her time came she asked to be carried to the highest part of the palace, "whence she suddenly disappeared amid thunder and lightning". This is a typical Chinese or Japanese dragon story of which versions are given by De Visser.[2]

A famous statue of Tlaloc, preserved in the National Museum, Mexico, shows him as a human-shaped god in semi-recumbent attitude, as if he had been awakened and was about to rise. He grasps a water pot, and a little serpent lies beside him. Apparently he is here a *nāga* in human form who stores and controls the supply of life-giving water.

Like Indra, Tlaloc had his own particular paradise. It was called Tlalocan, and was the source of rivers that nourished the earth. Eternal summer prevailed, and all the crops and fruits were in as great abundance as in the paradise of the Egyptian Osiris. Tlalocan was specially reserved for "those who had been killed by lightning, the drowned, those suffering from itch, gout, tumours, dropsy, leprosy, and other incurable diseases. Children also, at least those who were sacrificed to the Tlalocs, played

---

[1] *The Pacific States*, Vol. III, p. 485.   [2] *The Dragon in China and Japan.*

about in its gardens, and once a year they descended among the living in an invisible form to join in their festivals." [1]   This paradise was, of course, situated in the East.   The interpreter of *Codex Vaticanus*, dealing with *Chalmecaciuatl* (" children's paradise "), says : " This was the place . . . to which the souls of children who died before the use of reason went.   They feigned the existence of a tree from which milk distilled where all children who died at such an age were carried.   They also thought that the children have to return from thence to re-people the world after the third destruction which they suppose it has to undergo, for they believe that the world has been twice destroyed. . . . *Chichiualquauitl* signifies the tree of milk which nourishes children who die before attaining the use of reason." [2]

Clavigero describes a second paradise called " House of the Sun ", resembling the solar-cult's paradise in Egypt. It was reserved for soldiers who died in battle or in captivity, and for women who died on child-bed.   " Every day, at the first appearance of the sun's rays, they hailed his birth with rejoicings and with dancing and the music of instruments and voices. . . . These spirits, after four years of glorious life, went to animate clouds, and birds of beautiful feathers and of sweet song, but were always at liberty to rise again to heaven, or to descend upon the earth to warble and suck honey-flowers."   Honey and rain (from clouds) were thus the elixirs for the souls. Rain was produced by shedding human blood.

A third paradise allotted for souls was Mictland, a place of utter darkness like the Babylonian Underworld. This paradise was in the North.

[1] Bancroft, *The Pacific States*, Vol. III, pp. 523-4.
[2] Kingsborough, *Antiquities of Mexico*, Vol. VI (the translation of the explanation of the Mexican paintings of the *Codex Vaticanus A*, Plate V, p. 171).

CHAPTER XV

White Missionaries and White Gods

Spaniards as "White Gods"—Mexicans and an Ancient Prophecy—
Spanish King as Quetzalcoatl—Quetzalcoatl as Man, God, and Dragon—A
Peace-loving and Pious Cult—Quetzalcoatl as a Missionary—Expulsion of
Missionary King—Quetzalcoatl as a Buddha—Origin of Quetzalcoatl—The
Toltecs—Quetzalcoatl as Star God of the East—As God of the West—As
Wind God—As Creator—As Feathered-serpent Dragon—Legends of Sea-
farers reaching America—Votan, God and Missionary—The Oajacan Mis-
sionary—The Zapotec Missionary—Gucumatz, Kukulcan, and Itzamna—
South American Culture Heroes and Gods—White Strangers and Buddhist
Missionaries.

WHEN Cortez, the Spanish conqueror of Mexico, was
advancing with his small but comparatively powerful
army from Vera Cruz towards the capital of the Aztecs,
Montezuma and his subjects were greatly perturbed,
because it seemed to them that an ancient prophecy was
about to be fulfilled, and that the downfall of the Aztec
Empire was at hand. To them the Spaniards were
"white gods", or at any rate "white men from the East",
and it was remembered that their hero god or culture
god, Quetzalcoatl, who had lived for a time among men,
had departed eastward and set out to sea from Vera
Cruz. When taking leave of his disciples, Quetzalcoatl
told them "that there should surely come to them in
after times, by way of the sea where the sun rises, certain
white men with white beards, like him, and that these
would be his brothers and would rule that land". The
Mexicans are said to have long looked forward to the
arrival of these strangers.

Montezuma consulted the priestly astrologists when word was brought to him of the landing of Cortez. From them he received little comfort. Certain extraordinary happenings and signs had for some time engaged their attention. In 1510, nine years before Cortez set out as captain-general of the expedition, the lake of Tezcuco had overflowed its banks and devastated part of Mexico city. A mysterious fire broke out in the chief temple in the following year. Then no fewer than three comets appeared in the sky; and, shortly before the Spaniards landed, a strange pyramid of light appeared in the eastern sky which "seemed thickly powdered with stars"—a phenomenon probably caused by the eruption of a volcano. At the same time stories were circulated regarding voices and wailings that filled the air, foretelling approaching calamities. Some even told and believed that Montezuma's sister had, four days after her burial, risen from her grave to warn the monarch that his empire was soon to be plunged in ruin. It is not surprising therefore to read that Montezuma and his councillors should have been greatly agitated when the Spaniards made their appearance, some of them mounted on horses, which seemed to be dragon gods, and equipped with weapons that flashed like lightning and roared like thunder.

The Aztec monarch, being a fatalist, remained in a vacillating state of mind until the Spaniards had arrived in his capital. At first he endeavoured to persuade them to leave the coast by sending them presents of gold and gems, including the great gold and silver wheels referred to in my first chapter. He made a show of resistance which was speedily overcome.

The Spaniards had been opposed by the Tlascallans, who were heavily defeated after being terrified by the artillery bombardment. Then the Tlascallans made peace with the invaders and became their allies. Montezuma had the direct road to his capital blocked, but the obstacles were removed by Cortez, who was afterwards allowed to pursue his march free from molestation and enter the capital. The Spaniards seemed indeed to be " the men of destiny " whose coming had been foretold by Quetzalcoatl. It was useless, Montezuma thought, to attempt to resist them.

When Cortez was received in audience by Montezuma that monarch confessed that his ancestors were not the original owners of Mexico.[1]

" They had occupied it but a few ages, and had been led there by a great being, who, after giving them laws and ruling over the nation for a time, had withdrawn to the regions where the sun rises. He had declared, on his departure, that he, or his descendants, would again visit them and resume his Empire. The wonderful deeds of the Spaniards, their fair complexions, and the quarter whence they came, all showed they were his descendants. If Montezuma had resisted their visit to his capital, it was because he had heard such accounts of their cruelties—that they sent their lightning to consume his people, or crushed them to pieces under the feet of the ferocious animals on which they rode. He was convinced that these were idle tales; that the Spaniards were kind and generous in their nature; they were mortals, of a different race, indeed, from the Aztecs, wiser and more valiant—and for this he honoured them."

Tears streamed from the monarch's eyes as he spoke. " It is true ", he said, " I have a great empire inherited from my ancestors; lands, and gold, and silver. But your sovereign beyond the waters is, I know, the rightful lord of all. I rule in his name."[2] To Montezuma the King of Spain was the living representative of Quetzalcoatl.

[1] Perhaps he did not wish the Aztecs to be blamed for having expelled Quetzalcoatl.
[2] Prescott, *History of the Conquest of Mexico*, Book III, Chapter IX.

FIGURES OF QUETZALCOATL SHOWING BUDDHIST INFLUENCE

1, Quetzalcoatl representing Xipe Totec, from pyramid at San Dieguito, near Tezcoco.
2, Quetzalcoatl resembling Chinese Buddhist image.   3, Quetzalcoatl Buddhist-like figure
in Trocadéro Museum, Paris.   4, Quetzalcoatl sphinx from same locality as No. 1.   A
characteristic of all the images is the hooked ear-plugs which have a solar significance.
Nos. 1 and 4 have winding snakes above the wigs and "star-fish shaped" breast ornaments.
On breast of No. 2 is the "sliced-shell" symbol called in Japan the "maga-tama".

Now Quetzalcoatl, the "great being" referred to by Montezuma, comes before us for consideration in three aspects: (1) as a man, (2) as a culture god, and (3) as a dragon god of complex character. It would seem that he represents an intruding people who contributed to the culture complexes of pre-Columbian America, and not only the artisans and priests of that people, but also the god or gods they had imported from their area of origin. Before the intruders reached Mexico, their beliefs were of highly complex character. Their King-priests, who were called Quetzalcoatls, that is "feathered serpents" or "bird serpents", were, like the Emperors of China, also "Sons of Heaven"—that is human forms of the winged dragon god of their religion. An outstanding difference between the Quetzalcoatl cult and the other cults of the pre-Columbian Americans was that it was opposed to war and human sacrifice. According to the Aztec legends, Quetzalcoatl was ultimately expelled from the Mexican plateau, but, before leaving, foretold, as has been indicated, that either he or his descendants would return again.

The human Quetzalcoatl, Torquemada tells, was said to have been a tall, large-bodied white man, broad-browed, great-eyed, with long black hair and heavy beard. Some say that his face was red, and that he wore a long white robe or a black robe, adorned with crosses. He was reputed to have introduced the calendar, and to have taught the people agriculture, the art of government, stone-cutting, engraving, the craft of setting of precious stones, and the silversmith's craft, &c. He himself lived a chaste life, was given to the practice of penance, and to drawing blood from his ears and from beneath his tongue, because of the sinful things he had heard and uttered. He abstained from intoxicating drinks, and was a celibate. Mild and gentle, he hated war and violence, and, instead of offering up in sacrifice animals or human beings, he gave to the gods offerings of bread, roses and other flowers, and perfumes, and incense. He taught virtue and established good laws that promoted trade and peace.

At Tulla, where Quetzalcoatl reigned as a priest-king, maize was grown and fruit trees cultivated in great abundance. Cotton was produced in various colours. In the woods were many birds of rich plumage that sang sweetly. "This Quetzalcoatl had all the riches of the world, of gold and silver, of green stones called *chalchiuites* (*chalchiuitls*), and of other precious things, and a great abundance of cocoa-nut trees of divers colours."[1] He reigned for twenty years. When, in the end, he was compelled to retire eastward by his enemies, he threw precious stones at a tree which was remembered and reverenced as "the tree of the old man". When he came to a mountain near the city of Tlalnepantla, two leagues from Mexico city, he sat down on a stone and wept. He left the mark of his hand on the stone, and the place was called Temacpalco, which means "in the palm of the hand". At another place "he set up and balanced a great stone, so that one could move it with one's little finger, yet a multitude could not displace it". According to one account, he set to sea in a raft of snakes—which may refer to a "dragon ship" or "serpent ship", as ships were called by such far-separated seafarers as those of China and Norway. Another account, given by Mendieta, states that Quetzalcoatl died on reaching the seashore and that his disciples burned his body, thus inaugurating the custom of cremation. The heart of Quetzalcoatl was supposed to have ascended from the pyre to become the morning star. That was why the Mexicans called him "Lord of Dawn".

---

[1] Bancroft, *The Pacific States*, Vol. III, p. 241.

It may be that the Quetzalcoatl cult was of Buddhist origin. An interesting representation of him, preserved in the Ethnographical Department of the Trocadéro Museum, Paris, reveals him, indeed, as a Buddha sitting with legs crossed in quite the Hindu fashion, with downcast eyes, tranquil face, and arms hanging limp, as if engaged in meditation. Pious Brahmans can still be seen in this pose on the banks of the Ganges, meditating on the supreme soul, Brahma, oblivious to all that is happening about them.

Although some Americanists dismiss as "absurd" the view that there are traces of Buddhist influence in the Quetzalcoatl cult and legends, the evidence of this little art relic cannot be ignored, especially as another Quetzalcoatl image bears a remarkable resemblance to Chinese Buddhist art in clay images, and has the "magatama" symbol (the "sliced-shell" symbol of the Americanists) on the breast cloth. In China the white "magatama" was a symbol of *Yang* and the black "magatama" of *Yin*.

There are various Mexican legends as to the origin of Quetzalcoatl. One is that he had a virgin mother; another makes him the son of Iztacmixcoatl, the Mexican patriarch, by his second wife Chimamatl; another makes him a Culhuacan prince who preached a new religion, proscribing warfare and human sacrifices and encouraging penance. One of the interpreters of the codices states that he was created by Tonacatecotle (god of heaven), who was also called Citinatonali, "not by connection with woman, but by his breath alone. . . ." "Citinatonali sent his son into the world to reform it." Quetzalcoatl was usually associated with the pre-Aztec cult or people called Toltec. The Toltecs were supposed to have come from Hue-hue-tlapallan ("Old Red Land") in the north, and to have settled at Tulla, where Quetzalcoatl is said to have reigned as priest-king.

At the time of the Spanish conquest Tlapallan was supposed to be some area in the direction of Honduras, in the Maya country. There was also a Tlapallan-conco ("Little Tlapallan"), which was founded by Toltecs from "Old Tlapallan". It may be that in the Quetzalcoatl myth we have embedded legends regarding a god who came from the east and returned to the east in the Old Tlapallan mythology, and that it did not necessarily have its origin in America, although it was ultimately located there and influenced by traditions of American race-migrations.

When the Pandava brothers in the *Mahá-bhárata* set out to walk to paradise, they first go eastward until they reach the mythical "Red Sea"; then they turn south-ward, and from the south they go by way of the west to the northern paradise. The "Old Tlapallan" of the north may have simply been a mythical place like the Aztlan, the homeland of the Aztecs.

According to one of the expulsion myths already referred to, Quetzalcoatl became a god after he was cremated. He was supposed to have been invisible for four days, and to have dwelt in the underworld for eight days, before he appeared as the morning star.

The Spanish monks believed that Quetzalcoatl was no other than St. Thomas, who had crossed the Atlantic to preach Christianity. This theory explained, to the satisfaction of many at the time, why the cross (originally the symbol of the four quarters) was closely associated with Quetzalcoatl.

As a god Quetzalcoatl was of complex character. He was, in the first place, connected with both the east and the west, a fact which suggests that the ancient controversy regarding the importance of these cardinal points had been introduced into America by the Quetzalcoatl cult. In China there was a western paradise, in which grew the Peach Tree of Life, and the eastern paradise of the Isles of the Blest; in India, as far back as Vedic times, the cult of the west was represented by Varuna and that of the east by Indra. The Buddhists adopted the idea of a western paradise, and the Amida cult believed in "the Great Buddha of the Western Regions". Other Buddhists looked for comfort to the eastern "Isles of the Blest". In Ancient Egypt Osiris, "First of the Westerners", represented a cult opposed to Ra, the sun god of the Easterners, and the rivalry of the two cults is enshrined in a Pyramid text in which "the dead is adjured to go to the west in preference to the east".[1] The various paradises in India and pre-Columbian America appear to represent rival cults that had been fused by theorizing priests for political purposes.

As a god of the east Quetzalcoatl was identified, as has been noted, with the morning star. In the myths he came from the east and departed eastward. Under the sign *ce cipactli* ("one crocodile") he is shown in the codices with Huaxtec cone-shaped hat, and standing on the surface of water as ruler of the east; he is also shown in the east below the sign *eecatl* ("wind").[2]

As a god of the west, "the region of abundant water", Quetzalcoatl is sometimes a wind god and sometimes a rain and thunder god, who wears a chain of *chalchiuitl* jewels, and blows fire from his mouth before a fire vessel on which is a rubber ball and coiled snake.[3]

---

[1] Breasted, *Development of Religion and Thought in Ancient Egypt*, pp. 99 *et seq.*; *Chinese Myth and Legend*, pp. 60–61.

[2] *Codex Vaticanus B*, pp. 7, 87, 286.   [3] *Ibid.*, pp. 202, 243, 297.

Although shown as a god, his priestly character, however, always "clings to him", as Seler notes. He was reputed to be the introducer of "penitential exercises and mortifications, of the blood-letting and the offering of one's own blood" when lord and king of the Toltecs. By his prayers and practices he "ensured for his people the rain required for the growth of their crops", as did the Buddhist worshippers of the nāgas and dragons in India, China, and Japan. He was likewise, as a wind god, "the forerunner and sweeper of the rain god".[1] In India the rain god Indra absorbed the attributes of the wind god Vayu.

Quetzalcoatl was also worshipped as the creator, the giver of the breath of life. He, indeed, was the god of wind, fire, and rain; and Tlaloc was but a form of him. The explanation may be, as suggested, that the priest and penitent, Quetzalcoatl, took the place of all the deities worshipped by his cult. He was thus as the "feathered snake" the combined Garuda and nāga, the winged dragon, a personification of the complex dragon god. Being a nāga, he was a giver of children, and was prayed to by barren women, as are the nāga gods in India to this day. "Quetzalcoatl, whose name", says Seler, "properly means 'quetzal—feather snake', may also be translated 'the costly twins'." His array is worn by Xolotl, "the god of twins".[2]

The quetzal bird, with which the god was connected, belongs to the Trogon family. It is about the size of the magpie, and the male has gorgeous curving tail-feathers of emerald colour, about three feet in length. A trogon is a climber with grasping feet, and at first sight looks like a woodpecker. It feeds on fruit. Quetzalcoatl was a cultivator of fruit trees at Tulla, and these trees, no

[1] *Codex Vaticanus B*, pp. 136 *et seq.*   [2] *Ibid.*, pp. 220, 270.

doubt, attracted the quetzals, which may have been oracular birds. Their connection with serpents is quite arbitrary. According to Seler, the tail-feathers of the male bird denote costliness, plenty of water and vegetation, and a child.[1]

Another bird with which Quetzalcoatl was connected was a bird which Acosta thought resembled a sparrow. In America the native "sparrow" is really a bunting, and a variety of the bunting is found as far north as Alaska. In China the green sparrow is a messenger from the supernatural world and a foreteller of "good luck", or of the coming of the goddess of the west, in whose garden paradise it nests and feeds. Sparrows, buntings, linnets, &c., are supposed to foretell rain when they chirp with unusual vigour and clamour. In India the small birds symbolize fecundity.

The images and pictures of Quetzalcoatl are numerous and varied. He is shown in human form as a shield-bearing warrior grasping a thunderbolt, as a god with protruding bird's beak, as a priest god performing penance, as a sphinx-like human-headed animal, as a naked man, as a man with prominent breasts like the Nile god Hapi; and frequently, when shown in human form, he has prominent ear plugs and solar ear discs. Of special interest is the fact that he invariably wears Huaxtec attire. Seler's view in this connection is that Quetzalcoatl "was held to be the lord and prince of the earliest inhabitants of the land, that is, from the Mexican standpoint, the first immigrants. And, according to a widespread belief, this first immigration followed the route through the Huaxtec territory." Seler quotes the following significant Mexican hymn:

Over the water in ships came numerous tribes,
To the coast they came, to the coast situate in the North,

[1] *Codex Vaticanus B*, pp. 23, 116, 135.

And where with ships they landed—
That was called Panutla ("where they go over the water"),
  that is now called Pantla.
Then they followed the coast,
They behold the mountains, especially the Sierra Nevada and
  the Volcano (Popocatepetl),
And came, still following the coast, to Guatemala;
Thereafter they came and reached
The place called Tamoanchan (" we seek our home "),
And there they tarried long. [1]

Seler identified Panutla (Pantla) with the present Pánuco in Huaxtec territory, and writes:

"The districts inhabited by the Huaxtec peoples—Tuxpan and Papantla and the conterminous coast lands, the land of the Totonacs and of the Olmeca Uixtotin—were the seat of a very ancient and highly developed culture, and from the early times carried on an active intercourse with the Mexicans of the central tableland. By the Mexicans the Huaxtecs were also called Toueyô, which in his ethnographic chapter Sahagun explains with the term touampô, 'our next', 'our neighbour'. But in reality toueyô means 'our greater', probably in the sense of 'our elder brother', and by Molina is translated 'stranger', 'alien' (advenedizo estrangero), only because those designated by this term belonged to a foreign population of different speech." [2]

Whence came the highly cultured aliens whose civilization is represented by Quetzalcoatl? They were evidently seafarers who settled on the coastlands and introduced the dragon beliefs so like those found in India, China, and Japan; they introduced various arts and crafts and well-defined laws, and their Quetzalcoatl priests were penitents given to self-mortification like the Indian Brahmans; they hated war and violence, and instead of sacrificing animals made offerings of flowers, jewels, &c., to their deities. That they came under

[1] *Codex Vaticanus B*, pp. 141–2.   [2] *Ibid.*, pp. 142–3.

Hindu or Buddhist influence, as did sections of the Chinese people, is a view which cannot be lightly dismissed, except by those who cling to the belief in the spontaneous generation in different parts of the world of the same groups of highly complex beliefs and practices.

Like the Buddhist missionaries, the disciples of Quetzalcoatl, the Toltec priest-god, "went forth at the command of their master to preach his doctrines". They founded several centres of worship in Oajaca. At Achiuhtla, the centre of Mixtec religion, there was a cave with idols in which religious ceremonies were performed.[1] "A large transparent *chalchiuitl*, entwined by a snake whose head pointed towards a little bird", was a specially sacred relic which was worshipped as "the heart of the people". The relic was, according to Burgoa, supposed to support the earth. Quetzalcoatl was represented as an Atlas in Mexico.[2] The "heart" symbolism is met with in Japanese Buddhism. "The Essence of Zenshuism," writes Professor Arthur Lloyd, "is the 'Heart of Buddha'. But what that 'heart' is cannot exactly be said."[3]

The cave jewel serpent has been linked by not a few Americanists with Votan, "the heart", a Maya god. As we have seen, the *chalchiuitl* jewel was, like the green scarab of Egypt, regarded as the heart—the seat of life, and was placed in the mouths of the Mexican dead like the jade tongue amulet in China. It contained "life substance" (*yang*).

Votan was, like Quetzalcoatl, "the first historian of his people, and wrote a book on the origin of the race, in

[1] The Buddhist clergy greatly favoured caves in which they meditated and performed ceremonies.   [2] *Codex Vaticanus B*, p. 93.

[3] *The Formative Elements of Japanese Buddhism* (*Transactions of the Asiatic Society of Japan*), Vol. XXXV, Part II, p. 218.

which he declares himself a snake, a descendant of Imos, of the line of Chan, of the race of Chivim ". Unfortunately the book was burned by the Spaniards, but extracts from it have been preserved. According to Brasseur de Bourbourg (*Popol Vuh*, p. 109), "Chan" signified "snake", and applied to the Colhuas, Chancs, or Quinames. Cabrera believed that "Chivim" referred to Tripoli, and that it is the same as Hivim or Givim, the Phœnician word for snake, which again refers to Hivites, the descendants of Heth, son of Canaan. Votan's expression, as given in his book, "I am a snake, a Chivim", signifies, "I am a Hivite from Tripoli".[1]

Whatever may be thought of this view, the interesting fact emerges that there was a snake people in America as there were and are Nāga peoples in India.

The Votan peoples were seafarers who settled on various islands, and were called by one of the peoples with whom they mixed the Tzequiles ("men with petticoats") because they wore long robes. Votan is said to have returned to Palenque, where he found that "several more of the natives had arrived; these he recognized as 'Snakes', and showed them many favours".[2]

A tradition among the Oajacans told of the coming from the south-west by sea of "an old white man, with long hair and beard", who preached to the people. "He lived a strict life, passing the greater part of the night in a kneeling posture and eating but little. He disappeared shortly afterwards as mysteriously as he came." He left a cross as a memento of his visit.

A similar personage, if not the same, called Wixepecocha by the Zapotecs, who arrived by sea from the south-west, was a celibate. He called for repentance and expiation.

---

[1] Bancroft, *The Pacific States*, Vol. III, pp. 451-2, and Note 54.
[2] Bancroft, *op. cit.*, Vol. III, pp. 452-3.

Persecuted and driven from province to province, he took refuge on the summit of Mount Cempoaltepec, vanishing like a shadow and "leaving only the print of his feet upon the rock"—quite a Buddhist touch![1] Votan was supposed to have "hollowed out of a rock his cave temple by blowing with his breath".[2] There are also references to him entering the Underworld through a subterranean passage—one of the passages so familiar in Old World mythologies.

Other "feathered serpents", or "bird serpents", were Gucumatz and Kukulcan. Gucumatz was a ruler and god of the Quiche-Cakchiquel empire in Guatemala, which "was, at the coming of the Spaniards," says Bancroft, "the most powerful and famous in North America, except that of the Aztecs in Anáhuac, with which it never came into direct contact, although the fame of each was well known to the other, and commercial intercourse was carried on almost constantly. The southern empire . . . was about three centuries old in the sixteenth century."[3]

The monarch called Gucumatz was able to transform himself like Indra and Odin, and like them, and the Egyptian king Rhampsinitus, referred to by Herodotus, he visited the lower regions.

"In seven days he mounted to the skies—ascended the mountain heights—and in seven days he descended to the region of Xibalba (the Underworld). In seven days he took upon himself the nature and form of a serpent, and again of an eagle, and of a tiger; and in seven days he changed himself into coagulated blood."[4]

The god Gucumatz was a culture god like the Babylonian Ea. He was closely connected with Hurakan, the

---

[1] Bancroft, *op. cit.*, Vol. III, pp. 454-5. The superhuman Buddha, who was 16 feet high, left the marks of his feet in Japan on a great stone "in front of the Zojoji Temple in Shiba Park" (*Transactions of the Asiatic Society of Japan*, Vol. XXXV, Part II, p. 236).   [2] Brinton, *Myths of the New World*, p. 324.
[3] Bancroft, *The Pacific States*, Vol. V, pp. 540-1.   [4] *Ibid.*, Vol. V, p. 581.

god of tempest, thunder, rain, and the sky, who had the significant title "Heart of Heaven"; he was also the "Bowels of Heaven" and the "Bowels of Earth" and the god of "the four ends of heaven" (the four quarters).

In the *Popol Vuh*, the sacred book of the Quiches, Gucumatz has three manifestations, as has Hurakan, who is represented by (1) the thunder, (2) the lightning, and (3) the thunderbolt; or by (1) the lightning flash, (2) its track, and (3) the bolt. In the account of creation in the *Popol Vuh* it is said:

"At first there was stillness and darkness in the shades, in the night. Alone also was the Creator, the Former, the Dominator, the Serpent covered with feathers. Those who fertilise, those who give life, are upon the water like a growing light. They are enveloped in green and blue (*de vert et d'azur*); hence their name is Gucumatz."

A footnote explains: "Gucumatz is a serpent covered with green and blue. . . . They are also called by this name because they are enveloped, shadowed in green and blue." [1]

A temple oracle was a polished stone by which the gods made known their will. Quetzalcoatl was, in like manner, represented by a flint, a black stone, or by green stones (jadeite).

Kukulcan of the Maya, who links with Quetzalcoatl in Cholula, Gucumatz in Guatemala, and Votan in Chiapas, was supposed to come from the west and found or re-found the city of Mayapan. He had nineteen followers, "all with long beards and dressed in long robes and sandals, but bare-headed". He introduced the rites of confession, and modified the existing religious beliefs. According to Herrera he had two brothers, and all were celibates.

[1] Abbé Brasseur, *Popol Vuh, Le Livre sacré et les Mythes de l'Antiquité Américaine*, 1861.

Another Maya culture hero was Zamna or Itzamna, a priest and law-giver, who came from the west accompanied by priests, artisans, and even warriors; he invented the hieroglyphics. He bore a close resemblance to Votan.

Bancroft draws attention to the interesting fact that all the American culture heroes present the same general characteristics :

"They are all described as white, bearded men, generally clad in long robes; appearing suddenly and mysteriously upon the scene of their labours, they at once set about improving the people by instructing them in useful and ornamental arts, giving them laws, exhorting them to practise brotherly love and other Christian virtues, and introducing a milder and better form of religion; having accomplished their mission, they disappear as mysteriously and unexpectedly as they came; and finally, they are apotheosized and held in great reverence by a grateful posterity."[1]

In addition to those already given there are also Viracocha in Peru, Sumé and Paye-tome in Brazil, a mysterious visitor to Chili, and Bochica in Columbia.

Viracocha was supposed to have come from the west and to have returned westward, disappearing in the ocean. Another myth makes him emerge from Lake Titicaca as the creator of the sun and moon, and another makes him the sun which emerged from Pacari, the cave of dawn. Evidently the culture hero was confused with the sun god and creator of his cult. Peruvian legends, according to Torquemada, tell of giants who came across the Pacific, conquered Peru and erected great buildings.[2] There were

[1] *The Pacific States*, Vol. V, p. 23.

[2] The superhuman Buddha was, as has been noted, a giant. Stone circles, &c., were supposed to have been erected by giants in Britain. The Cyclopean style of building was in Greece attributed to giants. China and Japan have legends of giants. The remote prototype of the superhuman Buddha was the Egyptian Horus, who "attained," as Breasted reminds us, "a stature of eight cubits (nearly fourteen feet)".

also "numerous vague traditions of settlements or nations of white men, who lived apart from the other people of the country, and were possessed of an advanced civilization".[1]

Sumé of Brazil was a white, bearded man who, however, came from the east, not the west. He introduced agriculture, and had power to raise and still tempests. The Caboclos of Brazil persecuted him, and, before he retired from their country, he left the prints of his feet on rocks as did Buddha in Ceylon and elsewhere. Payetome was also a white man.

The apostle of the Chilians was a white man who performed miracles and cured the sick; he caused rain to fall and crops to grow, and kindled fire at a breath. In like manner Buddhist priests "caused rain" by repeating *sutras* as rain charms.

Bochica, who gave laws to the Muyscas, was a white, bearded man, wearing long robes, who regulated the calendar, established festivals, and vanished in time like the others. He was supposed to be a "son of the sun".[2]

It is remarkable that these legends of white, bearded men, wearing long robes, should be so widespread and persistent over wide areas in America. In all cases they are seafarers, teachers, and preachers, like the Buddhist missionaries who for centuries visited distant lands and left the impress of their teachings and the memory of their activities in the religious traditions of many different and widely-separated peoples.

---

[1] Bancroft, *The Pacific States*, Vol. V, p. 24.
[2] Authorities quoted by Bancroft in *The Pacific States*, Vol. V, pp. 23–24, and Notes 53–58.

CHAPTER XVI

Two Great Gods

Tezcatlipoca as Persecutor of Quetzalcoatl—As a Wizard—As a Yama—
The "Smoking Mirror"—Indian Wonder-working Stones—Chinese Mirrors
of Stone and Jade—New Fire procured by Stone Mirrors in Peru—Greek
Fire-procuring Crystal—Siamese and Chinese procured Fire by Mirrors—
Tezcatlipoca's Mirror as a Symbol of War—Its Connection with Fire and the
Sun—The Winter Sun and Summer Sun—Tezcatlipoca as God of Fire,
Drought, Death, &c.—Tezcatlipoca and the Indian Krishna—Black Forms
of Tezcatlipoca—His Gold Mirror called "The Viewer"—Spider's Web
Myth—Repulsive Forms of Tezcatlipoca, the Indian Kubera, and the Greek
Plutus—Huitzilopochtli the War God—Bird and Serpent Connections—The
Oracular Humming-bird—Huitzilopochtli as God of the Left and the
South—Tezcatlipoca as God of the Right and the North—God-eating
Festivals—Paynalton the Substitute War God—Huitzilopochtli and the
Indian Shiva—Skull Oracles—Skulls and Rain-getting—Human Sacrifices
in New and Old Worlds.

IN the Mexican legend of Quetzalcoatl, the god Tezcatlipoca figures as the persecutor who contrives to make
the white-bearded and aged priest-king depart from Tulla
towards the east. In this connection he is a wizard who
can change his form at will. As a god, however, Tezcatlipoca absorbs certain of the attributes of Quetzalcoatl,
and he even appears as his companion. An obscure
myth, which is illustrated in one of the codices, makes
Tezcatlipoca visit Hades, accompanied by Quetzalcoatl,
certain of whose symbols he has assumed. It would
appear that, like the Indian Yama and the Egyptian
Ap-uat, Tezcatlipoca was regarded as the first man to
"open the way", or discover the road to Hades.[1] This

[1] Seler, *Codex Vaticanus B*, p. 119.

phase of his character may have been derived from Xipe
Totec, who figures, indeed, as the " Red Tezcatlipoca " in
association with Quetzalcoatl, performing acts of penance
in the " House of Sorrow " and on the summit of Cat-
citepulz ("the mountain which speaks"), a mountain
covered with thorns, from which he calls on the people
of Tulan to do penance with him on account of their sins.
The interpreter of *Codex Vaticanus* states : " They held
Xipe Totec in the utmost veneration, for they said that
he was the first who opened to them the way to heaven,
for they were under this error amongst others—they supposed that only those who died in war went to heaven ".[1]

As a rule, Tezcatlipoca is shown as a god of the
north, but he is also found sometimes in the south and
in the east.[2]

An outstanding symbol of this god is the "smoking
mirror", which, in fact, gives him his name, and must
therefore be regarded as of first importance.   This mirror
is of polished black obsidian, and recalls at the outset the
polished stone in the temple of the Maya god, Gucumatz
(as Tohil), by means of which the gods made known
their will, as well as the black stone, the flint, and the
green stones (jadeite) of Quetzalcoatl, and the large
transparent *chalchiuitl* (a gem of some kind) entwined by
the Votan snake god of the Mixtecs.   As Tezcatlipoca
was a wizard and seer, and had, as will be shown, a
gold mirror named "Viewer", the obsidian mirror was
no doubt used, as Sahagun indicates, for purposes of
divination.

Crystallomancy (crystal gazing) by means of precious
stones, mirrors, &c., is of great antiquity, and the object

---

[1] Kingsborough, *Antiquities of Mexico*, Vol. VI, p. 50.
[2] *Codex Vaticanus B*, pp. 8, 77, 200–210, 320 (for the north), 81 (for the south),
and 95–96 (for the east).

FORMS OF TEZCATLIPOCA

1, Xipe Totec, who in one of his forms is the Red Tezcatlipoca (*Codex Vaticanus A*).
2, Tezcatlipoca as purple jaguar, with blue markings and eagles' claws (*Codex Vaticanus A*).
3, Tezcatlipoca as purple bird god (*Codex Vaticanus A*). 4, Blindfold Tezcatlipoca (*Codex Vaticanus B*).

used had to be of spherical or oval shape and finely polished. As those who used the crystal or mirror had to be penitents given to fasting, prayer, and contemplation, and had to face the east, the possibility cannot be overlooked that Tezcatlipoca's mirror was, like the Quetzalcoatl stones and those of Gucumatz and Votan, introduced from Asia. It does not follow, however, that Tezcatlipoca's mirror was borrowed from Quetzalcoatl. As a crystal gazer Tezcatlipoca may represent an intruding cult which had acquired the divination mirror from the same source as did the Buddhists.

An interesting fact about crystallomancy is that the stone or mirror, before revealing anything, was supposed to be obscured by mist or smoke. Tezcatlipoca's "smoking mirror" may therefore have been a mirror which was about to reveal to the magician the will of the gods, the future, or some sort of knowledge of special importance. "Adam's jewel", for instance, was used to light the way to the Underworld. It was used by the emissary of Alexander the Great, who passed through the dark mountain tunnel in quest of the Well of Life.

Divination and "luck stones" were also used for other purposes. Krishna, the Hindu man-god, became the possessor of a "wonder-working stone", and "its properties of procuring plenty to the country of its possessor, and of bringing down rain when needed, ally it", as Wilson says, "to the marvellous stone, for the acquisition of which the Tartar tribes not infrequently had recourse to hostilities".[1] Another famous Indian stone was the Chandrakánta ("moon gem"), "which was supposed to absorb the rays of the moon and to emit them again". The same properties were possessed by the moon pearl or "dragon pearl". Cooling and heating

[1] *Essays on Sanskrit Literature*, Vol. I, pp. 132–3.

jades are referred to in the jade lore of China and Japan. Chessmen of black and white jade were "warm in winter, cool in summer, and known as cool and warm jade".[1]

References are made in Chinese texts to mirrors of jade and stone which were placed in graves. These may have been intended to light the way to Hades, to assist the pilgrim by making revelations for his guidance, and to indicate, like the Gucumatz polished stone, the will of the gods. The Buddhists had various modes of sitting in meditation. One mode was: "Moondisk Contemplation, gazing fixedly at a disk of the bright full moon suspended in front of the devotee's breast."[2]

Mirrors and crystals were also used to procure fire from heaven, and especially from the sun. Laufer notes, in this connection, that "stone mirrors were known in ancient Peru". These were "of a circular form", with "one of the surfaces flat with all the smoothness of a crystal looking-glass". Others were "oval and something spherical and the polish not so fine". One Peruvian stone mirror referred to was of "Inca stone", the other being of Gallinazo stone. The latter was "very hard, brittle as flint and of black colour", and may have been, as Laufer suggests, of black obsidian. The mirrors were of various sizes, generally three or four inches in diameter, but reference is made to one a foot and a half; "its principal surface was concave, and greatly enlarged objects".[3]

The virgin priestesses of the Incas of Peru procured new fire at midsummer by holding towards the sun a hollow mirror, which reflected its beams on a tinder of cotton-wool. Sir James G. Frazer notes in this connection

[1] Laufer, *Jade*, p. 353.

[2] *Transactions of the Asiatic Society of Japan*, Vol. XXXVIII, Part II, p. 29.

[3] Laufer, *Jade*, p. 20, and Note 1.

in *The Golden Bough*[1] that the Greeks lit sacred fires by means of a crystal. "Nor", he writes, "were the Greeks and Peruvians peculiar in this respect. The Siamese and Chinese have also the habit of kindling a sacred fire by means of a metal mirror or burning glass." Copper was used in China as a substitute for jade, as jade was for gold, silver, pearls, gems, &c.

Tezcatlipoca's mirror is sometimes shown with clouds of flame or smoke issuing from it. In *Codex Borgia* (fig. 289, *Codex Vaticanus B*) the flames are combined with a water vessel. Seler's view is that the intention was to represent water and fire, "the symbol of war", and that the "smoking mirror" at the temple of the god's head and in the *Codex Borgia* "is itself nothing more than a symbol of war". It would appear, however, that the fire connection is important in itself. The mirror may have been used like the Peruvian "stone mirror" to procure new fire from the sun. Tezcatlipoca was the ruler of the winter-sun period, and his brother, Huitzilopochtli— who was associated with the fire god and was, indeed, himself, among other things, a fire and solar god—was the ruler of the summer-sun period. The "smoking mirror" may have been a relic—that is, Tezcatlipoca may have originally been prominent as a solar fire god before he was given a place in the later Aztec pantheon, which no doubt reflected local politics after the Aztec power became supreme in Mexico and the gods of the conquerors and the conquered were shown in a new association. As in Asia and Europe, the summer-sun period and the winter-sun period were ushered in by lighting sacred fires.

There are points of resemblance between Tezcatlipoca and the fire god Huehueteotl ("the ancient god"), who was celebrated at two annual festivals and had associations

[1] ("The Magic Art"), Vol. II, pp. 243–5, and Note 1, p. 244 (3rd edition).

with the god of war.   Tezcatlipoca was depicted as a creator of fire who used the fire drill.   He was, therefore, connected with lightning as well as the sun.   The interpreter of *Codex Telleriano-Remensis* states that "they paid Tezcatlipoca great reverence, for they kept lights and fires burning in his honour in the temples".

Although, in one of his aspects, a god of drought, Tezcatlipoca was also a rain-bringer.   His cold northern rain caused the maize ears to freeze.   Like Tlaloc he was connected with the rain-bird, the turkey ("the jewel fowl").   Withal, he was the god of the Great Bear constellation which in China regulates the seasons ; he helped at birth as the love god ; he slew the pulque god ; he was a wind god ; with Huitzilopochtli, he was a god of the upper heaven ; and he was the blind god of justice (the Avenger) and the black god of death, while, like the fire god, he was intimately associated with the god of war.[1]

Clavigero says that Tezcatlipoca was the greatest god adored by the Aztecs "after the invisible God or Supreme Being. . . . He was the god of Providence, the soul of the world, the creator of heaven and earth, and master of all things.   They represented him as always young to denote that no length of years ever diminished his power; they believed that he rewarded with various benefits the just, and punished the wicked with diseases and other afflictions."

The original Tezcatlipoca appears to be revealed by the young man who impersonated him for a year and was then sacrificed.   This victim behaved in a manner which recalls the black Hindu man-god Krishna, who played on the flute, was given to wearing jewels and flower garlands,

---

[1] *Codex Vaticanus B*, pp. 171, as a rain god ; 38, as a fire god ; 96 and 256, as a star god ; 40–51 and 234–5, as a love god ; 167, as a slayer of the pulque god ; 171, as a god of justice ; 69–90, for association with war god.

and to making love to many girls. For the year during which he masqueraded as Tezcatlipoca, the Mexican youth was greatly honoured. He went about playing a flute, wearing flower garlands, or carrying flowers, attended by eight pages who were clad like princes. Four girls were his temporary wives. Nobles and princes entertained him, and in the streets he was saluted as a god. It is of special importance to note that his body and face were painted black, and that his ornaments included sea shells, gold bells, precious stones, and a large gem on his breast. In the end a great feast, attended by elaborate ceremonies, was held, and the youth was sacrificed by having his heart torn out and his head cut off.

Clavigero has interesting things to say about the flute. He tells that ten days before the festival in honour of Tezcatlipoca the priest assumed the habits and badges of the god. "He went out of the temple with a bunch of flowers in his hands, and a little flute of clay which made a very shrill sound. Turning his face towards the east, and afterwards to the other three principal winds, he sounded the flute loudly, and then taking up a little dust from the earth with his finger, he put it into his mouth and swallowed it. On hearing the sound of the flute all kneeled down. . . . The sound of the flute was repeated every day until the festival." Evidently the god was summoned by the flute. In China white jade "male" and "female" flutes and bamboo flutes were used in religious ceremonies. "Jade flutes," says Laufer, "are frequently alluded to in Chinese literature. The *Si king tsa ki* relates that at Hien-yang there was a jade flute with twenty-six holes. When the Emperor Kao-tsu first went to that place, he spied it in the treasury and played on it, whereupon mountains and groves with horses and chariots appeared in a mist, vanishing altogether when he ceased playing."[1] Flutes were used in religious ceremonies in Babylonia. Tammuz was mourned annually to the music of the flute. In Syria and Asia Minor flutes were played in connection with the festivals of the mother goddess and of Attis, as they still are in connection with Krishna rites in India. A famous flute player was Marsyas, who is sometimes referred to in the classics as a shepherd and sometimes as a Phrygian satyr or Silenus. He challenged Apollo to a musical contest and, being vanquished, was mutilated and flayed. Herodotus (VII, 26) tells that in the market-place of Celænæ, in which the Cataract stream rises, "is hung to view the skin of the Silenus Marsyas, which Apollo, as the Phrygian story goes, stripped off and placed there". The skin was kept in a cave, and used to thrill when Phrygian music was played. Xipe Totec (the red Tezcatlipoca) was a flayed god, and the skins of his victims were deposited in a cave. The flute-playing Mexican god appears to bear traces of the influence of the ancient Old-World cult of the god who spent part of his year in Hades and part in this world, and figures as Tammuz in Babylonia and as Attis and Adonis in Syria, Anatolia, and Greece. The original flute-playing god may have given origin to the legends of the Pied Piper of Hamelin order. In Sardinia, on St. John's Day, a young man selected a *comare* (gossip and sweetheart), and marched with a long retinue headed by children to a church, where they broke against the door a pot of earth in which barley seeds had been sown. Thereafter they sat on the grass and ate eggs and herbs to the music of flutes, and then drank wine and danced.[2]

As a Pied Piper Tezcatlipoca (as Xipe Totec) destroys

[1] Laufer, *Jade*, pp. 332–3. Bishop, *Investigations and Studies in Jade* (New York, 1906), Vol. I, p. 49.

[2] *The Golden Bough* ("Adonis, Attis, Osiris" vol.), 3rd edition, pp. 7, 202, 222, 223, 225, 228, 242.

the adults of Tulan by causing them to fall into a cavity
between two mountains which closed together and buried
them; none but children remained alive. The interpreter
of *Codex Vaticanus*, dealing with this incident, says that
the people went forth "dancing and jesting," the devil
(Tezcatlipoca) "leading the way directing the minuet or
dance". Plate XIV is said to refer to the two masters
of penance Quetzalcoatl and Xipe Totec (Tezcatlipoca),
"who having taken the children and the innocent people
who remained in Tulan, proceeded with them peopling
the world and collecting along with them other people
whom they chanced to find". It is further added:
"Journeying in this manner with these people they
arrived at a certain mountain which, not being able to
pass, they feign that they bored a subterranean way through
it and so passed. Others say that they remained shut up
and that they were transformed into stones, and other
such fables."

An interesting collection of Pied Piper stories is given
in his *Curious Myths of the Middle Ages*[1] by the Rev. S.
Baring-Gould. He has found the belief in the super-
natural flute-call even in Yorkshire. "A Wesleyan," he
writes, "told me one day that he was sure his little ser-
vant-girl was going to die; for the night before, as he
had lain awake, he had heard an angel piping to her in
an adjoining room; the music was inexpressibly sweet, like
the warbling of a flute. 'And when t' aingels gang that
road,' said the Yorkshire man, 'they're boun' to tak'
bairns' souls wi' 'em.'"

Baring-Gould thinks that the flute or pipe player "is
no other than the wind". He sees in the Greek Hermes
two entirely distinct deities "run into one"—the Pelasgic
Hermes, the solar generator of life, who is "a tricksy,

---

[1] London, 1906, pp. 417 *et seq.*

thievish youth", and the other Hermes, the impetuous wind, "whose representative Saramâ exists as the gale in Indian mythology. Hermes Pyschopompos is therefore the wind bearing away the souls of the dead." The Mexican Hermes, Tezcatlipoca, was made up of several deities "run into one".

In the city of Mexico the chief images of Tezcatlipoca were fashioned in *itzli*, a shining black variety of obsidian, the "divine stone" (*teotelt*). The god was also shown as a black deity in the codices; at any rate, his face and arms were black, although his legs were white and red-striped. In this form (*Codex Borgia*, 21) he recalls the Indian Shiva as well as the black Krishna. Shiva was a "destroyer" as Tezcatlipoca was an "avenger". There was also, as has been stated, a red Tezcatlipoca who, according to Seler, was a form of Xipe Totec.[1] The devotees of the Indian Vishnu cult had perpendicular streaks of white clay and red chalk on their foreheads.[2]

The ears of the black Mexican idol of the young god Tezcatlipoca were adorned with symbolic ornaments of gold and silver, and a crystal tube was thrust through his lower lip; this tube enclosed a green or blue feather, as if to indicate its connection with the heart (soul). His hair, drawn into a queue, was bound with gold and decked with feathers, while a great jewel of gold suspended from his neck covered his breast. There were gold bracelets on his arms, and in his left hand a gold mirror which was called *itlachia* ("the viewer"). As the south was on "the left" the mirror had, no doubt, a solar significance. A green stone was set in his navel. The metals, gems, and feathers "adorning" the idol, indicate that the god had many attributes, and was, like the Indian Shiva, con-

---

[1] *Bureau of American Ethnology* (Bulletin 28), pp. 61, 68.
[2] Wilson, *Essays on Sanskrit Literature*, Vol. I, p. 57.

nected with the sun and moon and with live-giving water. His right foot was supposed to have been cut off in Hades, owing to the door having closed quickly as he emerged, and was sometimes replaced by a stump of flint shaped like a knife, by the "smoking mirror", or by a deer's foot, or a serpent for a foot. As a god of the night-wind, he was a speedy traveller. It may be, however, that Tezcatlipoca's connection with the deer had a deeper significance, and that it referred to his connection with fire (lightning) and rain. Stone seats were placed at street corners for the god, who was supposed to need rest in the course of his wanderings.

Tezcatlipoca was one of the gods who sacrificed himself to enable the sun to rise at the beginning. An obscure myth relates that he descended from heaven by a rope made from a spider's web. Some of the super-natural beings in India, especially the star maidens, reach the earth in like manner during the night, to bathe in sacred pools. In this connection Seler notes that "a spider (*tocatl*) is figured wherever a god is represented who was regarded as one of the Tzitzimimê, the forms descending from above, the stellar gods and demons of darkness".[1] Like the Japanese Susa-no-wo, Tezcatlipoca sinned in heaven and was cast out. From the war in heaven " sprung the wars below ". According to the interpreter of *Codex Vaticanus*, Tezcatlipoca was in one of his forms " Lord of Sin or Blindness " who " committed sin in Paradise" and had his eyes bandaged. His star proceeds in a "backward course". This star may have been the planet Mars. As a cock he " deceived the first woman who committed sin ". He was sometimes depicted with the foot of a cock or an eagle. The cock is a sinister bird in China and is associated with Hades.

[1] *Codex Fejérváry-Mayer*, London, p. 55.

As the persecutor of Quetzalcoatl, Tezcatlipoca appeared first as an old man, a sorcerer, who gave the good god an intoxicating drink that would renew his youth. It was necessary, however, that Quetzalcoatl should depart from Tulla. "On thy return", the sorcerer assured him, "thou shalt be as a youth, yea, a boy." The elixir was pulque; it made Quetzalcoatl drunk and moved him to go away.

As a love god Tezcatlipoca appeared in the marketplace of Tulla stark naked. He was a handsome but poor young foreigner who sold green chilly pepper. The daughter of the Toltec king fell in love with him, and was smitten with sickness because the stranger suddenly disappeared. When he was discovered, he was given suitable clothing and taken before the princess, whom he cured and married.

Owing to this marriage of royalty with a poor foreigner a rebellion broke out. Tezcatlipoca, assisted only by dwarfs and lame men, won a great victory, being matchless in war. He afterwards invited the Toltecs to a great festival, which lasted from sunset till midnight. He sang and danced, and induced the people to follow him. When, however, the crowd was massed on a bridge above a ravine through which a river flowed, Tezcatlipoca broke down the bridge and caused great slaughter. He was the destroyer of the Toltecs. On another occasion he slew many in a flower garden— evidently the flower garden of the love goddess. Various wonders, that inevitably resulted in the slaughter of Toltecs, were performed by the sorcerer god in human form. On one occasion he caused stones to fall from heaven; on another he made all food unfit to be eaten.

Like the Indian Krishna, Tezcatlipoca revelled in sensuality and the slaughter of human beings, but he had also, as had Krishna, a lofty side to his character. With the goddess Tlaelquani, he eradicated sins after confession by penitents, and figured as the turkey (the "jewel fowl"), which ensured immortality as well as rain.[1]

An interesting fact about Tezcatlipoca and Quetzalcoatl is that both had repulsive forms. In the city of Cholula, Quetzalcoatl's image "had a very ugly face". This image "was not set on its feet but lying down and covered with blankets".[2] The repulsive Tezcatlipoca is met with in a story, which depicts him as a sorcerer who appeared in Tulla with Huitzilopochtli as a manikin dancing on his hand.[3] He asks the people to stone him and kill him. The body of the sorcerer afterwards lay in the market-place and the smell of it tainted the air. This evil-smelling corpse was so heavy that it could not be moved. Ropes were fastened to it and pulled by crowds, but rope after rope broke and many who pulled were killed. At length the horrible corpse was dragged out of the city.

The Hindu god Kubera, who, like Tezcatlipoca, was a god of the north, had a variety of names. One, expressive of his deformity, was derived from the words for "vile" and "body". Wilson notes that, in Hindu mythology, Kubera performs the functions of the Grecian Plutus. He is the god of wealth, and master of nine inestimable treasures. . . . "Plutus is described as blind, malignant, and cowardly." Kubera had a garden in his northern paradise. In Brahmanic times he became associated with Shiva. In Tezcatlipoca there are traces of a blending of not only Krishna and Shiva, but the vile form of Kubera, the god of treasure, and the blind Plutus.

---

[1] *Bureau of American Ethnology* (Bulletin 28), p. 281.

[2] Bancroft, *The Pacific States*, Vol. III, p. 260.

[3] In a Gaelic story Finn-mac-Coul is similarly exhibited on the hand of a giant.

The red Tezcatlipoca's connection with Xipe is of interest, as Xipe resembles Kubera as the god of gold.

Not only have we in Mexico the blending of deities, forming complex gods, but the blending of deities who were of highly complex character before they were transported across the Pacific, to be ultimately fitted into a mythology which was framed to suit local conditions. The struggle between Tezcatlipoca and Quetzalcoatl was in a sense a reflection of American climatic phenomena; it was also a reflection of political conditions—the struggle between rival cults and rival tribes.

Huitzilopochtli was associated not only with Tezcatlipoca, but with the rain god Tlaloc. He was thus localized. The process of localization has, as in the case of Tezcatlipoca, somewhat obscured his original character. He appears to have been the chief god of the Aztecs, but after settling in Mexico the Aztecs embraced the beliefs and customs of their predecessors and mixed them with their own, forming a highly complex amalgam.

Like all the great gods of pre-Columbian America, Huitzilopochtli was connected with the widespread and ancient bird-and-serpent myth. His particular bird was the humming-bird, which took the place of some other bird. "The English traveller Bullock", says Bancroft, "tells how this bird distinguishes itself for its extraordinary courage, attacking others ten times its own size, flying into their eyes and using its sharp bill as a most dangerous weapon. Nothing more daring can be witnessed than its attack upon other birds of its own species when it fears disturbance during the breeding season. The effects of jealousy transform these birds into perfect furies. . . . The small but brave and warlike woodpecker stood in a similar relation to Mars, and it is accordingly termed *picus martius*."[1]

[1] *The Pacific States*, Vol. III, pp. 301–2.

The humming-birds resemble the brilliantly coloured sun-birds of Africa. They vary in size from that of the humble-bee to that of a wren, and have great beauty of form and plumage. They are peculiar to the Americas, and, although their range extends to Alaska, their head-quarters are in the neo-tropical region, where four-fifths of the species are found. Humming-birds feed on insects found inside brilliantly coloured flowers; they also suck honey and carry it to their young, into whose mouths they thrust their honey-smeared tongues. They never alight to feed, but hover before the flowers into which they dip their beaks. A loud humming noise is made by their rapidly moving wings.

The bird of the Aztec god was an oracle. In a myth about a man named Huitziton, who is usually regarded as Huitzilopochtli in human form, it is told that when the Aztecs lived in their northern homeland of Aztlan, he heard a bird which cried "tihui" ("let us go").[1] He asked the people to leave Aztlan, and this they did. It is not stated how Huitziton, like Siegfried, the dragon slayer and devourer of its heart, came to understand "the language of birds". His name signifies "small humming-bird". Huitziton was the soothsayer and bird in one. The Celtic Druids understood "the language" of the wren, and, according to Whitley Stokes, the Gaelic names of wren and Druid are derived from the root *dreo*, which is cognate with "truth". The soothsayer was the "truth-sayer".

The Aztecs were guided to Mexico by this god, and, as has been indicated, founded the city of Tenochtitlan (Mexico) on the site where they saw the eagle, with the serpent in its talons, perched on a nopal (Opuntie) growing

---

[1] This is the third bird connected with the god, the humming-bird and the eagle being the others.

upon a rock. The broad wings of the serpent were spread out to the rising sun. It formed "the winged disc"—the ancient bird, serpent, and sun symbol of Egypt, Assyria, &c., as has been already indicated.

According to Acosta the chief idol in Mexico was that of the war god Huitzilopochtli. It was made of wood in human shape, and was seated on an azure stool in a litter with serpents' heads at each corner.

"This idol had all the forehead azure and had a band of azure under the nose from one ear to another. Upon his head he had a rich plume of feathers, like to the beak of a small bird. . . . He had in his left hand a white shield, with figures of five pine-apples, made of white feathers, set in a cross; and from above issued forth a crest of gold, and at his sides he had four darts which (the Mexicans told) had been sent from heaven. . . . In his right hand he had an azure staff, cut in the fashion of a waving snake."

There was also in Mexico a famous temple of the god.

"It was built of great stones, in the fashion of snakes tied one to another, and the circle was called Coatepantli, which is, a circuit of snakes. . . . There were four gates or entries, at the east, west, north, and south. Upon the top of the temple were two idols, . . . Vitziliputzli (Huitzilopochtli) and his companion, Tlaloc."

According to Sahagun, Huitzilopochtli was originally a human being resembling Hercules, who performed great feats, especially as a slayer and destroyer. He carried a fiery dragon symbol. As a sorcerer he could transform himself into birds and wild beasts. Camaxtli of Tlascala resembled him closely.

Another name of the god was Mexitli, and from it the name of Mexico was supposed to have been derived.

A myth makes the war god a son of Coatlicue, the serpent goddess ("earth beast") of serpent mountain.

One day when walking in the temple she saw a ball of feathers falling from the sky. She picked it up and placed it in her bosom, and then became pregnant. Her children, unaware of the miraculous happening, regarded her condition with indignation, and, to avert the impending dishonour to the family, plotted to kill her. As they came against her she gave birth to Huitzilopochtli. Like the Indian Karna, the Teutonic Siegfried, &c., he came into the world fully armed and with lines of blue on his face, arms, and thighs. He attacked and slew his mother's persecutors.

In another version of the myth the war god has two mothers, Teteionnan, the goddess, and Coatlicue. Osiris was similarly "the bull begotten of the two cows Isis and Nephthys". The Hindu warrior, Jarasandha, had likewise two mothers. Bancroft notes in this connection that Aphrodite and Athena had different fathers.[1]

A good deal of speculation has been indulged in as to the meaning of Huitzilopochtli's name, which is translated "Humming-bird to the left". When he was born his left leg and head were adorned with the green plumes of the humming-bird. In Aztec mythology the left (opochtli) was the south, and the humming-bird god was the god of the southern region as, in China, the god of the south was the Red Bird. Huitzilopochtli's temple in Mexico city faced the south, which was "to the left" or "on the left hand". The god was connected with fire—he was the discoverer of fire—and the summer sun. Opposite Huitzilopochtli, on the north and "to the right", was the blind form of Tezcatlipoca as the god of justice and death and drought, Quetzalcoatl being on the east, and Xipe Totec on the west. There were other arrangements of the deities in the complicated and perplexing Mexican

[1] *The Pacific States*, Vol. III, p. 311.

systems, often so obscure, which varied according to cult, astrological views, season, and age. Similar complex ideas are to be met with in India, where the Brahmans wove mystifying allegories as assiduously as did the Mexican priests; these became, in the process of time, obscure to even their successors. In his name of Huitzilopochtli, the so-called "war god" of Mexico was essentially the guardian of the south.

The bird "on the left" is met with in India. This is the chátaka, a bird supposed to drink no water except rain water. It is always "a prominent figure in the description of wet and cloudy weather", and is invariably referred to as being "left", that is, "on the left side". An interesting statement by a native commentator in this connection is:

"Peacocks, chátakas, cháshas (blue jays), and other male birds, occasionally also antelopes, going cheerfully along the left, give good fortune to the host".

The late Professor H. H. Wilson, who occupied the Sanskrit chair at Oxford University, wrote in this connection:

"The Greek notions agreed with those of Rámanátha, and considered the flight of birds upon the right side to be auspicious; the Romans made it the left; but this difference arose from the situation of the observer, as in both cases the auspicious quarter was the east. In general among the Hindus, those omens which occur upon the left side are unpropitious." [1]

Rámanátha, the Hindu commentator who contended that to be auspicious the birds should be "upon the right side, not upon the left", was evidently unaware that to some Indian cults the left was more sacred than the right. The conflict between the cults of east and west was of

---

[1] *Essays on Sanskrit Literature*, Vol. II, pp. 325–6, London, 1864.

great antiquity. In Mexico, the original Huitzilopochtli cult of the Aztecs appears to have favoured the west, the south being on the left, and the north on the right. The Tlaloc cult held the east to be the most sacred region. It may be that the Old-World struggle between the ancient cults of east and west is also reflected in the myths about Quetzalcoatl, who sometimes comes from the west and sometimes from the east.

Not only was Huitzilopochtli the god of the south, of fire, and the sun of summer, he was also a rain-bringer who was associated with Tlaloc. In Mexico, as in China, the south was the region assigned to summer, and the north the region assigned to the god of winter, drought, and death. In Mexico, however, the summer is the rainy season. It is during the rainy season that the humming-bird becomes active. According to ancient Mexican belief, the humming-bird is featherless during winter and hangs limp and lifeless from a tree ; it renews its youth in the rainy season at the beginning of summer.

Huitzilopochtli was further given a stellar significance. With Quetzalcoatl, Tezcatlipoca, and other deities, he is found included among the group of star gods whose ruler is Itzpapalotl, the obsidian butterfly female demon or goddess. As the butterfly was a form of fire, it would appear that its connection with obsidian was due to the use of the obsidian mirror for the purpose of procuring fire.

The humming-bird, which thrusts its long beak into flowers and feeds on honey-devouring insects and carries honey to its young, nests in the agave plant. It is not surprising, therefore, to find traces of belief in the honey elixir of life in connection with Huitzilopochtli rites. In India the oblation called Argha or Arghya consisted of "water, milk, the points of Kuśa-grass, curds, clarified butter, rice, barley, and white mustard", or "saffron, the

Bel, unbroken grain, flowers, curds, Dúrba-grass, Kuśa-grass, and Sesamum". The oblation to the sun was "Tila, flowers, barley, water, and red sanders", or "water mixed with sandal and flowers". The Greeks offered "libations of honey, milk, oil, and water", and "the solid parts of an offering consisted of herbs, grains, fruits, flowers, and frankincense".[1]

In Mexico images of Huitzilopochtli were made of dough prepared from seeds and edible plants, or from maize, and mixed with honey and blood. The images were ceremonially eaten. In India rice cakes, which were offered as substitutes for human beings, were supposed to be transformed by the Brahmans, as were the dough images of Huitzilopochtli by the Mexican priests. The Hindu priest declared that "when it (the rice cake) still consists of rice meal, it is the hair. When he pours water on it, it becomes skin. When he mixes it, it becomes flesh: for then it becomes consistent; and consistent also is the flesh. When it is baked, it becomes bone. And when he is about to take it off (the fire) and sprinkles it with butter, he changes it into marrow. This is the completeness which they call the five-fold animal sacrifice."[2]

The images of Huitzilopochtli were made and eaten twice a year—in December, the beginning of winter, and May, the beginning of summer.

At the December festival various seeds were kneaded into dough and mixed with the blood of sacrificed children, the bones being represented by bits of acacia wood. The king burned incense before the image, as incense was burned before Egyptian mummies to impart vitality

---

[1] Works by H. H. Wilson (*Essays on Sanskrit Literature*, Vol. II, pp. 320–21), London, 1864.

[2] *The Satapatha Bráhmana* ("Sacred Books of the East", Vol. XII), Part I, p. 51.

to the corpse by restoring the body heat and odours. Next day, a priest, who impersonated Quetzalcoatl, "killed the god so that his body might be eaten" by piercing the breast of the dough image with a flint-tipped arrow. Then the heart was cut out and given to the king, who ate it. Men, youths, boys, and even male infants were given portions of the image to swallow. Females did not partake of the god's body, however.

Another account states that the December feast was called Panquetzaliztli ("the elevation of banners"). Cakes were baked and these were broken in pieces.

"These the high priest put into certain very clean vessels, and with the thorn of the maguey, which resembles a thick needle, he took up with the utmost reverence single morsels, and put them into the mouth of each individual, in the manner of communion." [1]

The May ceremony was of elaborate character. Two days before the *teoqualo* ("the god is eaten") ceremony, an image of the deity was prepared by nuns—the secluded virgin priestesses of the war god's temple—who made dough by mixing seeds of the beet and roasted maize with honey. A great idol was formed of the dough, the eyes being formed with green, blue, and white stones, and the teeth with grains of maize. Clothed in rich raiment and seated in a blue chair, the image was carried forth by the nuns, who wore white attire and new ornaments, were crowned with garlands of maize, and had their cheeks stained with vermilion and their forearms adorned with red parrot feathers. The nuns were the "sisters" of the god. They gave the idol to youths who were attired in red robes, and they carried it to the base of the pyramid-shaped temple, and drew it up the steps to the accompaniment of music, the silent worshippers mean-

[1] Bancroft, *The Pacific States*, Vol. III, p. 323.

time standing in the court "with much reverence and fear".

The image was deposited in "a little lodge of roses" on the temple summit, and offerings of flowers were made. Then the nuns brought pieces of dough, which were shaped like bones, from their convent, and gave them to the young men who deposited them at the feet of the idol.

Thereafter the priests of the various orders, which were indicated by the colours of their sacred vestments, wearing garlands on their heads and chains of flowers round their necks, worshipped the gods and goddesses, and sang and danced round the idol; consecrating the dough bones and flesh. Human sacrifices were then offered up, the hearts of victims being torn out. A sacred dance was subsequently performed by the youths and young nuns, who also sang sacred songs; while the great men of the kingdom, forming a circle round them, sang and danced also.

All the worshippers fasted until after midday. The ceremony ended by breaking up the idol and eating it. The greatest were served first, and all men, women, and children were given portions to swallow. They received each their portion with "tears, fear, and reverence . . . saying that they did eat the flesh and bones of God, wherewith they were grieved. Such as had any sick folks demanded thereof for them, and carried it with great reverence and veneration."[1] The body of the youth who impersonated Tezcatlipoca was eaten by his cannibal worshippers.

Sir J. G. Frazer gives in *The Golden Bough*[2] a large

---

[1] J. de Acosta, *National and Moral History of the Indies*, Book V, Chapter 24, Vol. II, pp. 356–60 (Hakluyt Society, London, 1880).

[2] ("Spirits of the Corn and of the Wild "), Vol. II, pp. 48 *et seq.*, London, 1912.

AZTEC SACRIFICIAL STONE, FROM TEMPLE IN MEXICO

This single block of carved porphyry is now in the National Museum of Mexico.

number of examples of the customs of eating the new corn and first fruits, &c., in a chapter entitled " Eating the God ". In some cases, as in Sweden, the grain of the last sheaf of the new harvest was used to make a loaf in the shape of a girl. The loaf was divided among the members of the household and eaten by them. In the Hindu Kush the new corn was roasted and steeped in milk. The Nandi of East Africa similarly favoured milk. Oil was used by other peoples. New friction fires were lit in different areas in connection with this ceremony. As we have seen, Huitzilopochtli was in one of his aspects a fire god, and was also the first to give fire to men.

Paynal, or Paynalton (" Little Paynal "), was a deputy god who acted for Huitzilopochtli in cases of emergency, or when the elder god was unable to give aid. Sahagun's view is that Huitzilopochtli acted as chief captain, and the deputy Paynal, whose name means " swift " or " hurried ", carried out his commands. A war god who was supposed to remain in a state of suspended animation for part of the year had need of a substitute. Apparently after the wandering Aztecs settled down in Mexico as the over-lords of other tribes, Huitzilopochtli became a highly complex deity, having absorbed the attributes of other gods. He, however, never displaced Tlaloc with whom he was closely associated. The Mexicans accounted for the association by explaining that the war god stirred the rain god into activity.

In some respects Huitzilopochtli bears a resemblance to the Hindu god Shiva, whose cult was for a period highly influential in India. Human sacrifices were of-fered to Shiva, who was associated with the goddess Black Kali, the terrible, blood-thirsty avenger who wore a waist-belt of skulls and hands, and a long necklace of skulls, while her body was smeared with blood. Shiva had likewise a necklace of skulls. Huitzilopochtli had, as Bancroft notes, "a band of human hearts and faces of gold and silver, while various bones of dead men, as well as a man torn in pieces, were depicted on his dress ".[1]

The skull oracle was known in Mexico as elsewhere. A Tezcatlipoca skull incrusted with mosaic is preserved in the British Museum. It represents Tezcatlipoca as a god of death, but it was apparently also a skull which revealed the will of the deities. The dead were able to foretell events as did the ghosts to Odysseus and Æneas when they visited Hades.

According to Boturini, Huitziton ("the small humming-bird "), who guided the Aztecs during their wandering period, died before the site of Mexico city was reached. The Mexicans, however, carried his skull and bones, "and the devil spoke to them", as the Spanish writer put it, "through this skull of Huitziton, often asking for the immolation of men and women, from which thing originated those bloody sacrifices practised afterwards by this nation with so much cruelty on prisoners of war. . . . This deity was called, in early as well as in late times, Huitzilopochtli, for the principal men believed that he was seated on the left hand of Tezcatlipoca."[2]

Large numbers of skulls were collected at the temple of Huitzilopochtli.

The skull oracle was of considerable antiquity in Asia. The Semites had a custom of killing a man who was a first-born son; they "wrung off his head and seasoned it with salt and spices, and wrote upon a plate of gold the name of an unclean spirit (a pagan god) and worshipped it". Davies tells in his *History of Magic* of the custom of

[1] *The Pacific States*, Vol. III, p. 306.   [2] *Ibid.*, p. 291.

making bronze heads under certain constellations; these gave answers. St. Thomas is said to have destroyed an image of this kind "because he could not endure its excess of prating".[1]

Rain-getting ceremonies were in New Caledonia performed before ancestral skulls. Frazer gives instances of the use of skulls in Armenian and Indian rain-getting ceremonies.[2]

The altars of Huitzilopochtli reeked with human blood, as did those of other deities. Tlaloc and his spouse claimed the sacrifice of many innocent children, as well as the blood and hearts of men. But pre-Columbian America was not the only sinner in this respect. The Phœnicians, Greeks, Celts, and Romans, also sacrificed human beings. It was not until the first century B.C. that a Roman law was passed to forbid human sacrifice.[3] In a play by the poet Ennius a banquet of human flesh is prepared. The Carthaginians sacrificed human beings, including children, to their god Baal. Sir James Frazer gives a number of instances of human sacrifices among peoples who were as refined and highly civilized as were the Mexicans, as well as among savages.[4] An early Spanish historian says of the Peruvians that "they have disgusting sacrifices. . . . Every month they sacrifice their own children, and smear with the blood of the victims the faces of the idols and the doors of the temples."[5]

---

[1] Godwyn, *Moses and Aaron.*
[2] *The Golden Bough,* Vol. I, pp. 163 and 285 (3rd edition).
[3] Pliny, *Hist. Nat.,* XXX, 3, 4.
[4] *The Golden Bough* ("The Dying God"), pp. 160 *et seq.* (3rd edition).
[5] *Ibid.,* p. 185.

CHAPTER XVII

Motives for Migrations

Ancient Movements of Peoples—Origin of Seafaring—Search for Precious Substances—Psychological Side of Problem—Natural Barriers—Ocean less Dangerous than Land—The Lure of Pearls—Distribution of Pearl-shell—Pearl and Shell Beliefs and Customs in Old and New Worlds—Shell Dyes in Europe, Asia, and America—Arts, Customs, and Beliefs associated with Pearls and Shells—Gold Finds in Peru—Peruvian Mining—Why Gold was Valued and Searched for—American and European Bronze—Metals used chiefly for Ornaments in America—No Originality in American Metal Symbolism—World-wide Search for Elixir of Life—American Traditions—Links between Peru and Indonesia—Gold as Trees and Plants—Gem Trees—Souls and Gods as Gems—Complex Ideas regarding Gems, Metals, Flowers, &c.—Culture Mixing in America—The Greatest of all Mysteries.

" THE movements of peoples which are sufficiently dramatic for the ordinary historian to record are ", writes Dr. A. C. Haddon, " often of less importance than the quiet steady drift of a population from one area into another, as, for example, in the emigration from Europe to America in modern times. . . . Although immigrant peoples may bring a culture and language permanently affecting the conquered peoples, yet the aboriginal population, if allowed to survive in sufficient numbers, will eventually impair the racial purity of the new-comers, and there is a tendency for the indigenous racial type to reassert itself and become predominant once more." [1] The change of culture may or may not be found to have been accompanied by a change of language. " Nothing is commoner in the

[1] *The Wanderings of Peoples*, pp. 4, 5.

history of migratory peoples", Professor J. L. Myres comments in this regard, "than to find a very small leaven of energetic intruders ruling and organizing large native populations, without either learning their subjects' language or imposing their own till considerably later, if at all."[1]

There were definite reasons for migrations in ancient as in modern times, and the migrations were, of course, controlled in a measure by geographical conditions. It is necessary therefore, at the outset, when dealing with the migration of the carriers of a complex culture across Asia towards the Pacific, and across the Pacific towards America, to discover the motives that caused even energetic minorities to venture into unexplored areas, and to overcome the natural barriers that restricted the ordinary movements of increasing tribes in the hunting or pastoral stages of civilization.

"Men did not take to maritime adventure", as Professor G. Elliot Smith reminds us, "either for aimless pleasure or for idle adventure. They went to sea only under the pressure of the strongest incentives."[2] They must have been prompted, as Laufer argues in connection with the search for jade in early Europe, by motives "pre-existing and acting" in their minds; the impetus of searching for something which could be found, and apparently was found, in America, must have been received "somehow from somewhere". They found that something "only because they sought it. . . . This is the psychological side of the historical aspect of the problem."[3]

In the first chapter it has been shown that the pre-

---

[1] *The Dawn of History*, p. 199.

[2] *Ships as Evidence of the Migrations of Early Culture* (Manchester and London, 1917), pp. 5–6.   [3] *Jade*, p. 4.

Columbian Americans who searched for and found gold had attached to that useless metal an arbitrary and religious value, and that they utilized it in precisely the same manner as did the progressive peoples of the Old World. It does not follow that they were attracted by gold simply because it was to be found. Laufer, writing regarding jade, shows that even a useful material may be quite abundant in a country and yet escape the attention of its inhabitants. He instances the case of kaolinic clay, as has been shown, and here the quotation may be given in full:

"Why did the Romans discover the Terra Sigillata on the Rhine and in other parts of Germany unknown to the indigenous population? Because they were familiar with this peculiar clay from their Mediterranean homes, because they prized this pottery highly and desired it in their new home. Let us suppose that we should not possess any records relating to the history of porcelain. The chief substance of which it is made, kaolin, is now found in this country (America), Germany, Holland, France, and England, all of which produce objects of porcelain; consequently porcelain is indigenous to Europe and America, because the material is found there. By a lucky chance of history we know that it was made in neither country before the beginning of the eighteenth century, and that the incentive received from China was the stimulus to Boettger's rediscovery in Dresden. Of course, arguing *a priori*, the peoples of Europe and America could have made porcelain ages ago; the material was at their elbows, but the brutal fact remains that they did not, that they missed the opportunity, and that only the importation and investigation of Chinese porcelain were instrumental in hunting for and finding kaolinic clay."

Laufer then writes regarding jade:

"Nothing could induce me to the belief that primitive man of Central Europe incidentally and spontaneously embarked on the laborious task of quarrying and working jade. The psychological motive for this act must be supplied and it can be deduced only from the source of historical facts. . . . There is, in the light of historical facts and experiences, no reason to credit the prehistoric and early historical populations of Europe with any spontaneous ideas relative to jade; they received these, as everything else, from an outside source; they gradually learned to appreciate the value of this tough and compact substance, and then set to hunting for natural supplies." [1]

The pre-Columbian American searched for and found not only gold, but silver, copper, and tin. Although, however, iron existed and could easily have been found and utilized, they did not search for it, find it, or use it; they left it *in situ*, as did the early Europeans the kaolinic clay, and it was not until after the Spaniards came that they discovered it and worked it.

A difficulty experienced by not a few, regarding the migration of even small groups of peoples from Asia to America, is the great distance that had to be covered by the ancient mariners. The Pacific was undoubtedly a formidable natural barrier. It was, however, a less formidable one than the mountain ranges and extensive deserts of the Old World, and even than the more formidable barriers formed by organized communities in fertile valleys, because these communities were invariably armed and had to be overcome in battle. On the trackless ocean nature alone, a less formidable enemy than man, had to be contended with. That the ocean was traversed by considerable numbers of seafarers in ancient times is demonstrated by the fact that Polynesia was peopled by Indonesians and others, and that even Easter Island was colonized. The distance from the Malay peninsula to Easter Island, as has been already indicated, is vastly greater than from Easter Island to America.

[1] *Jade*, pp. 4, 5.

Indeed longer voyages were made by Polynesians within the limits of Polynesia than those which were necessary to cross from their islands to the New World. The Pacific barrier was no more formidable than was the barrier of the Indian Ocean. If the voyage was longer it was not less possible of achievement, and the wide distribution of islands must have enticed and encouraged explorers to venture farther and farther to sea. Withal, having gained experience in making long voyages, the exploring mariners were not likely to have been discouraged by the fact that their voyages were becoming of increasing length. After shipbuilding and navigation had been developed, a breed of seafarers came into existence who migrated more rapidly and sometimes in greater numbers than did those of their fellows who inhabited the plains and river valleys of the great continents. Voyages of from four hundred to seven hundred miles were, as has been shown, common in Polynesia when the early Christian missionaries began to settle and preach on the coral islands. No inland peoples could have ventured so far from home with any hope of ever returning again. Forests, deserts, and mountain ranges have restricted migrations more than have perilous and trackless belts of ocean.

No American records survive, save in the vague traditions about " white men " from the west, those mysterious " snake peoples ", regarding the voyages made across the Pacific to America by ancient Asiatic mariners. It is not impossible, however, to supply the motives for such migrations as appear to have taken place.

In the first place consideration should be given to the distribution of pearl-shell. It is found in the Red Sea, the Persian Gulf, and thence round the coasts of India, Burma, Siam, throughout Indonesia, Melanesia and Polynesia, and from Indonesia to the Philippine Islands. It is also found in Japan, and in the New World from Peru northward along the Central American coast to the north-western sea-coast of Mexico, round the Gulf of Mexico, and northward through river valleys in the United States, to nearly the borders of Canada. Pearls and pearl-shell were searched for and found by the ancient Asiatic mariners.

It has been shown that in Mexico, as in China, Europe, and Ancient Egypt, green stones were interred with the dead. In Mexico, indeed, they were, as in China, placed in the mouths of the dead. Now pearls were used in precisely the same way. A Chinese first-century text, already referred to, says in this connection:

"On stuffing the mouth of the Son of Heaven with rice, they put jade therein; in the case of a feudal lord they introduce pearls; in that of a great officer, and so downwards, as also in that of ordinary officials, cowries are used to this end".[1]

In India pearls were likewise placed in the mouths of the dead, as Marco Polo has stated. In Japan as in India pearls were placed in the mouths of even the dead who were cremated. Pearls, pieces of *Haliotis* shell, and rice, were interred with the dead in Korea. In the New World pearls and shells were freely used at burials. Objects inlaid with *Haliotis* shell have been found in graves on the islands of Santa Catalina and Santa Cruz. W. K. Moorhead, who examined the Ohio mounds, found pearls in the mouths of the dead or on their wrists and ankles. Pearls were deposited with the dead in the mounds of Illinois. In Virginia pearls, copper, &c., were used to stuff mummies. G. B. Gordon, who explored ancient Maya tombs at Copan in Western Honduras, found besides polished jadeite amulets "pearls and trinkets

[1] De Groot, *The Religious System of China*, Vol. I, p. 277.

carved from shell ". In Yucatan and British Honduras Thomas Gann found pearl-shell and amulets in sepulchral mounds. Pearls and pearl-shell were greatly esteemed by the Aztecs of Mexico. According to Mrs. Zelia Nuttall women of the higher classes wore them as drop-ear-rings and pendants. " Among the pre-Columbian antiquities found in Ecuador associated with burials was a little box or receptacle cut from Cassis shell, the cover of which was a fragment of the valve of the pearl oyster." The Peruvians valued pearls and pearl-shell.[1] ·

Murex purple, which had a religious value, was used in the New World as in the Old. It appears to have been first introduced in Crete as far back as 1600 B.C. On Leuke, an island off the south-east coast and at the ancient sea-port of Palaikastro, Professor Bosanquet discovered a bank of crushed murex shell associated with Kamares pottery.[2] The Phœnicians of Tyre and Sidon adopted the industry and " Tyrian purple " became famous. Other dyeing centres were established. The purple of Laconia in the Gulf of Corinth was greatly esteemed. Purple-yielding shells were searched for far and wide and in the western Mediterranean. Tarentum, the modern Otranto, became an important dyeing town. Bede, " the father of English history ", tells that on the British coasts were found, not only mussels which yielded pearls of all colours, including red, purple, violet, green, and white, but also cockles, " of which the scarlet dye is

---

[1] Kunz and Stevenson, " Folklore of Precious Stones " (*Memoirs of the International Congress of Anthropologists*), Chicago, 1894, pp. 241, 255–259, 493, 510 *et seq.* W. K. Moorhead, *Prehistoric Implements*, New York, 1900, p. 376. G. B. Gordon, " The Mysterious City of Honduras" in *The Century Magazine*, Vol. IV, p. 417. W. H. Holmes, " Art in Shell of the Ancient Americans" in *Second Annual Report of the Bureau of Ethnology*, Washington, p. 256, and others quoted by J. Wilfrid Jackson in *Shells as Evidence of the Migrations of Early Culture*, London and Manchester, 1917, pp. 89–90, 100–101, 106, 114 *et seq.*, and 204.

[2] R. C. Bosanquet, *British Association Report*, 1913, p. 817.

made: a most beautiful colour which never fades with the heat of the sun or the washing of the rain, but the older it is the more beautiful it becomes ".[1] "Purpura mounds" have been discovered in Ireland. A large number of purple-yielding shells, which had all been broken, from a Caithness broch were exhibited at the meeting of the British Association in Edinburgh in 1921. "Kitchen middens" in Cornwall and elsewhere have likewise yielded traces of the ancient industry. The Phœnicians are believed to have obtained from the British Isles a dark shade of shell purple called " black purple ".[2]

Shells yielding purple were searched for and found and used, as far east as China and Japan. An interesting fact about the shells discovered in the mounds of Omori, Japan, is that many of them had a portion of the body-whorl broken away " as if for the purpose of more conveniently extracting the animal ".[3] The Caithness broch shells were broken in like manner.

Traces of the purple industry have been found, as has been said, in the New World. Mrs. Zelia Nuttall has published a paper entitled " A Curious Survival in Mexico of the use of the Purpura Shell-fish for Dyeing ".[4] She shows that in the *Nuttall Codex* there are " pictures of no fewer than thirteen women of rank wearing purple skirts, and five with capes and jackets of the same colour. In addition, forty-six chieftains are figured with short, fringed, rounded purple waist-cloths, and there are also three examples of the use of a close-fitting purple cap." Some priests and other personages have faces painted purple. The Romans used purple for staining cheeks

---

[1] *Ecclesiastical History*, Chapter I.

[2] *Manual of Ancient History of the East*, London, 1870, Vol. II, p. 217.

[3] Professor E. S. Morse, *Memoirs of the Scientific Department of the University of Tokio*, Vol. I, Part I, No. 2539, 1879.

[4] *Pullman Anniversary Volume*, 1909, pp. 368–384.

and lips.   Mrs. Nuttall points out that " the shade of the purple paint is identical with that of the purpura dye ". Broken purpura shells have been taken from Inca graves in North Chile, and broken purple-yielding shells from North American " kitchen middens ".   Mr. J. Wilfrid Jackson, who has collected much important evidence regarding shells and the religious uses to which they were put in ancient times, writes as follows regarding the New World finds: [1]

" This purple industry is closely associated, both in the Old and in the New World, with the appreciation of pearls and the use of the artificially devised conch-shell trumpet.   Each of these cultural elements had their origin in the Eastern Mediterranean stations for the purple industry . . . and were established by the early Mediterranean mariners in several places in the Old World.   In addition we find that an intimate relationship existed between this art and skill in weaving, as well as the mining, working, and trafficking in metals, such as gold, silver, and copper.   In the New World the purple industry is associated with similar pursuits."

Mrs. Nuttall's view in this connection is of special interest.   " It seems ", she writes, " almost easier to believe that certain elements of an ancient European culture were at one time, and perhaps once only, actually transmitted by the traditional small band of . . . Mediterranean seafarers, than to explain how, under totally different conditions of race and climate, the identical ideas and customs should have arisen ".   Professor G. Elliot Smith writes regarding the murex industry:

" If it be argued that purple was invented independently in the New World, it must be remembered that the method of its production is a complex and difficult process, which in itself is sufficient

[1] *Shells as Evidence of the Migrations of Early Culture* (Manchester and London, 1917), p. 27.

to raise a doubt as to the likelihood of such a discovery being made more than once ".

He shows that the same people who settled in isolated spots " to work the gold and copper, and incidentally to erect megalithic tombs and temples, were also searching for pearls and making use of shell trumpets ", and adds:

" There are reasons for believing that all these special uses of shells were spread abroad along with the complex mixture of arts, customs and beliefs associated with the building of megalithic monuments.

" The earliest use of the conch-shell trumpet was in the Minoan worship in Crete. Thence it spread far and wide, until it came to play a part in the religious services, Christian and Jewish, Brahman and Buddhist, Shinto and Shamanistic, in widely different parts of the world—in the Mediterranean, in India, in Central Asia, in Indonesia and Japan, in Oceania and America. In many of these places it was supposed to have the definite ritual object of summoning the deity. . . . Like the cowry it was used in marriage and funeral ceremonies, in connection with harvest rites and circumcision,[1] in the ritual of initiation into secret societies, in the ceremonials before sacred images, in the rites of drinking (such as soma-worship and kava) and of head hunting. It was also used in India as the receptacle for libations which . . . was one of the essential ritual procedures for animating the dead, and in course of time for performing the same devotional act for the deity. Thus it was intimately interwoven into the very texture of the remarkable culture complex of which these practices represent a few of the ingredients."

Professor Elliot Smith goes on to say that "in attempting to form some conception of the mode of the easterly spread of these cultural developments which originated in the Eastern Mediterranean and the Red Sea, it is impor-

---

[1] Circumcision was practised in pre-Columbian America. This rite originated in Ancient Egypt in pre-Dynastic times.

tant to remember that it was the pearl fishers themselves who played the chief part in the Wanderings".[1]

The importance attached to murex purple cannot be accounted for on other than religious grounds. Before the purple attracted attention in the Old World, the shell itself, it must be noted, had acquired a religious value. In Egypt and elsewhere it had been connected with the mother-goddess—the virgin who gave origin to all life and fed her children, especially with milk. She was, as has been shown, the cow-mother in Egypt, the sow-mother in Troy, Crete, and Greece, the wolf-mother in Rome, the tiger-mother in China, and the bear-mother in north-eastern Asia and in north-western America. As has been brought out in the chapter dealing with the Mexican goddess Mayauel, she was connected with "milk-yielding" plants and trees.

In Japan, India, and elsewhere, the milk-elixir was obtained not only from the plants and trees of the goddess but from her shells. In the Japanese sacred book, the Ko-ji-ki,[2] the slain god Ohonamochi is brought back to life by an elixir prepared by burning and grinding cockleshell and mixing the powder with water. The mixture is called "mothers' milk" or "nurses' milk". A similar "elixir" is still prepared in the Scottish Highlands for weakly children.

It was first discovered in ancient Crete that the murex-shell fish secreted a fluid in a *sac* or vein. "The matter", says Rawlinson, "is a liquid of a creamy consistency, and, while in the *sac* or vein, is of a yellowish

---

[1] Introduction to Jackson's *Shells as Evidence of the Migrations of Early Culture.* See also Elliot Smith, *Ships as Evidence of the Migrations of Early Culture,* Manchester and London, 1917, and *Migrations of Early Culture,* 1915. W. J. Perry, *Relationship between the Geographical Distribution of Megalithic Monuments in Ancient Mines,* Manchester, 1915, and *The Megalithic Culture of Indonesia,* London and Manchester, 1918.

[2] See my *Myths of China and Japan,* Index, under *Ohonamochi.*

white colour; on extraction, however, and exposure to the light, it becomes first green, and then purple. . . . The season for collecting the purple dye was the end of winter, or the very beginning of spring, just before the molluscs would naturally have set to work to lay their eggs."[1]

Apparently the ancients were greatly impressed by the fact that a shell-fish yielded a milky fluid during the very season in which the fig-tree exuded its "milk"— that is, in the spring when the mother goddess, having given birth to her "children" in the world of vegetation, provided as nourishment for them the "milk" which flowed from the "Milky Way" and appeared in rivers as foam and as yellowish or whitish mud and also exuded from various plants and trees.

It was found that the shell-fish "milk", after being exposed to the light, first turned green, and then, although Rawlinson does not mention the fact, assumed a bluish tint before it finally became a fixed purple-red.

The doctrines of colour symbolism had already been well established. According to these the attributes of a deity, and the properties and influences of all substances connected with deities, were revealed by colours. The colours were in themselves operating influences. Importance was therefore attached to the revelation made by shell-fish milk which assumed various colours.

It has been suggested by Besnier that shell-purple, which "was considered a noble and sacred colour by the ancients and emblematic of the power of the gods", was esteemed because it resembled "the colour of blood, the principle of life".[2] The writer's fuller explanation is that purple-red was, in the first place, given a religious

[1] G. Rawlinson, *Phœnicia* ("The Story of the Nations" Series), pp. 277–8.
[2] Quoted by Jackson in *Shells as Evidence of the Migrations of Early Culture*, pp. 7–8.

value because it was produced by the shell-fish form of the goddess, and, in the second place, because it was regarded as her milk. The colours of the fluid suggested to the ancients that this "milk" from the shell ultimately assumed the properties of life-blood. The "milk" of the deity "made" blood.

In Ancient Egypt the riddle of life was read in the Nile which, as it rose in flood, turned green, red, yellowish, and blue. The fluid from the murex-shell similarly revealed by its sequence of colours the various attributes of the deity who had had her origin in water, was connected with shells, plants, and trees, and was the source of blood-making milk. Her trees, which yielded "milk", also yielded "blood" as sap; her shell, it was discovered, displayed similar properties. The sanctity of shell-purple thus appears to have had its origin in the idea of a milk-yielding goddess who was connected with life-giving water, the sky, and the heavenly bodies, and whose "milk" nourished vegetation and human beings and produced sap and blood and flesh.

In America, as has been shown in the Mayauel chapter, the cult of the milk-yielding goddess was well established. The Zuni Indians, like the Mexicans, were fully acquainted with the complex ideas connected with the ancient Old-World conception of the nourishing All-mother whose milk and blood and flesh were in all vegetation. This fact is brought out clearly in the following extract from the Zuni creation myth:

"Corn shall be the giver of milk to the youthful and of flesh to the aged, as our women folk are the givers of life to our youth and the sustainers of life in our age; for of the mother-milk of the Beloved Maidens is it filled, and of their flesh the substance".[1]

[1] Cushing, *Outlines of Zuni Creation Myth*, in 13*th Annual Report of the Bureau of American Ethnology*, 1891–2, p. 397.

Nothing could be clearer and more emphatic. The milk of the mother, or group of mothers, was to the Zuni Indians, as to the Hindus, Greeks, Egyptians, and others, the life-fluid which sustained human beings and, indeed, all living creatures. As we have seen, Mayauel gave milk even to fish as the Egyptian Neith gave hers to crocodiles.

The rain-god Tlaloc, who provided the life-fluid, including "milk", in the form of rain, is shown shut in his shell (*Codex Bologna*, 8), and in one illustration (*Codex Vaticanus*, No. 3773) the particular shell that encloses the deity is the *Murex Trunculus*. A conch-shell with the apex replaced by a snake's head—the serpent-dragon form of the rain-god—is found in *Codex Vaticanus B* (66). In the *Dresden MS*. 38, 6, a Maya deity is seen emerging from a shell. The Mexican moon-god similarly emerged from a shell.

The shell form of the mother was worn by women in the Old as in the New World to assist birth as well as to give protection. This fact is brought out clearly in the explanation of Plate XXVI of the *Codex Vaticanus* translated in Kingsborough's *Antiquities of Mexico* (Vol. VI, p. 203):

"They believed the moon presided over human generation, and accordingly they always put it by the sign of the sun. They placed on its head a sea-snail to denote that in the same way as this marine animal creeps from its integument or shell, so man comes from his mother's womb."

The interpreter of *Codex Telleriano-Remensis* (Plate XI, Kingsborough, *op. cit.*, p. 122) states that Mexitli was otherwise called Tectziztecatl

"because in the same way that a snail creeps from a shell so man proceeds from his mother's womb. They placed the moon opposite to the sun because its course continually crosses his; and they believed it to be the cause of human generation."

The goddess of the shell was in the Old World associated with the moon as well as with the starry sky. It is incredible that the same arbitrary connections should have had spontaneous origin in the New World. Complexes which have a history in the Old World cannot possibly have "cropped up" by accident in the New World. It was surely something more than a "coincidence" that the pre-Columbian Americans connected shells, shell-purple, pearls, precious stones, and precious metals with their deities just as did the progressive peoples of the Old World. The doctrines regarding "shell-milk", "river-milk", and vegetation "milk" arose in Egypt where the domesticated cow was connected with the sycamore fig tree and with shells. How came it about that the same doctrines were promoted in Mexico? They could not have originated there among a people who did not have domesticated animals; they must have been imported with much else because they are fundamental doctrines—the very "sap" of the mythological tree.

The connection between metal working and pearl gathering, as between beliefs associated with metals and pearls, obtained in pre-Columbian times in both South and North America. In 1920 the American Museum obtained twelve gold objects of ancient Peruvian manufacture, found by treasure seekers in Peru, that had been offered for sale in New York. These had originally been worn as ornaments of religious value, or were used for religious purposes, and included breastplates, discs, and small water jars with combined handle and spout.

"The material of which these objects are composed is an alloy of gold, silver and copper, varying somewhat in proportions but averaging about 60 per cent gold, from 20 to 30 per cent silver, and from 6 to 20 per cent copper. One of the breastplates with alternating bands of light and dark metal gave interesting results upon analysis. The yellower metal was 80 per cent gold, 13 per cent silver, and 7 per cent copper, while the lighter bands were 47 per cent gold, 44 per cent silver, and $8\frac{1}{2}$ per cent copper. Such alloys are fairly hard and cannot be beaten with the same ease as purer gold. It appears that these objects were first cast in a prepared mould and then finished by hammering, and perhaps re-touched with an engraving tool." [1]

These finds alone afford sufficient evidence to show that the Peruvians were highly skilled and experienced in the sciences of mining and metallurgy. There is no recorded evidence, however, to indicate how or why the pre-Columbian Americans began to collect and utilize this precious metal or, indeed, any other metals. From the outset they appear to have searched for metals as the early Europeans searched for jade—that is, not "incidentally and spontaneously", but because of an influence operating from "an outside source", which directed their attention to metals, and at the same time provided the necessary instruction how to obtain them. "Their mining", says one writer, dealing with the Mexicans, "was doubtless carried on by the fire-and-water process used by the northern people, while gold from the river beds was possibly obtained in much the same manner as I have been told the Amerinds of Peru get it. Selecting a river that was known to be rich in the metal, a series of stone 'riffles' would be arranged in the best place at the very lowest stage of the water. Then when the freshets came and swept the gravel across these rude affairs the gold would remain lodged there, and on subsidence of the stream could be readily taken out". [2]

[1] *Natural History* (*Journal of the American Museum of Natural History*, New York, September-October, 1921, Vol. XXI, No. 5).

[2] F. L. Dellenbaugh, *The North Americans of Yesterday* (New York and London, 1901), p. 299.

"Rude" as the riffles may have been, they betoken an advanced skill and knowledge in the collection of gold, and this is further made manifest by the statement that the river selected "was known" to be a gold-yielding one.

In an interesting article on "Prehistoric Mining in Western South America", Mr. Charles W. Mead writes:[1]

"Many of the quartz lodes of gold-bearing ores were formerly worked by the Incas or their predecessors, as the remains of their old workings show. These excavations are often of considerable extent, but do not go below the oxidized zone. Finds in these works show how the gold was extracted. The crushing was done on a large, hollowed-out block of granite with a heavy rocking stone, three or four feet in diameter.[2] To operate this rocking stone required the labour of more than one man. The present Indians make use of such a prehistoric 'stamp' whenever they find one. The early historians tell us that in the dry season the Indians covered a part of the beds of streams with stones to arrest the particles of gold brought down by floods during the rainy season. On the return of the dry season the gravel between these stones was washed or panned and the gold obtained. Before the coming of Pizarro the Peruvians had reached a very high degree of skill in working gold."

Mr. Mead does not deal with the question as to how the Peruvians first came to display much interest in so useless a metal as gold. The problem, however, is touched upon by Mr. Pliny Goddard in the same publication.[3] He shows that the Peruvians had reached a high stage of civilization ; they cultivated "maize, beans, squash, pumpkins, the potato, cassava, cotton and many other plants"; had irrigation systems "requiring great industry

[1] *Natural History*, Vol. XXI, No. 5, pp. 453 *et seq.* (New York, 1921).

[2] The people of Luzon in Indonesia crushed ore by means of "a stout rock in certain large receptacles fixed firmly in the ground."—W. J. Perry, *The Megalithic Culture of Indonesia*, pp. 171–2.

[3] "Peruvian Gold of the Chinese Kingdom" in *Natural History*, Vol. XXI, No. 5, p. 449.

ANCIENT WALLS OF THE INCA FORTRESS AT CUZCO, PERU

No cement was used in the construction of these walls, so wonderfully exact was the
mason-work on the massive blocks of which they are composed.

and considerable engineering skill"; had many of the arts "highly developed", wonderful skill as architects and builders in stone, while they made pottery beautifully decorated, and were excellent weavers and dyers. He proceeds :

"It is not surprising, then, that the people in this particular region had made considerable progress in working with metals. Gold seems to have been generally common in the sands of the coastwise streams. Its sparkle undoubtedly attracted the eye of the people, and, when it was found to be easily malleable, its use in the arts was appreciated. It may be that copper was also first found in a pure state. By the time the Spaniards entered the region, however, considerable progress had been made in taking silver and copper ore out of the rock of the mountains and reducing the metals by means of blast furnaces."

Mr. Goddard thus assumes that from the outset gold appealed to the æsthetic sense of the ancient Peruvians, and he appears to consider that this view is strengthened by the fact that it was used for ornaments. It is difficult to believe, however, that men and women pierced their ears, noses, and lips to disfigure their faces with even exquisitely-worked jewels in response to a dormant or cultivated æsthetic sense. The fact that they were attracted by bright colours in gems, or that they produced beautiful dyes, does not add weight to such a hypothesis, for, as has been shown, gems possessed a religious value, and colours symbolized ideas, and were in themselves supposed to radiate influences. Gold, like the *chalchiuitl*, was a depository of life substance. As we have seen, it possessed the same arbitrary value to the Mexicans, and to less highly civilized Americans, including, it may here be added, the Isthmians. "According to Peter Martyr", writes Bancroft, "the embalmed and be-jewelled bodies of ancestors were worshipped in Comagre, and in Veragua gold was invested with divine qualities, so that the gathering of it was attended with fasting and penance."[1]

In dealing with the origin of gold working in America, consideration must be given to the religious as well as to the æsthetic use of gold and other metals. How came it about that in the New as in the Old World precisely the same beliefs were attached to gold, and that it was collected and utilized in precisely the same way? The blast furnaces were similar to those used from Japan to India and from India to Britain and in Ancient Egypt. These have been fully dealt with by Professor Gowland.[2] The Egyptian blow-pipe was also used in America.

In addition to gold, the Peruvians worked silver, the mines of Porco being one of the chief sources of supply. They also used copper and they manufactured bronze. "Analysis of 171 objects of copper and bronze, in the American Museum's collection, found in ancient Peruvian graves, shows", writes Mr. C. W. Mead, the assistant curator of Peruvian archæology, "that the bronze pieces average between 6 and 7 per cent of tin." This is less than the European average, which is 10 per cent, but as low proportions of tin as 1·09, 2·78, 4·56, 5·09, 5·15, and 7·19 have been found in ancient British and Irish bronzes.[3] The proportion of tin used depended, no doubt, on the skill possessed by individual craftsmen, the uses to which bronze artifacts were to be put, and the quality of the copper, for some coppers are softer than others.

Of more importance than the proportion of tin used

[1] *The Pacific States*, Vol. III, p. 500.
[2] "The Metals in Antiquity", Huxley Memorial Lecture in *The Journal of the Royal Anthropological Institute*, Vol. XLII, 1912, p. 244.
[3] Dr. Daniel Wilson, *Prehistoric Man*, p. 198.

by the Peruvians in manufacturing bronze is the remarkable fact that they used it at all. "No vessels or other objects made entirely of tin", writes Mr. Mead, "have been found in the ancient graves." If the Americans had been originators and not copyists, they would surely have displayed some originality in this connection.

"The Amerinds", Mr. Frederick L. Dellenbaugh reminds us, "were practically all in the so-called Stone Age of culture; that is, they were unacquainted with the *common use* of metals. Some tribes worked silver, gold, and copper to a limited extent and in an ornamental way."[1] Weapons and implements of flint, which was chipped, of obsidian, and of stone were exceedingly common. The old Egyptian "throwing stick" was used by some tribes. Metals, however, were mainly used for religious purposes, that is, to protect and animate the living and the dead; they were accumulated, as has been shown in the first chapter, because they possessed "merit", and they were offered with gems to the deities.

The earliest trace of this habit of offering life-giving and life-sustaining metals to gods and the dead is found in Ancient Egypt. In a Solar-Osirian chapter of the *Book of the Dead* the soul of the dead Pharaoh who is being initiated into the mysteries of the Otherworld is informed:

"Brought to thee are blocks of silver and [masses] of malachite. Hathor, mistress of Byblos, she makes the rudders of thy ship. . . . It is said to thee 'Come into the broad-hall', by the Great who are in the temple. Bared to thee are the Four Pillars of the Sky, thou seest the secrets that are herein, thou stretchest out thy two legs upon the Pillars of the Sky and the wind is sweet to thy nose."[2]

---

[1] *The North Americans of Yesterday* (London and New York), 1901, p. 248.
[2] Breasted, *Religion and Thought in Ancient Egypt*, p. 279.

No trace of originality in the matter of metal symbolism, or in that of colour symbolism, is to be discovered in the New World which, indeed, appears merely "as an appendix to Asia". To quote from Laufer once again, "Originality is certainly the rarest thing in the world, and in the history of mankind the original thoughts are appallingly sparse". As he finds it impossible to credit the early Europeans with "any spontaneous ideas relative to jade", so does the writer find it impossible, especially in view of the evidence dealt with in the foregoing chapters, to credit the pre-Columbian Americans with "any spontaneous ideas" relative to precious metals, pearls, pearl-shell, precious stones, jade or jadeite, and herbs and milk-yielding plants. All these things were searched for in the New World as in the Old and for the same reasons, and these are set forth by Professor Elliot Smith, who writes:

"In delving into the remotely distant history of our species we cannot fail to be impressed with the persistence with which, throughout the whole of his career, man (of the species *sapiens*) has been seeking for an elixir of life, to give added 'vitality' to the dead (whose existence was not consciously regarded as ended), to prolong the days of active life to the living, to restore youth, and to protect his own life from all assaults, not merely of time, but also of circumstance. In other words, the elixir he sought was something that would bring 'good luck' in all the events of his life and its continuation. Most of the amulets, even of modern times, the lucky trinkets, the averters of the 'Evil Eye', the practices and devices for securing good luck in love and sport, in curing bodily ills, in mental distress, in attaining material prosperity, or a continuation of existence after death, are survivals of this ancient and persistent striving after those objects which our earliest forefathers called collectively the 'givers of life'." [1]

The pearl and coral were called *margan* (life-giver) by

[1] *The Evolution of the Dragon*, p. 145.

Persians and Arabians, and gold likewise ensured immortality, as Hindu and Chinese texts state clearly:

" The gold, of beauteous colour of the sun, that men of old with their progeny sought—that, shining, shall unite thee with splendour; of long life becomes he that wears it ".[1]

De Groot quotes texts to show that in China the ancient peoples " were fully imbued with the belief that jade and gold could prolong life by strengthening the vital energy, and thus protecting the body against decay. Both minerals have indeed for a long series of ages held a prominent place in alchemy, or the great art of preparing the elixir of life and the philosophers' stone. . . . The same reasons why gold and jade were used for stuffing the mouth of the dead hold good for the use of pearls."[2]

Sahagun[3] tells, as has been stated, that the ancestors of the Nahua crossed the ocean and moved southward in America searching for the earthly paradise. According to Torquemada the strangers were silversmiths and goldsmiths and accomplished artisans, and collected and worked precious stones. As has been shown in the chapter devoted to Quetzalcoatl, they introduced religious beliefs and practices of distinctive character from the Old World. Dragon and nāga myths were imported among other things, as is shown in the Tlaloc chapter. The Maya god B was undoubtedly of Indian origin and connected with the elephant-headed god Ganesha and the god Indra, as has been shown.

In Peru the searchers for sacred gold practised irrigation. The searchers for sacred gold in Indonesia did likewise, connecting gold with the chiefs and the sky-

---

[1] Whitney, *Atharva Veda Samhita*, XIX, 26, p. 937 (Cambridge, Mass., 1905).

[2] *The Religious System of China*, Vol. I, pp. 273–275.

[3] Quoted by Brasseur de Bourbourg, *Popol Vuh* (Paris, 1861), pp. lvii, lviii, lxxiv, cliii.

world, just as it was connected with the Incas, "the children of the sun" and the sky-world in Peru.[1]

In the New World as in the Old it was believed that gold grew like a tree and that it was, indeed, a tree, just as coral was to the Chinese and others a sea-tree form of the mother goddess.[2] A Moorish author, quoted by Chénier, writes as follows regarding Paradise:

"Adam, after having eaten the forbidden fruit, sought to hide himself under the shade of the trees that form the bowers of Paradise: the Gold and Silver trees refused their shade to the father of the human race. God asked them, why they did so? 'Because', replied the Trees, 'Adam has transgressed against your commandment'. 'Ye have done well', answered the Creator; 'and that your fidelity may be rewarded, 'tis my decree that men shall hereafter become your slaves, and that in search of you they shall dig into the very bowels of the earth'."

Peter Martyr wrote regarding American "gold trees":

"They have found by experience, that the vein of gold is a living tree, and that the same by all ways that it spreadeth and springeth from the root by the soft pores and passages of the earth, putteth forth branches, even unto the uppermost parts of the earth, and ceaseth not until it discover itself unto the open air: at which time it showeth forth certain beautiful colours in the stead of flowers, round stones of golden earth in the stead of fruits, and thin plates instead of leaves. They say that the root of the golden tree extendeth to the centre of the earth, and there taketh nourishment of increase: for the deeper that they dig, they find the trunks thereof to be of so much the greater, as far as they may follow it, for abundance of water springing in the mountains. Of the branches of this tree, they find some as small as a thread, and others as big as a man's finger, according to the largeness or straightness of the rifts and clefts. They have sometimes chanced upon

---

[1] W. J. Perry, *Megalithic Culture in Indonesia*, pp. 135, 170-3.

[2] Laufer, *Sino-Iranica*, p. 524, note 8. The coral tree on the coral island takes the place of the Egyptian sycamore tree of life on the island of the Celestial Paradise. This tree was a form of the mother goddess Hathor.

whole caves, sustained or borne up as it were with golden pillars, and this in the ways by which the branches ascend; the which being filled with the substance of the trunk creeping from beneath, the branch maketh itself way by which it may pass out.   It is oftentimes divided, by encountering with some kind of hard stone, yet is it in other clefts nourished by the exhalations and virtue of the root."

Herrera wrote in similar strain:

" Metals are like plants hidden in the bowels of the earth, with their trunk and boughs, which are the veins; for it appears in a certain manner, that like plants they go on growing, not because they have any inward life, but because they are produced in the entrails of the earth by the virtue of the sun and of the plants; and so they go on increasing.   And as metals are thus, as it were, plants hidden in the earth; so plants are animals fixed to one place, sustained by the aliment which Nature has provided for them at their birth.   And to animals, as they have a more perfect being, a sense and knowledge hath been given to go about and seek their aliment. . . . Barren earth is the support of metal, and fertile earth of plants, and plants of animals: the less perfect serving the more perfect."

Paradise had its gem trees, as has been shown, in Buddhist literature, and these were guarded by dragons. Such trees were, however, much older than Buddhism. In the Babylonian epic of Gilgamesh a wonderful tree grows in the seashore Paradise of the West.

Precious stones it bore as fruit,
Branches hung from it which were beautiful to behold.
The top of the tree was *lapis lazuli*,
And it was laden with fruit which dazzled the eye of him
that beheld.[1]

In India plants and shells and flowers and precious stones were connected as symbols of the deities whose influences radiated from them, because the divine "life

[1] King, *Babylonian Religion*, p. 167.

substance" was contained in them. Thus at certain ceremonies "the Dhátri flower, the Sálagrám stone, the
various kinds of Sálagrámas, the conch shell, the Tulasi
plant, various perfumes, as sandal, agallochum, and different fragrant flowers . . . are dedicated to Vishnu and
are to be worshipped or offered in worship ".[1]

Of as much importance in India as fasting, silent
prayer and drinking holy water, was "wearing necklaces
and chaplets of the woods and seeds of the Tulasi" by the
worshippers of Vishnu. Offerings included "flowers,
fruits, cakes, vessels, gems, gold, &c.".[2]

Souls might assume animal, plant, or gem forms.
Torquemada (Book VI, Chapter 47) tells that "the
Tlascallans believed that the souls of chiefs and princes
became clouds, or beautiful birds, or precious stones;
whereas those of the common people would pass into
beetles, rats, mice, weasels, and all vile and stinking
animals". The precious stone, like the transparent gem
in the Votan cave, might contain the deity, as in Japan the
spirit of the deity might inhabit the *tama* (pearl). According to Hebrew belief Noah's ark was lit by a gem, because
day and night ceased during the flood. "The universal
spirit, fixed in a transparent body, shines like the sun in
glory", a commentator has written, "and this was the
light which God commanded Noah to make."

The arbitrary association of gems, metals, plants, &c.,
with the heavenly bodies and the source of life was
productive of myths and beliefs that became widely
prevalent, and can be detected in the religious symbolism
and religious texts and in the folk-lores of different
peoples and different lands. Pearls and precious stones
had in the myths nocturnal luminosity because they were
identified with the stars, the moon, or the sun, and with

---

[1] Wilson, *Essay on Sanskrit Literature*, Vol. I, p. 66.   [2] *Ibid.*, pp. 57, 73, 104.

the deities of which they were manifestations. They were also connected with plants, and the light of the jewel was regarded as a manifestation of life substance, which in the plant revealed itself by colours and existed as sap and the fire obtained by friction. The sap was regarded as identical with life blood[1] and with the fertilizing water which fell from the sky as rain, bubbled up from the earth forming a sacred well, or came down from the mountains as a river. Foam and fogs were likewise forms assumed by the "life substance" deposited in gems, in plants, and in animal, insect, and reptile life. It was because fire and heat were identified with colours, with sunlight, moonlight, starlight, and lightning, that the Mexicans, like the Gaelic-speaking Scots, regarded the butterfly as an insect form assumed by fire, and symbolized the flame produced by friction of fire-sticks as a red butterfly. As we have seen, the butterfly might be a god or a human soul. It was a manifestation of the principle of life, as was also the green pebble or pearl placed in the mouth of the dead and regarded as a substitute for the heart, the seat of life. Birds that nested in trees or fed on honey, the vital essence of flowers—forms assumed by the "fire of life"—were connected with the sacred plants and the deity of plants, and their highly coloured feathers were as sacred as gems, because they were supposed to be impregnated with "life substance". Feathers were worn by Mexican devotees for the same reason as were flowers, shells, and jewels. In

[1] Kingsborough provides interesting American evidence in this connection which is precisely similar to Old-World evidence. In his translation of the explanation of the Mexican paintings of the *Codex Vaticanus* (*Antiquities of Mexico*, Vol. VI, Plate XLVI, p. 211) he deals with the Rose Tree called Xuitlicastan and quotes: "They painted this tree distilling blood". It was a blood-yielding tree as other trees were "milk-yielding trees", and as the agave plant was a "milk plant", the "milk" being pulque. Blood was drawn from the pulque pot, as has been shown. Milk, blood, water, sap, oil, and honey were all liquids impregnated with "life substance".

Polynesia a log of wood into which feathers were stuck was regarded as the god Oro. Bunches of feathers were in America "badges" of deities, whose attributes and moods they revealed by their colours. It was not merely because green and blue jewels suggested water and vegetation that they were sacred; like water they were supposed to contain "life substance".

Seler, discussing the forms and symbols of the goddess Chalchiuhtlicue as revealed by illustrations in the Codices, shows that she sometimes wears flowers, or feathers, or coloured symbols, as substitutes for one another or for jewels, and that jewels, feathers, and flowers may symbolize water or blood. The following extract is of importance in this connection :

"As a symbol of the element, of which Chalchiuhtlicue is the image and embodiment, we see beside the *Codex Borgia* figure (fig. 429) a jewel (*chalchiuitl*), from within which a stream of water gushes forth. But here this stream of water is not set at the ends in the usual way with round or longish white snail-shells, but with yellow *cuitlatl*-like objects which, as we know, denote ordure, dirt, filth, and metaphorically 'sin'. This means that here this *chalchiuhatl*, or 'jewel water', is again conceived, not as the moisture that fertilises the fields, but, like 'jewel water' shown with the *chalchiuhtotlin*, emblem of the eighteenth day-count, as the moisture that cleanses from the dirt of sin, that is, the blood of mortification. This metaphorical meaning continually presents itself more and more to the artists of these picture-writings. Accordingly in our manuscript (fig. 430), beside the Water Goddess, we see depicted a ring of flowers from within which a flowering tree breaks out. The stem of this flowering tree is certainly painted the colour of the water, i.e. blue. But as in these manuscripts the flower is so often placed simply for blood, here, too, we shall have to think of the metaphorical significance of the *chalchiuhatl*. And should we still feel inclined to doubt this view, all doubts will be dispelled by the *Codex Fejérváry* picture (fig. 431). For here beside the flowering tree growing up from the jewelled bowl we see realistically reproduced the blood itself, with a heart figured in it." [1]

Seler shows, too, that the deity of the evening star, Xipe, god of earth (and gold), and the goddess Chalchiuhtlicue, the goddess of water, "are all alike equally significant for the quarter of the west"—the star, gold, the gem, moisture and the products of moisture, and earth, and the colours green and blue, are all connected in the complex Mexican symbolism, while, as shown in the long extract from Seler, blood, water, jewels, feathers, flowers, and plants, are regarded as manifestations of life substance, which is a purifier of sin, sin being a byeproduct of death, and, therefore, an evil influence.

The sacred things which cleansed human beings from sin also protected them, and were consequently worn as "ornaments" or placed on weapons and armour. Peter Martyr informs us that among the presents which Cortez sent to Spain were:

"two helmets covered with blue precious stones; one edged with golden bells and many plates of gold, two golden knobs sustaining the bells. The other covered with the same stones, but edged with 25 golden bells, crested with a green fowl sitting on the top of the helmet, whose feet, bill, and eyes were all of gold; and several golden knobs sustained every bell."

As the voices of birds were the voices of the gods, the tinklings of bells were calls made by the deity who was in gold and was manifested by the bird with golden eyes. In Ancient Egypt the deity was summoned by the sistrum.

The serpent was, in America, a form of the deity, and the serpent jewel contained the life substance, or "external soul" of the deity. These serpent jewels were the same

[1] *Codex Vaticanus B*, pp. 204, 205.

as the Chinese dragon pearls and the Asiatic and European gems produced by serpents, frogs, otters, &c.   Mortals who obtained one of these gems used it for enchantment, as the poet Gower informs us, to protect themselves from wounds, ill-health, &c., or to guide them by its light in dark places.   Jewels and feathers were connected.   The Mexicans made artificial feathers of gems and of gold as they made golden flowers.   It was not merely for æsthetic reasons that jewels were manufactured in imitation of flowers, shells, &c.

As gems enabled men to work enchantment, or to become prophets and seers, because these gems possessed life substance and shed light, herbs likewise inspired them with divine wisdom and knowledge.   Sacred intoxicants were prepared from sacred herbs.   Early Christian missionaries in Mexico were supposed to ask members of their flocks,

"Hast thou drunk *peyotl*, or hast thou given it to others to drink, in order to find out secrets, or to discover where stolen or lost articles were?   Dost thou know how to speak to vipers in such words that they obey thee?"

Sahagun has recorded that the intoxicant *peyotl* was made from a plant with a white tuberous root, and he states:

"Those who eat or drink of this *peyotl* see visions, which are sometimes frightful and sometimes ludicrous.   The intoxication it causes lasts several days.   The Chichimecs believed that it gave them courage in time of danger and diminished the pangs of hunger and thirst."

Father Augustin de Vetancurt, who lived in Mexico in the middle of the seventeenth century, tells that the pagan priests made an intoxicating ointment from the ashes of insects and worms and green leaves and seeds.

The influence exercised by this mixture was "attributed by them to divine agency". In southern Mexico and Yucatan an intoxicating drink was prepared from the bark of a tree. The natives "attribute to it a sacred character, calling it *yax ha*, the first water, the primal fluid. They say", the priestly recorder states, "that it was the first liquid created by God, and when He returned to His heavenly home He left this beverage and its production in charge of the gods of the rains, the four Pah-Ahtuns (i.e. Chacs)." The gems (*chalchiuitl*), usually jadeite, turquoise, emerald, chlormelanite or precious serpentine, not only protected human beings but provided nourishment. Spanish missionaries asked at the confessionary :

"Dost thou believe and hold for very truth, that these green stones give thee food and drink, even as thy ancestors believed, who died in their idolatry? Dost thou believe that they give success and prosperity and good things and all that thou hast or wishest?"

Brinton, from whom these quotations are made,[1] states that "down to quite a recent date, and perhaps still, these green stones are employed in certain ceremonies among the Indians of Oxaca in order to ensure a plenteous maize harvest. The largest ear of corn in the field is selected and wrapped up in a cloth with some of these chalchiuitles. At the next corn-planting it is taken to the field and buried in the soil." In his *The Evolution of the Dragon* (pp. 225 *et seq.*) Professor Elliot Smith shows that the mother goddess was the thunder-stone, the meteoric stone, the moon stone, &c. All these were "life-givers". As surrogates of the Great Mother they promoted fertility.

[1] *Nagualism*, Philadelphia, 1894, pp. 6–9, 43–47.

Similar ideas and practices were widespread in the Old World, and we cannot dismiss them as "simple", "natural", or "inevitable", in the manner that some confident theorists are so prone to do. The various complexes have a history; they were evidently the products of prolonged and diverse experiences in various centres of civilization in which cults met and mingled and attempted to harmonize their creeds. The various cults had one thing in common. All their members feared death and pain, and searched for the animating and life-prolonging elixir of life—the divine fluid or substance containing the vital principle, the herbs, stones, metals, &c., which possessed the colours, the light (i.e. fire), the shapes, odours, &c., of divine life. Gems were coagulated life blood, or "life substance", like the red jasper called by the Egyptians "Blood of Isis", the various jades supposed by the Chinese to be hardened "grease" issuing from rock, the crystal supposed by Camillus Teonardus, physician of Pizarro, as he states in his *Mirror of Stones*, to be "snow turned to ice which has been hardening thirty years", the precious stones, "and even flint in small masses" which Buffon regarded as "only exudations" from rock, and the American jadeite, &c., which, as we have seen, exuded water which was blood (jewel water). Feathers, flowers, gold, plants, &c., likewise had, as was supposed, their origin from divine fluid and yielded that fluid, or radiated the protecting and animating power of coagulated "life substance". It was after gold had been identified with life substance that gold was widely searched for.

These conceptions and practices lie behind the great mythologies of pre-Columbian America as they do behind many Old-World mythologies. They are really of more importance than the deities themselves. Gods may differ in appearance; they may speak different languages, but they are all intimately connected in Mexico, as in China and India, with the complex lore regarding the elixir of life.

Considered apart from or along with Old-World lore regarding precious metals, precious stones, &c., the American evidence appears but as a part of a whole, and not as a complete and isolated system in itself. That the Old-World lore and the associated beliefs and practices were introduced into America by the searchers for elixirs of life in the form of precious metals, stones, pearls, wells, feathers, plants, &c., there can be little doubt. Before and after the ancient mariners reached America the process of culture mixing was in active operation. India inherited much and contributed much, and as the migratory waves of humanity swept into China and beyond, and into Indonesia and Polynesia towards the American continent, fresh material was added and beliefs and customs were localized and influenced by local phenomena.

In Mexican mythology, as in other American mythologies, the influences of various local cults can be traced. It does not follow, however, when allowance is being made for development in America, that the highest conceptions were necessarily the latest, or that the New-World theologians were not stimulated by outside influences. The pantheon of the Aztecs, for instance, had, as has been indicated, its political and tribal aspect; after the theologies of the conquerors and conquered became fused, it reflected local politics as well as the views of the various cults. This process of arbitrary fusion is reflected by many complexities, obscurities, and contradictions. The gods sometimes tramp on one another's heels and their precise locations become uncertain. Further, the Mexican pantheon is found to include a god who hated war and human sacrifices, while the Aztec tribal deities required much human blood and promoted war so that victims might be obtained. The refined ideas of the searchers for elixirs in the form of precious metals and precious stones were mixed up with the older and more savage ideas of the blood drinkers and head hunters, who regarded blood as the elixir.

This process of culture mixing is not peculiar to America. Both in China and Japan much confusion and spiritual unrest existed during the early centuries of our era in consequence of the importations of all sorts of religious ideas. Rival cults and sects exercised so baneful an influence on social life that it became absolutely essential to impose harmonizing systems by law. Individual teachers, accustomed to "a jumble of religious notions", sometimes attempted to introduce harmony by promoting a cult which drew upon various religious systems. Cubricus, the Babylonian, who called himself Manes and founded in the third century the cult of Manichæism, was one of these. He mixed up the old Babylonian religion with Buddhism, Zoroastrianism, and early Christianity, and after his death his faith spread far and wide, reaching China, Japan, Tibet, Southern India, and Ceylon, and passing westward to Syria, Anatolia, Egypt, and even to France and Spain. St. Augustine was a Manichæan before being converted to Christianity. That individual teachers similarly arose in America to promote new systems framed from existing cults is highly probable. It may be that, as a result of the religious disturbances in Asia, there were companies of persecuted teachers who sought refuge in the New World in the early part of the Christian era, as did the Puritans of England in later times.

Those who contend that the pre-Columbian mythologies and religious systems were of spontaneous generation, or, as they put it, of "independent origin", base their hypothesis on an insufficient knowledge of the activities, movements, religious practices, and mythologies of the peoples of the Old World, as well as on hazardous assumptions regarding that greatest of all mysteries, the workings of the human mind.

INDEX

Absolution, in Mexico, 230.
Agave plant, animal connected with, in codices, 181.
— — as " Tree of Life ", 192.
— — description of, 178.
— — goddess of, 177. See *Mayauel*.
— — sap of, as pulque (vegetable milk), 178, 179. See *Milk*.
— — Spanish reference to " milk " of, 186, 187.
Aleutian Islands route to America, 116.
Amber, as " life giver " (*margan*), 12.
American civilization, beginnings of, 15 *et seq.*
American races, Asiatic race-cradle of Red Indians, 116.
— — Celtic theory, 95.
— — Gaelic numerals in Central America, 96.
— — Intercourse of, with Asia, 102 *et seq.*
— — Irish in America, 97.
— — Madoc legend, 95.
— — Norsemen in America, 97 *et seq.*
— — Phœnician theory, 92 *et seq.*
— — Theories as to the origin of, 81 *et seq.*
— — Welsh in America, 95, 96.

Amrita (Hindu elixir), milk and honey as, 185, 186.
Amulets, as tutelary spirits, 21.
— in Old and New World burial customs, 301, 302. See *Gems*.
Animal forms of mother goddess, 187, 188.
Armour, American and Asiatic, 106–9.
Artemis, the goddess, bee symbol of, 185.
— — connected with fish like American Mayauel, 193, 194.
— — the American, 181. See *Mayauel*.
— — tree and serpent connected with, 182.
— — " winged disc " symbol and, 63. See *Mother Goddess*.
Artemesia, the herbs called, Chinese and American symbolism of the same, 204. See *Mugwort*.
Asia, American intercourse with, by Behring Straits, 102, 103.
— American links in Northeastern, 112, 113.
— Aztec birth symbols, same as Japanese, 209.
— boat links, 108. See *Boats*.
— " Celestial Dog " of China in America, 246, 247.

331

INDEX

A CATALOG OF SELECTED DOVER
BOOKS IN ALL FIELDS OF INTEREST

CONCERNING THE SPIRITUAL IN ART, Wassily Kandinsky. Pioneering work by father of abstract art. Thoughts on color theory, nature of art. Analysis of earlier masters. 12 illustrations. 80pp. of text. 5⅜ × 8½. 23411-8 Pa. $3.95

ANIMALS: 1,419 Copyright-Free Illustrations of Mammals, Birds, Fish, Insects, etc., Jim Harter (ed.). Clear wood engravings present, in extremely lifelike poses, over 1,000 species of animals. One of the most extensive pictorial sourcebooks of its kind. Captions. Index. 284pp. 9 × 12. 23766-4 Pa. $12.95

CELTIC ART: The Methods of Construction, George Bain. Simple geometric techniques for making Celtic interlacements, spirals, Kells-type initials, animals, humans, etc. Over 500 illustrations. 160pp. 9 × 12. (USO) 22923-8 Pa. $9.95

AN ATLAS OF ANATOMY FOR ARTISTS, Fritz Schider. Most thorough reference work on art anatomy in the world. Hundreds of illustrations, including selections from works by Vesalius, Leonardo, Goya, Ingres, Michelangelo, others. 593 illustrations. 192pp. 7⅛ × 10¼. 20241-0 Pa. $9.95

CELTIC HAND STROKE-BY-STROKE (Irish Half-Uncial from "The Book of Kells"): An Arthur Baker Calligraphy Manual, Arthur Baker. Complete guide to creating each letter of the alphabet in distinctive Celtic manner. Covers hand position, strokes, pens, inks, paper, more. Illustrated. 48pp. 8¼ × 11. 24336-2 Pa. $3.95

EASY ORIGAMI, John Montroll. Charming collection of 32 projects (hat, cup, pelican, piano, swan, many more) specially designed for the novice origami hobbyist. Clearly illustrated easy-to-follow instructions insure that even beginning papercrafters will achieve successful results. 48pp. 8¼ × 11. 27298-2 Pa. $2.95

THE COMPLETE BOOK OF BIRDHOUSE CONSTRUCTION FOR WOOD-WORKERS, Scott D. Campbell. Detailed instructions, illustrations, tables. Also data on bird habitat and instinct patterns. Bibliography. 3 tables. 63 illustrations in 15 figures. 48pp. 5¼ × 8½. 24407-5 Pa. $1.95

BLOOMINGDALE'S ILLUSTRATED 1886 CATALOG: Fashions, Dry Goods and Housewares, Bloomingdale Brothers. Famed merchants' extremely rare catalog depicting about 1,700 products: clothing, housewares, firearms, dry goods, jewelry, more. Invaluable for dating, identifying vintage items. Also, copyright-free graphics for artists, designers. Co-published with Henry Ford Museum & Green-field Village. 160pp. 8¼ × 11. 25780-0 Pa. $9.95

HISTORIC COSTUME IN PICTURES, Braun & Schneider. Over 1,450 costumed figures in clearly detailed engravings—from dawn of civilization to end of 19th century. Captions. Many folk costumes. 256pp. 8⅜ × 11¾. 23150-X Pa. $11.95

CATALOG OF DOVER BOOKS

STICKLEY CRAFTSMAN FURNITURE CATALOGS, Gustav Stickley and L. & J. G. Stickley. Beautiful, functional furniture in two authentic catalogs from 1910. 594 illustrations, including 277 photos, show settles, rockers, armchairs, reclining chairs, bookcases, desks, tables. 183pp. 6½ × 9¼. 23838-5 Pa. $9.95

AMERICAN LOCOMOTIVES IN HISTORIC PHOTOGRAPHS: 1858 to 1949, Ron Ziel (ed.). A rare collection of 126 meticulously detailed official photographs, called "builder portraits," of American locomotives that majestically chronicle the rise of steam locomotive power in America. Introduction. Detailed captions. xi + 129pp. 9 × 12. 27393-8 Pa. $12.95

AMERICA'S LIGHTHOUSES: An Illustrated History, Francis Ross Holland, Jr. Delightfully written, profusely illustrated fact-filled survey of over 200 American lighthouses since 1716. History, anecdotes, technological advances, more. 240pp. 8 × 10¾. 25576-X Pa. $11.95

TOWARDS A NEW ARCHITECTURE, Le Corbusier. Pioneering manifesto by founder of "International School." Technical and aesthetic theories, views of industry, economics, relation of form to function, "mass-production split" and much more. Profusely illustrated. 320pp. 6⅛ × 9¼. (USO) 25023-7 Pa. $9.95

HOW THE OTHER HALF LIVES, Jacob Riis. Famous journalistic record, exposing poverty and degradation of New York slums around 1900, by major social reformer. 100 striking and influential photographs. 233pp. 10 × 7⅞. 22012-5 Pa $10.95

FRUIT KEY AND TWIG KEY TO TREES AND SHRUBS, William M. Harlow. One of the handiest and most widely used identification aids. Fruit key covers 120 deciduous and evergreen species; twig key 160 deciduous species. Easily used. Over 300 photographs. 126pp. 5⅜ × 8½. 20511-8 Pa. $3.95

COMMON BIRD SONGS, Dr. Donald J. Borror. Songs of 60 most common U.S. birds: robins, sparrows, cardinals, bluejays, finches, more—arranged in order of increasing complexity. Up to 9 variations of songs of each species.
Cassette and manual 99911-4 $8.95

ORCHIDS AS HOUSE PLANTS, Rebecca Tyson Northen. Grow cattleyas and many other kinds of orchids—in a window, in a case, or under artificial light. 63 illustrations. 148pp. 5⅜ × 8½. 23261-1 Pa. $4.95

MONSTER MAZES, Dave Phillips. Masterful mazes at four levels of difficulty. Avoid deadly perils and evil creatures to find magical treasures. Solutions for all 32 exciting illustrated puzzles. 48pp. 8¼ × 11. 26005-4 Pa. $2.95

MOZART'S DON GIOVANNI (DOVER OPERA LIBRETTO SERIES), Wolfgang Amadeus Mozart. Introduced and translated by Ellen H. Bleiler. Standard Italian libretto, with complete English translation. Convenient and thoroughly portable—an ideal companion for reading along with a recording or the performance itself. Introduction. List of characters. Plot summary. 121pp. 5¼ × 8½. 24944-1 Pa. $2.95

TECHNICAL MANUAL AND DICTIONARY OF CLASSICAL BALLET, Gail Grant. Defines, explains, comments on steps, movements, poses and concepts. 15-page pictorial section. Basic book for student, viewer. 127pp. 5⅜ × 8½. 21843-0 Pa. $4.95

BRASS INSTRUMENTS: Their History and Development, Anthony Baines. Authoritative, updated survey of the evolution of trumpets, trombones, bugles, cornets, French horns, tubas and other brass wind instruments. Over 140 illustrations and 48 music examples. Corrected and updated by author. New preface. Bibliography. 320pp. 5⅜ × 8½. 27574-4 Pa. $9.95

HOLLYWOOD GLAMOR PORTRAITS, John Kobal (ed.). 145 photos from 1926–49. Harlow, Gable, Bogart, Bacall; 94 stars in all. Full background on photographers, technical aspects. 160pp. 8⅜ × 11¼. 23352-9 Pa. $11.95

MAX AND MORITZ, Wilhelm Busch. Great humor classic in both German and English. Also 10 other works: "Cat and Mouse," "Plisch and Plumm," etc. 216pp. 5⅜ × 8½. 20181-3 Pa. $5.95

THE RAVEN AND OTHER FAVORITE POEMS, Edgar Allan Poe. Over 40 of the author's most memorable poems: "The Bells," "Ulalume," "Israfel," "To Helen," "The Conqueror Worm," "Eldorado," "Annabel Lee," many more. Alphabetic lists of titles and first lines. 64pp. 5³⁄₁₆ × 8¼. 26685-0 Pa. $1.00

SEVEN SCIENCE FICTION NOVELS, H. G. Wells. The standard collection of the great novels. Complete, unabridged. First Men in the Moon, Island of Dr. Moreau, War of the Worlds, Food of the Gods, Invisible Man, Time Machine, In the Days of the Comet. Total of 1,015pp. 5⅜ × 8½. (USO) 20264-X Clothbd. $29.95

AMULETS AND SUPERSTITIONS, E. A. Wallis Budge. Comprehensive discourse on origin, powers of amulets in many ancient cultures: Arab, Persian, Babylonian, Assyrian, Egyptian, Gnostic, Hebrew, Phoenician, Syriac, etc. Covers cross, swastika, crucifix, seals, rings, stones, etc. 584pp. 5⅜ × 8½. 23573-4 Pa. $12.95

RUSSIAN STORIES/PYCCKNE PACCKA3bl: A Dual-Language Book, edited by Gleb Struve. Twelve tales by such masters as Chekhov, Tolstoy, Dostoevsky, Pushkin, others. Excellent word-for-word English translations on facing pages, plus teaching and study aids, Russian/English vocabulary, biographical/critical introductions, more. 416pp. 5⅜ × 8½. 26244-8 Pa. $8.95

PHILADELPHIA THEN AND NOW: 60 Sites Photographed in the Past and Present, Kenneth Finkel and Susan Oyama. Rare photographs of City Hall, Logan Square, Independence Hall, Betsy Ross House, other landmarks juxtaposed with contemporary views. Captures changing face of historic city. Introduction. Captions. 128pp. 8¼ × 11. 25790-8 Pa. $9.95

AIA ARCHITECTURAL GUIDE TO NASSAU AND SUFFOLK COUNTIES, LONG ISLAND, The American Institute of Architects, Long Island Chapter, and the Society for the Preservation of Long Island Antiquities. Comprehensive, well-researched and generously illustrated volume brings to life over three centuries of Long Island's great architectural heritage. More than 240 photographs with authoritative, extensively detailed captions. 176pp. 8¼ × 11. 26946-9 Pa. $14.95

NORTH AMERICAN INDIAN LIFE: Customs and Traditions of 23 Tribes, Elsie Clews Parsons (ed.). 27 fictionalized essays by noted anthropologists examine religion, customs, government, additional facets of life among the Winnebago, Crow, Zuni, Eskimo, other tribes. 480pp. 6⅛ × 9¼. 27377-6 Pa. $10.95

CATALOG OF DOVER BOOKS

FRANK LLOYD WRIGHT'S HOLLYHOCK HOUSE, Donald Hoffmann. Lavishly illustrated, carefully documented study of one of Wright's most controversial residential designs. Over 120 photographs, floor plans, elevations, etc. Detailed perceptive text by noted Wright scholar. Index. 128pp. 9¼ × 10¾.
27133-1 Pa. $11.95

THE MALE AND FEMALE FIGURE IN MOTION: 60 Classic Photographic Sequences, Eadweard Muybridge. 60 true-action photographs of men and women walking, running, climbing, bending, turning, etc., reproduced from rare 19th-century masterpiece. vi + 121pp. 9 × 12.
24745-7 Pa. $10.95

1001 QUESTIONS ANSWERED ABOUT THE SEASHORE, N. J. Berrill and Jacquelyn Berrill. Queries answered about dolphins, sea snails, sponges, starfish, fishes, shore birds, many others. Covers appearance, breeding, growth, feeding, much more. 305pp. 5¼ × 8¼.
23366-9 Pa. $7.95

GUIDE TO OWL WATCHING IN NORTH AMERICA, Donald S. Heintzelman. Superb guide offers complete data and descriptions of 19 species: barn owl, screech owl, snowy owl, many more. Expert coverage of owl-watching equipment, conservation, migrations and invasions, etc. Guide to observing sites. 84 illustrations. xiii + 193pp. 5⅜ × 8½.
27344-X Pa. $8.95

MEDICINAL AND OTHER USES OF NORTH AMERICAN PLANTS: A Historical Survey with Special Reference to the Eastern Indian Tribes, Charlotte Erichsen-Brown. Chronological historical citations document 500 years of usage of plants, trees, shrubs native to eastern Canada, northeastern U.S. Also complete identifying information. 343 illustrations. 544pp. 6½ × 9¼.
25951-X Pa. $12.95

STORYBOOK MAZES, Dave Phillips. 23 stories and mazes on two-page spreads: Wizard of Oz, Treasure Island, Robin Hood, etc. Solutions. 64pp. 8¼ × 11.
23628-5 Pa. $2.95

NEGRO FOLK MUSIC, U.S.A., Harold Courlander. Noted folklorist's scholarly yet readable analysis of rich and varied musical tradition. Includes authentic versions of over 40 folk songs. Valuable bibliography and discography. xi + 324pp. 5⅜ × 8½.
27350-4 Pa. $7.95

MOVIE-STAR PORTRAITS OF THE FORTIES, John Kobal (ed.). 163 glamor, studio photos of 106 stars of the 1940s: Rita Hayworth, Ava Gardner, Marlon Brando, Clark Gable, many more. 176pp. 8⅜ × 11¼.
23546-7 Pa. $11.95

BENCHLEY LOST AND FOUND, Robert Benchley. Finest humor from early 30s, about pet peeves, child psychologists, post office and others. Mostly unavailable elsewhere. 73 illustrations by Peter Arno and others. 183pp. 5⅜ × 8½.
22410-4 Pa. $5.95

YEKL and THE IMPORTED BRIDEGROOM AND OTHER STORIES OF YIDDISH NEW YORK, Abraham Cahan. Film Hester Street based on Yekl (1896). Novel, other stories among first about Jewish immigrants on N.Y.'s East Side. 240pp. 5⅜ × 8½.
22427-9 Pa. $6.95

SELECTED POEMS, Walt Whitman. Generous sampling from *Leaves of Grass.* Twenty-four poems include "I Hear America Singing," "Song of the Open Road," "I Sing the Body Electric," "When Lilacs Last in the Dooryard Bloom'd," "O Captain! My Captain!"—all reprinted from an authoritative edition. Lists of titles and first lines. 128pp. 5³⁄₁₆ × 8¼.
26878-0 Pa. $1.00

THE BEST TALES OF HOFFMANN, E. T. A. Hoffmann. 10 of Hoffmann's most important stories: "Nutcracker and the King of Mice," "The Golden Flowerpot," etc. 458pp. 5⅜ × 8½. 21793-0 Pa. $8.95

FROM FETISH TO GOD IN ANCIENT EGYPT, E. A. Wallis Budge. Rich detailed survey of Egyptian conception of "God" and gods, magic, cult of animals, Osiris, more. Also, superb English translations of hymns and legends. 240 illustrations. 545pp. 5⅜ × 8½. 25803-3 Pa. $11.95

FRENCH STORIES/CONTES FRANÇAIS: A Dual-Language Book, Wallace Fowlie. Ten stories by French masters, Voltaire to Camus: "Micromegas" by Voltaire; "The Atheist's Mass" by Balzac; "Minuet" by de Maupassant; "The Guest" by Camus, six more. Excellent English translations on facing pages. Also French-English vocabulary list, exercises, more. 352pp. 5⅜ × 8½. 26443-2 Pa. $8.95

CHICAGO AT THE TURN OF THE CENTURY IN PHOTOGRAPHS: 122 Historic Views from the Collections of the Chicago Historical Society, Larry A. Viskochil. Rare large-format prints offer detailed views of City Hall, State Street, the Loop, Hull House, Union Station, many other landmarks, circa 1904–1913. Introduction. Captions. Maps. 144pp. 9⅜ × 12¼. 24656-6 Pa. $12.95

OLD BROOKLYN IN EARLY PHOTOGRAPHS, 1865–1929, William Lee Younger. Luna Park, Gravesend race track, construction of Grand Army Plaza, moving of Hotel Brighton, etc. 157 previously unpublished photographs. 165pp. 8⅞ × 11¾. 23587-4 Pa. $13.95

THE MYTHS OF THE NORTH AMERICAN INDIANS, Lewis Spence. Rich anthology of the myths and legends of the Algonquins, Iroquois, Pawnees and Sioux, prefaced by an extensive historical and ethnological commentary. 36 illustrations. 480pp. 5⅜ × 8½. 25967-6 Pa. $8.95

AN ENCYCLOPEDIA OF BATTLES: Accounts of Over 1,560 Battles from 1479 B.C. to the Present, David Eggenberger. Essential details of every major battle in recorded history from the first battle of Megiddo in 1479 B.C. to Grenada in 1984. List of Battle Maps. New Appendix covering the years 1967–1984. Index. 99 illustrations. 544pp. 6½ × 9¼. 24913-1 Pa. $14.95

SAILING ALONE AROUND THE WORLD, Captain Joshua Slocum. First man to sail around the world, alone, in small boat. One of great feats of seamanship told in delightful manner. 67 illustrations. 294pp. 5⅜ × 8½. 20326-3 Pa. $5.95

ANARCHISM AND OTHER ESSAYS, Emma Goldman. Powerful, penetrating, prophetic essays on direct action, role of minorities, prison reform, puritan hypocrisy, violence, etc. 271pp. 5⅜ × 8½. 22484-8 Pa. $5.95

MYTHS OF THE HINDUS AND BUDDHISTS, Ananda K. Coomaraswamy and Sister Nivedita. Great stories of the epics; deeds of Krishna, Shiva, taken from puranas, Vedas, folk tales; etc. 32 illustrations. 400pp. 5⅜ × 8½. 21759-0 Pa. $9.95

BEYOND PSYCHOLOGY, Otto Rank. Fear of death, desire of immortality, nature of sexuality, social organization, creativity, according to Rankian system. 291pp. 5⅜ × 8½. 20485-5 Pa. $8.95

A THEOLOGICO-POLITICAL TREATISE, Benedict Spinoza. Also contains unfinished Political Treatise. Great classic on religious liberty, theory of government on common consent. R. Elwes translation. Total of 421pp. 5⅜ × 8½. 20249-6 Pa. $8.95

MY BONDAGE AND MY FREEDOM, Frederick Douglass. Born a slave, Douglass became outspoken force in antislavery movement. The best of Douglass' auto-biographies. Graphic description of slave life. 464pp. 5⅜ × 8½. 22457-0 Pa. $8.95

FOLLOWING THE EQUATOR: A Journey Around the World, Mark Twain. Fascinating humorous account of 1897 voyage to Hawaii, Australia, India, New Zealand, etc. Ironic, bemused reports on peoples, customs, climate, flora and fauna, politics, much more. 197 illustrations. 720pp. 5⅜ × 8½. 26113-1 Pa. $15.95

THE PEOPLE CALLED SHAKERS, Edward D. Andrews. Definitive study of Shakers: origins, beliefs, practices, dances, social organization, furniture and crafts, etc. 33 illustrations. 351pp. 5⅜ × 8½. 21081-2 Pa. $8.95

THE MYTHS OF GREECE AND ROME, H. A. Guerber. A classic of mythology, generously illustrated, long prized for its simple, graphic, accurate retelling of the principal myths of Greece and Rome, and for its commentary on their origins and significance. With 64 illustrations by Michelangelo, Raphael, Titian, Rubens, Canova, Bernini and others. 480pp. 5⅜ × 8½. 27584-1 Pa. $9.95

PSYCHOLOGY OF MUSIC, Carl E. Seashore. Classic work discusses music as a medium from psychological viewpoint. Clear treatment of physical acoustics, auditory apparatus, sound perception, development of musical skills, nature of musical feeling, host of other topics. 88 figures. 408pp. 5⅜ × 8½. 21851-1 Pa. $9.95

THE PHILOSOPHY OF HISTORY, Georg W. Hegel. Great classic of Western thought develops concept that history is not chance but rational process, the evolution of freedom. 457pp. 5⅜ × 8½. 20112-0 Pa. $9.95

THE BOOK OF TEA, Kakuzo Okakura. Minor classic of the Orient: entertaining, charming explanation, interpretation of traditional Japanese culture in terms of tea ceremony. 94pp. 5⅜ × 8½. 20070-1 Pa. $3.95

LIFE IN ANCIENT EGYPT, Adolf Erman. Fullest, most thorough, detailed older account with much not in more recent books, domestic life, religion, magic, medicine, commerce, much more. Many illustrations reproduce tomb paintings, carvings, hieroglyphs, etc. 597pp. 5⅜ × 8½. 22632-8 Pa. $10.95

SUNDIALS, Their Theory and Construction, Albert Waugh. Far and away the best, most thorough coverage of ideas, mathematics concerned, types, construction, adjusting anywhere. Simple, nontechnical treatment allows even children to build several of these dials. Over 100 illustrations. 230pp. 5⅜ × 8½. 22947-5 Pa. $7.95

DYNAMICS OF FLUIDS IN POROUS MEDIA, Jacob Bear. For advanced students of ground water hydrology, soil mechanics and physics, drainage and irrigation engineering, and more. 335 illustrations. Exercises, with answers. 784pp. 6⅛ × 9¼. 65675-6 Pa. $19.95

SONGS OF EXPERIENCE: Facsimile Reproduction with 26 Plates in Full Color, William Blake. 26 full-color plates from a rare 1826 edition. Includes "The Tyger," "London," "Holy Thursday," and other poems. Printed text of poems. 48pp. 5¼ × 7. 24636-1 Pa. $4.95

OLD-TIME VIGNETTES IN FULL COLOR, Carol Belanger Grafton (ed.). Over 390 charming, often sentimental illustrations, selected from archives of Victorian graphics—pretty women posing, children playing, food, flowers, kittens and puppies, smiling cherubs, birds and butterflies, much more. All copyright-free. 48pp. 9¼ × 12¼. 27269-9 Pa. $5.95

PERSPECTIVE FOR ARTISTS, Rex Vicat Cole. Depth, perspective of sky and sea, shadows, much more, not usually covered. 391 diagrams, 81 reproductions of drawings and paintings. 279pp. 5⅜ × 8½. 22487-2 Pa. $6.95

DRAWING THE LIVING FIGURE, Joseph Sheppard. Innovative approach to artistic anatomy focuses on specifics of surface anatomy, rather than muscles and bones. Over 170 drawings of live models in front, back and side views, and in widely varying poses. Accompanying diagrams. 177 illustrations. Introduction. Index. 144pp. 8⅜ × 11¼. 26723-7 Pa. $8.95

GOTHIC AND OLD ENGLISH ALPHABETS: 100 Complete Fonts, Dan X. Solo. Add power, elegance to posters, signs, other graphics with 100 stunning copyright-free alphabets: Blackstone, Dolbey, Germania, 97 more—including many lower-case, numerals, punctuation marks. 104pp. 8⅛ × 11. 24695-7 Pa. $8.95

HOW TO DO BEADWORK, Mary White. Fundamental book on craft from simple projects to five-bead chains and woven works. 106 illustrations. 142pp. 5⅜ × 8. 20697-1 Pa. $4.95

THE BOOK OF WOOD CARVING, Charles Marshall Sayers. Finest book for beginners discusses fundamentals and offers 34 designs. "Absolutely first rate . . . well thought out and well executed."—E. J. Tangerman. 118pp. 7¾ × 10⅝. 23654-4 Pa. $5.95

ILLUSTRATED CATALOG OF CIVIL WAR MILITARY GOODS: Union Army Weapons, Insignia, Uniform Accessories, and Other Equipment, Schuyler, Hartley, and Graham. Rare, profusely illustrated 1846 catalog includes Union Army uniform and dress regulations, arms and ammunition, coats, insignia, flags, swords, rifles, etc. 226 illustrations. 160pp. 9 × 12. 24939-5 Pa. $10.95

WOMEN'S FASHIONS OF THE EARLY 1900s: An Unabridged Republication of "New York Fashions, 1909," National Cloak & Suit Co. Rare catalog of mail-order fashions documents women's and children's clothing styles shortly after the turn of the century. Captions offer full descriptions, prices. Invaluable resource for fashion, costume historians. Approximately 725 illustrations. 128pp. 8⅜ × 11¼. 27276-1 Pa. $11.95

THE 1912 AND 1915 GUSTAV STICKLEY FURNITURE CATALOGS, Gustav Stickley. With over 200 detailed illustrations and descriptions, these two catalogs are essential reading and reference materials and identification guides for Stickley furniture. Captions cite materials, dimensions and prices. 112pp. 6½ × 9¼. 26676-1 Pa. $9.95

EARLY AMERICAN LOCOMOTIVES, John H. White, Jr. Finest locomotive engravings from early 19th century: historical (1804–74), main-line (after 1870), special, foreign, etc. 147 plates. 142pp. 11⅜ × 8¼. 22772-3 Pa. $10.95

THE TALL SHIPS OF TODAY IN PHOTOGRAPHS, Frank O. Braynard. Lavishly illustrated tribute to nearly 100 majestic contemporary sailing vessels: Amerigo Vespucci, Clearwater, Constitution, Eagle, Mayflower, Sea Cloud, Victory, many more. Authoritative captions provide statistics, background on each ship. 190 black-and-white photographs and illustrations. Introduction. 128pp. 8⅞ × 11¾. 27163-3 Pa. $13.95

EARLY NINETEENTH-CENTURY CRAFTS AND TRADES, Peter Stockham (ed.). Extremely rare 1807 volume describes to youngsters the crafts and trades of the day: brickmaker, weaver, dressmaker, bookbinder, ropemaker, saddler, many more. Quaint prose, charming illustrations for each craft. 20 black-and-white line illustrations. 192pp. 4⅝ × 6. 27293-1 Pa. $4.95

VICTORIAN FASHIONS AND COSTUMES FROM HARPER'S BAZAR, 1867–1898, Stella Blum (ed.). Day costumes, evening wear, sports clothes, shoes, hats, other accessories in over 1,000 detailed engravings. 320pp. 9⅜ × 12¼.
22990-4 Pa. $13.95

GUSTAV STICKLEY, THE CRAFTSMAN, Mary Ann Smith. Superb study surveys broad scope of Stickley's achievement, especially in architecture. Design philosophy, rise and fall of the Craftsman empire, descriptions and floor plans for many Craftsman houses, more. 86 black-and-white halftones. 31 line illustrations. Introduction. 208pp. 6½ × 9¼. 27210-9 Pa. $9.95

THE LONG ISLAND RAIL ROAD IN EARLY PHOTOGRAPHS, Ron Ziel. Over 220 rare photos, informative text document origin (1844) and development of rail service on Long Island. Vintage views of early trains, locomotives, stations, passengers, crews, much more. Captions. 8⅞ × 11¾. 26301-0 Pa. $13.95

THE BOOK OF OLD SHIPS: From Egyptian Galleys to Clipper Ships, Henry B. Culver. Superb, authoritative history of sailing vessels, with 80 magnificent line illustrations. Galley, bark, caravel, longship, whaler, many more. Detailed, informative text on each vessel by noted naval historian. Introduction. 256pp. 5⅜ × 8½. 27332-6 Pa. $6.95

TEN BOOKS ON ARCHITECTURE, Vitruvius. The most important book ever written on architecture. Early Roman aesthetics, technology, classical orders, site selection, all other aspects. Morgan translation. 331pp. 5⅜ × 8½. 20645-9 Pa. $8.95

THE HUMAN FIGURE IN MOTION, Eadweard Muybridge. More than 4,500 stopped-action photos, in action series, showing undraped men, women, children jumping, lying down, throwing, sitting, wrestling, carrying, etc. 390pp. 7⅞ × 10⅝.
20204-6 Clothbd. $24.95

TREES OF THE EASTERN AND CENTRAL UNITED STATES AND CANADA, William M. Harlow. Best one-volume guide to 140 trees. Full descriptions, woodlore, range, etc. Over 600 illustrations. Handy size. 288pp. 4½ × 6⅜.
20395-6 Pa. $5.95

SONGS OF WESTERN BIRDS, Dr. Donald J. Borror. Complete song and call repertoire of 60 western species, including flycatchers, juncoes, cactus wrens, many more—includes fully illustrated booklet. Cassette and manual 99913-0 $8.95

GROWING AND USING HERBS AND SPICES, Milo Miloradovich. Versatile handbook provides all the information needed for cultivation and use of all the herbs and spices available in North America. 4 illustrations. Index. Glossary. 236pp. 5⅜ × 8½. 25058-X Pa. $6.95

BIG BOOK OF MAZES AND LABYRINTHS, Walter Shepherd. 50 mazes and labyrinths in all—classical, solid, ripple, and more—in one great volume. Perfect inexpensive puzzler for clever youngsters. Full solutions. 112pp. 8⅛ × 11.
22951-3 Pa. $4.95

CATALOG OF DOVER BOOKS

PIANO TUNING, J. Cree Fischer. Clearest, best book for beginner, amateur. Simple repairs, raising dropped notes, tuning by easy method of flattened fifths. No previous skills needed. 4 illustrations. 201pp. 5⅜ × 8½.   23267-0 Pa. $5.95

A SOURCE BOOK IN THEATRICAL HISTORY, A. M. Nagler. Contemporary observers on acting, directing, make-up, costuming, stage props, machinery, scene design, from Ancient Greece to Chekhov. 611pp. 5⅜ × 8½.   20515-0 Pa. $11.95

THE COMPLETE NONSENSE OF EDWARD LEAR, Edward Lear. All nonsense limericks, zany alphabets, Owl and Pussycat, songs, nonsense botany, etc., illustrated by Lear. Total of 320pp. 5⅜ × 8½. (USO)   20167-8 Pa. $6.95

VICTORIAN PARLOUR POETRY: An Annotated Anthology, Michael R. Turner. 117 gems by Longfellow, Tennyson, Browning, many lesser-known poets. "The Village Blacksmith," "Curfew Must Not Ring Tonight," "Only a Baby Small," dozens more, often difficult to find elsewhere. Index of poets, titles, first lines. xxiii + 325pp. 5⅜ × 8¼.   27044-0 Pa. $8.95

DUBLINERS, James Joyce. Fifteen stories offer vivid, tightly focused observations of the lives of Dublin's poorer classes. At least one, "The Dead," is considered a masterpiece. Reprinted complete and unabridged from standard edition. 160pp. 5³⁄₁₆ × 8¼.   26870-5 Pa. $1.00

THE HAUNTED MONASTERY and THE CHINESE MAZE MURDERS, Robert van Gulik. Two full novels by van Gulik, set in 7th-century China, continue adventures of Judge Dee and his companions. An evil Taoist monastery, seemingly supernatural events; overgrown topiary maze hides strange crimes. 27 illustrations. 328pp. 5⅜ × 8½.   23502-5 Pa. $7.95

THE BOOK OF THE SACRED MAGIC OF ABRAMELIN THE MAGE, translated by S. MacGregor Mathers. Medieval manuscript of ceremonial magic. Basic document in Aleister Crowley, Golden Dawn groups. 268pp. 5⅜ × 8½.   23211-5 Pa. $8.95

NEW RUSSIAN-ENGLISH AND ENGLISH-RUSSIAN DICTIONARY, M. A. O'Brien. This is a remarkably handy Russian dictionary, containing a surprising amount of information, including over 70,000 entries. 366pp. 4½ × 6⅛.   20208-9 Pa. $9.95

HISTORIC HOMES OF THE AMERICAN PRESIDENTS, Second, Revised Edition, Irvin Haas. A traveler's guide to American Presidential homes, most open to the public, depicting and describing homes occupied by every American President from George Washington to George Bush. With visiting hours, admission charges, travel routes. 175 photographs. Index. 160pp. 8¼ × 11. 26751-2 Pa. $10.95

NEW YORK IN THE FORTIES, Andreas Feininger. 162 brilliant photographs by the well-known photographer, formerly with *Life* magazine. Commuters, shoppers, Times Square at night, much else from city at its peak. Captions by John von Hartz. 181pp. 9¼ × 10¾.   23585-8 Pa. $12.95

INDIAN SIGN LANGUAGE, William Tomkins. Over 525 signs developed by Sioux and other tribes. Written instructions and diagrams. Also 290 pictographs. 111pp. 6⅛ × 9¼.   22029-X Pa. $3.50

ANATOMY: A Complete Guide for Artists, Joseph Sheppard. A master of figure drawing shows artists how to render human anatomy convincingly. Over 460 illustrations. 224pp. 8⅜ × 11¼. 27279-6 Pa. $10.95

MEDIEVAL CALLIGRAPHY: Its History and Technique, Marc Drogin. Spirited history, comprehensive instruction manual covers 13 styles (ca. 4th century thru 15th). Excellent photographs; directions for duplicating medieval techniques with modern tools. 224pp. 8⅜ × 11¼. 26142-5 Pa. $11.95

DRIED FLOWERS: How to Prepare Them, Sarah Whitlock and Martha Rankin. Complete instructions on how to use silica gel, meal and borax, perlite aggregate, sand and borax, glycerine and water to create attractive permanent flower arrangements. 12 illustrations. 32pp. 5⅜ × 8½. 21802-3 Pa. $1.00

EASY-TO-MAKE BIRD FEEDERS FOR WOODWORKERS, Scott D. Campbell. Detailed, simple-to-use guide for designing, constructing, caring for and using feeders. Text, illustrations for 12 classic and contemporary designs. 96pp. 5⅜ × 8½. 25847-5 Pa. $2.95

OLD-TIME CRAFTS AND TRADES, Peter Stockham. An 1807 book created to teach children about crafts and trades open to them as future careers. It describes in detailed, nontechnical terms 24 different occupations, among them coachmaker, gardener, hairdresser, lacemaker, shoemaker, wheelwright, copper-plate printer, milliner, trunkmaker, merchant and brewer. Finely detailed engravings illustrate each occupation. 192pp. 4⅝ × 6. 27398-9 Pa. $4.95

THE HISTORY OF UNDERCLOTHES, C. Willett Cunnington and Phyllis Cunnington. Fascinating, well-documented survey covering six centuries of English undergarments, enhanced with over 100 illustrations: 12th-century laced-up bodice, footed long drawers (1795), 19th-century bustles, 19th-century corsets for men, Victorian "bust improvers," much more. 272pp. 5⅜ × 8¼. 27124-2 Pa. $9.95

ARTS AND CRAFTS FURNITURE: The Complete Brooks Catalog of 1912, Brooks Manufacturing Co. Photos and detailed descriptions of more than 150 now very collectible furniture designs from the Arts and Crafts movement depict davenports, settees, buffets, desks, tables, chairs, bedsteads, dressers and more, all built of solid, quarter-sawed oak. Invaluable for students and enthusiasts of antiques, Americana and the decorative arts. 80pp. 6½ × 9¼. 27471-3 Pa. $7.95

HOW WE INVENTED THE AIRPLANE: An Illustrated History, Orville Wright. Fascinating firsthand account covers early experiments, construction of planes and motors, first flights, much more. Introduction and commentary by Fred C. Kelly. 76 photographs. 96pp. 8¼ × 11. 25662-6 Pa. $8.95

THE ARTS OF THE SAILOR: Knotting, Splicing and Ropework, Hervey Garrett Smith. Indispensable shipboard reference covers tools, basic knots and useful hitches; handsewing and canvas work, more. Over 100 illustrations. Delightful reading for sea lovers. 256pp. 5⅜ × 8½. 26440-8 Pa. $7.95

FRANK LLOYD WRIGHT'S FALLINGWATER: The House and Its History, Second, Revised Edition, Donald Hoffmann. A total revision—both in text and illustrations—of the standard document on Fallingwater, the boldest, most personal architectural statement of Wright's mature years, updated with valuable new material from the recently opened Frank Lloyd Wright Archives. "Fascinating"—*The New York Times.* 116 illustrations. 128pp. 9¼ × 10¾.
27430-6 Pa. $10.95

CATALOG OF DOVER BOOKS

PHOTOGRAPHIC SKETCHBOOK OF THE CIVIL WAR, Alexander Gardner. 100 photos taken on field during the Civil War. Famous shots of Manassas, Harper's Ferry, Lincoln, Richmond, slave pens, etc. 244pp. 10⅝ × 8¼.
22731-6 Pa. $9.95

FIVE ACRES AND INDEPENDENCE, Maurice G. Kains. Great back-to-the-land classic explains basics of self-sufficient farming. The one book to get. 95 illustrations. 397pp. 5⅜ × 8½.
20974-1 Pa. $7.95

SONGS OF EASTERN BIRDS, Dr. Donald J. Borror. Songs and calls of 60 species most common to eastern U.S.: warblers, woodpeckers, flycatchers, thrushes, larks, many more in high-quality recording.
Cassette and manual 99912-2 $8.95

A MODERN HERBAL, Margaret Grieve. Much the fullest, most exact, most useful compilation of herbal material. Gigantic alphabetical encyclopedia, from aconite to zedoary, gives botanical information, medical properties, folklore, economic uses, much else. Indispensable to serious reader. 161 illustrations. 888pp. 6½ × 9¼. 2-vol. set. (USO)
Vol. I: 22798-7 Pa. $9.95
Vol. II: 22799-5 Pa. $9.95

HIDDEN TREASURE MAZE BOOK, Dave Phillips. Solve 34 challenging mazes accompanied by heroic tales of adventure. Evil dragons, people-eating plants, bloodthirsty giants, many more dangerous adversaries lurk at every twist and turn. 34 mazes, stories, solutions. 48pp. 8¼ × 11.
24566-7 Pa. $2.95

LETTERS OF W. A. MOZART, Wolfgang A. Mozart. Remarkable letters show bawdy wit, humor, imagination, musical insights, contemporary musical world; includes some letters from Leopold Mozart. 276pp. 5⅜ × 8½.
22859-2 Pa. $7.95

BASIC PRINCIPLES OF CLASSICAL BALLET, Agrippina Vaganova. Great Russian theoretician, teacher explains methods for teaching classical ballet. 118 illustrations. 175pp. 5⅜ × 8½.
22036-2 Pa. $4.95

THE JUMPING FROG, Mark Twain. Revenge edition. The original story of The Celebrated Jumping Frog of Calaveras County, a hapless French translation, and Twain's hilarious "retranslation" from the French. 12 illustrations. 66pp. 5⅜ × 8½.
22686-7 Pa. $3.95

BEST REMEMBERED POEMS, Martin Gardner (ed.). The 126 poems in this superb collection of 19th- and 20th-century British and American verse range from Shelley's "To a Skylark" to the impassioned "Renascence" of Edna St. Vincent Millay and to Edward Lear's whimsical "The Owl and the Pussycat." 224pp. 5⅜ × 8½.
27165-X Pa. $4.95

COMPLETE SONNETS, William Shakespeare. Over 150 exquisite poems deal with love, friendship, the tyranny of time, beauty's evanescence, death and other themes in language of remarkable power, precision and beauty. Glossary of archaic terms. 80pp. 5³⁄₁₆ × 8¼.
26686-9 Pa. $1.00

BODIES IN A BOOKSHOP, R. T. Campbell. Challenging mystery of blackmail and murder with ingenious plot and superbly drawn characters. In the best tradition of British suspense fiction. 192pp. 5⅜ × 8½.
24720-1 Pa. $5.95

THE WIT AND HUMOR OF OSCAR WILDE, Alvin Redman (ed.). More than 1,000 ripostes, paradoxes, wisecracks: Work is the curse of the drinking classes; I can resist everything except temptation; etc. 258pp. 5⅜ × 8½. 20602-5 Pa. $5.95

SHAKESPEARE LEXICON AND QUOTATION DICTIONARY, Alexander Schmidt. Full definitions, locations, shades of meaning in every word in plays and poems. More than 50,000 exact quotations. 1,485pp. 6½ × 9¼. 2-vol. set.
Vol. I: 22726-X Pa. $16.95
Vol. 2: 22727-8 Pa. $15.95

SELECTED POEMS, Emily Dickinson. Over 100 best-known, best-loved poems by one of America's foremost poets, reprinted from authoritative early editions. No comparable edition at this price. Index of first lines. 64pp. 5³/₁₆ × 8¼.
26466-1 Pa. $1.00

CELEBRATED CASES OF JUDGE DEE (DEE GOONG AN), translated by Robert van Gulik. Authentic 18th-century Chinese detective novel; Dee and associates solve three interlocked cases. Led to van Gulik's own stories with same characters. Extensive introduction. 9 illustrations. 237pp. 5⅜ × 8½.
23337-5 Pa. $6.95

THE MALLEUS MALEFICARUM OF KRAMER AND SPRENGER, translated by Montague Summers. Full text of most important witchhunter's "bible," used by both Catholics and Protestants. 278pp. 6⅝ × 10. 22802-9 Pa. $11.95

SPANISH STORIES/CUENTOS ESPAÑOLES: A Dual-Language Book, Angel Flores (ed.). Unique format offers 13 great stories in Spanish by Cervantes, Borges, others. Faithful English translations on facing pages. 352pp. 5⅜ × 8½.
25399-6 Pa. $8.95

THE CHICAGO WORLD'S FAIR OF 1893: A Photographic Record, Stanley Appelbaum (ed.). 128 rare photos show 200 buildings, Beaux-Arts architecture, Midway, original Ferris Wheel, Edison's kinetoscope, more. Architectural emphasis; full text. 116pp. 8¼ × 11. 23990-X Pa. $9.95

OLD QUEENS, N.Y., IN EARLY PHOTOGRAPHS, Vincent F. Seyfried and William Asadorian. Over 160 rare photographs of Maspeth, Jamaica, Jackson Heights, and other areas. Vintage views of DeWitt Clinton mansion, 1939 World's Fair and more. Captions. 192pp. 8⅞ × 11. 26358-4 Pa. $12.95

CAPTURED BY THE INDIANS: 15 Firsthand Accounts, 1750–1870, Frederick Drimmer. Astounding true historical accounts of grisly torture, bloody conflicts, relentless pursuits, miraculous escapes and more, by people who lived to tell the tale. 384pp. 5⅜ × 8½. 24901-8 Pa. $8.95

THE WORLD'S GREAT SPEECHES, Lewis Copeland and Lawrence W. Lamm (eds.). Vast collection of 278 speeches of Greeks to 1970. Powerful and effective models; unique look at history. 842pp. 5⅜ × 8½. 20468-5 Pa. $14.95

THE BOOK OF THE SWORD, Sir Richard F. Burton. Great Victorian scholar/adventurer's eloquent, erudite history of the "queen of weapons"—from prehistory to early Roman Empire. Evolution and development of early swords, variations (sabre, broadsword, cutlass, scimitar, etc.), much more. 336pp. 6⅛ × 9¼. 25434-8 Pa. $8.95

AUTOBIOGRAPHY: The Story of My Experiments with Truth, Mohandas K. Gandhi. Boyhood, legal studies, purification, the growth of the Satyagraha (nonviolent protest) movement. Critical, inspiring work of the man responsible for the freedom of India. 480pp. 5⅜ × 8½. (USO)   24593-4 Pa. $8.95

CELTIC MYTHS AND LEGENDS, T. W. Rolleston. Masterful retelling of Irish and Welsh stories and tales. Cuchulain, King Arthur, Deirdre, the Grail, many more. First paperback edition. 58 full-page illustrations. 512pp. 5⅜ × 8½.
26507-2 Pa. $9.95

THE PRINCIPLES OF PSYCHOLOGY, William James. Famous long course complete, unabridged. Stream of thought, time perception, memory, experimental methods; great work decades ahead of its time. 94 figures. 1,391pp. 5⅜ × 8½. 2-vol. set.
Vol. I: 20381-6 Pa. $12.95
Vol. II: 20382-4 Pa. $12.95

THE WORLD AS WILL AND REPRESENTATION, Arthur Schopenhauer. Definitive English translation of Schopenhauer's life work, correcting more than 1,000 errors, omissions in earlier translations. Translated by E. F. J. Payne. Total of 1,269pp. 5⅜ × 8½. 2-vol. set.   Vol. 1: 21761-2 Pa. $11.95
Vol. 2: 21762-0 Pa. $11.95

MAGIC AND MYSTERY IN TIBET, Madame Alexandra David-Neel. Experiences among lamas, magicians, sages, sorcerers, Bonpa wizards. A true psychic discovery. 32 illustrations. 321pp. 5⅜ × 8½. (USO)   22682-4 Pa. $8.95

THE EGYPTIAN BOOK OF THE DEAD, E. A. Wallis Budge. Complete reproduction of Ani's papyrus, finest ever found. Full hieroglyphic text, interlinear transliteration, word-for-word translation, smooth translation. 533pp. 6½ × 9¼.
21866-X Pa. $9.95

MATHEMATICS FOR THE NONMATHEMATICIAN, Morris Kline. Detailed, college-level treatment of mathematics in cultural and historical context, with numerous exercises. Recommended Reading Lists. Tables. Numerous figures. 641pp. 5⅜ × 8½.   24823-2 Pa. $11.95

THEORY OF WING SECTIONS: Including a Summary of Airfoil Data, Ira H. Abbott and A. E. von Doenhoff. Concise compilation of subsonic aerodynamic characteristics of NACA wing sections, plus description of theory. 350pp. of tables. 693pp. 5⅜ × 8½.   60586-8 Pa. $14.95

THE RIME OF THE ANCIENT MARINER, Gustave Doré, S. T. Coleridge. Doré's finest work; 34 plates capture moods, subtleties of poem. Flawless full-size reproductions printed on facing pages with authoritative text of poem. "Beautiful. Simply beautiful."—Publisher's Weekly. 77pp. 9¼ × 12.   22305-1 Pa. $6.95

NORTH AMERICAN INDIAN DESIGNS FOR ARTISTS AND CRAFTS-PEOPLE, Eva Wilson. Over 360 authentic copyright-free designs adapted from Navajo blankets, Hopi pottery, Sioux buffalo hides, more. Geometrics, symbolic figures, plant and animal motifs, etc. 128pp. 8⅜ × 11. (EUK)   25341-4 Pa. $7.95

SCULPTURE: Principles and Practice, Louis Slobodkin. Step-by-step approach to clay, plaster, metals, stone; classical and modern. 253 drawings, photos. 255pp. 8⅛ × 11.   22960-2 Pa. $10.95

CATALOG OF DOVER BOOKS

THE INFLUENCE OF SEA POWER UPON HISTORY, 1660–1783, A. T. Mahan. Influential classic of naval history and tactics still used as text in war colleges. First paperback edition. 4 maps. 24 battle plans. 640pp. 5⅜ × 8½.
25509-3 Pa. $12.95

THE STORY OF THE TITANIC AS TOLD BY ITS SURVIVORS, Jack Winocour (ed.). What it was really like. Panic, despair, shocking inefficiency, and a little heroism. More thrilling than any fictional account. 26 illustrations. 320pp. 5⅜ × 8½.
20610-6 Pa. $8.95

FAIRY AND FOLK TALES OF THE IRISH PEASANTRY, William Butler Yeats (ed.). Treasury of 64 tales from the twilight world of Celtic myth and legend: "The Soul Cages," "The Kildare Pooka," "King O'Toole and his Goose," many more. Introduction and Notes by W. B. Yeats. 352pp. 5⅜ × 8½.
26941-8 Pa. $8.95

BUDDHIST MAHAYANA TEXTS, E. B. Cowell and Others (eds.). Superb, accurate translations of basic documents in Mahayana Buddhism, highly important in history of religions. The Buddha-karita of Asvaghosha, Larger Sukhavativyuha, more. 448pp. 5⅜ × 8½. ,
25552-2 Pa. $9.95

ONE TWO THREE . . . INFINITY: Facts and Speculations of Science, George Gamow. Great physicist's fascinating, readable overview of contemporary science: number theory, relativity, fourth dimension, entropy, genes, atomic structure, much more. 128 illustrations. Index. 352pp. 5⅜ × 8½.
25664-2 Pa. $8.95

ENGINEERING IN HISTORY, Richard Shelton Kirby, et al. Broad, nontechnical survey of history's major technological advances: birth of Greek science, industrial revolution, electricity and applied science, 20th-century automation, much more. 181 illustrations. ". . . excellent . . ."—Isis. Bibliography. vii + 530pp. 5⅜ × 8¼.
26412-2 Pa. $14.95

Prices subject to change without notice.

Available at your book dealer or write for free catalog to Dept. GI, Dover Publications, Inc., 31 East 2nd St., Mineola, N.Y. 11501. Dover publishes more than 500 books each year on science, elementary and advanced mathematics, biology, music, art, literary history, social sciences and other areas.